WHOSE REALITY COUNTS?

WHOSE REALITY COUNTS?

Putting the first last

ROBERT CHAMBERS

INTERMEDIATE TECHNOLOGY PUBLICATIONS

Intermediate Technology Publications
103–105 Southampton Row, London WC1B 4HH, UK

© Intermediate Technology Publications 1997

Reprinted 1997, 1999

A CIP record for this book is available from the British Library

ISBN 1 85339 386 X

Typeset by Dorwyn Ltd, Rowlands Castle, Hants
Printed in Great Britain by The Bath Press, Bath

Contents

For Jenny Chambers

and

to the memory of

Selina Adjebeng-Asem and Steven Treagust

List of Figures

List of Tables

Abbreviations and Addresses

Addresses given include organizations with several available publications listed in the references.

Action Aid	Hamlyn House, MacDonald Road, Archway, London N19 5PG, UK
AKF	Aga Khan Foundation, PO Box 2369, 1211 Geneva 2, Switzerland
AKRSP	Aga Khan Rural Support Programme (India), Choice Premises, Swastik Cross Road, Navrangpura, Ahmedabad 380009, India
BRAC	Bangladesh Rural Advancement Committee, 66 Mohakhali Commercial Area, Dhaka 12, Bangladesh
CDR	Complex, Diverse and Risk-prone
CGIAR	Consultative Group on International Agricultural Research, CGIAR Secretariat, 1818 H Street, NW Washington DC 20433, USA
CPRs	Common Property Resources
DANIDA	Danish Agency for International Development, Environment Secretariat, Ministry of Foreign Affairs, Asiatisk Plads 2, DK 1448 Copenhagen, Denmark
ERR	Egocentric Reminiscence Ratio
EU	European Union
FAO	Food and Agriculture Organisation, Via delle Terme di Caracalla, Rome 00100, Italy
FF	Ford Foundation, 320 East 43rd Street, New York, NY 10017, USA
FINNIDA	Finnish International Development Agency, Mannerheimintie 15C, SF-00260, Helsinki, Finland
GIS	Geographic Information Systems
GTZ	Deutsche Gesellschaft für Technische Zusammenarbeit, GmbH, Postfach 5180, D-65726, Eschborn, Germany
HYV	High-Yielding Variety
ICRISAT	International Crops Research Institute for the Semiarid Tropics Patancheru P.O., Andhra Pradesh 502 234, India
IDRC	International Development Research Centre, 250 Albert St, PO Box 8500, Ottawa, Canada, K1G 3H9

IDS	Institute of Development Studies, University of Sussex, Sussex, Brighton BN1 9RE, UK
IFAD	International Fund for Agricultural Development, 107 Via del Serafico, 00142, Rome, Italy
IFPRI	International Food Policy Research Institute, 1200 Seventeenth Street, N.W., Washington, DC 20036–3006, USA
IIED	International Institute for Environment and Development, 3 Endsleigh Street, London WC1H ODD, UK
IIMI	International Irrigation Management Institute, P.O. Box 2075, Colombo, Sri Lanka
ILEIA	Information Centre for Low-External-Input Agriculture, Kastanjelaan 5, P.O. Box 64, NL-3830, AB Leusden, Netherlands
IRDP	Integrated Rural Development Project
ITK	Indigenous Technical Knowledge
lcddu	Local, Complex, Diverse, Dynamic and Uncontrollable and/or Unpredictable
LFA	Logical Framework Analysis
MANAGE	National Institute of Agricultural Extension, Rajendra Nagar, Hyderabad 500 030, Andhra Pradesh, India
NGO	Non-Governmental Organization
NTFPs	Non-Timber Forest Products
M and E	Monitoring and Evaluation
MYRADA	MYRADA, 2 Service Road, Domlur Layout, Bangalore 560 071, India
NOVIB	NOVIB, Amaliastraat 7, 2514 JC The Hague, Netherlands
ODA	Overseas Development Administration, 94 Victoria Street, London SW1E 5JL, UK
ODI	Overseas Development Institute, Portland House, Stag Place, London SW1E 5DP, UK
OUTREACH	109 Coles Road, Fraser Town, Bangalore 560 005, India
PAR	Participatory Action Research
PLA	Participatory Learning and Action
PPA	Participatory Poverty Assessment
PRA	Participatory Rural Appraisal
REFLECT	Regenerated Freirian Literacy through Empowering Community Techniques
RRA	Rapid Rural Appraisal
SCBA	Social Cost Benefit Analysis

SDC	Swiss Agency for Development and Cooperation, Eigerstrasse 73, 3003 Berne, Switzerland
SIDA (now Sida)	Swedish International Development Authority, Klarabergsgatan 23, 10525 Stockholm, Sweden
SPEECH	Society for People's Education and Economic Change, 14 Jeyaraja Illam, Opp. Kasirajan Hospital, Titupali, Madurai 625 014, India
T and V	Training and Visit
TOT	Transfer of Technology
UNDP	United Nations Development Programme, One United Nations Plaza, New York, NY 10017, USA
UNICEF	United Nations Children's Fund, UNICEF House, 3 United Nations Plaza, New York NY 10017, USA
USAID	United States Agency for International Development, Washington DC, 20523, USA
World Bank	The World Bank, 1818 H Street NW, Washington DC 20433, USA
ZOPP	Ziel-Orientierte Projekt Planung

Glossary of Meanings

Words mean different things to different people. To make what is being said clearer to myself and to the reader, here are some meanings and descriptions. These are not necessarily what the words *ought* to mean, or how others use them. Rather they sketch what I have struggled, however fallibly, to be consistent in meaning by them in this book. To avoid confusion, I have tried to keep close to common usage where there is one.

Altruism	unselfish concern and action for the welfare of others
Capability	the quality of being capable; the ability to do something
CDR agriculture	agriculture which is complex, diverse and risk-prone, contrasting with industrial agriculture and Green Revolution agriculture which are relatively simple, uniform and risk-free
Complex	having many parts, categories, linkages and relationships a) within a system and/or b) between it and its parts and the surrounding environment. Causality is complex when there are many actual or potential causes of an effect, many effects of a cause, and/or backward linkages
Development	good change
Deprivation	lacking what is needed for well-being. Deprivation has dimensions which are physical, social, economic, political and psychological/spiritual. It includes forms of disadvantage such as social inferiority, physical weakness, isolation, poverty, vulnerability, powerlessness and humiliation
Diverse	having variety, differentness, with many different things and/or forms of the same type of thing
Emic	expressing the views, concepts, categories and values of insiders
Epistemology	the theory of knowledge, and especially the critical study of its validity, methods and scope
Etic	expressing the views, concepts, categories and values of outsiders

Generosity	willingness and liberality in sharing and giving things away
Ill-being	the experience of bad quality of life
Institution	has two meanings: an organization; and rules-in-use. The latter refers to working rules, procedures and norms expressed in repeated actions and relationships between individuals in organizations (see also Thompson 1995:1545, from whom these meanings have been adapted)
lcddu	local, complex, diverse, dynamic, and uncontrollable or unpredictable
Local	pertaining to a particular rural or urban place or area
Local people	people who live in a particular rural or urban place or area
Lowers	people who in a context are subordinate or inferior to uppers. A person can be a lower in one context and an upper in another.
Model–T	the mass-produced Ford motorcar of which Henry Ford is supposed to have said something like: 'Americans can have their Model–T any color they like as long as it is black'. Model–T is used to describe standardized top-down packages for the transfer of technology or of procedures
Myth	misguided belief
Normal professionalism	the concepts, values, methods and behaviour dominant in a profession or discipline, often positivist and placing high value on measurement.
Normative	expressing value judgements or prescriptions as opposed to stating facts
Paradigm	a coherent and mutually supporting pattern of concepts, values, methods and action, amenable or claiming to be amenable, to wide application
Poor	has its common and wide meaning. This goes beyond its use as the adjective for poverty (see below) to include the broader sense of being deprived, in a bad condition, and lacking basic needs.
Positivism	a form of empiricism which holds to scientific method as means of establishing objective reality
Poverty	a condition of lack of physical necessities, assets and income. It includes, but is more than, income-poverty. Poverty can be distinguished from other dimensions of deprivation (see above)

Quadrat	a square area selected to sample vegetation in a larger area
Reality	has two senses: physical and personal. Physical reality is the world of things 'out there'. Personal reality is an individual person's perception and interpretation of physical and social realities outside her or himself. 'Reality' as in 'Whose reality counts?' refers to personal realities, including personal constructs, perceptions and values (see also pages 56–8)
Reductionism	reducing the diverse and complex to the standard and simple for purposes of analysis, or studying part of a system separately from the whole
Relevance	practical utility for learning and acting
Serendipity	making discoveries by accident
Transfer of technology (TOT)	the approach to development in which packages are developed in central, controlled environments, and then transferred to other environments and people for adoption
Triangulation	seeking multiple perspectives through different methods, analysts, entities sampled, locations, points in a distribution, sources of information, and/or disciplinary perspectives, leading to crosschecking, successive approximation and/or appreciation of ranges of variance
Trustworthiness	the quality of deserving to be believed; how believable a representation of reality deserves to be (see also pages 158–61)
Uppers	people who in a context are dominant or superior to lowers. A person can be an upper in one context and a lower in another
Vulnerability	means exposure and defencelessness. It has two sides: the external side of exposure to shocks, stress and risk; and the internal side of defencelessness, meaning a lack of means to cope without damaging loss
Well-being	the experience of good quality of life

Preface

This is a good time to be alive as a development professional. For we seem to be in the middle of a quiet but hugely exciting revolution in learning and action. That is what this book is about.

In 1983 I wrote in the preface of an earlier book *Rural Development: Putting the Last First*, that it was 'only a stage in a journey in which there is far still to go'. *Whose Reality Counts? Putting the First Last* is about another stage of that journey. And there will perhaps always remain far, far to go.

Five years ago, I began writing about the methods and approaches of participatory rural appraisal (PRA). Like others, I had been astonished by the analytical abilities of poor people. Whether literate or not, whether children, women or men, they showed that they could map, list, rank, score and diagram often better than professionals. That experience of PRA remains central, the empirical core of this book. But PRA has evolved and spread in many directions and into many domains: from NGOs to government organizations, universities and research institutes; from a few countries and sectors to many; from rural to urban; from South to North; from appraisal to longer processes of planning, negotiation, action, monitoring and evaluation; from field programmes to policy and theory; from methods to organizational procedures and cultures, and above all to personal behaviour and attitudes. PRA has come to impinge on much development practice, professionalism, research, education, training, management and institutions, and to raise questions about what sort of people we are. All this has happened fast, driven by innovating colleagues in the South. Trying to keep up and think this through has been at once daunting and exhilarating.

The PRA experience has led into wider questions about development and about the human condition. It has pointed towards a gap in the writing about development: the lack of analysis of how error, professionalism, power and personal interactions interlink. Reflective and self-critical PRA practitioners are evolving a philosophy and behaviours which seem to promise better performance. These resonate with other contemporary trends as part of a broader, deep shift in ways of thinking, seeing, acting and being in the world. So the book has come to be about more than PRA and more than just development.

Labels are a problem. As a term, 'participatory rural appraisal' no longer describes what is happening. 'Participatory' fits, with its implications of interaction and empowerment; but 'rural' is wrong because of innumerable applications in urban areas, organizations, adult literacy, policy and so on; and 'appraisal' implies only finding out and assessment, when many want PRA to describe a much longer process. Perhaps a new term is needed or, in the spirit of decentralized empowerment and local creativity, a plurality of new terms. 'Participatory learning and action' (PLA) may come to take the place of PRA, but at the time I am writing, PRA is the term people are using.

Activities described as PRA have become fashionable. The astonishment, wonder and admiration remain, and the methodological revolution continues. But as described in Chapter 10, bad practice is rife. The big question is whether PRA can be self-improving as it spreads; whether self-critical awareness, embracing error, and changing behaviour and attitudes can be part of its genes, expressing themselves through individual practice, understanding and better performance, and influencing organizational cultures and professional methods and values.

I hope readers will find the book accessible, in price, organization, language and style. Its price should be low, thanks to the publishers, and to organizations named below. Its gist can be grasped in minutes, without the bore of having to read the main text, by going to the first paragraphs of Chapter 6 and to the abstracts at the start of each chapter.

Language has posed dilemmas. I have tried to write for both academics and practitioners. The glossary says what I mean by some words and phrases. I have tried to stick close to common usage and not to invent new terms, but UPPERS and LOWERS seemed unavoidable. In writing I used lcddu for local, complex, diverse, dynamic and unpredictable, but I have put the words in full in most of the text. Nor have I been able to resist having fun with words, images and occasional verse. Despite good advice, much of that remains, though some has been quarantined in notes at the end of the book. Readers for whom notes distract may wish to scan them before reading the main text. I hope the lapses from dry prose will not undermine the arguments and evidence.

This book tries to express how I see things, but there is hubris and hypocrisy in what I write: hubris because who am I, who have been wrong so often, to examine others' errors?; hypocrisy because I do not live what I say. But hubris and hypocrisy are bad reasons for keeping quiet. If something seems right, it has to be said.

Like others, I am trapped inside a skin, a separate, fallible, self-centred person. I see and construe things in a personal way, unable to escape being who I am, moreover a white, Anglo-Saxon, educated male. Others have other realities and see and construe things differently. And our different realities evolve. In what follows, I have been driven and drawn along, not always willingly, by the logic and learning of writing. This has led me to join others in asking:

○ whether the best way forward is to engage and reflect – to experience, listen, learn and share, to be self-critical and embrace error, and to be willing to change;

○ whether for each of us there is no permanent reality, no final truth, no ultimate correct behaviour or belief, but rather, always doubt, stumbling and search;

○ whether much meaning and fulfilment are to be found in exploring and sharing better ways of learning, living and being, and in celebrating the realities of others.

Readers will have their own answers, their own realities, their own ideas of well-being and fulfilment. Let me invite them, then, to reflect critically on what is in this book, to improve on it, and to go beyond it.

Robert Chambers
July 1996

Acknowledgements

Much of this book is the outcome of collective effort. It originates in the field experience, innovations, research and writings of many people in NGOs, government organizations and universities. The Administrative Staff College of India in Hyderabad gave me a base, legitimacy and support for two years in 1989–91, and above all the freedom to travel and pursue an open-ended agenda of trying to keep up with developments. To those who were pioneering PRA in India at that time, who welcomed me as a colleague and with whom I have worked subsequently I shall always be indebted, not least to John Devavaram, Sheelu Francis, Ravi Jayakaran, Sam Joseph, Kamal Kar, James Mascarenhas, Neela Mukherjee, Anil K. Shah, Meera Kaul Shah, and Parmesh Shah. I have been fortunate in receiving comments from colleagues on earlier drafts, and help with sources and references from many people. Gordon Conway has given consistent encouragement and support. For constructive criticism which has helped in adding, revising, and avoiding traps, I am grateful to Heidi Attwood, Bob Baulch, Fiona Chambers, Tim Dyson, David Evans, Anne-Marie Goetz, Martin Greeley, Irene Guijt, Melissa Leach, Simon Maxwell, Robin Mearns, Ben Osuga, Jules Pretty, Anna Robinson-Pant, Ian Scoones, Meera Kaul Shah, John Thompson, Karen Twining and Norman Uphoff. I am also much obliged to publishers' anonymous reviewers for pertinent comments, and to Meg Howarth who as copy editor corrected many errors. I have a special thanks to Robin Mearns for reading the book, seeing it as a whole, and giving wise advice and good suggestions.

Above all my debt is to Jenny Chambers. Neither this book, nor its predecessor *Rural Development: Putting the Last First*, would have been written without her insights, ideas, inspiration and understanding. It is unfair that she has the ideas, and I write about them. I have no words adequate to express what this book owes to her.

That said, the usual disclaimers apply. Responsibility for errors and omissions, of which there are surely many, is mine and mine alone.

I am embarrassed by the way the names of co-authors and co-editors have been edited out of the text as I wrote it and reduced to *et al.* reinforcing the unfair visibility of one whose surname begins with an early letter in the alphabet. There is also an excess of self-referencing for which I have little excuse. Parts of this book draw on earlier publications, rewritten and updated. These include: 'Rural Development in India: reversals for diversity', *ASCI Journal of Management*, Vol. 21, No. 1 (1991); 'The Self-deceiving State', in Robin Murray ed., *New Forms of Public Administration*, *IDS Bulletin*, Vol. 23, No. 4 (1992); 'All Power Deceives', in Susanna Davies ed., *Knowledge is Power?*, *IDS Bulletin*, Vol. 25, No. 2 (1994); three articles on PRA in *World Development*, Vol. 22, Nos 7, 9 and 10 (1994);

and 'Poverty and Livelihoods: whose reality counts?' *IDS Discussion Paper* 347 (1994), which was originally commissioned by UNDP. Permissions to use the material are gratefully acknowledged.

Fieldwork and writing have been made possible by support from the Aga Khan Foundation, the Ford Foundation's offices in India, Bangladesh and East Africa, NOVIB, the Overseas Development Administration (UK), the Paul Hamlyn Foundation, SAREC, SIDA, and Swiss Development Cooperation. All these, together with the Ford Foundation, New York, have helped to keep the retail price of this book low. I thank them for their generosity and patience, and for the freedom they have given me. I am also grateful to Helen McLaren and Jenny Skepper for their capable, willing and trouble-free support, in working on text and tables, and helping to bring this to completion.

1

The Challenge to Change

Nothing is permanent but change
Heraclitus, c.500 BC

In the last years of the twentieth century, change accelerates and the future becomes harder to foresee. As instant communications spread, and power and wealth concentrate, so ideas spread faster. A balance-sheet of development and human well-being shows achievements and deficits. Power and poverty are polarized at the extremes, with a global overclass and a global underclass. An evolving consensus converges on well-being, livelihood, capabilities, equity, and sustainability as interlinked ends and means. Huge opportunities exist to make a difference for the better. The challenge is personal, professional and institutional, to frame a practical paradigm for knowing and acting, and changing how we know and act, in a flux of uncertainty and change.

An overview

As we approach the end of the twentieth century and the start of the twenty-first, we, humankind, have more power and more control over things, and are more closely and instantly connected with each other, than ever before. At the same time, more people than ever before are wealthy beyond any reasonable need for a good life, and more are poor and vulnerable below any conceivable definition of decency. New power, knowledge and social and economic polarization coexist on an unprecedented and scandalous scale.

Many of the hopes of earlier decades have faded and many beliefs have been challenged and changed. The visions of the 1950s and 1960s for a better world with full employment, decent incomes, universal primary education, health for all, safe water supplies, a demographic transition to stable populations, and fair terms of trade between rich and poor countries, have in no case been realized. The beliefs of those times – in linear and convergent development through stages of growth, in central planning, in unlimited growth, in industrialization as the key to development, in the feasibility of a continuous improvement in levels of living for all – these now have been exposed as misconceived and, with the easy wisdom of hindsight, naïve. Hundreds of millions of people are worse off now than twenty years ago. That some nations should be rich and others poor can even seem inevitable as we watch, year by year, the indicators of well-being improve in some, and decline in others, with lower incomes, fewer children in school, deteriorating services in health, mounting civil disorder, lower expectation of life, and greater vulnerability.

1

These deep divisions seem rooted in the sort of people we are. It is tempting then to accept and excuse them as unavoidable. The truisms trot off the tongue – 'There always have been rich and poor . . . There always have been wars . . . You can't change human nature'. So we accept the unacceptable, telling ourselves we are bowing to the inevitable. But the coexistence of extremes of wealth and poverty, or of power and vulnerability, is not inevitable. It is the result of innumerable human choices, actions and non-actions. We do not bow to physical diseases as inevitable – polio, measles, malaria, TB. Nor is there any reason to bow to social sicknesses and discords, as many millions of courageous and committed people show through the lives they live. The challenge, as with all that is not right, is to analyse, reflect and act to make things better.

The problem has many levels – international, national, regional, community, household, and individual; many dimensions – of gender, class, caste, age, occupation, and physical and mental capability; and many implications in domains which are political, legal, economic, social, psychological and ethical. All of these have a bearing. All of these present points of entry and leverage for change for the better. Nor is this all. Some would say that no book about deprivation and development is complete without chapters on war and civil disorder, on bad and worsening international terms of trade for what poor countries produce, on debt and the bad effects on poor people of policies of structural adjustment, on the insults to the environment by the affluent North, on the practices and impacts of transnational corporations, and on the ideology of greed implicit in neo-liberal economics. These are surely all relevant. All demand analysis and action. Nothing in this book should be taken as undervaluing them. Nothing written here should be taken as an excuse for ignoring them. To offset them, and to augment positive aspects and trends, have to be priorities.

I have chosen, though, a different focus. This starts with 'us', with development professionals. It asks about failures, errors and learning, about what we do and do not do, and how we can do better. The argument is that we are much of the problem, that it is through changes in us that much of the solution must be sought. An earlier book (Chambers, 1983) was subtitled 'Putting the Last First'.[1] But to put the last first is the easier half. Putting the first last is harder. For it means that those who are powerful have to step down, sit, listen, and learn from and empower those who are weak and last.

So this book is concerned as much with those who are first, with 'us' and our errors, omissions, delusions and dominance, as with 'them', the last. We are many. We are from both North and South. We include political leaders, writers, lawyers, film makers, businessmen, and bankers; students and teachers in schools, colleges, polytechnics, training institutes and universities; researchers in all development disciplines – agriculture, animal sciences, botany, ecology and other environmental sciences, economics, education, engineering, fisheries, forestry, geography, health, human nutrition, irrigation, management, political science, public administration, sanitation, social anthropology, sociology and others; all who influence or work for and with the multilateral agencies – the IMF and the World Bank, the regional Development Banks, and that litany of acronyms – the

2

CGIAR, FAO, the FAO Investment Centre, IFAD, the ILO, UNDP, UNESCO, UNHCR, UNICEF, WFP, and WHO, to name but some of the larger and better known; all those, too, who influence or work for and with bilateral aid agencies and international NGOs; we include senior decision-makers in all countries; and most numerous of all, those who are closest to the action, the fieldworkers and headquarters staff of government departments and agencies and of NGOs in the South who are directly engaged with poor people and development.

I am referring to us as a group, as 'we' and 'us'[2], after this point without inverted commas. The radical activist in a remote village in Bihar may not identify with the president of the World Bank; nor he with her. But we are all actors in the same 'upper' system of organization and communication which is ever better linked; and our decisions and actions impinge on those in the 'lower' system of local rural and urban people and places. We are all trying to change things for others, we say for the better. We are all development professionals.

There are many starting points. Each chapter is in a sense a start on its own. But I hope to show that all chapters converge. To begin, let us set the scene by examining the context of contemporary conditions and change within which this book is written.

Accelerating change

Most ages have had their chroniclers who see themselves living through times of exceptionally rapid change, and facing imminent doom. But continuous change is a natural condition of physical, biological and social systems; and fears of doom are endemic. So given that change is inherent in nature, and in human society, one can ask whether change in the mid-1990s is different.

It seems to be different in its combination of scale, speed, global scope, and unpredictability. More seems to be changing and changing faster; changes are more interconnected and more instantly communicated; and the future is harder to foresee.

This is a view from a 'core', from a place which in our terminology is called central, in a rich country, linked in with global communications, and in the mid-1990s. The waves on which we find ourselves swept along are political, economic, technological, environmental and social, and they seem to be ever accelerating. If this book survives into the twenty-first century, anyone reading it may find of historical interest the changes which seem so dynamic in the mid-1990s.

Politically, the effects of the end of the Cold War have been dramatic. Global power is now concentrated in the North, and especially in Washington. The North is now less concerned with what happens in the South. The relative stability of the Cold War has given way to flux. Against expectations, multi-party democracy is in process in more and more countries. The plural nation-state has found it harder to hold together: some countries have fallen apart and split up, peacefully or with violence – Czechoslovakia, Ethiopia, Somalia, the USSR, Yugoslavia; and many have unresolved conflicts involving violence – Afghanistan, Angola, Burundi,

Cambodia, Chechenya, Georgia, India, Indonesia, Iraq, Liberia, Rwanda, Sierra Leone, Sri Lanka, Sudan and the UK, to mention only some of those more often in the news. Against this dismal backdrop, the liberating achievements of South Africans have given the human spirit a huge lift.

Economically, power relations have polarized. The North is no longer inhibited by post-colonial guilt; the countries of the South have become weaker; and the North now more freely imposes its latest economic ideologies on the countries of the South. Globalization of the free market means that economic change is less subject to human control, and states have less control over their economies. At the same time, in the 1980s and 1990s, the World Bank, the IMF and other banks and donors have set conditions for domestic economic policies in the South to a degree unthinkable in the 1960s or 1970s. More than ever before, power is concentrated in the cores of the North, including power to determine national policies in the South.

Technological change has, if anything, been even more rapid and startling than political and economic change. Its effects on the Northern view have been strong, through accelerating rates of innovation and obsolescence especially in microprocessing and communications. Instant communication has spread to those connected through E-mail, fax and Internet, and instant news comes from CNN and the BBC. Television has shrunk our world to a visual village.

Environmentally, as every Northern schoolchild now knows, change is upon us, much of it threatening, through air, sea, water and soil pollution, through global warming and rising sea levels, through the thinning of the ozone layer, through the dangers of disarming and disposing of nuclear weapons, through nuclear waste disposal, and through deforestation and erosion.

Socially, in terms of well-being, for many in the North the experience is of increasing unemployment, job insecurity, crime, drug abuse, and anti-social anomie. Simultaneously, for the privileged of both North and South, the visual social reality perceived or repressed includes mass slaughter, genocide, starvation, child soldiers, mutilation by land mines, and the like, brought literally home on television screens.

All this is how things appear from a stance in a core, that is, either in the North or in a position of power and privilege in the South. Contrast the view from the other end, from the remote (that is, remote from many of us) peripheries in the South. From there, there is no one view, but a multiplicity. Social change is rapid in almost every part of the globe, though largely unperceived in the cores. Tens of millions are deprived and marginalized each year through political, economic and physical disasters. More, not fewer, people become refugees; more, not fewer, migrate each year in desperation and distress, hoping for a less bad life. For others, from the farming or fishing village, the pastoralists' camp, the small town or the city slum, the details differ, for each is local and special. For them, the world is not a global presence that has penetrated the living room, as in the North, but a specific outside, a particular surrounding of people, resources, services, opportunities, threats and conditions.

There is, though, one meaning, shared by the majority who live in the peripheries. For them, 'remote' refers to the cores, to the places of wealth, power and privilege which are far away. For those in the cores, 'remote' is

4

reversed, and refers to the peripheries, the places of poverty, weakness and deprivation. For the powerful minority of the cores and the powerless majority of the peripheries, the world is opposite ways round.

Both perspectives, from Northern cores and Southern peripheries, are tied to a time in history, the present. What they share, and what will persist, is the unpredictability of the future. The faster the change, the less secure the forecasts; and the quicker and more global the communication, so the greater the costs of error. Futurologists are discredited: they have been spectacularly wrong, and the errors of economic forecasters have not been few. William J. Baumol (1991: 1) has expressed the uncertainty that many feel with his statement that 'I feel obliged to confess that I can offer with any degree of confidence only one prediction – that the future will surprise me'. New humility, sensitivity, nimbleness and willingness to change are needed for the more fluid and transient conditions of contemporary life in the North. And in the peripheries of the South, the world remains uncertain, as in the past, subject to sudden changes in markets, prices, services, supplies, institutions, government staff, weather, and civil order. At any time, the world outside the local community can bring human-made or natural threat and disaster.

Polarization: overclass and underclass

Accelerating change sharpens the challenges of social and economic 'development'. The faster the change, the greater are both opportunities and dangers. Just how acute these challenges are can be gauged from progress and regress in the human condition over recent decades. These show striking contrasts: huge successes and achievements; and disastrous failures and shortcomings.

Let us start conventionally, with statistics. These are notoriously flawed and liable to mislead. The multiple and diverse realities of poverty and well-being defy capture by standard measures. Reported improvements or declines can be fictions. Yet for all their limitations, conventional figures can at least suggest some orders of magnitude, trends and contrasts. Aggregate figures for some common indicators show average improvements, as in Table 1.1. But any complacency would mislead: gross deficits

Table 1.1: Reported improvements in indicators of human well-being

	Least-developed countries		All developing countries	
	1960	1993	1960	1993
Life expectancy (years at birth)	39	51	46	61.5
Infant mortality per 1000 live births	173	110	150	70
Adult literacy rate (per cent)	29	46.5	46	69
Real GDP per capita $US	580	900*	950	2700*

Source: HDR, 1995, 1996   * rounded

remain; achievements are unstable and need to be maintained; as populations rise, absolute numbers deprived can rise even when averages improve; and deprivations interlock, making it harder at the margin to help those who are badly off.

In each sector the record is mixed. The glass that looks half full, with the achievements reported, is also half empty, with what has not been achieved for basic well-being.

In health, life expectancy in all developing countries reportedly rose, between 1960 and 1993, from 46 to 61.5 years (HDR, 1995; 1996) and infant mortality per 1000 live births reportedly more than halved, from 150 to 70. Smallpox was eradicated from the earth, and polio and Guinea Worm disease greatly reduced. In little more than a generation the proportion of rural families with access to safe water was reported to have risen from less than 10 per cent to more than 60 per cent.

On the other hand, there has been a resurgence of malaria and tuberculosis, the time bomb of HIV menaces whole peoples and economies with its insidious spread, and in some countries with civil disorder, famine and breakdown in government services, life expectancy has fallen.

In education, the adult literacy rate in developing countries reportedly rose, between 1960 and 1993, from 46 to 69 per cent, and in little more than a generation, the proportion of children in primary school is said to have risen from less than a half to more than three-quarters.

On the other hand, nearly one billion people remain illiterate, and the primary school drop-out level is said to be 30 per cent. The goal of universal primary education is not remotely in sight.

On females,[3] from 1970 to 1992, in low- and middle-income countries, rises were reported in female life expectancy at birth from 56 to 64.5 years, and in the ratio of female to male literates from 54 to 71 per cent.

On the other hand, the enormity of discrimination and violence against females is simply outrageous. In 1993, two-thirds of all illiterates were reported to be women (HDR, 1993: 12). The abuse, sexual and other, of girl children is still largely concealed by the sacred secrecy of the family, and is only beginning to come to light. India is not alone in exhibiting discrimination against females on a scale which beggars the imagination. The bad effects of dowry in India intensify as lower castes and economic groups adopt and exploit it, contributing to the selective abortion of perhaps a million female foetuses a year following prenatal sex-determination. The liberal-democratic traditions of South Asia, especially India, have allowed these issues to be exposed and debated. Bangladesh, Pakistan, and China are also implicated. At the sub-Saharan African sex ratio of 102 females to 100 males, India had 41 million missing females in 1992 and China 48 million.[4] Comparing the female:male ratios of developing countries as a whole (96 to 100) with those of industrialized countries (104 to 100) presents the staggering figure for the developing countries of over 170 million females missing.

On the military, in recent years, global military expenditures, the numbers of people in armed forces, and the numbers employed in arms industries, have all declined (HDR, 1993: 9–10), and the nuclear arsenals of the United States and the former USSR are gradually being reduced.

On the other hand, civil wars break out, some like Yugoslavia and Rwanda in the world's eye, and others like Angola, Liberia and Sudan largely forgotten in the world of international communications. Whole peoples, ethnic groups and cultures, for example the Tibetans, the Marsh Arabs of Iraq, the Kurds, the South Sudanese, and the people of East Timor are still, in the mid-1990s, oppressed and persecuted. Thirty-five million people were estimated to be refugees or displaced within their countries in 1993 (HDR, 1993: 12) and their numbers have continued to rise.

On economy, from 1960 to 1993, in developing countries as a whole, real GDP per capita nearly trebled, from US$950 to $2,700. On the other hand, the rise in the least developed countries was much more modest, from US$580 to only $900. In 36 of the 83 low-income economies and lower/middle-income economies per capita GNP from 1980 to 1991 was reported to have declined. The number of people in the world who are defined as in absolute poverty has increased and is increasing.

Globally, too, personal deprivation more broadly defined has in many places deepened. This can be understood through the interlinked dimensions of physical weakness, isolation, income-poverty, vulnerability and powerlessness (Chambers, 1983: 108–39). In any balance sheet, vulnerability is easily overlooked, yet its spread and aggravation have been widespread (see e.g. Davies, 1996; Scoones, 1995b). Hundreds of millions have become more vulnerable. They are more exposed to risks, shocks and stresses; and with the loss of physical assets and fewer and weaker social supports, they have fewer means to cope without damaging loss.

Deprivation has become more regional, concentrated more in those countries which have the least capability to improve conditions, as in many of sub-Saharan Africa, or in regions within countries, as with BIMARU (Bihar, Madhya Pradesh, Rajasathan and Uttar Pradesh) in India, with its population of some 370 million. Typically, the countries most affected are heavily in debt. Many are politically unstable and have had declining levels of living. The terms of trade for their exports are subject to long-term decline so that they have to run harder just to stay in the same place, let alone progress. Donors and creditors who proclaim their commitment to anti-poverty programmes nevertheless require poor debtor countries to pursue policies which further weaken and impoverish the poorest. A new underclass of countries has evolved, mirroring the dimensions of personal deprivation – physically weak, isolated, poor, vulnerable and powerless.

Even though the trends and tendencies are mixed, the polarization of humankind between privilege and deprivation, between security and vulnerability, and between power and impotence, seems to be intensifying. Within countries, income disparities have tended to widen. When SIDA reviewed the 21 countries which it had been aiding, it found that income inequalities had grown in all of them (pers. comm. Gunilla Olsson, 1995). In general, the distribution of income has become increasingly more unequal since 1960 (Tabatabai, 1995). There are now more very poor and vulnerable people in the world than ever before; and they are more and more concentrated in regions and nations which are themselves weak and deprived, lacking resources, or the capacity or will to act, or impoverished

Table 1.2: World Classes 1992

Global class	Overclass	Middle	Underclass
Category of consumption	Overconsumers (1.1 billion)	Moderates (3.3 billion)	Marginals (1.1 billion)
Income per capita	over US$7500	US$700–7500	less than US$700
Diet	meat, packaged food, soft drinks	grain, clean water	insufficient grain, unsafe water
Calories consumed[5]	too many	about right	too few
Transport	private cars	bicycles, public transport	on foot
Materials	throwaways	durables	local biomass
Shelter	spacious climatized	modest	rudimentary
Clothing	image conscious	functional	secondhand or scraps

Adapted from Korten, 1995: 6 and Durning, 1992: 27

by debt and declining terms of trade, or racked by civil disturbance, or suffering combinations of these. Personal deprivation is nested within national deprivation.

With the withering away of Marxism, the usefully vague word class has gone out of fashion. Humankind can, though, be seen to have two polar concentrations – an overclass with wealth and power, and an underclass which is poor and weak, with a mixed and mobile middle. In 1992, this was described by Alan Durning (1992: 27) as three World Consumption Classes, whose characteristics are elaborated in Table 1.2.

The overclass of overconsumers is the same size as the underclass of marginals. The income taken home by the wealthy overclass is not twice, or 4 times, or 8 times, or 16 times, but 32 times that of the poor underclass.

The overclass is a majority within the countries of the North, and a minority within the countries of the South. There is a 'South', perhaps 20 per cent of the population, in the North, and there is a 'North', again perhaps 20 per cent of the population, in the South. In the North, the overclass makes up a democratic majority which votes for its own interests against the smaller underclass, and luxuriates in a 'culture of contentment' (Galbraith, 1992). This overclass gained from the neo-liberal right-wing governments of the 1980s. And the North as a whole has gained from its dominant position *vis-à-vis* the South. Despite this, the minority overclass in the South finds common interests with the overclass in the North. Wherever it is, the overclass holds power, and bears the main responsibility for what is done and not done.

The categories of overclass and underclass dramatize the polarization of our world. Like all such categories, and all statistics about complex realities, they simplify the reality. Conditions, people, trends, resource endowments, and relationships, are diverse – within families, groups, communities, regions, and nations. All the same, the overclass and underclass are stable: the overclass has multiple interlocking privileges, securities and advantages which keep it on top; and the underclass has multiple interlocking disabilities, vulnerabilities and deprivations which hold it under. The question is how to help them converge, how to narrow the gap, how to enable the overclass to accept less, and how to enable the underclass to gain more.

An evolving consensus

Faced with many shifting dimensions, the temptation is to simplify or despair. Ambiguity, diversity and plural realities can be difficult to tolerate. Refuge can be sought in negativism. The outside cover of *The Development Dictionary: A Guide to Knowledge as Power* (Sachs, 1992) asserts that 'The idea of development stands today like a ruin in the intellectual landscape'. That is no grounds for pessimism. Much can grow on and out of a ruin. Past errors as well as achievements contribute to current learning. So it is that in the mid-1990s a consensus may be evolving on concepts, objectives and actions for a better future.

It seems bold to assert that in conditions of accelerating change, concepts may be stabilizing. Ideas for development policy and practice have continuously changed, not least in response to the conditions from which they derive and on which they act. With the extension of instant over-communication on the cybernetic superhighway, and with new concentrations of intellect and power in central places, Northern and donor-driven lurches of policies to promote and fashions to follow can now spread faster. At any time there have coexisted a range of vocabulary, concepts, and values, some considered old-fashioned, some current, and some avant-garde. So it is only to be expected that the frontier words of the mid-1990s, such as accountability, ownership, stakeholder and transparency will be followed and perhaps superseded by others. All the same, certain other words, concepts and phrases have gradually grown in usage and have a generality and utility which seem to fit them for survival even in volatile and turbulent conditions and debates.

At a general level, there is putting people first, featuring in the titles of at least two books (Cernea, 1985 and Burkey, 1993). A massive shift in priorities and thinking has been taking place, from things and infrastructure to people and capabilities. Consonant with this shift, five words, taken together, seem to capture and express much of an emerging consensus. These are well-being, livelihood, capability, equity and sustainability. Each is linked with the others, as in Figure 1.1.

Each word can be presented in a statement:

○ *The objective of development is well-being for all.* Well-being can be described as the experience of good quality of life. Well-being, and its opposite ill-being, differ from wealth and poverty. Well-being and ill-being are words with equivalents in many languages. Unlike wealth, well-being is open to the whole range of human experience, social,

9

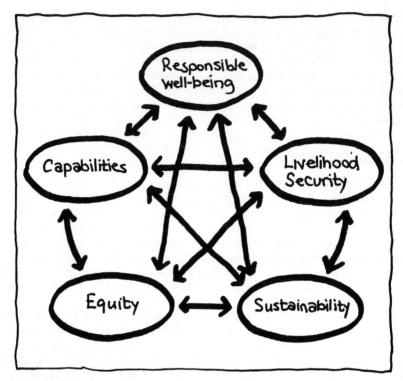

Note: The overarching end is well-being, with capabilities and livelihood as means. Equity and sustainability are principles which qualify livelihood to become livelihood *security*, and well-being to become *responsible* well-being.

Figure 1.1: The web of responsible well-being

mental and spiritual as well as material. It has many elements. Each person can define it for herself or himself. Perhaps most people would agree to include living standards, access to basic services, security and freedom from fear, health, good relations with others, friendship, love, peace of mind, choice, creativity, fulfilment and fun. Extreme poverty and ill-being go together, but the link between wealth and well-being is weak or even negative: reducing poverty usually diminishes ill-being, but amassing wealth does not assure well-being.

○ *Livelihood security is basic to well-being.* Livelihood can be defined as adequate stocks and flows of food and cash to meet basic needs and to support well-being. Security refers to secure rights and reliable access to resources, food and income, and basic services. It includes tangible and intangible assets to offset risk, ease shocks and meet contingencies.[6] Sustainable livelihoods maintain or enhance resource productivity on a long-term basis and equitable livelihoods maintain or enhance the livelihoods and well-being of others.

○ *Capabilities are means to livelihood and well-being.*[7] Capabilities refers to what people are capable of doing and being. They are means to

10

livelihood and fulfilment; and their enlargement through learning, practice, training and education are means to better living and to well-being.
o *The poor, weak, vulnerable and exploited should come first.* Equity
qualifies all initiatives in development. Equity includes human rights,
intergenerational and gender equity, and the reversals of putting the last
first and the first last, to be considered in all contexts. The reversals are
not absolute, but a means of levelling.
o *To be good, conditions and change must be sustainable – economically,
socially, institutionally, and environmentally.* Sustainability means that
long-term perspectives should apply to all policies and actions, with
sustainable well-being and sustainable livelihoods as objectives for present and future generations.

Each word relates to the others, but they are of different sorts. Equity and
sustainability are principles. They also combine in intergenerational equity,
the principle of assuring the rights and opportunities of future generations.
For their part, capabilities and livelihood security are intermediate ends as
means to well-being. The overarching end is well-being, qualified by equity
and sustainability to be responsible. This means that well-being is not at the
cost of equity and sustainability, but is enhanced when it contributes to
them. Responsible well-being recognizes obligations to others, both those
alive and future generations, and to their quality of life. In general, the
word 'responsible' has moral force in proportion to wealth and power: the
wealthier and more powerful people are, the greater the actual or potential
impact of their actions or inactions, and so the greater the need and scope
for their well-being to be responsible. The objective of development
around which consensus might coalesce is then *responsible well-being by
and for all.*

When it comes to policies and practice, less agreement can be expected.
What ought to be done, and how it should be done, is sensitive to conditions. Any tentative outline of consensus here is more open to challenge,
and more likely to shift and vary. Still, some elements in a mid-1990s view
of how to achieve well-being, livelihoods, enhanced capabilities, equity and
sustainability, might include:

o combining and balancing the state and the market, to benefit, serve and
empower the poor;
o seeking livelihood-intensity in social and economic change;
o securing human rights for all, including peace, the equitable rule of law,
and secure rights of property and access for the poor;
o ensuring means of livelihood for all, comprising access to livelihood
resources and/or employment, together with safety nets;
o providing basic services for all, including health, education, water, housing; and
o facilitating participation, with approaches which are bottom up with
processes of learning, rather than top-down with blueprints.

On concepts and objectives, and on policies and actions, there is no final
word. There are, as it were, two polarized paradigms: one with a structure
which is linear, organized, predictable and converging on equilibrium; and

11

one with a form which is non-linear, chaotic, unpredictable, divergent and non-equilibrium. In the latter, everything is provisional and subject to review. Change and learning know no boundaries. Realities are multiple. But some elements of learning do persist; and time will show whether those above will be among the survivors.

The power and will to act

A basic question is what power and will there are to act to put people first, and poor people first of all. Among the conditions affecting power and will, three deserve note:

1. Much that happens on a vast scale is neither accountable nor under effective control. Uncontrolled globalization adds to uncertain or negative outcomes for the poor. Transnational corporations (TNCs) are footloose, shifting nimbly to their advantage from country to country, and subject to little regulation. Foreign-exchange speculations on an unprecedented scale cream off fortunes for a few at the expense of the many. Whether the poor gain or lose from TNCs depends hardly at all on any regulation; and profits from currency speculation would appear to be at the cost of the whole of the rest of humankind, including the poor. Such global trends present themselves, like the weather, as hazards to be observed and forecast fallibly, but seemingly outside human control.
2. Fundamentalisms are divisive, and weaken any sense that individuals can make a difference. They lure the unsuspecting and insecure into belief systems which separate people into 'either/or' groups – believers and unbelievers, the saved and the damned, the chosen and the rest, the proletariat and the bourgeoisie, the ideologically sound and the ideologically unsound, often with closed categories. Caricatured in their vulgar forms, both neo-classical and Marxist theory render the individual virtually powerless to change the course of human affairs. What happens is determined by self-interested maximizers and historical forces respectively. The human world can then appear a neo-classical system driven inexorably by greed, or a Marxist zero-sum game in which gain for one is loss for another. In neither case would the overclass willingly accept loss or forgo gain so that the underclass could be better off. For fundamentalist cynics, the global haves will always hold on to what they have, and never give over anything for the global have-nots; and the individual is largely impotent.
3. Fine rhetoric is rarely matched by equivalent action. In words, aid agencies have been squarely for the underclass. The Overseas Development Administration of the British government has had as its declared policy: 'The purpose of our overseas aid for developing countries is to promote sustainable economic and social development and good government in order to reduce poverty, suffering and deprivation and to improve the quality of life for poor people' (FCO, 1993: 40).
  Successive presidents of the World Bank have repeatedly stated their similar commitment, as for example Lewis Preston in 1993: 'Sustainable

poverty reduction is the World Bank's fundamental objective. It is the benchmark by which our performance as a development institution should be judged' (Preston, 1993); and at the Social Summit in Copenhagen in 1995, leaders of the world's richest and most powerful countries committed themselves to: '. . . the goal of eradicating poverty in the world, through decisive national actions and international co-operation, as an ethical, social, political and economic imperative for humankind' (WSSD, 1995).

Yet reviews (ActionAid, 1994; 1995) by NGOs found 17 out of 21 donor countries cutting aid, with a 6 per cent decline between 1992 and 1993, leading to the conclusion that 'Despite many assertions that poverty focus is the priority of official aid, there is little hard evidence that money is actually following the rhetoric' (ActionAid, 1994). The problem is to make rhetoric bite in the real, messy world.

Interpenetrating these negative conditions are others that are positive. Much, but not all, that TNCs do is bad for the poor. Much, but not all, of the windfall profits of currency speculators, is used selfishly: George Soros,[8] gave away some of the billions of pounds he made out of British devaluation to support education and development in Eastern Europe. He did not have to do that. But there are others in the overclass who go much further, who organize and work for the underclass and who inspire through their vision, lives and leadership, not just those like Gandhi, Freire, Schumacher, Mother Theresa and Mandela who are well known, but those unnamed millions who work for NGOs, in governments and in other organizations, in a spirit of service. And even if the quantity of aid stagnates or declines, some of its quality improves.

The key is personal choice. The actions of TNCs, of currency speculators, of UN agencies, of governments, of NGOs are all mediated by individual decisions and action. The point is so obvious and so universal it pains to have to make it. People are complex and diverse. People can choose how to behave and what to do. The assumption of pervasive selfishness and greed in neoliberal and male-dominated thought, policy and action supports a simplistic view of human nature. This overlooks or underestimates selflessness, generosity and commitment to others, and the fulfilment that these qualities bring. Development theorists have neglected the drives and pleasures of generosity and altruism, and the personal trade-offs between satisfactions.

As words go, 'altruism' is a Cinderella of development. It provokes the cynic to see through to other, less flattering, realities. Human motivation is many-sided, and almost any act can be seen in a good or bad light. Whatever other negative interpretations may also apply, there is a level at which part of the motivation for many actions is to help others, to make things better for those who are less fortunate or in need. Altruism is a fact of human behaviour, and can be chosen. The huge achievements of recent decades in health had many causes, but the desire to reduce suffering, to cut infant mortality, to make life better for those who are deprived, was surely one. No one is fully determined; no one is immune from altruism.

Beyond this, the new concentrations of power in the 1990s present new opportunities for action. The unipolar focus of power, influence and decision-making in the eastern United States presents new opportunities for individual intervention. Washington is the home of the United States government, of the World Bank, and of the IMF. New York is the headquarters of the United Nations. In the democratic environment of the United States, all of these can be confronted and pressured.[9] A busy small group of committed NGO lobbyists in Washington has an influence far out of proportion to its numbers. Moreover, like their colleagues in other countries, it has shown repeatedly that policy and practice are not fully determined, can be changed, and flow from accumulations of individual decisions about what to say and do. Humankind is closer together, and the peripheries are closer to the centres of power, than ever before. And the changes with which we are concerned are not between political Left and Right, or between states and markets. They are between the priorities of the powerful and those of the weak.

The potential for deliberate, chosen change is there. If the levers of power are stronger, so too is the potential for change. Many are now better placed to act than were their predecessors. Whether they now act in favour of the weak and poor depends on many motivations. The choices are real; for all actors there is an agenda for personal fulfilment and responsible well-being through generosity, vision, commitment and courage.

The challenge to change

The problem is how, in conditions of continuous and accelerating change, to put people first and poor people first of all; how to enable sustainable well-being for all. The thesis of this book is that solutions can be sought in a new paradigm and a new professionalism.

Basic to a new professionalism is the primacy of the personal. This recognizes the power of personal choice, the prevalence of error, and the potential for doing better in this thing called development. The personal, professional and institutional challenge is learning how to learn, learning how to change, and learning how to organize and act.

The new paradigm needs change and adaptability in its genes: for if nothing is permanent but change, then managing and coping with change has to be inherent in the paradigm itself. In this respect, it is a meta-paradigm, a paradigm about paradigms. Different elements will have different degrees of robustness and permanence. Which will endure is not knowable. That they will change is the only certainty. The analytical challenge is to frame a practical paradigm for knowing and acting, and changing how we know and act, in a flux of uncertainty and change.

2

Normal Error

. . . a waste of money and a bloody mess.
Official of a multilateral agency on
Integrated Rural Development Projects

Some of the potential gains from personal and professional change can be gauged through analysis of error. Errors in development are so common as to be normal. Some are embraced and lead to quick learning; others are embedded and sustained. Past errors are evident in many domains. Examples include: macro-policies; beliefs about food and famines; projects, programmes and packages; science and technology; and beliefs about people and the environment. The puzzle is why we, development professionals, have been wrong so often and for so long. Learning has been slow. The challenge is to learn faster and better.

Errors: embraced or embedded?

'To err is human' is oddly absent from *The Methuen Dictionary of Clichés* (Ammer, 1992). Yet Alexander Pope's phrase is common currency in colloquial English, and error is normal in all domains of human activity. That the history of development is littered with errors is, then, scarcely surprising. The other side of the coin is that if we could learn from errors and avoid them in future, 'development' would be transformed. This chapter presents and analyses examples of error to provide a basis for seeing how to do better.

Errors in development lie on a continuum between two poles: at one pole embraced errors which lead to learning; at the other, embedded errors which sustain mistakes.

Errors which are recognized and embraced can lead quickly to better understanding and performance. Faced with the complexity, diversity and dynamism of people, conditions, institutions and actions, it is only to be expected that mistakes will be made. Those who take responsibility and act have to learn, adapt and adjust on the run. For them, lessons from mistakes are needed for learning to do better. There is, then, a class of errors which can lead to quick improvements. They are short-term and reversible. They are known as trial-and-error, learning-by-doing, and successive approximation, and found and expected in pilot projects and in a learning process approach (Korten, 1980, 1984; Rondinelli, 1983). The opportunity they present is to 'fail forward' (Peters, 1989: 261–2). They are errors for learning.

Embedded errors go deeper, last longer, and do more damage. Often they reflect widely held views, and are generalized. Often they fit what powerful people want to believe. They tend to spread, to be self-

15

perpetuating, and to dig themselves in. Embedded error proliferates and sustains failures.

This chapter is concerned more with embedded errors. Some academics delight in exposing them, and I am not guiltless on that score. But the consummation sought is not an orgy of morbid glee. It is to understand how and why we, development professionals, so often get it wrong while so sure we are right.

Effective action requires understanding of the physical and social world on which we seek to act. We have to know what works and what does not. The presumption has been strong among development professionals that we do know what we are doing. But many beliefs, policies, projects and programmes which have been part of conventional wisdom at one time have proved later to have been false or flawed. Those which follow are a few, selected because they are accessible, and have been well analysed and documented. The aim is to understand how these errors arose and were so deeply embedded, and how similar errors can be avoided.

Macro-policy

The most serious such errors in scale of impact have been in macro-policy prescriptions for development, since these have affected so many people so much. In the 1950s industrialization was seen as key to progress for the underdeveloped countries. A linear view of development was concerned with a convergent evolution of economies, with 'catching up', with, in Rostow's (1960) term, 'take-off into sustained growth' which would pass through standard stages of development. Infant industries were protected. National planning was prestigious and the norm. Parastatals proliferated. But in the 1970s, much prescription changed. Natural resource endowments were seen to be crucial, and agriculture and rural development were stressed. Large-scale loans were disbursed for capital investment. The 1980s followed with heavy indebtedness and the neo-liberal lurch, leading to the imposition on weak, impoverished and now deeply indebted governments, especially in sub-Saharan Africa, of policies of structural adjustment by their creditors. These policies, it was hoped, would enable their economies to recover and their debts to be repaid. Markets were to be freed. State bureaucracies, which had earlier been encouraged to swell, were now to be shrunk. So the development dogmas of the powerful did a U-turn, from a neo-Fabianism of direct government action and of parastatals, in which the state did more and more, to a neo-liberalism of privatization and a free market, in which the state did less and less.

To be fair, policies make more sense in their contemporary conditions than they seem to later. Also, whatever policies are followed, some people will usually be hurt and so the policies will be open to criticism. All the same, with hindsight, one can see a succession of massively damaging mistakes: first, to expect weak states to do so much through central planning and direct government action; then to drive them deep into debt with enormous loans; and then, when they were in no position to argue, to thrust on them policies of structural adjustment which made life worse for the poorest. The policies were flawed, but at the time most professionals, especially economists,

16

thought them right. The puzzle is how such errors, so obvious after the fact, could have occurred, and on such a phenomenal scale. And since the confidence and conviction of the powerful seem sustainable in the face of such errors, the questions are how much they and other development professionals are still wrong, and may continue to be wrong, while sure they are right; and how we can all of us learn to be less wrong in the future.

Integrated Rural Development Projects

The literature on development errors is neither sparse nor all of it recent (see for example Wood, 1950; Baldwin, 1957; Hirschman, 1967; Chambers, 1973; Cassen et al. 1986; Hill, 1986; Porter, Allen and Thompson, 1991; Morse and Berger, 1992). Errors and failures are found in the work of all development organizations, not just in international agencies, bilateral donors, and host governments, but also in NGOs and banks. The project and programme errors considered here involve the World Bank, because it combines huge scales of operation with self-critical transparency in sharing some of its learning with others.

Following Robert McNamara's speech in Nairobi in September 1973, rural poverty and rural development became priorities for World Bank lending. Smallholder farming and farmers were identified as the main target. Since rural development and smallholder farming had many related aspects, it was considered that many of these should be tackled simultaneously. To make this manageable, bounded geographical areas were identified for integrated rural development projects (IRDPs). The designs sought to combine simultaneous and co-ordinated actions, often by different organizations and departments, but with an on-site project management.

Between 1973 and 1986, the Bank lent US$19 billion for nearly five hundred (498) rural development projects, the total costs of which were estimated at $50 billion (i.e. averaging about $100 million each). Area development projects were 40 per cent of the portfolio. The outcome for these was a large proportion of failures, especially in sub-Saharan Africa (World Bank, 1988 *passim*). In the words of the Bank's own, commendably self-critical evaluation: 'the Bank apparently lost sight of the reality that the cost of failures, in what were identified from the outset as risky experiments, would be borne by borrower countries and not by the Bank' (ibid. xviii).

The evaluation concludes that there are many lessons to be learnt. They included problems arising from:

○ institutional and managerial complexity;
○ lack of the viable technical packages which had been assumed; and
○ supply-driven lending, high targets, and urgent large-scale action without pilot projects.

Beliefs about food and famine

Few fields are of more intense concern for human well-being and development than food. Lay people can be forgiven for supposing that human nutritional requirements would have long since been established by hard

17

science, and would be universally recognized. This, however, has not been so, either with the composition of diet, or with calorie requirements.

On diet, it was believed in the 1950s that protein deficiency was the major cause of malnutrition, and that the solution was to increase the intake of protein. This led to feeding undernourished children with expensive high-protein foods. Then it came to be understood that the main deficiency was usually calories, not proteins. In consequence, feeding priorities shifted from proteins to ensuring adequate calories through carbohydrates, which were also cheaper. Although some debate continues about how important proteins are, adequate calories are still recognized as usually the top priority.

Micronutrients have been another big change. In the past decade, vitamin A, vitamin C, thiamine and niacin, and iodine, iron and zinc, have been found to matter more to physical well-being than earlier thought (Uvin, 1992: 39–50; 1994: 20–26). Micronutrient additions to the diet, especially vitamin A, can reduce morbidity and mortality among many children (Beaton et al. 1993). On current form, it would be surprising if coming decades did not see yet further discoveries about diet and nutrition.

On calorie requirements, the belief current in the 1950s and 1960s was that these were around 3000kcal or more. This was for an active male in the North. When the figures were applied worldwide, very large numbers of people were classified as seriously malnourished. In 1950 Lord Boyd-Orr, the first Director-General of FAO, wrote in *Scientific American* (cited in Uvin, 1994: 63) that 'a lifetime of malnutrition and actual hunger is the lot of at least two-thirds of mankind'. But since then estimates of individual nutrient requirements have shown a long-term downward trend. The National Academy of Sciences estimates of food energy requirements for a moderately active man of 70kg bodyweight declined from 3200kcal in 1958 to 2700kcal in 1974 (see Table 2.1), and FAO estimates for a moderately active man of 55kg declined from 2830kcal in 1957 to 2450kcal in 1985.

The technical issues are not simple, given variances by body weight, basic metabolic rate, sex, life cycle (including pregnancy and lactation), season, physical activity, climate and state of health. These variables give experts plenty of leeway to choose between alternative estimates. It seems that estimates of requirements, and of numbers of people undernourished, have been influenced not just by research, but by a shifting climate of opinion, judgements by individuals and committees, and political considerations (Pacey and Payne, 1985 ch. 1; Uvin, 1994 ch. 3). One fear was that if estimated calorie requirements were reduced, the numbers for the hungry would decline, and support for international agencies and aid would be undermined.

Even more radical changes have taken place in the understanding of famines. For many years, the received wisdom was three commonsense beliefs: first, that famines resulted from a shortage of food; second, that deaths in famines resulted from starvation; and third, that the action required was to supply food when people could no longer feed themselves. In his 1981 book *Poverty and Famines*, Amartya Sen challenged the first belief, arguing that famines were more the result of lack of entitlements – the lack of the ability to command and obtain food, than of lack of food or

Table 2.1: Some estimates of food energy requirements

Year	Kcal	A: Male, bodyweight 70kg
1958	3200	NAS moderately active
1968	2800	NAS moderately active
1974	2700	NAS moderately active
		B: Male, bodyweight 55kg
1957	2830	FAO moderate activity
1965	2500	active, in Africa
1973	2530	FAO moderate activity
1983	2400	ICMR[1] recommended daily intake adult, moderate physical activity
1985	2450	WHO/FAO/UNU ditto (est. 2710, corrected for overestimate of BMR[2])
1985	2200	as above, with minimal activities
1985	1960	as above, with body weight adjusted to 44kg
1985	1550	as above, 'survival' requirement

Sources: Pacey and Payne 1985: 23 and Payne 1990: 15 citing various sources.
[1]ICMR = Indian Council for Medical Research; [2]BMR = basic metabolic rate.

decline in food availability. In his 1989 book *Famine that Kills* Alexander de Waal challenged the second belief, arguing on the basis of extended field-work that in Darfur in 1984–85, that disease, often water-borne, was the overwhelmingly important killer in the famine, not hunger. In her 1996 book, *Adaptable Livelihoods*, Susanna Davies has challenged the short-term reductionism of the third belief. Drawing on research and experience in Mali and elsewhere, she establishes the case for earlier interventions, and for a shift to save livelihoods, not just lives. These three books, and the research on which they are based, change the way famines are viewed and the prescriptions for actions to be taken in response and in anticipation. But none of these new received wisdoms is itself final, and each is subject to continuing debate.

The learning from all this is that what appear to be hard scientific facts and figures can be selected according to the climate of opinion and to political considerations; that combinations of scientific knowledge and common sense can be wrong; and that in matters as complex and locally and individually variable as the relations between human physiology, deprivation, famine, food and livelihoods, there is much to doubt and probably much still to learn.

Post-harvest losses of grain

In matters amenable to investigation by hard science, development professionals are inclined to believe that 'we know', and that our technology is superior. There are areas where this is well established and credible, and where modern scientific knowledge has an advantage over local knowledge. This is especially the case with the very small and microscopic, as with viruses, bacteria, and their related diseases; and with the very large and macroscopic, as with comparative conditions in other places. There are other areas where accurate knowledge has been claimed, or has appeared to have been established, but where there is actually uncertainty and error. An example is village-level post-harvest losses of foodgrains. On this, the principal sources used here are Martin Greeley's (1980, 1982, 1986, and 1987 Ch. 2) analyses of the origins and explanations of estimates of village-level post-harvest losses of grains.

Post-harvest losses of food at the village level became a major focus of attention in the 1970s, especially following the World Food Conference of 1974. They were identified as 'the neglected dimension in increasing the world's food supply' (Bourne, 1977, cited in Greeley, 1986: 333). Estimates were high. The most extreme, cited by Lester Brown (*Seeds of Change*, 1970) was where 'according to one calculation, based on local reports, 50 per cent of the grain crop of India was lost to rodents, 15 per cent was lost during milling and processing, 15 per cent was lost to cows, birds and monkeys, 10 per cent was lost to insects and 15 per cent was lost during storage and transit – a grand total of 105 per cent'. Less extreme but still high figures were taken more seriously and widely quoted. Parpia (1977: 20) argued that 'In most of the food-deficit countries, actual shortages (of food) represent 4–6 per cent, while losses have been estimated at 20–40 per cent of production'. The figures of 30 and 40 per cent were widely and loosely quoted in many different contexts. Typically, an account of participatory research concerned with post-harvest losses in Tanzania opens with the statement that 'As much as 30–40% of grain harvests in Tanzania have been lost annually' (SPRA 1982: 6).

The belief in such huge post-harvest losses of grains at the village level led to the establishment of large-scale programmes of intervention. FAO set up a Post-harvest Loss Prevention Programme, and its budget for postharvest-related programmes rose from US$2.5 million in 1976/77 to over $19 million in 1981. USAID tripled its authorized expenditure between 1976 and 1978, from nearly US$5 million to nearly $15 million.

When careful multi-disciplinary field-level research was later carried out village-level post-harvest losses were found in practice, again and again, to be low. Tyler and Boxall (1984) reviewing ten storage loss studies reported that 'the results from nine of the ten farm-loss studies showed that losses appear to be fairly well contained about or below the 5 per cent level over the storage season'.

The wrong belief appears to have had several sources. One was losses of high-yielding varieties in the Green Revolution which led to large marketed surpluses for which storage was a problem, and which were more vulnerable to pest attack. Another source was on-station research conducted by de Padua (1976) at IRRI. This measured losses in harvesting, handling, threshing, drying, storage and milling. The aim was to see how losses varied with time of harvesting. The results gave ranges of loss. Summing the lows gave 10 per cent; summing the highs gave 37 per cent. A technical critique (Greeley 1986, 1987) shows these figures were themselves high (correct multiplying

20

gives 32 per cent, not 37, etc). Though derived from an on-station experiment to determine ranges of losses under different, including suboptimal conditions, the figures were subsequently quoted by others as applying to the farm level, and as late as 1985 as evidence of up to 37 per cent losses at the farm-level in South-east Asia (ASEAN 1985).

The belief in high losses proved resiliently sustainable. Commercial interests had no cause to underestimate losses, since silos and other storage technology lent themselves to profits from capital-aid programmes: in Bourne's laconic words (1977: 15): 'figures that have been obtained by careful measurement are manipulated for various reasons'. Rural development tourists were vulnerable to the way in which 'farmers, usually village leaders, will often oblige the visiting post-harvest 'experts' by displaying the severity of their post-harvest problems (perhaps the few remaining insect-damaged, rodent-chewed cobs from a harvest long since past)' (Greeley 1986). Thirty per cent and 40 per cent were easy figures to remember and repeat for those who write general development briefs, compose speeches for ministers, and personally pontificate at conferences. Moreover, high farm-level losses were attractive because they blamed the farmer and invited a modern technological fix. There were many reasons for wanting to believe in high losses.

The learning is that vested interests and professional predispositions can sustain an entrenched belief long after it has been repeatedly exposed as false.

Animal-drawn wheeled toolcarriers

The source for this section is Paul Starkey's scholarly and sobering study *Animal-Drawn Wheeled Toolcarriers: Perfected yet Rejected* (1988).

Wheeled toolcarriers are multipurpose implements that can be used for ploughing, seeding, weeding and transport. In the three decades to 1987 about 10 000 wheeled toolcarriers of over 45 designs were made, mainly in and for Africa and Asia. The toolcarriers were designed by agricultural engineers, developed and tested in workshops and on research stations, and then passed on to farmers for trials and to manufacturers for production. The International Crops Research Institute for the Semiarid Tropics (ICRISAT) developed toolcarriers which received much publicity. Up to 1200 were distributed to farmers through credit and subsidies of up to 80 per cent. Worldwide, more than one hundred senior person-years, and several hundred person-years of less senior staff, were devoted to the development of these toolbars, and the cost at 1987 prices was estimated to be over US$40 million (ibid: 142).

Wheeled toolcarriers were rejected by farmers. The reasons were high cost, heavy weight, lack of manoeuvrability, inconvenience, complication of adjustment, difficulty in changing between modes, and higher risk and less flexibility than with a range of single-purpose implements. Their design was a compromise between the many different requirements. Farmers did better, by their criteria, with single-purpose implements. Of the 10 000 or so toolcarriers made, Starkey found that the number ever used by farmers as multipurpose implements for several years was negligible (ibid: 9). Wheeled toolcarriers were, in sum, a resounding failure.

Farmer rejection was apparent from the early 1960s. At a conference at ICRISAT in 1979, an economic analysis (Binswanger *et al.*, 1979) cautiously supported further development, but on a field visit during that conference farmers who had been trying out the ICRISAT toolcarrier embarrassingly rejected it, on three grounds: the strong bullocks needed to draw it, its cost, and the large area required for it to be economical. Nevertheless, work on the toolcarrier continued. After his careful comparative research, Starkey concluded that 'No wheeled toolcarrier has yet been proven by sustained farmer adoption in any developing country'. Yet as late as 1987 'Research, development and promotional activities (were) continuing in at least twenty countries in Africa, Asia and Latin America' (ibid. 131).

Much technically expert work was done; but, to borrow the title of Starkey's book, the wheeled toolcarriers were 'perfected yet rejected'. There was a collective myth. When Starkey corresponded with those who were developing and testing these implements, a common reply was that they were facing difficulties, but that they knew toolcarriers had been successful elsewhere.

The learning is that we have a puzzle: to understand how so many able agricultural engineers, scientists and researchers, and so many donor agencies, were able to persist in the face of negative evidence, how they could have gone on being, for so long, so wrong. It seems that personal, professional and institutional commitment to a failure can be sustained in many ways.

Woodfuel forecasts

Mistakes in forecasting are normal, but the errors in forecasting the wood-fuel crisis in African and some other countries crossed the boundary into pathology. The forecasts were documented and critiqued by Gerald Leach and Robin Mearns in *Beyond the Woodfuel Crisis: People, Land and Trees in Africa* (1988) (see also Dewees, 1989b and Mearns, 1995).

The woodfuel crisis was 'discovered' in the mid-1970s after the oil price rises of 1973 and 1974. Evidence had been accumulating of deforestation and of increasing shortages of fuelwood. The problem was analysed according to 'woodfuel gap theory'. This estimated current and projected consumption of woodfuels set against current stocks and a projected growth of trees. In the first half of the 1980s, this type of demand and supply analysis for woodfuels was conducted in the sixty-odd UNDP/World Bank energy-sector assessments for African and other countries in the South (ibid: 6). Typically, consumption was found greatly to exceed the annual growth of trees. This led to predictions that the last tree in Tanzania would disappear in 1990 and in Sudan in 2005. Leach and Mearns' observation in 1988 (ibid: 7) that 'There are still many trees in Tanzania' remains true in the mid-1990s.

The gap calculations were multifariously flawed in terms of both supply and consumption:

Supply
o total tree stocks were usually grossly underestimated by forest departments since they knew little about trees outside forests, for example on farm, fallow and village common lands;

22

o natural regeneration was usually omitted, although 'tree regrowth can soften dramatically the dire predictions of gap forecasts' (ibid: 8);
o surpluses were not accounted for arising from land-clearing, often the largest source of woodfuel;
o farmers plant and protect trees to provide for their needs and also to meet market opportunities;
o much tree-based fuel is, in practice, dead branches, twigs and leaves, and does not entail depletion of living stock.

Consumption
o woodfuel consumption figures were unreliable and conclusions were sensitive to small differences in assumptions;
o consumption was assumed to rise in proportion to population, but people have many coping strategies for substitutions and economizing in face of scarcity. Substitutions occur, and change over time, between tree-based fuel of different sorts, dung, crop residues and fuels such as kerosene. For example, Patrick Darling (1993: 2) has reported for Ethiopia that: 'Western economists . . . calculated tree requirements, assuming that Highland people had similar per caput fuel consumption levels as those elsewhere in Africa. Had they consulted local people, they would have found that fermentation and rapid cooking of *t'ef enjera* pancakes has reduced per caput fuel consumption by a factor of up to ten';
o woodfuel and other fuel-consumption patterns are highly variable locally and seasonally, making averages of aggregates misleading, and defying generalization (Mearns, 1995). For example, in a survey of 38 villages in Ethiopia (CESEN, 1986 cited by Mearns), energy consumption was found to vary between 4 and 38 gigajoules per person.

Few would deny that rural energy is often a problem or that it bears heavily on women. That the problem was grossly misperceived and exaggerated by planners also seems beyond dispute. Some of the prescriptions that flowed from these analyses were for urgent top-down large-scale afforestation in Africa. The need now perceived is for actions which are small-scale and local.

The learning is that central planners, cut off from local conditions, confined with their computers, uncritical of bad data and ignorant of how people live, are prone to construct for themselves and their colleagues costly worlds of fantasy, prophesying doom and prescribing massive programmes which are neither needed nor feasible.

People and the environment

The view is widespread that poor people are bad for the environment and more poor people are worse. The following quotes illustrate:

The interaction of poverty and environmental destruction sets off a downward spiral of ecological deterioration that threatens the physical security, economic well-being and health of many of the world's poorest people (Leonard, 1989: 6).

The human factors responsible for this degradation are becoming increasingly apparent. High rates of population growth destroy the land and our future capacity to respond to the world's needs (CGIAR, 1993).

Others have seen a process in which a critical human mass is exceeded globally, leading to a 'gigantic, and widely synchronized population crash' (Pennycuick, 1992: 104 cited in Darling, 1993: 13).

The implicit simple feedback loop is:

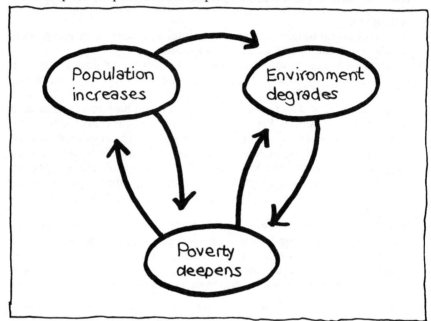

Figure 2.1: The population–poverty–environment stereotype

An authoritative statement of this view, carefully written and qualified, is UNICEF's 1994 *The State of the World's Children.* This posits a Population-Poverty-Environment (PPE) spiral which has multiple negative causation. Part of this is a negative link between population and the environment. More people causes environmental degradation which in turn causes more poverty and so a larger population.

This is sometimes true. Moreover, UNICEF's policy prescriptions are generally sound, as far as they go. The problem is that these negative relationships are stated as universals, implying that more people always and necessarily means more environmental degradation. There is much evidence of professional error in this belief, and much local contrary evidence (see e.g. Binns, 1995). Let us examine some examples.

Planting and protecting trees

Trees are planted and protected by small farmers in many parts of the world. Preconditions are secure rights to land and trees, and a need for tree products or opportunities for their sale. But in countries and conditions as diverse as those of Kakamega, Kisii, Murang'a and Machakos in Kenya, of the hills of Nepal, and of Haiti, farmers have confounded the prophets of doom by planting and protecting trees to increase their density.

Research conducted by the Kenya Woodfuel Development Programme (Bradley *et al.*, 1985; Bradley, 1991) in the 1980s in three densely populated districts – Kakamega, Kisii and Murang'a – used a careful combination of methods, including aerial surveys, questionnaire surveys, and less formal RRA-type investigations. Especially but not only in Kakamega District, it found denser population associated with more, not fewer, trees. The denser the population and the smaller the farms, so the denser were the trees per unit area: 'As farm sizes become smaller with increasing population density, the proportion of the farm devoted to tree management increases' (ibid: 134–5). Further, not only did the gross quantity of woody biomass increase, but a greater proportion of it was deliberately cultivated. There was reason to expect the same higher woody biomass with denser population in most of the high-potential lands of the Kenya highlands (Bradley, 1991: 280) as was found also in the more marginal agroecological conditions of Machakos District (Mortimore, 1991; Tiffen *et al.*, 1993: 213–25). A national-scale aerial sample survey of high potential land in Kenya, comparing photographs taken in 1986 and 1991, combined with fieldwork, showed an annual increase of 4.7 per cent in planted woody biomass, leading to the conclusion that:

> Instead of increasing fuelwood deficit and land degradation following rapid population growth, Kenyan farmers seem to apply wise and sustainable-management practices, including tree growing.
>
> (Holmgren *et al.*, 1994: 390)

In Nepal, as supplies of non-timber forest products (NTFPs), especially fodder and fuelwood, diminished from forests and from common property resources, farmers have planted and protected trees on their own land to provide substitutes; and with changes in tenure and community-forest management, forest degradation has been observed to be reversed (Gilmour 1988; Carter and Gilmour 1989; Gilmour 1989; Fox 1993; Shrestha 1996). Gerard Gill has slides of two aerial photographs of the same land in Nepal, taken ten years apart. One has many trees, the other few. He asks audiences which is the later photograph. They guess the one with fewer trees; but it is the one with more.

More people, less erosion: Machakos District, Kenya

The universality of core professional beliefs about people and the environment has been challenged by research in Kenya, conducted in the later 1980s by the Overseas Development Institute, London and the University of Nairobi (Gichuki, 1991; Mortimore, 1991; Tiffen, 1992; Tiffen and Mortimore, 1992; Tiffen, 1993; Tiffen *et al.*, 1993). This investigated changes over a 60-year period, 1930–90 in Machakos District. During this period the population of the district rose almost six-fold (from 240 000 in 1932 to

25

1 393 000 in 1989). During the first three decades, there was acute official alarm at soil erosion. Describing the condition of the district in 1937, Colin Maher (1937: 3 quoted in Thomas, 1991) wrote:

> The Machakos Reserve is an appalling example of a large area of land which has been subjected to uncoordinated and practically uncontrolled development by natives whose multiplication and the increase of whose stock has been permitted, free from the checks of war and largely from those of disease, under benevolent British rule. Every phase of misuse of land is vividly and poignantly displayed in this Reserve, the inhabitants of which are rapidly drifting to a state of hopeless and miserable poverty and their land to a parching desert of rocks, stones and sand.

By 1990, erosion was sharply reduced; the density of trees had increased; almost all cultivation was on terraced land; labour-intensive composting and stall-feeding of cattle were common; and agricultural output (in maize equivalents) had risen more than threefold per capita and more than five-fold per square kilometre. The explanations identified by the researchers include infrastructural investment, capital inflows from earnings outside, the proximity of the Nairobi market, and marketed crops (coffee, horticulture etc). Perhaps most, though, they stress a rapidly rising population and labour force. Indeed, the principal researchers entitled their book *More People, Less Erosion: Environmental Recovery in Kenya* (Tiffen *et al.*, 1993).

People and forests in Guinea

In Guinea, too, conventional wisdom about bad effects of people on the environment has been turned on its head. Meticulous research conducted by James Fairhead and Melissa Leach with their co-researchers Marie Kamano and Dominique Millimouno (Fairhead *et al.*, 1992a and b; Leach and Fairhead, 1992, 1994; Leach *et al.* 1994; Fairhead and Leach, 1995) in the Kissidougou Prefecture has led to one of the most dramatic reversals of professional wisdom in the history of rural development.

The Kissidougou Prefecture consists largely of savannah grassland with islands of forest. The researchers reported in 1992 that:

> Ecologists, botanists, agronomists and social scientists, whether expatri-ate or Guinean, all share the view that Kissidougou Prefecture is under-going rapid and potentially disastrous environmental change. Their various works are mutually reinforcing in this conviction. The region is believed to be undergoing a transition from forest to savanna, with the relics of its once-extensive humid forest cover now found only as small islands around villages, in small reserves, and in inaccessible places.
>
> These forest islands have been believed by botanists, foresters, ecolo-gists, development planners and policy-makers to be relics of a recently much more extensive humid forest cover. This degradation is considered anthropogenic, and to be aggravated by economic and social modernity and by increasing population pressure. (Fairhead *et al.*, 1992a: 1)

The researchers' in-depth research methods included archival research, analysis of aerial photographs, oral histories, and extended participant observation. Their findings flatly contradict the professional view. When they examined archival evidence

> We ourselves were shocked to find that there has been virtually no significant change in the distribution and extent of the vegetation types in Kissidougou Prefecture during this century. We were equally shocked to have these conclusions from the archives validated by oral histories. (ibid: 33)

They conclude that the woody vegetation cover of savannahs has been increasing during the period when policymakers have believed the opposite; that the island forests, far from being remnants, have been created by people around their settlements; and that people have sophisticated and labour-saving ways to protect forests from fire by grazing cattle and cultivating near forest fringes, and by pre-emptive burning of grass when it is short and damp with dew and the fire is less hot; and that fires are used to help establish forests. During periods when this controlled early burning has been banned, fires have come later in the season, and with the higher grass and drier conditions have been hotter and worse and have done more damage. The presence of people, and their use of controlled burning, has, then, preserved, not destroyed, the forest, which was threatened not by local people but by fire control policy, at least in the North. When, as part of government policies, people moved to larger settlements near roads, protection of old forests became less effective, but new forest islands have been formed around the new sites. It was not population pressure that limited the forest area, but lack or absence of people; and it was not the people's management practices that were the problem, but those of government.

In their parallel study of the history of the Ziama Reserve, Fairhead and Leach (1994) found another misperception of history. What is now regarded by professionals as pristine forest, a relic of the diverse and species-rich original forest, actually supported a dense human population in the nineteenth century, as recorded in detail by colonial travellers; and they cite other evidence that most of West Africa's high forests contain old abandoned village sites (*ibid*: 481–4). Human and ecological history, when carefully and sensitively investigated, was found to be more complicated, dynamic, changing and locally specific than scientists and administrators had ever supposed, and to contradict many of their beliefs.

The authors stress that they are not saying there is no deforestation, nor that all forest patches are created by people, and they caution against dangers of overgeneralizing. Nevertheless, evidence is amassing that the Guinea perspective is relevant across the forest-savannah transition zone of West Africa, with local variations (Fairhead and Leach, forthcoming). They find widespread evidence across the zone of forest advance into savannah over the last few centuries, assisted by both people and climate. Their re-evaluation suggests that recent forest loss in West Africa has been massively exaggerated and during the present century may be only about 15 per cent of the usual estimates.

The main source for this section is research by Gerard Gill (1992, 1993a and b, 1995) and Devika Tamang (1992, 1993).

The received wisdom about Nepal has been that increasing population has led to the cultivation of more land, the degradation of forest, and declining woody biomass. A 1991 report bearing the authority of the National Agricultural Research Council and of the Asian Development Bank put it thus:

> Continued population pressure on land resources in the hills and mountains has resulted in expansion of farming onto marginal cultivable land, with ensuing environmental degradation – soil erosion, losses of soil fertility, a deterioration of forests and forest covers. (NARC-ADB 1991: 15).

This view was supported by official statistics for cultivated area which indicated a steady annual increase. But as Gill has shown, this trend has an origin both curious and spurious. The figures derive from two sources for cultivated land: the decennial National Agricultural Census, which has lower figures, and the ongoing Cadastral Survey which gives higher figures. The Cadastral Survey raises the figure for cultivated area on average by a factor of 3.7. Each year it covers one or two more hill districts and their totals are added to the national figure. The source of the upward trend in cultivated area has, then, been these annual additions to the total. The trend was not field reality but professional artefact, based on method and ignorance.

A different field reality is reported by Tamang (1992, 1993) and Carson (1992, cited in Gill, 1993a), both of whom travelled extensively in the hill areas, in Tamang's case conducting a 400km transect through the hills. Their more credible reality is that cultivated land in the hills is declining. This is a consequence of loss of organic matter, soil acidification, build-up of aluminium toxicity, and outmigration. Shortage of labour through seasonal or permanent outmigration means less organic matter collected from forests, less maintenance of terraces, and abandonment of land which is marginal because distant from the homestead, difficult to work or infertile, while cultivation concentrates more intensively on smaller areas. Terraces break and erode for lack of maintenance. There are many causal linkages and there have been historical sequences. Perhaps population pressure has historically led to an expansion of cultivated land in the hills. Currently, it seems, the process is in reverse. Erosion and degradation are linked with lack of labour. Hedged with qualifications about likely local variations and about oversimple statements, one dimension of the problem can, then, be hypothesized as not too many people but too few.

The lessons from the planting and protecting of trees, and the upending of conventional wisdom about people and the environment in parts of Kenya, West Africa and Nepal, are sobering. Environmentally, each zone deserves separate understanding in its own right, informed by local knowledge and historical evidence. A more general conclusion, when such widely-held beliefs prove wrong, is that all embedded beliefs deserve repeated sceptical scrutiny, including those which have just been established as the latest conventional wisdom. With processes as complex and dynamic as the interactions of people and environments, there may be some underlying principles with some stability, but current realities are diverse. The easiest error is to overgeneralize from particular cases and assume uniformity.

The puzzle: why were we wrong?

Nor are these isolated examples of error. I have chosen them for their diversity, and variously for their scale of impact, the tenacity with which they have been upheld, their topical relevance and the credibility with which they have been qualified or overturned. Other examples might have been human-made desertification (Darling, 1993; Swift, 1996), the theory of Himalayan environmental degradation (Ives, 1987), soil erosion in Africa (Stocking, 1996), pastoralism (Scoones, 1995c, d and f), the Integrated Rural Development Programme in India (Dreze, 1990), or others, e.g., in Leach and Mearns (eds) book, *The Lie of the Land* (1996). Patrick Darling has concluded from his review of Western myths on the population–environment interface in Africa, that

> where they have been challenged by indigenous technical expertise and tested seriously by time-series studies, the main thrusts of their past analyses are proving to be incorrect in every major vegetation zone in Africa.

Errors and myths have persisted through decades, reinforced and reasserted by intelligent, highly educated people across the range of disciplines and professional occupations.

Learning and change have been slow and often resisted. Some changes and modifications, as with errors in macro-policy and projects, were provoked by feedback and failures, learning from experiences, and effects in the field. Some were so deeply entrenched that it required long-term, meticulous and versatile research and lobbying to modify or overturn them. The processes differed. Sometimes the research was largely through the insightful analysis of secondary data, as with Amartya Sen's entitlement theory of famine, and Gerald Leach's and Robin Mearns' demystifying of the woodfuel crisis; sometimes through personal social-anthropological field research, as with Alexander de Waal's identification of disease, not hunger, as the main killer in most famines; sometimes through extended multi-disciplinary research with scrupulous measurement, as with Martin Greeley's and others' findings of low post-harvest losses; sometimes through research and correspondence, as with Starkey's discovery that multi-purpose wheeled toolcarriers were everywhere rejected by farmers; sometimes through combinations of multi-disciplinary historical, archival, ecological and social-anthropological field research, as by Mary Tiffen, Michael Mortimore and F.N. Gichuki for Machakos in Kenya and by Melissa Leach, James Fairhead and their colleagues for the forest–savanna zone in Guinea. The researchers used different combinations and sequences of methods. All were methodological pluralists. All invested much time and effort in their research and analysis. And all their insights met opposition from the development establishment.

In most of these domains, new understandings are now quite widely accepted. The puzzle is how and why errors were so deeply entrenched in the first place in the beliefs, thinking, values and actions of development professionals. These included managers, scientists, planners, academics and consultants, of many disciplines, and working in many organizations, such as aid agencies, national bureaucracies, research and training institutes, universities and colleges, and private firms. How could they all have been so wrong, and wrong for so long? How were these errors possible, and why were they so sustained?

How could it have been supposed that complex large-scale IRDPs could be implemented rapidly and would work well? That the priority for hungry children was proteins more than calories? That post-harvest grain losses at the village level were 5 to 10 times higher than they were? That multi-purpose wheeled toolbars were a good idea accepted by farmers? That fuelwood would run out and trees would disappear? That Machakos District in the 1930s had exceeded its human carrying capacity? That people in Guinea turned forest into savannah? That cultivated area in the hills of Nepal was expanding and it was the expansion that was causing erosion?

Different observers would give different answers. There are multiple shifting realities. We choose answers which fit our constructs and predispositions. I am no different from others in having a personally idiosyncratic view and wanting to believe some things more than others. The mix of explanations can be expected to vary.

A first answer lies in the political economy of received narrative, in who gains materially from what is believed. When myth supports policies, projects and programmes, many stand to gain. These are both individuals and organizations: bureaucrats, politicians, contractors, consultants, scientists, researchers and those who fund research; and their organizations – national and international bureaucracies, political systems, companies, firms of consultants, research institutes and research-funding agencies. Any one, or several, or all of these, can benefit from the acceptance of wrong ideas, projects or policies.

Conditions vary. Where commercial and political interests dominate in large projects, myths may scarcely be needed: the Pergau Dam in Malaysia, financed illegally by the British government to assist the sale of arms, may be an example. Where commercial and political interests are weaker or combine less, myth and bureaucratic interests can play a bigger part. The IRDPs were sustained by donor and host-country bureaucracies, which gained variously by disbursing and receiving large loans. The beliefs that protein was the priority for starving children, and that post-harvest village-level grain losses were high, were good for those who made and sold milk powder and silos respectively. Those who invented multi-purpose wheeled toolcarriers had personal interests in renewals of project funding. With natural resources, those who seize land and exploit forests can divert attention from their rapacity by blaming the poor for erosion and deforestation. And to add an example, the myth of desertification in the Sahel, as carefully documented and analysed by Jeremy Swift (1996), was sustained through a convergence of the interests of three main constituencies: national governments in Africa; international-aid bureaucracies, especially United Nations agencies and some major bilateral donors; and some groups of scientists.[1]

Nothing in this book should detract from the significance of vested interests and the distortions and distractions to which they give rise.

The puzzle and the challenge

But as an explanation, the 'who gains and who loses?' approach of political economy takes us only part way in understanding the genesis and longevity of myth; it is relatively weak with some myths, such as the forecasts of fuelwood shortages or locally erroneous beliefs that overpopulation was degrading the environment. To complement vested interests, three other explanations stand out: professionalism; distance; and power.

Professionalism is concerned with our knowledge, and how we learn, analyse and prescribe. In all these examples, the erroneous beliefs were embedded in the concepts, values, methods and behaviour normally dominant in disciplines and professions. Those who were wrong had had long education and training, whether as macro-economists, engineers, agronomists, ecologists, foresters, administrators or social scientists. Most were highly numerate. Most were specialists. All were linked in with other professional colleagues around the world. Through letters, the telephone, workshops, conferences, professional journals and papers, they were in touch with their professional peers and with current dominant values and beliefs. Their learning was, then, more likely to come laterally or from above than from below, and to follow current ideologies and fashions. This leads us, in Chapter 3, to the analysis of professional realities.

Distance blocks, blurs and distorts vision, and distance is institutionalized. Most of those who were wrong were physically, organizationally, socially and cognitively distant from the people and conditions they were analysing, planning and prescribing for, and making predictions about. Physically, they were centrally placed, in headquarters, in offices, in laboratories and on research stations, far from and isolated from local, complex, diverse, dynamic and unpredictable rural realities. Organizationally, they were trapped by norms of behaviour, by routines and by resources (or their lack), which kept them in central places and rewarded them for working there. Socially, they were different and apart from rural people. Their contact, if any, was confined to short special occasions, as development tourists. Cognitively, they were distant, having different categories, criteria, values and life experiences.

Being distant, they relied on secondary data. They calculated with the figures that were to hand, and treated numbers as reality. Fuelwood projections were made far from the sources of fuelwood or the users. Analysis, planning and action were top-down and centre-outwards. In the IRDPs it was assumed that technological packages were available. Centrally-determined packages could be transferred to and imposed on local conditions. This leads us to explore, in Chapter 4, the transfer of reality.

31

Power hinders learning. Those who were wrong were powerful. They were senior, almost all men, mostly white, and influential, whether through age, professional authority, control of funds, or position in a hierarchy. Their very power conditioned their perceptions and prevented them from learning. This leads us to examine, in Chapter 5, how power deceives.

Professionalism, distance and power can combine with vested interests to offer spirited resistance to new insights. Old professionals deny new understandings and realities. At the same time, the acceleration of change, the concentration of power and the diversity of people and conditions now make error both easier and more dangerous. It is easier because through new communications, professionals in central places have more instant power, and still little direct contact with the realities their actions affect. It is more dangerous because those who may be affected are more numerous and likely to be affected more quickly. So being right matters now more than ever.

The question remains how correct, in their turn, new insights are. One conclusion has to be self-doubt. We have to ask how and why we construct our realities, how and why we learn and mislearn. 'Self-critical epistemological awareness' is an ungainly phrase but its acronym is apposite – SEA. For when faced with the complexity, diversity and dynamism of human and local conditions, there is no normal bedrock on which to anchor, and few fixed points. Rather, we need a repertoire of skills for staying afloat, steering, finding our way and avoiding shipwreck on a turbulent and transient flux. So much we thought we knew we did not know, or were wrong about; and very likely much we now think we know we still do not know, or have got wrong; and what we need to know is constantly changing. I have found myself repeatedly revising the section in this chapter about Nepal, and am still in doubt about it; the reader will note the words 'it seems' near the end. The realities of life and conditions are elusive: they are local, complex, diverse, dynamic and unpredictable (or lcddu for short). Central professionals are pervasively ignorant, out-of-touch and out-of-date, about lcddu realities.

It is not 'them', those who are peripheral, poor, weak and vulnerable, who are responsible for these problems of knowing, acting and error. For it is not they who have been wrong, but us. The first step, then, is humbling. It is to recognize our ignorance and error. Gradually, and none too soon, development professionals are coming to see that the problem is more 'us' than 'them'. It is with ourselves that we have to start.

3

Professional Realities

Thomas Gradgrind, sir, A man of realities. A man of facts and calcula-tions, a man who proceeds upon the principle that two and two are four, and nothing over, and who is not to be talked into allowing for anything over . . . With a rule and a pair of scales, and the multiplica-tion table always in his pocket, sir, ready to weigh and measure any parcel of human nature, and tell you exactly what it comes to. It is a mere question of figures, a case of simple arithmetic.

Charles Dickens, *Hard Times*, Chapter 2

Normal professionalism – the ideas, values, methods and behaviour accepted and dominant in professions or disciplines – is a means to status, power and wealth. Commonly, its elements derive from, and fit, things more than people. Universals are valued, based on measurement in controlled conditions. Special-izations and reductionism separate parts from wholes. Complex realities are simplified and ordered in single scales such as poverty lines, and measures of production and employment. In the social sciences and policy, economics domi-nates, and gives primacy to mathematical analysis; what has been measured and counted becomes the reality. All this makes it hard for normal professionals to understand and serve the local, complex, diverse, dynamic and unpredictable realities of the conditions, farming systems and livelihood strategies of poor people. Normal professionalism creates and sustains its own reality.

The purpose of this chapter is to examine us, development professionals, as a type, group or class. Professionals, like others, seek to order and make sense of their experience. Like others, they construct realities, their inter-pretations and ways of construing the world. To understand their realities, a starting point is to ask what ideas, values, methods and behaviour are accepted, dominant and rewarded in a profession or discipline, or in profes-sions and disciplines as a whole. These can be described as normal professionalism.[1]

Normal professionals, like other people, can be expected to have com-mon preferences which are physical, financial, and social and psychological. Physically, these include comfort, security, cleanliness, and access to good services and facilities; financially – money, and more rather than less; so-cially and psychologically – status and esteem, being accepted, valued and respected.

Three characteristics commonly distinguish professionals from other people: (i) extended education and training when young, delaying respons-ibility and exposure to the real world; (ii) later, livelihoods gained in organ-izations with fellow professionals with shared values; and (iii) throughout their lives, ambition to do well, not just with good grades in school and college, but also through rising in status within discipline, profession and organization. As values and status are closely linked, we can start by asking what values are reflected in the relative status of different professions.

Normal professional status

For purposes of analysis, status can be taken as a central thread around which values cluster. Relative status as between the practising professions and sub-professions in health and agriculture, and then between some academic disciplines, is presented in Table 3.1. This shows contrasts between the practising and academic professions. They differ in the value they place on practice and theory. The practising professions are concerned more with action; the academic more with understanding. It is, then, not surprising that highest status in medicine and agriculture goes to those able to produce the most dramatic physical effects – saving human lives through surgery, and engineering new organisms through biotechnology; and that highest status in the academic professions goes to those able to make the most dramatic breakthroughs in understanding and theory, as in physics (especially astrophysics and small-particle physics), and in the computer sciences.

The practical and academic professions differ also in what they sometimes see as mildly pathological in each other. Some academics regard the practical professions as philistine, too close to their practical work to be able to take a wider view. Some practitioners, for their part, see academic disciplines as abstruse, too theoretical and too far from practical realities. This is not least because of the high status enjoyed by theory in academic discourse. 'A bit weak on theory' is dismissive, 'with significant theoretical

Table 3.1: Relative status in medicine, agriculture and some academic disciplines (each column to be read separately: there is no horizontal comparison)

Medicine	Agriculture	Academic disciplines
HIGH STATUS		
Micro and organ-transplant surgeons	Biotechnologists/genetic engineers	Small-particle physics
Surgeons/consultants	HYV Seed breeders	Computer sciences
General practitioners	On-station researchers	Economics
Hospital nurses	Off-station researchers with farmer researchers	
Community health workers		Sociology/social anthropology
	Agricultural extensionists	
Traditional healers	Farmer experimenters	Social work
Sick men	Male farmers	Students
Sick women	Female farmers	
LOW STATUS		

Table 3.2: Contrasting correlates of higher and lower professional status

Characteristic	High status	Low status
Education, training and induction	Prolonged	Brief
Competence	Specialist	Generalist
Gender	More men	More women
Influence	Powerful	Weak
Income, wealth	Higher	Lower
Location	Central, urban	Peripheral, rural
Concerned more with	Things	People
Working environments	Controlled Standardized Simplified	Uncontrolled Diverse Complex
Approaches, methods and values	Measurement Reductionism Precision	Judgement Holism Fitness

Note: These are general tendencies not absolutes.

implications' an accolade. Those with the highest academic reputations for theory are also sometimes difficult to understand. Academic status can vary inversely with intelligibility and perhaps utility: Levi-Strauss in social anthropology, Talcott Parsons in sociology, and miscellaneous post-modernists, combine high status, obscure language and opaque syntax. The line between academic brilliance and thought disorder is not always sharp. Being hard to fathom can be profound; it can also be bottomless.

Apart from this practice–theory contrast, it is striking how much the practising professions and the academic disciplines share characteristics which vary in a polar fashion between high and low status. Some of these are indicated in Table 3.2.

Of these, five are widely evident and recognized:

○ *education, training and induction.* Those with high status have prolonged education, training and induction; for those with low status, these are brief.
○ *competence.* Those with high status are specialists, with claims to universal competence in narrow areas; those with low status are generalists, with claims to local and specific competence across a broader range.
○ *gender.* The high-status professionals are mainly men, while those of lower status are mainly women, or have a higher proportion of women.
○ *influence and wealth.* These are concentrated among those with high status, through patriarchy, professional authority, high salaries, clients among the rich, commercial consultancies, and the like. Their services are in demand in different places. In contrast, weakness and poverty are found more among those with low status, whose salaries are less and the demand for whose services is more local.

o *location.* Those with higher status tend to be located in central urban places and to work more there, while those with lower status include a higher proportion who are rural, or part of whose work is rural or in peripheral urban areas.

Less obvious, less analysed, but at least as important, are other linked dimensions which correlate with high and low status: things and people, and control and lack of control; measurement and judgement; and reductionism and holism.

Things and people

The highest-status disciplines and professions are concerned either with things or with people as though they were things. Physicists are pre-eminently concerned with the physical world. Biotechnologists are concerned with genetic engineering, with treating living matter as composed of molecules and genes, reduced almost to the level of things. Surgeons need anaesthetists to reduce people to 'things' so that they can operate. Transplant surgeons go further in treating the human body like a machine with interchangeable spare parts, analogous to the 'cannibalizing' of a motor vehicle.

In contrast, the lowest-status disciplines and professions are concerned with people as people. Social workers, nurses, traditional medical practitioners, and agricultural extensionists are confronted by and have to cope with, variously, individuals, families, communities, and farming and livelihood systems.

The working environments of higher-status disciplines and professions are standardized, controlled and predictable. Laboratories for physics and biotechnology, greenhouses for plantbreeding, operating theatres for surgery, are indoors and usually sealed off, providing environments which are clean, sterile and dust-free, with controlled temperature and humidity and specially protected from human contamination: scientists wear white coats or protective clothing; surgeons wear face masks. Agricultural research stations, too, are often simplified, standardized and protected from risk, with flat fields and irrigation.

In contrast, the lower-status disciplines and professions work in environments which are diverse, dynamic and uncontrollable. Social workers, community-health workers and agricultural extensionists face the open and often dusty, dirty and polluted conditions of villages, slums, and poor dwellings, dealing with unpredictable families, sick people, communities, conflict, and risk-prone rainfed farming at the mercy of the seasons.

The higher-status disciplines and professions are specialized and reductionist, and rely on precise measurement and mathematics. The longer the training, the more specialized they are. As the cliché has it, they know more and more about less and less. They deal, too, with parts more than wholes. In their controlled conditions they simplify, and manipulate only one or a few variables. The transplant surgeon changes only a kidney or heart; the genetic engineer intervenes only with one gene or set of genes; the physicist focuses sharply on one or only a few sets of conditions. In contrast, the low-status disciplines and professions have to be generalists

36

and holistic. Their training is shorter, but they have to deal with conditions which are irreducibly complex, diverse and unpredictable. In dealing with people's different and difficult problems, most of their work is qualitative, cannot easily or usefully be measured, and demands judgement.

The academic disciplines confirm these polar dimensions of things versus people, and of quantification versus judgement. Hard physics has high status, with things as its subject matter. Computer sciences are much concerned with mathematics. Economics comes next, quantifying, and dealing with people as numbers and their behaviour as describable in laws and equations; and the other social sciences, dealing though they do with the greater complexities, diversity and uncontrollability of people, have lower status, with social work, which tries to help people as people in society, lowest of all.

The contrasts must not be overdrawn. Of course, high-status professionals also have to exercise judgement, and social workers sometimes make measurements. Nor do all academics accept the values which prevail as normal and prestigious. Some reverse them. But professionally they tend to be scattered and peripheral, usually a dispersed and marginal subculture looked down on for their lack of logic and rigour. Meanwhile, the traditional concepts, values, methods and behaviour of their conventional colleagues continue to dominate. Normal rigour rules.

In the things–people contrast, the gender dimension is pervasive. Men are socialized more to deal with things, and women are socialized more to deal with people. The middle-class boy is given a tractor and trailer; the middle-class girl, a nurse's dress, with toy bandages and syringe. More controversial is whether males have an innate bent towards things and

Table 3.3: Two paradigms – of things and people*

Point of departure and reference	Things	People
Mode	Blueprint	Process
Keyword	Planning	Participation
Goals	Pre-set, closed	Evolving, open
Decision-making	Centralized	Decentralized
Analytical assumptions	Reductionist	Systems, holistic
Methods, rules	Standardized, universal	Diverse, local
Technology	Fixed package (*table d'hôte*)	Varied basket (*à la carte*)
Professionals' interactions with local people	Instructing, 'motivating'	Enabling, empowering
Local people seen as	Beneficiaries	Partners, actors
Force flow	Supply-push	Demand-pull
Outputs	Uniform	Diverse
	Infrastructure	Capabilities
Planning and action	Top-down	Bottom-up

* This table has been adapted from the work of David Korten.

37

Table 3.4: Nobel prizes awarded to women

	Women	of which shared with men	Total	Women as per cent of total
Peace	9	(3)	80	11
Literature	8	(1)	91	9
Physiology or medicine	5	(4)	158	4
Chemistry	4	(2)	121	3
Physics	2	(2)	146	1
Economic sciences	0	0	38	0

Source: HDR, 1995: 37, citing Siegman, 1992.

working with the physical environment, and females towards people and relating to the social environment. Empirically, men dominate the 'things' and 'numbers' professions and activities (for example, engineering, physics, chemistry, accountancy, economics) and the senior posts, while the proportion of women is higher in the 'people' professions and activities (the so-called 'caring' professions – nursing, psychotherapy, social work) and in the lower posts. This is especially marked among economists: most economists are men, and almost all the recognized 'great names' of economics have been men.

Startling confirmation of these biases comes from the award of Nobel prizes. Only 28 out of 634 individual recipients of Nobel prizes by 1992 had been women, and these were concentrated in peace (9) and literature (8), while physics had only 2, both shared with men, and economic sciences had no woman at all.

There are many reasons why women are less numerous in senior posts and in 'things-and-numbers' professions. These are extensively elucidated and detailed in feminist literature. Prominent reasons include social and role norms, and a larger and longer investment in boys' than in girls' education. Perhaps most decisive has been the career chasm into which educated women have often crashed when they start the cycle of pregnancy, birth and childcare, leading to professional re-entry, later if at all, at a lower level than they would otherwise have reached. This tends to be in relatively junior jobs which deal face-to-face with clients, rather than the senior managerial jobs to which their male contemporaries have in the meantime risen.

So those, often men, in the clean, controlled and comfortable conditions of the centre, in their dark suits, white coats and black shoes, receive recognition and reap rich rewards for their work with things, and with people as though they were things; and those, often women, in the dirty, chaotic and uncomfortable conditions of the periphery, in their work-a-day clothes and sensible shoes or sandals, are poorly paid, looked down on, and little recognized or rewarded for their work with people as people. Were this paradox not so universal and familiar, its unfairness would seem grotesque.

Measurement

Perhaps the most pervasive value of normal professionalism concerns measurement. Many physical things are amenable to measurement. They are part of the practical Newtonian universe of everyday life. They can be controlled, counted, compared, manipulated and their behaviour predicted. They are subject to the universal methods and norms of engineering – blueprints, schedules, targets, and physical outputs to predetermined standards. The problem is that the idiosyncratic attributes of people are, in contrast, difficult to measure; their individual behaviour is unpredictable; and the approaches and methods for handling them are in continuous evolution and change.

Within and between professions, status and respectability are sought and can be gained through quantification, mathematical techniques, and precision. Professions or disciplines which develop or adopt skilled techniques of measurement move upwards: in the UK, clinical psychology rose with psychological testing and mechanistic behaviour-therapies; sociologists have sought 'scientific' respectability through questionnaire surveys which generate numbers for statistical analysis; and farming systems researchers likewise have conducted surveys to produce figures for multivariate analyses which impress or bemuse their colleagues. Operations research was meant to be multidisciplinary, but when Paul Spencer, as a social anthropologist, joined a team he found it actually dominated by mathematics (pers. comm.). For those with mathematical skills and with work where they make sense and can be applied, quantitative methods are empowering; for those without mathematical skills, and with work where they do not make sense and can be applied only with difficulty, quantitative methods can be disabling, a threat, a means by which others dominate.

Not surprisingly, low-status professionals seek to promote themselves by using quantitative methods. Some social anthropologists confess to conducting surveys in order to raise the respectability of their work. Wolf Bleek records of his fieldwork in Ghana that he was often chided by colleagues about the statistical weakness of his research:

> Because my sample consisted of only 42 adults, its representativeness was challenged. I was advised to include a survey of a larger sample of the town population, selected in an orthodox way. And so, a budding academician, I yielded to the statistical temptation.
>
> (Bleek, 1987: 317)

Cultural anthropology, one might have supposed, would be immune from this temptation. But in the November 1990 issue of the *CAM (Cultural Anthropology Methods) Newsletter* four of the five articles were concerned with statistical approaches. One (Otterbein, 1990), contrasting the deductive with the inductive style of cross-cultural research, asserts that the deductive,. in which hypotheses derived from theories are tested through statistical analysis, 'is vastly superior'. The reader might then suppose that the contrasting inductive style would entail field research, exposure to cultural differences, and analysis based on reflection, comparison and judgement. Not so. The inductive style employs a standard sample, precoded data and variables selected to create a matrix of correlations. Throughout, the manipulation and analysis of numbers prevails. In this sort of cross-cultural anthropology, mathematical methods manifest a near-monopoly.

Quantification and statistics can mislead, distract, be wasteful, simply not make sense, or conflict with common values. When Wolf Bleek saw the survey-interview responses by women whom he knew well, he reports: '. . . I was abashed. They had lied lavishly' (Bleek, 1987: 319). As we saw in Chapter 2, widely quoted figures such as those for human nutritional requirements, post-harvest grain losses at the village level, woodfuel shortages, and the expansion of agricultural land in Nepal, can give a false authority and exactness to misleading information, leading to wrong policy. What is measured may also not be what matters. Real per capita GDP (Gross Domestic Product) is still widely used as an indicator of how well a country is doing; yet much ill-being contributes to GDP. In the accounts, much of the bad life is counted as positive.[2]

Yet professionals, especially economists and consultants tight for time, have a strong felt need for statistics. At worst, they grub around and grab what numbers they can, feed them into their computers, and print-out not just numbers but more and more elegant graphs, bar-charts, pie diagrams and three-dimensional wonders of graphic myth with which to adorn their reports and to justify their plans and proposals. Gerry Gill (1993a) has said it all in his paper, '*OK, The Data's Lousy, But It's All We've Got*', a quote from an anonymous full professor of economics at a reputable US university. As Gill points out, this is not an isolated example but representative for a fairly wide cross-section of development experts; and 'wrong data are worse than no data' (ibid: 4); wrong numbers one might add, are worst of all because numbers pose as precisely true.

Nor can figures that are used and quoted be considered objective. There are always problems of measurement, representativeness and meaning. Though well known, these are rarely mentioned when results are reported and cited. Jack Ives (1987: 194) cites 'the 67 factor', estimates of fuelwood consumption in Nepal which differed by a factor of 67, that is to say, the highest was 67 times larger than the lowest. Michael Stocking (1993b, cited in Pretty, 1995a: 14) found that among at least 22 erosion studies in the Mahaweli catchment in Sri Lanka, there was a variation of some 8000-fold, from a low of 0.13t/ha per year to a high of 1026t/ha per year. The lowest was from a tea-research institute seeking to show that their land management was safe; the highest was from a development agency wishing to show how serious erosion was in the Third World. In Stocking's words: 'The researchers were not lying; they were merely selective'. When there is such a range, it is easy to choose and quote those figures that suit a purpose best.

Figures so selected are then accepted, repeated, cumulatively misquoted, and used, consciously or unconsciously, to reinforce predisposition and prejudice. In India in the 1980s, it became a commonplace that 10 million hectares of canal-irrigated land had become waterlogged (see e.g. Jayal, 1985), but the archeology of this figure suggested that it originated from the totals for waterlogging (6 million ha) and salinity (4 million ha). This involved double-counting and also inclusion of flooded land unconnected with canal irrigation (Chambers, 1988b: 27); but the figure appealed to the environmental lobby and the opponents of canal irrigation. So it became an often-quoted fact. The figure of village-level post-harvest losses of grain of 30 to 40 per cent, although partly, it would seem, originating in a time-of-harvesting trial on a research station, was repeated and believed all over the world. It met felt needs: it served commercial and professional interests, gave hope of big gains in food availability, and blamed the poor.

Numbers can also reassure by appearing to extend control, precision and knowledge beyond their real limits. Needing to calculate water availability on canal-irrigation systems, irrigation engineers adopt rules of thumb for transmission losses. These are sometimes applied with a wild universality at which a lay person can only boggle: in South Asia, some have taken a rule of thumb, such as 25 per cent losses in transmission, and applied this to a whole canal-irrigation system, regardless of variations in distance or seepage rates by soil type (Chambers, 1988b: 75–6). The professional culture of precision with static things, so essential for physical infrastructure, is thus spread to cover dynamic and variable flows. When a figure is needed but cannot be measured, there is an option of intelligent estimating, gauging effects of distance and local diversity. But instead, distance and diversity are smothered by a single ratio. It is as though a threshold of complexity triggers an irrational reflex to simplify and standardize. So it is that simplistic rules of thumb are applied across the board, without judgement of the local and diverse, to colonize the unmeasurable and make it mathematically manageable.

Mathematics then masquerades with bogus precision. Rules of thumb would often (but not always) be reasonable if the resulting calculations were treated as approximate. But usually this is not what happens. Thomas Mayer (1993: 56) has written that many economists

> act like the person who, when asked about the age of the Amazon river, replied that by now it is one million and three years old, because three years ago he was told that it was a million years old.

Mayer continues (ibid. 56–63) with his principle of the strongest link. This is the practice of focusing attention on the strongest link in an argument, or the part of a causal chain most amenable to precise measurement and analysis, and then attributing the certainty and precision of that link to the whole argument.

For the complex, diverse, dynamic and unpredictable realities of people, farming systems and livelihoods, comparisons and judgement are often more potent and practical than precise measurement. In counselling people, apart from some specialized aspects of psychological diagnosis, measurement has little part to play. In farming-systems research, and in understanding the livelihoods of the poor, the value of measurement is easily exaggerated. What often matter are judgements of trends and of relative amounts, and insights into causality. Numbers shown visually with seeds, stones or counters (see below pp. 135 and 174) can be used to make comparisons. These can show trends in ways not accessible through words alone without tortuous and torturing circumlocution. In the saying attributed to Lord Keynes: 'It is better to be approximately right than precisely wrong'. The problem, so often, is to prevent the approximation being treated as precise. The danger is that numbers, however bad, will downgrade and drive out judgement.

Not all normal professionalism suffers these defects. They are, though, common. They tend towards inbreeding, almost incest, a syndrome or self-sustaining system, with mutual reinforcement of concepts, values, methods and behaviours, each feeding back into the others. Combined, they narrow and distort the view of reality which professionals construct.

These criticisms do not question the power, relevance and utility of science, measurements and mathematics in many domains. The point is that their proven utility and the reverence attached to them also enable them to be misused and to mislead. In power and influence, counting counts. Quantification brings credibility. But figures and tables can deceive, and numbers construct their own realities. What can be measured and manipulated statistically is then not only seen as real; it comes to be seen as the only or the whole reality. Some professions are more vulnerable than others. Individuals and professional schools vary. But there may be some truth in the following:

> Economists have come to feel
> What can't be measured, isn't real.
> The truth is always an amount
> Count numbers, only numbers count.

Reductionism: simplifying the complex

Reductionism is reducing the complex and varied to the simple and standard. Its method is often to focus on parts instead of wholes.

In normal physical science reductionism has been immensely successful. It goes with specialization which focuses vision and concern on one or a few aspects of a whole. Narrowing attention to a part of a whole usually enables precise measurement. Predictable mathematical relationships have been established, as in Newtonian physics, where conditions can be controlled, for example between gases and temperature and pressure. In development, reductionist scientific method has been powerful with simple, uniform interventions. An example has been establishing the effects of Vitamin A supplements in reducing child mortality. The experimental method used a standard intervention and a placebo, double blind, with large comparable experimental and control populations, in different conditions and countries. Nothing that follows detracts from or undervalues the need for and value of such methods, well used, where they fit.

Problems arise because the simplifications, standardizations and controls which work in such cases have been transferred to the human sciences and to other more complex intersections of the ecological and biological sciences with people and their needs. In diverse, dynamic and uncontrollable conditions with continuous variance and multiple linkages, reductionist methods can be both costly and misleading. Yet many professionals seem driven compulsively to simplify what is complex and to standardize what is diverse. Five examples can illustrate.

ZOPP

In project planning, logical framework analysis and its variants ZOPP (GTZ, 1988) and GOPP have been widely adopted and required by donor agencies. They employ forms of logical analysis variously of objectives, purposes, inputs, assumptions, outputs, effects and impacts. This at first sight appears exemplary. The analysis forces staff to think through what they consider needed, to set targets, and to plan action. This may make sense in engineering, with things. There are, though, defects when this method is applied to projects and processes involving people. An overarching problem is that participatory development cannot be planned in this way: its course is not foreseeable; it is a sea voyage, not a Swiss[3] train journey.

In two respects, also, ZOPP has been reductionist. First, classical ZOPP forced analysts to identify *a single core problem*.

> Each member of the planning team first writes down just one problem which he/she deems to be the core problem . . . A brief substantiation is then given for each proposed core problem. In the following discussion we try to agree on what is the core problem. If agreement cannot be directly reached then arrange the proposed core problems above and below each other into causes and effects; try again to agree on the core problem on the basis of the overview achieved in this way. (GTZ, 1988: 6)

If still no consensus was achieved, brainstorming, role games, or other decision-making aids were advised, or the selecting of the best decision, for example by awarding points. The possibility of there being several or many problems was not allowed. Reductionism to one core problem was *de rigueur*.

Second, participants in the ZOPP process have not represented a diversity of interests, unless among outsiders. Typically, the most local stage of a ZOPP process has taken place in a hotel or institute, not in a village or slum. If villagers or slum-dwellers took part at all, they were not likely to be the poorer people or women. Here is an account of the later stages of a ZOPP process with a small NGO in Pakistan:

> . . . they began developing a Project Planning Matrix. Based on problems identified by the participants at this workshop this matrix listed the sectors in which [the NGO] would work over a certain period of time and set indicative targets. When this exercise began I protested, rather vociferously, that these decisions should not be taken in this room and argued for a more participatory, open-ended planning process. The outside facilitator tried to convince me that this exercise was in fact participatory since it involved 'representatives' of the local people! I pointed out that the 8 people – all males – from 12 'clusters' (each cluster consists of about 8–12 villages which means these 8 persons were in fact representing 49 villages!) could only represent their own view, or at best that of a certain group. I also argued that as they were outnumbered by the articulate [NGO] staff and may have found it difficult to follow all the written stuff (ZOPP makes profuse use of index cards) these so-called reps of local people had little opportunity to get in a word, leave alone participate, in deciding on the perceived problems of local people

43

and the sectors on which [the NGO] should concentrate! (pers. comm., Rashida Dohad, 1995)

The reductionism here is of realities. By confining participants to outsiders and (presumably élite) male villagers, and by using methods which tended to marginalize even them, so the view of problems and priorities was limited. Yet women and men, poor and rich, young and old, and those with different resources, rights, skills and occupations, have different realities – different needs, perceptions, and priorities, demanding what Alice Welbourn (1991, and pp. 183–7) has called 'the analysis of difference'. But class and gender biases were combined in the ZOPP participants. Where were the poor women? Narrow participation narrows outcomes. It manifests reductionism to the realities of 'uppers': of outsiders, of a local élite, and of men.

The reductionism of participation then supports the reductionism of the single core problem, opening the way for agreement on a relatively few simplistic gender- and class-biased priorities and plans. The construction of such an artificial reality can be painful and difficult, but has been achieved by allowing days, sometimes a whole week, for the ZOPP process. Ultimate consensus has been assured by verbal dominance, exhaustion and the bottom line that donors have the money:

By requiring their partners to ZOPP
Donors rule with their talkers on top
   That one problem is core
   For those absent and poor
Is agreed when thought comes to a stop.

Social cost-benefit analysis (SCBA)

There are many dimensions to the costs, benefits, effects and impacts of development projects. The more obvious costs include capital, recurrent and foreign-exchange, and the opportunity costs of foreign-exchange and of a range of physical, natural and human resources including staff and labour. They also include disbenefits which may be human and social (e.g., livelihoods, communities and institutions weakened or destroyed, people displaced), political, and environmental, especially in the long term. Benefits can include revenue-generation and returns on capital, incomes generated and services provided. In effects and impacts much else, too, matters: livelihood security, ownership and access, migration, health and nutrition, equity, gender relations, well-being as people themselves define it, and impacts outside a project area. And these lists could and should be lengthened. So the information for good judgements necessarily includes assessing and weighing many criteria within a broad span of relevance.

Confronting this plurality, SCBA is reductionist through conflation. Various factors, some of them shadow-priced, are merged into a single measure, either a benefit:cost ratio, or an internal rate of return. The procedures for doing this have been elaborated in a small library of manuals, especially during the 1970s. These and the practice of SCBA have provoked many criticisms, among others for neglecting political dimensions, for losing detail and failing to provide the range of information needed for decision-making (Carruthers and Clayton, 1977), for gender bias (Kabeer, 1994: 163–86), and for undervaluing the future and discriminating against sustainability. The response to objections that a significant cost or benefit was being overlooked has been to find ways of accommodating it in the method. The new factor was made commensurable, reduced to a form which could become part of the single measure, or, in the case of sustainability and the future, the discount rate was not abandoned but lowered (Cline, 1992); so the reductionist single scale could survive.

The obscurity of the process has made it vulnerable to manipulation (Self, 1975). It is sensitive to predictions which are imponderable: the same agricultural project in Lesotho, appraised by three teams from different donors, was given rates of return of 19 per cent, 13 per cent, and minus 2 per cent respectively. In practice, SCBA has often been done backwards.[5] A judgement is made about a suitable ratio or rate of return, and then assumptions adjusted to produce it.

In its proper and limited place, cost-benefit analysis has a part to play, as one contribution to judgements between alternatives. Unfortunately, it has not occupied its proper and limited place. Many have been trained in its application; and for many it remains *the* method in project appraisal.

Poverty-line thinking

Deprivation as poor people perceive it has many dimensions, including not only lack of income and wealth, but also social inferiority, physical weakness, disability and sickness, vulnerability, physical and social isolation, powerlessness, and humiliation (Beck, 1994; Chambers, 1995). In practice, much of this wide spectrum of deprivation and ill-being is covered by the common use of the word poverty. But poverty also has a narrow technical definition for purposes of measurement and comparison. In the words of one authority (Townsend, 1993: 3) ' "poverty" has to be given scientifically acceptable universal meaning and measurement'. Poverty is then defined as low income, or often as low consumption, which is more easily and reliably measured. Surveys are carried out and poverty lines constructed.

This limits much of the analysis of poverty to the one dimension that has been measured. Some analysts recognize explicitly the resulting bias to the measurable and what measures are available. In his review of studies on poverty in India, D.S. Thakur (1985) observed:

This review . . . has revealed that their major focus has been on the aspect of measurement. None of them, in fact, examined the conceptual issues underlining the definitions of poverty or explored the causal links in depth between the various factors underlying the phenomenon.

Thakur did not himself explore the implications of this oversight, but reverted to the normal in the very next sentence with 'Even in the aspect of measurement there are many issues to be resolved', and then continued in that vein. Like Thakur, those who study what has been studied are trapped by the biases of their material.

Or again, Montek Ahluwalia (1986: 59) acknowledges that 'longevity, access to health and education facilities, and perhaps also security of consumption levels from extreme shocks' are equally relevant in analysis of poverty. But he then points out that he is constrained because '. . . time-series data on all these dimensions are not available. Data from a series of consumption surveys conducted by the National Sample Survey Organization are available, and these data have been used in most of the studies of rural poverty in India', a pattern which he then repeats.

Similarly, Lipton and Ravallion (1993) acknowledge the potential breadth of a definition of economic welfare, but then continue:

> While recognizing the limitations of the concept of economic welfare as 'command over commodities', we will largely confine ourselves to that definition, in order to review the many important issues treated in the literature that has evolved around it. (Ibid: 1)

So the analysis of deprivation and poverty comes to be narrowed to what has been measured and is available in statistics. This has its uses. It enables central planners to make comparisons between regions and districts, and between different times. But it entails a double simplification. Only one dimension of deprivation is measured when there are so many, and so diverse a range; and the questionnaires used to assess consumption or income further simplify and miss much, not least by omitting or under-estimating multiple sources of money, materials and food.

The simple definition of the bad condition – poverty – is made, then, not by the poor, from their experience, but by the well-off, for their convenience. Planners' and academics' need for a single scale of numbers narrows, distorts and simplifies their perceptions. Deprivation and poverty come to be defined, not by the changing and varied wants and needs of the poor, but by the static and standardized wants and needs of professionals. Conceptually, professionals are then caught in their own reductionist poverty trap. Poverty becomes what has been measured.

Production thinking

It has been normal for economists and agricultural scientists to focus their attention on food production; and within food production, on foodgrains. So seed breeders concentrated on yield to the relative neglect of other characteristics. Breeders at one time competed to see who could achieve the most production per unit area for rice, or maize, or wheat. The one question asked, again and again, of varieties, was 'What's the yield?' And the one figure quoted and remembered as an indicator of annual agricultural performance, continues to be estimated and reported production of tonnes of foodgrains.

It is only common sense that enough food has to be produced to meet human food requirements, but making production a single objective has in practice three defects:

○ The first is the supposition that producing more food will prevent hunger and famine. As noted above (pp. 18–19) much evidence indicates that famines are more weakly linked with food availability than had been supposed, and that producing more food will not prevent famine unless poor people can obtain the food. What matters is not so much how much food is produced but who produces it, where it is produced, and who can command it once it has been produced.

○ The second defect of production thinking has been the preoccupation with yield per hectare, and the implicit assumption that this is all or most of what matters to farmers. In practice, farmers have many criteria, of which yield is only one. With open-ended matrix scoring, in countries as diverse as Bangladesh, Botswana, China, India, Sri Lanka, Tanzania and Zambia, farmers have listed criteria by which they compare varieties of the same crop. In farmers' matrix scoring for four varieties of bananas, facilitated by scientists from the Tamil Nadu Agricultural University, farmers' seven criteria did not include yield at all (Manoharan *et al.*, 1993). For three varieties of millet in Zambia, farmers had 16 criteria (Drinkwater, 1993), and elsewhere ten or more criteria have been common. Examples are: the range of soils in which varieties can be grown; timing of maturity and harvest; early yield; disease resistance; resistance to birds; not lodging; straw production for fodder; ease of weeding, not shedding; ease of harvesting; ease of threshing; storability; price; cooking quality; suitability for beer; and taste. Again and again, farmers have preferred and planted varieties which give less than the highest yields (e.g. Ashby *et al.*, 1989; Women of Sangams Pastapur etc. and M. Pimbert, 1991).

○ The third defect is treating estimated grain production as total food production. Grains, especially maize, rice and wheat, have often been accorded primacy to the neglect of other major sources of calories, which most obviously include root crops such as cassava (manioc), potatoes and sweet potatoes, bananas, tree foods and fruits like jack fruit, bread fruit, durian and mangoes, and many different vegetables. The produce of home gardens is often significant (Hoogerbrugge *et al.*, 1993). The 'hidden harvest' of wild foods (Scoones *et al.*, 1992; Hinchcliffe, 1995; Guijt *et al.*, 1995) is often another major source, especially for the poor and as fallback in times of shortage. Yet in authoritative texts on food production and availability (e.g. Pinstrup-Andersen and Pandya-Lorch, 1995) the words 'food' and 'grain' can alternate, leaving the reader unclear whether food means anything more than grain. Figures for grain production are conveniently available for use in texts and tables; those for other foods less so. The reality of food production becomes what has been measured.

Employment thinking

Most normal professionals have thought in terms of employment, and creating jobs. This was especially so in the 1970s. Of India, Schumacher wrote in 1973 that according to his estimates there was 'an immediate need for something like fifty million new *jobs*' (Schumacher, 1973: 162–3) (emphases in this paragraph are mine). The 1976 ILO Conference which launched basic needs was on world *employment*. The director-general of the ILO wrote at that time that the basic-needs approach 'implies that each person available for and willing to work should have an adequately remunerated *job*' (ILO, 1976: 7). The Nigerian Constitution of 1978 included a statement that the state 'shall direct its policy towards ensuring . . . that . . . a reasonable national minimum living *wage* . . . would be provided for all citizens' (quoted in ILO, 1981: v). The problems of the poor were seen as lack of employment, and solutions were seen in providing jobs with wages and salaries in workplaces.

Employment thinking is embedded in the language and concepts which persist in much discussion of poverty. Thus H. Jeffery Leonard (1989: 14)

> . . . the central task for the 1990s and beyond will be to create enough jobs to employ billions of new workers through the developing world . . . Job creation efforts for new labor-force entrants in many developing countries . . . must focus on both the urban and rural sectors.

The concepts and categories derive from the formal sector of the urban and industrial world of the North: the ideas of job, workplace, and workforce, and the objective of providing full employment by generating jobs for all workers. Earlier, Gunnar Myrdal had agonized over the misleading preconceptions of Western economics when applied to Asian conditions:

> When new data are assembled, the conceptual categories used are inappropriate to the conditions existing: as, for example, when the underutilization of the labour force in the South Asian countries is analysed according to Western concepts of unemployment, disguised unemployment, and underemployment. The resulting mountains of figures have either no meaning or a meaning other than that imputed to them . . . The very fact that the researcher gets figures to play with tends to confirm his original, biased approach . . . the continuing collection of data under biased notions only postpones the day when reality can effectively challenge inherited preconceptions. (Myrdal, 1968)

And he called for behavioural studies founded on observations of the raw reality (ibid., Vol. 2: 1027).

The raw reality for the majority of the very poor in the world, in the South, and either in rural areas or in the informal urban sector, is not one of jobs in the Northern, industrial sense. It is a reality of diverse livelihoods with multiple activities by different family members at different times, exploiting varied and changing resources and opportunities. But because such livelihoods are difficult to measure, and do not fit the familiar Northern frame, their reality has for long been under- and misperceived.

Since Myrdal wrote, the informal sector has been discovered and explored, and livelihood has been proposed as a better word than employment to capture the complex and diverse reality of the poor. But employment thinking remains alive, strong and, by some, universally applied. It featured prominently in the papers prepared for the Social Development Summit in Copenhagen in 1995. Whatever happens to the poor, full employment seems assured for conventional economists as they continue to analyse the available statistical data on employment and unemployment, and to project their categories and the concerns of the industrial North on to the different reality of most of the poor in the South. Myrdal would be sad to learn how little has changed.

So pervasive is reductionism that one can talk of it as a normal mode of analysis and thinking, especially in applied economics. The brutal conflations and simplifications of complex realities by ZOPP, cost-benefit analysis, poverty lines, production thinking and employment thinking mutilate and reframe the complex and diverse local and personal realities to which they refer. How is it that highly trained and intelligent professionals can indulge in such distortions?

It would itself be simplistic to attribute these forms of reductionism to simple-mindedness, emotional insecurity, a desire for power, or some combination of these. For those who use these methods and concepts are often highly educated and intelligent in the conventional sense of intelligence, well balanced and not manifestly striving to exercise power. Some explanations can be suggested: the pleasures of mathematics; addiction to computers and calculations; the transfer and application of the methods and mindsets of physical science to human conditions; the pressure of time for writing papers for conferences which prevents careful and complicating qualifications to texts and tables; the security, for teachers and practitioners alike, of stepwise procedures, straightforward and predictable both to teach and to use; the convenient practicality of single scales and single criteria through the scope they provide for longitudinal and cross-sectional comparisons; and the need for simple figures and 'facts' to present to policymakers. Perhaps most of all, the tension between complex diversity and practical action forces those with central power to simplify in order to see what to do.

Even after weighing these explanations, a puzzle remains. It is as though there is a single groove in the brains of some of the brilliantly intelligent which captures, confines and concentrates many streams. Perhaps there is a drive to find a unifying theory, a single explanation; perhaps, too, sometimes ambition and arrogance can be found in those who seek unifying theory. In reductionist thinking, in a mysterious way, intelligence and humane commonsense seem inversely related. And since intelligent people dominate the discourse of development, we can expect reductionism to remain robustly sustainable.

Economics: culture and cult

Among disciplines and professions concerned with poverty, deprivation and development, economics is the most influential. Economists dominate the World Bank at the cost of other social scientists. The world-views and values of economists matter to poor people more than those of, say, sociologists, for the simple reason that more economists hold power and determine policy, and are likely to continue to do so. In 1993, it was said that only about 20 World Bank professional staff were sociologists or social anthropologists practising their discipline, outnumbered by their economist colleagues by perhaps between 20 and 50 to 1 (see also SDN, 1993: 11).[6] In the words of a staff member: 'Only economists in the Bank are regarded as professionals'.[7] It is, mainly, economists who advise on economic policy; economists who have staffed the country missions of the IMF and the World Bank which have required structural adjustment policies for weak, indebted countries; and economists who generate, sustain and modify the dominant ideologies of development. It is important, then, to understand the strengths and weaknesses of contemporary economics and economists.

Among economists, those of the United States enjoy primacy, both academically and in their influence on the IMF and the World Bank.[8] The judgements, decisions and actions of those who are young economists now will in future decades powerfully affect, for better or for worse, the livelihoods and well-being of hundreds of millions of those who are most deprived. Their professional socialization and values are, therefore, a matter of concern to all who are committed to the reduction of deprivation and poverty.

A series of studies (e.g. Kamarck, 1983; Frey *et al.*, 1984; Klamer and Colander, 1990; Baumol, 1991; Frank *et al.*, 1993) has presented an alarming view of economists and of the normal high-status professionalism of economists, especially in the United States.

A review of several behavioural studies by an economist and two psychologists at Cornell University (Frank *et al.*, 1993) found that economists were more likely than non-economists to act in a non-trusting, non-cooperative, self-interested manner.[9] The median gift to big charities by economists among 1245 randomly selected college professors was substantially lower than for non-economists; and about 9 per cent of economics professors gave nothing, against a range for other disciplines of between 1 and 4 per cent. In a prisoners' dilemma game with options of trusting or not trusting, economics students defected 60 per cent of the time compared with 39 per cent for non-economists. In an experiment with students, those who received instruction in game theory and industrial organization tested as less 'honest' than those who were taught development in Maoist China or those who took a placebo (astronomy).

It can be asked whether there is a self-reinforcing culture here. The reductionism of Economic Man, the rational optimizer, misses much of the complexity of human behaviour. Economists tend to take a Pavlovian view of human nature which sees people as subject to reflexes which respond to economic incentives.[10] The danger is that assuming that other people are economic maximizers makes economic maximizers of those who make the assumptions.

The normal high-status professionalism of economists is reported in these studies to have clustered around formalist theory and mathematical modelling, in contrast with the empirical economics of the real world. According to Thomas Mayer (1993: 46–55) the ranking at the time he wrote was: (1) formalist theory; (2) empirical science theory; (3) policy advising and data gathering; and (4) history of economic thought and methodology.

The potential for erudite arrogance is not slight. Abstract mathematical modelling comes top; and a context for critical self-awareness and self-doubt through a historical perspective or reflection on methodology comes bottom. Much the same is evident in the values into which graduate students of economics in the USA are socialized. When economics graduate students at six leading universities (Chicago, MIT, Harvard, Stanford, Columbia and Yale) were asked 'Which characteristics will most likely place students on the fast track?' only 3 per cent chose 'Having a thorough knowledge of the economy', while 68 per cent thought that unimportant; in contrast 98 per cent thought excellence in mathematics either very important (57 per cent) or moderately important (41 per cent) (Klamer and Colander, 1990: 18).

The researchers reported that

> the interviews suggested a definite tension, frustration and cynicism that, in our view, went beyond the normal graduate school blues. There was a strong sense that economics was a game and that hard work in devising relevant models that demonstrated a deep understanding of institutions would have a lower payoff than devising models that were analytically neat; the facade, not the depth of knowledge, was important. (Ibid: 18)

One might have hoped, in the interests of a better world, that teaching and learning would stress a sense of historical context, an empirical understanding of real economies, and a broad competence as a basis for judgement. Not so. In the words of students 'Policy is for simpletons' and 'those who can't do economics do policy' (ibid.: 181).

The highest status is reserved for those who combine mathematics and theory. Even less accessible to the lay person, formalist economists who converse with colleagues in equations are respected and rewarded for their erudite obscurantism. Lay people assume that their failure to understand what is being said or shown is a sign of stupidity, and manifest a prudent reverence. The most brilliant and ambitious students are drawn to the master (more rarely mistress) and are clever enough to learn the language. Having invested time, effort and their not inconsiderable ability in learning, they are co-opted by the concepts, modes of thought and jargon, and are bright enough to be able to use them. In this way a school may coalesce which talks to itself and impresses others in proportion to its self-sustaining separation from the world of real people.

There are parallels between physics and economics. Physics has enjoyed high status among the physical sciences, as has economics among the social sciences. Theoretical physics and theoretical economics each has an esoteric mathematical language. Each is accorded high prestige within its related disciplines. In both, mathematics is applied at the level of the very large and very small: in physics, astrophysics and particle physics; in economics, macro-economics and micro-economics. In the middle of these polar scales comes the practical world of low-status applied physics and low-status policy economics. Both also suffer from the recalcitrant messiness of the revealed world: for physicists the mischievous refusal of God or nature to stop presenting new micro-particles; and for economists the obdurate refusal of people to behave as simple economic maximizers. In both physics and economics, the atoms persist in being naughty.

At their powerful extremes, both physicists and economists are dangerous. If economics is the physics of the social sciences, macroeconometrics is its nuclear physics. Macro-econometricians and nuclear physicists have both endangered life on a large scale but in different ways: nuclear physicists by being right about things and producing bombs, and macro-econometricians by being wrong about people and producing policies. Combining awesome power with a rarified atmosphere far from the effects of their actions, both are vulnerable to an ethical high-altitude deterioration.

The behaviour and values of high-status theoretical economists combine convenience and escapism. The convenience is that messy data are not needed. Being formal and logical, model-building is easy to organize and lecture on. In economics as in physics it has led to a higher rate of publication than dealing with time-consuming and laborious work on real-world problems. Over half the articles in the *American Economic Review* from 1972 to 1981 were on mathematical models without any data (Kamarck, 1983: 122–3).

The escapism is from the insecure and uncertain external world where opinions differ, judgement is needed and one may be wrong. On causalities and practical policies, a study published in 1984 found economists to differ, as illustrated in Table 3.5, to a degree which can only astonish the layperson. In 1996, Stephen Roach, the economist guru and advocate of 'downsizing' which laid off millions of workers in the North, changed his mind (Carlin, 1996). It would seem that practical economic policy is an area

Table 3.5: Degrees of disagreement among economists

Percentages of 936 economists in five countries

	Generally agree	Agree, with provisions	Generally disagree	Degree of consensus
Wage price controls should be used to control inflation	10	21	69	Highest of 27 questions
A minimum wage increases employment among young and unskilled workers	41	26	32	Close to median of 27
Inflation is primarily a monetary phenomenon	23	29	46	
Government should restructure the welfare system along the lines of a negative income tax	28	29	38	Lowest of 27

All figures rounded, 0.5 upwards. The return rate of complete replies to the mailed questionnaire was 45.2 per cent, without a reminder. Respondents were anonymous. The countries were the United States, France, the Federal Republic of Germany, Austria and Switzerland.

Source: Frey *et al.*, 1984: 986–9.

where economists can be deeply uncertain, widely divided and often wrong. They are dealing there, after all, not with the paradigm of controllable and predictable things, but with complex and unpredictable processes.

It is only human for some to seek refuge in theoretical models which are not only high status, but also secure. Starting conditions can then be set, assumptions specified, and procedures followed through to conclusions without the distress of contact with the recalcitrant untidiness of real economies or people. Formal mathematical models are then to formal economists what operating theatres are to surgeons and laboratories to bio-engineers: controlled environments, warm wombs, safe from invasion. The difference between these professions is in proximate responsibility: the surgeons deal with people, even if anaesthetized and so temporarily inert, like things; the bio-engineers deal with living organisms, even if temporarily separated into small bits; but the formal economists deal only with abstractions. Their models are secure, more controlled than an operating theatre or laboratory, safe for the display of precision, logic and elegance of rigour, vulnerable only to a computer crash or virus. The only problem is that their realities are artefacts, worlds of fantasy, esoteric works of art not practical tools.

The elevation and spread of formalist economics has not gone unchecked or unquestioned. Kamarck wrote that:

> Economic science is advanced by economist-practitioners who struggle with the economic models of the real world and not by those economists who live prestigious and happy lives playing with elegant models of comely shape but without vital organs. (Kamarck, 1983: 122)

In a ten-day workshop at the Santa Fe Institute in Arizona, in which physicists and economists met to brainstorm about their commonalities, differences and the emerging science of complexity, the physicists were astonished at the assumptions made by economists, such as perfect rationality among economic agents. This led to remarks by the physicists like 'You guys really believe that?' and 'You're solving the wrong problem if that's not reality' (Waldrop, 1994: 136ff).

As in other disciplines, so in economics reality is constructed. In disciplines dependent on numbers, causal significance in the theory is liable to vary with measurability. Economists, like others, are then forced into a self-sustaining circularity: what is measured generates theory which leads to more measurements which maintain the theory. An example would be the analysis of capital accumulation compared with other factors in economic growth (Woo, 1986, cited in Mayer, 1993: 57). Theory is then reinforced, as the measurable is measured and analysed more and more, and imputed more and more causal primacy. Measurable is sustainable. Irreverent imagery comes to mind: of a measurement-theory merry-go-round; of a dog chasing its tail.[11]

Economists differ from dogs in several ways.[12] But some behaviour can be similar, as in the principle of the lamp-post. Dogs leave boundary marking signatures on lamp-posts, and mad dogs chase their tails. Some economists look for answers not in the dark areas where they are to be found, but under the lamp-post where they can see numbers in light. They too mark their boundaries of professional specialization, illuminated by the circularity of reductionism and measurement. What lies outside in darkness, unseen and unmeasured, is assumed to be more of the same, describable in rules of thumb, unimportant, or simply not to exist. Reality is what the light shines on.

Now, in the mid-1990s, formal economics is increasingly challenged. The movement of socio-economics in the United States has sought to redress the balance and restore the prestige of empirical work. More practical journals challenge the primacy of those dominated by abstract theory. The World Bank talks more of human capital, social infrastructure, and people; James Wolfensohn, the president of the World Bank, embraces participation. Many economists are engaged with the practical mess of people and policies, and can in part or wholly except themselves from the criticisms of this section. Macro-economists are needed and will always have a vital role. What matters is that they should be in touch with 'the real world' of people. Unfortunately, elegant models still seduce and measurement merry-go-rounds still mesmerize. In both formal theory and practical policy, the danger is that high status will have its own circular, self-sustaining dynamic.

The professional prison

Much normal professionalism, then, creates and sustains its own reality. A core magnetic pull draws people inwards towards cities, offices, libraries, laboratories, hospitals, research stations and computers, and then holds them there. For many, this is the road to advancement. In the words of one: 'For me as a trained economist the easiest way to get promotion is to stay in my office and play with my computer, and not go out'. To get on, you have to stay in.

So professional methods and values set a trap. Status, promotion and power come less from direct contact with the confusing complexity of people, families, communities, livelihoods and farming systems, and more from isolation which permits safe and sophisticated analysis of statistics. The normal reflex of professionals faced with complexity – of people, environments, farming systems and so on – has been to extract, process and analyse data and use them to decide what to do to those people, environments and farming systems. The processing and analysis of data are private activities under the control of professionals: power, in the name of planning and science – the project plan, the district plan, the farm plan, even the national plan – is retained in their hands and expressed in prescriptions for others.

The methods of modern science then serve to simplify and reframe reality in standard categories, applied from a distance. ZOPP, social cost-benefit analysis, poverty lines, and production and employment thinking all do violence to complex, diverse and dynamic realities, and mutilate, massage and mould them to make countable packaged units. Those who manipulate these units are empowered and the subjects of analysis disempowered: counting promotes the counter and demotes the counted. Top-down, centre-outwards patterns are then self-reinforcing through rewards, status and power.

It is then the reductionist, controlled, simplified and quantified construction which becomes reality for the isolated professional, not that other world, out there. There is an analogy with Plato's cave in *The Republic*. Unwitting prisoners, professionals sit chained to their central places and mistake the flat shadows of figures, tables, reports, professional papers and printouts for the rounded, dynamic, multi-dimensional substance of the world of those others at the peripheries. But there is a twist in the analogy. Platonism is stood on its head. Plato's reality, of which the prisoners perceived only the shadows, was of essences, each simple, unitary, abstract and unchanging. The reality, of which core professionals perceive only the simplified shadows, is in contrast a diversity: of people, farming systems and livelihoods, each a complex whole, concrete and changing. But professionals reconstruct that reality to make it manageable in their own alien analytic terms, seeking and selecting the universal in the diverse, the part in the whole, the simple in the complex, the controllable in the uncontrollable, the measurable in the unmeasurable, the abstract in the concrete, the static in the dynamic, permanence in flux. For the convenience and control of normal professionals, it is not the local, complex, diverse, dynamic and unpredictable reality of those who are poor, weak and peripheral that counts, but the flat shadows of that reality that they, prisoners of their professionalism, fashion for themselves.

4

The Transfer of Reality

It appears that the act of extension, in whatever sector it takes place, means that those carrying it out need to go to 'another part of the world' to 'normalize it', according to their way of viewing reality: to make it resemble their world.

Paulo Freire, 1974: 95

Realities – the world as perceived and interpreted by individuals – are multiple but with commonalities. Human relationships can be seen as patterned by dominance and subordination, with people as uppers and lowers. Uppers experience and construct their realities and seek to transfer these to lowers. In normal teaching, adult realities are transferred to children and students. Normal successful careers carry people upwards in hierarchies and inwards to larger centres, away from the poor and the peripheries. In normal bureaucracy, central authorities simplify, control and standardize. In normal top-down, centre-outwards development, new technology is developed in central places by uppers and transferred to peripheral lowers. The resulting 'Model-T' standard packages often misfit diverse and unpredictable local conditions. Similarly, the transfer of procedures which require local people to conform to fixed timetables frequently fail. Normal professionalism, teaching, careers and bureaucracy help to explain errors in development, but not fully how and why they persist so long without uppers learning.

Realities

Since the word 'reality' is used much in this book, let me try to be clear about what I mean by it. Others may disagree with this use, but at least they will have a better sense of what I am trying to say. As I shall use it, the term has two clusters of meaning: 'physical' reality that exists outside us, the so-called 'real world' of physical things; and 'personal' reality that we construct for ourselves – what we perceive, know and believe. The physical reality that exists outside us is a commonplace of ordinary practical life. We live successfully on the basis that physical things exist independently of ourselves 'out there' and that many of them have predictable properties.

This idea of a solid objective physical reality is out of fashion. The reassuringly predictable world of Newtonian physics, with its notional billiard-ball atoms in regular mathematical orbits, has been dissolved once and for all. Relativity theory and quantum physics have replaced it with indeterminacy. The act of observation affects what is observed: according to the popular view of the celebrated Heisenberg uncertainty principle, this makes it impossible to observe both the position and velocity of a particle at the same time. But these ideas can go too far; the fact that we cannot measure or study something without altering it does not mean that it does not exist. Nor do indeterminacy and unpredictability in small-particle physics in any significant way affect our daily lives. We build dams, bridges and skyscrapers successfully on the basis of Newtonian physics. This fits our common experience, especially of solid objects. In the popular stereotype, professional philosophers are not outstanding for the practical competence of their mastery of the physical world; but even the most absent-minded and impractical among them conducts everyday life on the basis of commonsense assumptions about universally predictable physical realities.

In the social sciences, too, the solid ground of positivism has crumbled. In the 1920s, the famous experiments in the Western Electric Company's Hawthorne works in Chicago dramatized the finding that the act of observing people influences their behaviour: the productivity of a group of workers went up each time a new experimental change was introduced in their working conditions; they were responding to being studied. Objectivity in the social sciences is regarded as a mirage. Post-positivism, constructivism (Guba and Lincoln, 1989) and post-modernism (Harvey, 1990; Giddens, 1990) (itself separable into affirmative and sceptical post-modernism) (Rosenau, 1992) variously stress the limitations of 'scientific' method in the social sciences, holding that objectivity is not possible and that we have multiple realities, each of us constructing our own. These insights and ideas impel us to critical self-questioning and continual doubt about our perceptions and interpretations of what is outside ourselves, that is to say, about our personal realities.

A personal[1] reality is, then, reality as experienced and put together by an individual person. It is how a person construes experience, and the framework with which sense and coherence are made of the world. This refers to perceptions not just of things, but of people, processes and relationships. Perception is always selective, through the nature of our senses, through what we have contact with, through what we choose to perceive or expose ourselves to perceiving, through our methods and acts of observing, through our habits of thinking, and through the mental frames into which we fit information. Our personal mental frames are made up from our past learning and experience, and our constructs, beliefs, values and preferences. What we perceive and believe is also moulded by ego and power: ego in the sense of personal needs, as for self-esteem, rewarding social relations and peace of mind; and power in our relations with those who are weaker and stronger than ourselves (for which, see Chapter 5). From their nature, then, personal realities all differ. We all 'see things differently'. Personal realities are, in the terms used later in this book, complex, diverse and dynamic. We speak, then, of a world of multiple realities, in which each of us constructs our own and has our own way of construing what we perceive.

The distinction in Chapter 3 between things and people helps here. We have a personal reality about things. How we perceive and construe things we can call a 'personal physical reality'. And we have a personal reality about people, how we perceive and construe them, which we can call a 'personal social reality'.

With personal physical realities, there is much commonality between us. It makes practical sense to think in terms of a unitary and largely stable and predictable physical world. This relates to solids, and some dimensions of liquids and gases in the middle range of scale, but not to those where chaos theory better applies. With personal social realities, in contrast, there is more divergence and dynamism. It is in the social realm that it makes most sense to talk of multiple realities.

The distinctions are not absolute, but help in understanding ourselves. Personal physical realities are formed mainly through sensory experience of the predictable, regular, Newtonian physical world. Personal social realities are formed mainly through interaction with unpredictable, irregular and idiosyncratic people. Personal social realities are, then, influenced by interpersonal relationships; and to understand their formation and diversity it is to interpersonal relationships that we must turn.

Top-down: uppers and lowers, North and South

Many human relationships can be seen and understood in terms of hierarchies of power and weakness, of dominance and subordination. As Albert Camus (1956) put it:

> We can't do without dominating others or being served . . . Even the man on the bottom rung still has his wife, or his child, If he's a bachelor, his dog. The essential thing, in sum, is being able to get angry without the other person being able to answer back.

Power relations vary by person and context. There are various axes of power, and

> individual persons can occupy different positions along different axes of power at one and the same time. People are complicated enough, alas, to enjoy the various pleasures of domination while simultaneously suffering all the insults and injuries that subordination brings in its wake.
>
> (Cocks, 1989: 6)

Those who are powerful and dominant in a context are, then, 'uppers' and those who are weak and subordinate are 'lowers'. Like magnets, people are oriented in North–South fields of relationships, with uppers above and lowers below.[2] In the Bible, for example, St Paul is recorded as having written: 'Wives, submit yourselves unto your husbands as unto the Lord. For the husband is the head of the wife, even as Christ is the head of the church . . .' (Ephesians v.22). Hierarchy in the church, and the authority of Christ as the head of the church, was thus used to justify by analogy another authority, that of husband over wife. In such ways, different North–South magnetic fields are mutually reinforcing.

The North–South analogy resonates with two interlocking orientations. The first is the global polarization of wealth and power, with the temperate North dominating the tropical South. The second concerns normal professional maps. By near-universal convention, these have North at the top and

South at the bottom. Compasses are seen as showing North, and only secondarily South.[3]

At the personal level, the upper-lower magnetic field is present in many relationships between people. Some of these are shown in Table 4.1. Most people have uppers above them and lowers below them. Most are uppers at some times, in some roles and contexts, and lowers at others. Sources of upper-lower status and dominance include these eight:

(i) *biologically preset and socially determined* as with male-female, white-black, high caste-low caste, and ethnic group;

(ii) *socially inherited*, as with wealth-poverty, high and low class;

(iii) *accidental*, resulting from external events beyond personal control, such as disasters and windfall gains;

(iv) *personal*, based on individual aspects of personality, physical characteristics (height, strength, fierceness of eye, timbre of voice, etc.), behaviour, charisma, and so on;

(v) *acquired* through training, initiation and performance, as with professionals such as doctors, psychiatrists, priests and politicians;

(vi) *occupational*, associated with the relative status of a profession or occupation;

(vii) *sequential*, being part of life and domestic cycles, where status changes as children become adults and parents, daughters-in-law become mothers-in-law, and more generally young women and men become old women and men; and

(viii) *hierarchical*, derived from position in an organizational or political hierarchy.

Status, dominance and subordination which are biological, social and accidental in their origins are often quite largely given. The personal dimension is partly given but can be changed. Acquired, occupational, sequential and hierarchical status, dominance and subordination are more malleable and changeable; and it is with these four that this chapter is most concerned. Acquired and occupational are linked with normal teaching and professionalism, sequential with normal careers, and hierarchical with normal bureaucracy. These combine to enable uppers to dominate lowers in many ways. The more obvious include force, threats, orders and rewards. In addition, and consciously and unconsciously, uppers also deny the realities of lowers and seek to impose on them their own realities. In this chapter we will see how dominance and subordination lead to the question: whose reality counts?

Normal teaching

Almost all development professionals, in the conventional sense of professional, have received prolonged formal teaching and training. From early childhood, we have been 'schooled', and have faced tests and examinations. Patterns differ, but often parents have made sacrifices for our education. Parental approval and disapproval, as well as incentives and disincentives in school, made us try hard to do well. In school, we were rewarded for learning, and for reproducing what we had learnt. Some of

Table 4.1: North and South, uppers and lowers

Dimension/context	North, uppers	South, lowers
Spatial	Core (urban, industrial)	Periphery (rural, agricultural)
International and developmental	The North IMF, World Bank Donors Creditors Outsider, professional	The South Poor countries Recipients Debtors Local person
Inborn and social	Male White High ethnic or caste group	Female Black Low ethnic or caste group
Life cycle	Old person Parent Mother-in-law	Young person Child Daughter-in-law
Bureaucratic organization	Senior Manager Official Patron Officer Warden, guard	Junior Worker Supplicant Client 'Other rank' Inmate, prisoner
Social, spiritual	Patron Priest Guru Doctor, psychiatrist	Client Lay person Disciple Patient
Teaching and learning	Master Lecturer Teacher	Apprentice Student Pupil

our earliest learning and rewards were with the three Rs – reading, writing and arithmetic.

Most of our teaching has been top-down. In the archetypal school of Thomas Gradgrind in Charles Dickens' *Hard Times* (1854), education was about facts: 'Now, what I want is Facts. Teach these boys and girls nothing but Facts'. 'Fancy' was forbidden – 'You are never to fancy', and the pupils were seen as 'little vessels then and there arranged in order, ready to have imperial gallons of facts poured into them until they were full to the brim'. Gradgrindian education is commonly deplored, but its features of hierarchy, authority, discipline and a one-way flow of facts to fill empty vessels persist in much of the world, in what Freire has called the 'banking' system of education.

That education is a massive priority, especially for those children who are denied it, that it has a huge potential to liberate, especially girls and women, that it can open up opportunities and a wider world of experience, that it can empower and support social and economic development – none of these is being questioned. The question is, what else does normal teaching do to us.

Early in life, when most impressionable, we leave our families daily and go to school where we are oriented, together with our peer-mates, to respect and learn from those who are older, bigger, stronger, louder and more dominant than we are. For many this means sitting in rows, at desks, facing an adult who looks down, and who rewards and punishes according to how well rote is repeated and routines remembered. For India, Malcolm Adiseshiah (1983) lamented that: 'In the majority of schools, the technique of teaching is a one-way speaking style, with the teacher pouring forth "words of wisdom" and the students listening passively' and that a 'growth of not thinking out for oneself but repeating faithfully what someone else has said, now pervades the whole educational system'.

Such experience conditions behaviour and attitudes in later life. The empty vessels are not just filled; they are magnetized. The force field of the teacher orients them for the world beyond the classroom. They learn to face, fear and follow authority. The more Gradgrindian our schooling, and the more top-down, or North–South, our teachers, so the more top–down, or North–South we are when we leave school and education. Those who have had sticks waved at them in school go out and later wave sticks at others. Some rebel, but most learn the lesson, and grow up conditioned to fit into, and reinforce, the hierarchies of authority and obedience which they find again in work and life after their formal education.

Teachers and teaching are themselves standardized. Teacher training has progressed since the time when the teacher in Gradgrind's school, Mr M'Choakumchild 'and some one hundred and forty other schoolmasters had been lately turned at the same time, in the same factory, on the same principles, like so many pianoforte legs'. All the same, it can be asked whether repetition and routinization are as normal in teacher training as in teaching pupils, with the same lectures delivered at the same time in the same way to similar 'vessels' year after year until disability, dismissal, death or retirement terminates the teacher's treadmill. If so, the subjects preferred may be those which do not change, where there is a right and a wrong, and where the methods are immutable, as in practice in much mathematics;[4] textbooks, then, with luck will last a lifetime, marking is easier, and the teacher's authority less likely to be challenged.

In much teaching, other people are treated as entities. There are exceptions in history and civics. But generally, students are taught about people not as being infinitely diverse but as universally standard. They become entities to be counted, or objects to be dissected. So people become numbers in a census, completed schedules in a questionnaire survey, or cadavers in a medical students' laboratory. As the Goods (Good and Good, 1989) have shown, students at Harvard Medical School go through a process of redefining their relationship with people. At first touching another person in a physical examination may be felt to be invasive. But in 'the construction of the professional self' personal boundaries are changed. The patient is reconstructed 'as object of the medical gaze'. In the words of a student at Harvard Medical School:

I don't feel like another person's body is foreign to me now. The concept of the other body is changing. At first, you are very aware that you are dealing with another person. Now I just don't think about that any more. You just do the routine. If there's a head at the end of the body, that's better for the interview!

Whether in the counting of questionnaires, the correlations of regressions, the 'physical' or medical examination, or the dissections of surgery, the idiosyncratic, complex, dynamic individual with her or his miraculous and uncontrollable consciousness is reduced to, and treated as, standard and controllable. The person becomes thing.

Top-down teaching, and the transfer of knowledge of things, and of people as things, are, then, deeply rooted. There are exceptions, but the ghost of Gradgrind stalks the primary schools of much of the North as well as South, and quite often the secondary schools, training colleges and universities. In practice, institutions of education exist for teaching, rather than for learning or for learning to learn. What is learnt, above all, is information, routines and obedience, in other words, facts, procedures, and to do what one is told. The lesson is: obey, learn, repeat, and you will avoid penalties, get good marks, and be approved and rewarded for being a good little (or not so little) girl or boy.

Learning is then meant to be not lateral, from exploration, experience and peers, let alone from below or from beyond the classroom, but vertical, from above, from the voice of authority. A single, standard way of seeing and construing is instilled. Rarely is local people's knowledge taught, or their understanding of their world. The reality and understanding that are imprinted are alien and other, introduced from outside and above. So normal teaching transfers not just knowledge but a structured reality; and that is reality as defined through hierarchies based in the cores of power and wealth.

In this pattern and process, the more élite, privileged and long-drawn-out the education, the more highly magnetized the final product. Those who proceed to central high-status institutions – to better schools, and universities, and from South to North – gain confidence in their learning in proportion to their distance from the social realities of the poor and the peripheries. There are exceptions and dangers of caricature. But often, students' experience of being taught makes them more N–S, preparing them for the world of hierarchy to which they will progress.

The upper–lower structure of relationships is then repeated in later life. On leaving school, college or university, well-magnetized graduates join bureaucracies and orient themselves naturally in the new hierarchical fields. Their magnetism is reinforced. They now in turn transfer their constructions of reality to those they find below them. Those who were taught become teachers; those who were dominated, dominate. Now powerful, they disempower others. They impose their reality, treating that of their lowers as inferior or of no account. Nor is radical ideology a guarantee that teachers will abstain from didactic dominance. Higher education has much to answer for. In the lament of one Northern teacher reported by Anne Marie Goetz (pers. comm.): 'The people we have trained have stripped peasants of their power'.

Normal (successful) careers

A common hope of parents who get their children into school is that whatever their children can receive of primary, secondary and tertiary education will lead to a job in a bureaucracy, whether in government or the private sector. This will bring status and a secure and substantial income. And the top–down, upper–lower, N–S orientation of the teaching they receive in school, college and university does indeed magnetize them to fit into hierarchical organizations.

For professionals, normal (successful) careers present three interlocking trends: tying down; moving inwards; and moving upwards (Figure 4.1). In rural development, professionals gain direct field experience only early in a career, if at all. Not all marry, but most do. In their domestic cycle those who do marry search, appraise, negotiate and bond, and then usually have children. This interrupts most women's careers, and is a major reason why few women get to the top. Men, though less than women, are also progressively tied down by marriage and the care and education of children. For good schools, parents seek to live in larger towns or cities. Happily, as promotion moves them upwards in hierarchies, it also draws them inwards to larger urban centres with better schools and other facilities. The more successful a person is, the faster he or she moves away from the rural periphery. The centripetal tendency with age and seniority is also found among politicians, graduating from local to national politics, and academics, moving inwards from smaller to larger and more prestigious institutes, colleges and universities. In the end, power is concentrated in cities, especially capital cities, in the hands of those, mostly men, who reach the top. Success has made them confident in the superiority of their knowledge. To them might apply the verse about Jowett, the classics scholar, Master of Balliol College, Oxford, himself a multiple upper – white, male, Anglo-Saxon, highly educated, ageing, and Master of a superior college at a superior university:

> First come I; my name is Jowett.
> There's no knowledge, but I know it.
> I am Master of this college;
> What I don't know isn't knowledge
> (Beeching, late 1870s)

Unfortunately, they often do not know or are wrong. Their direct field experience, if any, was 20 to 30 years earlier. Their location, lifestyles, work pressures and power isolate them from field realities. Like Jowett, they are multiple uppers – male, ageing, senior and influential. So it comes about that in normal bureaucracy and normal successful careers, the central power is held by old men confident in their knowledge but often out of date and out of touch (see also pp. 91–93).

Normal development bureaucracy

The hierarchy of normal bureaucracy reinforces, and is reinforced by, four tendencies: to centralize, control, conserve and standardize. These

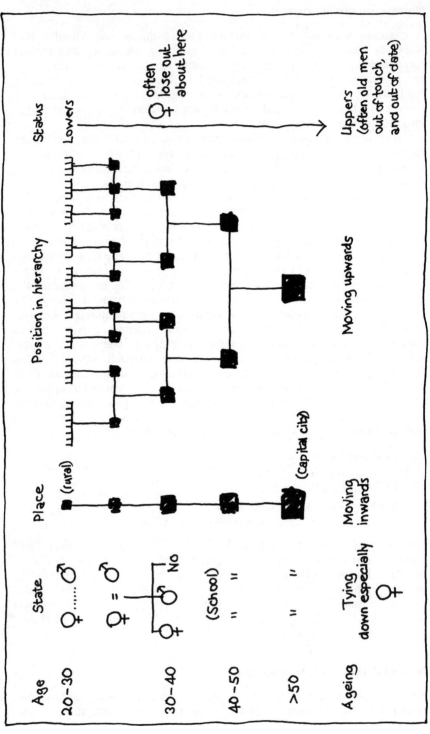

Figure 4.1: The pattern of normal (successful) careers

tendencies are found in no small measure in many of the field bureaucracies of the South.

Centralization and control are inherent in hierarchy and process. The
very language is loaded with messages about the relative status of uppers
and lowers. Officers (the quasi-military term often used) are senior and
junior, and have subordinates. There are many gradations of seniority, and
many designations of posts, each with its own level. Those who are most
senior (and also who have the authority of age) sit in the centre and
concentrate power in their hands. They control their subordinates through
written orders, budgets, authorities to incur expenditure, targets, transfers,
confidential reports, sanctions and promotions.

Conservatism is entrenched, especially in the repetitive rituals of the
lower levels of some bureaucracies. Rules and procedures are revered.
They may be bent or used in ways not intended, but the outward form is
respected, giving a sort of liturgical pleasure to those who master their
sequences and observances, even when they are exploited for private rents.
Procedures tend to be additive: new ones are superimposed upon old, while
the old are preserved. Rules and lists tend to be for ever, reproduced more
or less faithfully,[5] unless there is strong reason to change them; and when
there is reason to change, adding and patching are preferred to abolition or
restructuring.

Standardization is promoted and sustained by four factors:

(1) Standardization minimizes administration. To differentiate makes
work. The same instructions can be issued to cover a whole country or
region. Standard actions are easier to order, easier to supervise, and
easier to monitor. This would appear one reason why, in the Integrated
Rural Development Programme in India, there has been a tendency at
the village level for loans to be for the same item: for milch buffaloes,
for sewing machines or for credit for trading. Economies of standardization reduce the unit administrative load.

(2) Standardization has a certain democratic uniformity, in which all are
treated alike. It was politically safe for the Indian Integrated Rural
Development Programme to allocate an identical number of beneficiaries per year to every administrative block in the country. Standardization of benefits protects against accusations of political favouritism.
When universal rules do not fit local or personal needs or conditions,
there may be opportunities for modest, or not so modest, informal
rents to bend the rules. In contrast, formal differentiation requires the
complication, effort and risks of discrimination, judgement and
responsibility.

(3) Standardization simplifies supervision, monitoring and evaluation. It
is more straightforward to inspect, count, measure, estimate and
evaluate one type of item than many, whether it is seeds distributed,
trees planted, bunds constructed, pumps installed or clinics built.
Reports can more readily be analysed and tables of performance be
put together; standardization makes comparisons easier between the
performance of different provinces, districts and other administrative
areas.

(4) Perhaps most potently, standardization helps spend money fast. Pressures to disburse and spend have been common in donor funding, especially that of multilateral banks. Whatever the theory of management practice, multilateral bank staff members have tended to be evaluated and rewarded for the size of the loans and grants they negotiate, and then the speed with which these are disbursed. Delays have been seen not as savings, as necessary for participation, as economies or opportunities to learn, or as needed for local differentiation and fit, but as 'slippage'. Moreover, those who negotiate with representatives of the banks, the officials and political leaders of indebted countries, are often eager to obtain foreign exchange. Gains in personal income for officials and politicians are also not unknown. Between them, these interest groups – the bank staff of the North, and the officials and politicians of the South, for their different reasons – readily combine to agree on large sums to be lent and spent fast.

An example of speed and standardization comes from environmental loans from the Asian Development Bank and the World Bank to the Philippines for afforestation. The guidelines for the programme encouraged the use of multiple species, but Department of Environment and Natural Resources personnel had *gmelina arborea* seedlings and no time to develop others. The massive programme was under time pressure to disburse, so *gmelina* it was. This species, despite its commercial advantages, inhibited undergrowth which reduced its anti-erosion effects, and its widespread use increased the threat of pest and disease infestation. 'Given these problems, some analysts estimated that the disruption of grasslands involved in planting the trees would cause more soil loss than the surviving trees would prevent' (Korten, 1993). As so often, standardization had bad effects, and it was rapid scaling-up that forced the programme to abandon differentiation and diversity.

Similar pressures are found within host-country bureaucracies, and occur not only in donor-funded programmes and projects. In many field bureaucracies, unspent funds from one year's budget cannot be carried forward to the next. This creates an annual crisis where unspent money has to be 'saved' by spending it. Cement and other building materials are a convenient and fungible currency into which to convert cash balances. So they are purchased in the last days of the financial year, and then have to be used.[6] This accentuates the bias of development towards the construction of things. Off-the-shelf blueprint designs are the easiest and fastest to adopt. Expenditures are then concentrated on stock capital items for ease of implementation.

In sum, standard packages meet the needs of bureaucrats, enabling them to exercise authority and control, to set targets, to streamline monitoring and supervision, and to spend their budgets. Meeting these needs leads to the transfer of pre-set packages and patterns. These packages and patterns then act as carriers, the means by which bureaucratic centres extend their control and imprint their reality on peripheries.

Model-Ts and the transfer of technology

North–South dominance, normal professionalism, normal careers and normal bureaucracy interlock in the top-down, centre-outwards paradigm of the transfer of technology (TOT). In this pervasive paradigm, technology is developed by highly educated professionals in the controlled and well-endowed environments of central places – laboratories, workshops, research stations, greenhouses – and then passed to field staff to use or transfer. In the common mode, the technology is uniform: mass-produced as a standard package, a single variety of a tree or crop, a standard practice to be applied everywhere, or a mass-produced piece of hardware. These can be described as Model-T approaches,[7] programmes and packages, remembering Henry Ford's perhaps apocryphal remark that Americans could have their Model-T automobile any colour they liked as long as it was black.[8]

> Old Henry Ford the First, now dead
> reputedly, while living, said
> Americans should never lack
> their Model-Ts, so long as black.
>
> This way of acting still persists
> Professionals are reductionists
> And bureaucrats embrace the norm
> that programmes should be uniform.
>
> The poor are look-alikes and weak
> We know their needs. They need not speak.
> Our mass production's sure to please
> Let's make our programmes Model-Ts.

In the Indian Green Revolution, you could grow any wheat you liked as long as it was the new HYV Sonora; in social forestry you could grow any tree you liked as long as it was Eucalyptus – until eucalyptus fell from favour; you could plant any multi-purpose tree in agroforestry as long as it was Leucaena (*Leucaena leucocephala*) (but this has been partly abandoned because of vulnerability to pest attack); or you could establish any anti-erosion grass as long as it was the Vetiver grass (*Vetiveria zizanoides*) promoted by the World Bank.

The Model-T transfer-of-technology model has selective strengths. It can work or be made to work under three conditions:

○ Where a robust physical technology can be effective in a wide range of environments: in India, two examples have been blackboards for schools, and the India Mark 2 handpump for water.
○ Where there is a tightly regulated and predictable receiving environment. An example is the human or animal body, which has enabled immunization programmes, with their universal inputs, to be one of the big successes of development. The elimination of smallpox, and the near elimination of polio bear testimony to this.

67

o Where the receiving environment can be readily controlled and stand-ardized. This applied to some irrigated, fertilized land in the Green Revolution.

Often, though, receiving environments differ from those in which technologies have been developed, being more complex, more diverse, less controllable and more risk-prone. The technologies then cannot on any scale fit local conditions or human needs. Model-T misfits are many. It is almost morbid to review them. But they have to be faced. They are endemic in the TOT approach. To illustrate, examples will be taken from agriculture, and from management procedures.

Model-Ts in agriculture

Normally, seed-breeding has taken place on research stations and in laboratories. In the classical modes for industrial and green-revolution agriculture, as in India, conditions were controlled to maximize yield per unit area, but with attention to disease-resistance and other characteristics. By the eighth generation there could be over 200 lines. The breeder would then select from these a very few, perhaps three, to go for multi-locational testing. After those tests, a committee would decide which varieties could be certified, released, and made available for large-scale seed production. Typically, the result was a widely adaptable variety to be mass produced, and a package of practices through which the environment (E) was to be modified to fit the genotype (G), rather than a basket of different varieties from which farmers could choose to suit their diverse conditions.[9]

Bean breeding in Rwanda is an illustration. The formal breeding programme there focused efforts on yield, with disease resistance a secondary consideration. Breeders sought 'a few widely-adapted cultivars to accommodate large-scale centralized seed production' (Sperling et al., in press). Farmers were offered only two to five options, the tip of a selection funnel originally numbering some 200 entries (Sperling and Scheidegger, 1995). But a consequence of this search for Model-Ts was that only 10 per cent of the 50-odd bush bean cultivars tested on-farm in the previous decade were still being grown, with most on the decline. In contrast with scientists' limited criteria, farmers evaluated beans against at least 15 different criteria. A Rwandan farmer might test 75–100 varieties in her lifetime (Sperling, 1992). It was not wide adaptability but a wide choice for local and personal fit that they wanted, with the poor preferring short-cycle varieties.

Seed breeding in Europe presents a variant on these processes. To be certified, new seeds must usually pass a DUS test: they must be distinct (distinguishable from others on the market), uniform (all individuals of a variety must be the same), and stable (salient traits must be passed on from one generation to the next). In Europe, a variety which does not pass the DUS test may not legally be sold! This effectively excludes from the market a huge range of genetically diverse varieties of cereals, fruit, vegetables and other crops (Pimbert, 1993: 78). This is to the advantage of large-scale seed-breeding companies which can mass produce their (Model-T) seeds in large batches, and sell them through their distribution networks, while the

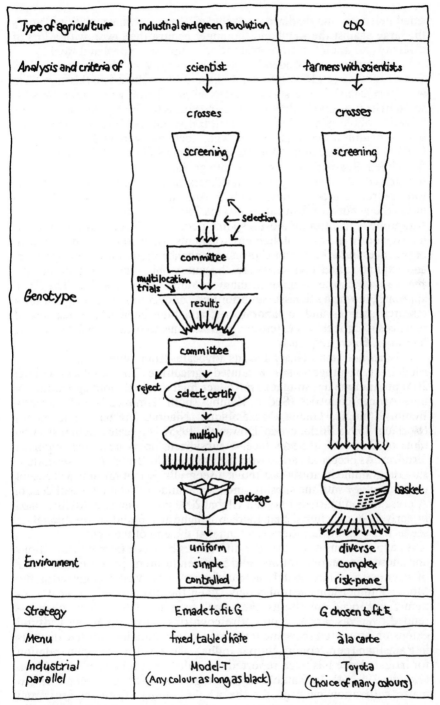

Figure 4.2: Strategies for crop breeding, selection and spread. E = Environment, G = Genotype, CDR = Complex, diverse and risk-prone

small person is marginalized or excluded. As so often, regulation favours the large against the small and the upper against the lower, with a loss of diversity and a reinforced centralization of power, control and wealth.

In agriculture, the Model-T approach has proved robustly sustainable. The classical Green Revolution in India and China, based on this approach, was spectacularly successful in increasing production where there was assured irrigation, good infrastructure, and access to inputs. This very success misled a whole generation of agricultural scientists. It reinforced beliefs that agricultural scientists knew what technology would be good for farmers in all conditions. What scientists were slow to realize was that in the Green Revolution, it was as though the research station itself was transferred: through irrigation, fertilizers and pesticides, its conditions were reproduced on farmers' fields. E (the environment) was modified to fit G (the genotype). But this is not feasible for the complex, diverse and risk-prone agriculture of most resource-poor and rainfed farmers who cannot so modify and control their environments. They do not need a package of practices but a basket of choices, to enhance their ability to respond to and exploit varied conditions. In the automobile analogy, they need a Toyota-type choice, coming in many colours, not a Model-T. The TOT approach, in which scientists set priorities, conduct research on agricultural research stations and in laboratories, and then hand over packages of practices to agricultural extension organizations to pass on to farmers, has, therefore, failed frequently.

This has not inhibited some of its advocates from attempting large-scale Model-T type programmes in rainfed agriculture. The Sasakawa Global 2000 programme has sought to introduce high external input agriculture in nine African countries (Sudan, Zambia (both terminated) and currently Benin, Ethiopia, Ghana, Mozambique, Nigeria, Tanzania and Togo) (Borlaug, 1992; Borlaug and Dowswell, 1995). Typically, demonstration plots of about 0.4 hectares receive subsidized inputs including imported fertilizer. As occurred earlier with the similar Indo-British Fertiliser Extension Programme in north-east India, it seems likely that farmers will accept the technology with the subsidy, and then abandon it when it is withdrawn. A presentation on the Ethiopian Global 2000 programme in Addis Ababa in early 1996 concluded that there was light at the end of the tunnel. It seems more likely that there is a tunnel at the end of the light.

As explanations of failure, the differences between farmers' conditions and those of research stations, and between farmers' priorities and those of scientists are now widely acknowledged. Less well recognized is the Model-T dimension. Astonishingly, given the diversity of physical, economic and social conditions, the same recommendations have been extended over vast areas, even entire countries. At one time, agricultural extension promoted the same fertilizer recommendations for five districts in Rajasthan (pers. comm. Narpat Jodha). The fertilizer recommendation for irrigated rice has been reported to be the same for the whole of Java (Roling, 1992: 4). In Zambia at one stage there was one recommended maize cultivation package for the whole country. Both scientists and agricultural bureaucracies have sought single solutions which could go to scale.

70

The transfer of procedures (TOP)

Standardization has been applied not only to physical technology, as with seeds and agricultural packages, but also to procedures and their sequencing. TOP (the Transfer Of Procedures) requires the implementation of standardized routines. These are types of activity in which I have myself indulged with, at best, mixed results (Chambers, 1974). It is true that standard sequences of procedure are essential in the context of many things: maintaining a car, carrying out surgery, getting into a computer programme, preparing a plane for take-off. Their strict performance is also vital in accounting. They can be essential in agriculture where there are strict imperatives of timing and quality for processing and marketing, as with smallholder tea in Kenya and elsewhere. The question is whether they make sense with people and with conditions which are local, complex, diverse, dynamic and unpredictable. Let us examine three examples of the transfer of procedures by uppers to lowers: the Training and Visit system of agricultural extension; the *warabandi* system for the distribution of irrigation water; and pastoral 'development' in Africa.

The training and visit system (T&V)

The T&V system of agricultural extension promoted by the World Bank was an attempt at bold and radical change. The aim was to streamline, routinize and regulate the activities of agricultural extension agents, simplifying the chain of command, and making their work predictable and manageable. In India, earlier, agricultural extension was undertaken by village level workers (VLWs) responsible not only to the Department or Ministry of Agriculture, but to other departments also. VLWs were often expected to implement an impossible number and variety of programmes. They were overwhelmed and buried under geological layers of instructions from different masters. Reporting requirements alone took much of their time. T&V was a management system (Benor and Harrison, 1977) which sought to make them responsible only for agriculture and only to one department, to programme their work so that their supervisors would know each day where they were and what they were doing, and to institute regular meetings and training. Under the system

> . . . schedules of work, duties and responsibilities are clearly specified and closely supervised at all levels . . . A specific schedule of visits to farmers' fields is rigidly followed. The ratios of supervisory staff are such that close supervision is easy. Frequent (weekly or fortnightly) one-day training sessions for field-level extension staff are an integral part of the system. In these training sessions, the extension agents are intensively instructed in the three or four most important recommendations for the forthcoming one or two weeks of the crop season. With this concentrated training received in digestible doses the extension agents can develop a better understanding of what they are recommending. This

enhances their confidence and makes them better able to convince the farmers. (Benor and Harrison, 1977: 12)

There was no doubt who were uppers and who lowers; who knew and who was ignorant.

With the weight and inducement of World Bank loans, T&V was introduced on an extraordinary scale in countries of the South, first in India and Asia, and then in Africa. By 1988 the Bank, through 512 projects, had disbursed about US$2 billion for reform and the strengthening of agricultural extension, primarily for the T&V model, or a somewhat modified version (Antholt, 1993: 12).

Evaluations of T&V have been numerous.[10] Three of the main assumptions of the system proved erroneous in practice. These are:

o that representative contact farmers would be identified. In practice they were usually better-off farmers;
o that a backlog of technology suitable for farmers was available from research, off the shelf. This was rare; and
o that agricultural extension staff would respond well to a regular routine and close supervision. They did not. A discussion group in Nigeria, for example, reported that: 'It is . . . rigid and there is little room for initiative. Fortnightly trainings often have nothing new to offer and people become bored' (ODA, 1995: 24).

T&V was a mechanistic management blueprint for the transfer of technology. As Antholt (1993: 14) observed, T&V projects had 'tended to further institutionalize hierarchical tendencies already existing for top-down, centralized management, despite clear aims to the contrary'. Standardized extension was built in, and could not fit diverse conditions and needs.[11]

T&V was welcomed and adopted by some bureaucrats who gained (or felt they gained) variously from its control orientation, the increases in staff, vehicles and other resources, career advancement and trips to Washington. Whatever the intentions, T&V seems to have benefited uppers rather than lowers.

By the late 1980s, the dominant discussion of the system in Asia had shifted from promotion to post-mortem. Relatively powerful countries like India, Malaysia and Thailand had rejected it and moved on to other approaches. For its part, the World Bank also moved on, to introduce the system into the weaker countries of sub-Saharan Africa.

> If Asian countries throw it out
> it's only they who have the clout
> In Africa you can insist
> they have no power to resist.

Warabandi in irrigation[12]

Warabandi is a system for allocating irrigation water between users. It was developed for and in the north-west Indian plains where the land is flat, rainfall low and water scarce. The system is based on timed shares of water, with each farmer taking water from a near-constant flow for a fixed length of time proportionate to his or her landholding. The system is routinized, regular and standardized over large areas in the north-west (Singh, 1981; Malhotra, 1982).

For the system of timed shares to be feasible requires four conditions: clear land rights, stable water scarcity, channels to carry water to farmers' fields, and a constant flow of water through a shared outlet. These conditions obtain in north-west India, where land has been adjudicated, there is little rain and so a stable shortage of water for much of the year, channels carry water to farmers' fields, and, above all, canal systems have been designed to provide a constant flow day and night to groups of farmers. To find these four conditions combined elsewhere in India is rare indeed. Yet in 1981 the secretary of irrigation went on record as saying:

> The Warabandi system should be introduced on a nation-wide basis after one year of assessment. You can introduce it on a pilot basis in a small area. And then you can seriously try it on the entire system. There is no reason why you should fail provided you take all appropriate steps . . . I think it will be a great success.
>
> (Patel, 1981: 9)

A meeting of the most senior irrigation officials decided in good faith to spread *warabandi* on a vast scale throughout the country. To my shame, I was present at the two-day workshop at which this was resolved and did not speak up as boldly as I now wish I had. I was a foreigner. I was not an engineer. I had never managed an irrigation system. I had been invited as a courtesy. And those taking part were senior government officials, older than me. So it is that a lower funks responsibility, lacking the guts, push and confidence to assert his or her reality. But even if I had spoken up more, I doubt whether it would have made any difference. The World Bank wanted a big programme, The government wanted a big programme. A big programme was what they got. The seventh Five Year Plan carried a target of 8 million hectares to be placed under *warabandi* (GOI, 1985: 96).

It was tragic. What could be transferred, and inspected, was the outward and visible sign of *warabandi*, the metal notice boards erected to show names and times of turns. But they were not timetables but tombstones, rusting relics for archeological students of error. The top-down, centre-outwards, standard Model-T was a misfit, and the ignorance and misperceptions on which this policy was based was little short of staggering.

Pastoral development

A history of pastoral 'development' in the drier areas of sub-Saharan Africa would read like the afflictions of Job. Few domains can claim such consistent failure. The ranch model was developed especially in the United States mainly for a single product, meat, and to be labour-sparing. The model was transferred to Kenya in the late 1950s and early 1960s, and christened the Texas system. The range was to be divided into four areas of roughly equal 'carrying capacity' for livestock. A fixed quota of animals was to be permitted. Each block was then to be depastured in rotation for exactly four months.[13] In this way, each block was to have 12 months rest before being grazed again. Whether such an astonishingly rigid system was ever used by ranchers in the United States may be questioned. It would be difficult to conceive a worse system for the conditions experienced by pastoralists in Africa. But visiting experts from the North sought to transfer to the powerless periphery of the South this engineering model of management, rigid, mechanical and insensitive, to be enforced for the good of the weak and ignorant. As Ian Scoones has written: '. . . the transfer of technology approach is wholly inappropriate for the highly variable, unpredictable and complex environments found in pastoral areas' (Scoones, 1994: 7).

To attempt, as I did, to introduce inflexible rules into such environments has to be seen as an act of extraordinarily insensitive arrogance. Not only was the rigid ranch model a mindless misfit, but the very idea of transfer was misguided. The reality of the experience of pastoralism in Africa has to generate its own solutions.

T&V, *warabandi*, and the rigid ranch model share common features: all are top-down, centre-outwards, control-oriented and intended to standardize and regulate behaviour. In practice, none could fit or serve local complex, diverse, dynamic and unpredictable conditions. All three required exact timing: in T&V, a regular and predictable weekly or fortnightly routine; in *warabandi*, taking water at the same time for the same duration each week; and in the rigid ranch model, opening and closing grazing blocks every four months. But conditions always varied by season, vagaries of weather, water supply, diseases, price and market, not to mention differences by household and farm. All three management systems concentrated power upwards; but only by shifting power downwards could local diversity be served. And all three demoralized front-line staff who found themselves more supervised and less trusted, were forced to dissemble to their superiors, and made to appear foolish to their clients by implementing programmes they knew made no sense. So, as attempts to impose procedures and transfer reality, T&V, *warabandi* outside north-west India, and the rigid ranch model have always or almost always failed and been abandoned.[14]

Dominant realities

Top-down centre–periphery transfers are found worldwide. They have benefits as well as costs. At their best, they can lead to huge gains like the elimination of smallpox, the sharp reduction of polio, and the spread of literacy. At their worst, Model-Ts, whether of technologies or of time-bound procedures, demoralize staff and harm people trying to gain livelihoods in local conditions. Normal professionalism, teaching, careers and bureaucracy help to explain how bad policies and programmes are generated, and how it is that uppers seek to implement them, and to transfer their realities to lowers. In part they help to understand the errors described in Chapter 2. But a puzzle remains. Inappropriate Model-T approaches have proved robustly sustainable. On a wide scale, they continue to override local priorities, inhibit participation, obliterate diversity, and disseminate technologies which do not fit the local needs of the poorer. How and why is it that error becomes so embedded? How and why is it that for so long we do not learn?

We can return to Charles Dickens for a clue. In *Hard Times*, Mr Gradgrind, several times an upper (male, middle class, middle-aged, and benefactor) speaks to Sissy Jupe, several times a lower (female, lower class, young, and dependent as a pupil in his charity school):

> 'Sissy is not a name,' said Mr. Gradgrind. 'Don't call yourself Sissy. Call yourself Cecilia.'
>
> 'It's father as calls me Sissy, sir,' returned the young girl, in a trembling voice, and with another curtsy.
>
> 'Then he has no business to do it,' said Mr. Gradgrind. 'Tell him he mustn't. Cecilia Jupe. Let me see. What is your father?'
>
> 'He belongs to the horse-riding, if you please, sir.'
>
> Mr. Gradgrind frowned, and waved off the objectionable calling with his hand.
>
> 'We don't want to know anything about that here. You mustn't tell us about that here . . .'.
>
> (*Hard Times*, Ch. 2)

The upper rejects discordant feedback. He relabels the lower and redefines her reality for her. He seeks to transfer his reality. He wants it to be his reality that counts. What prevents him learning in this case is not professionalism or bureaucracy. It is his dominant behaviour, person to person. It is his power.

5

All Power Deceives

In the final analysis, power is the right to have your definition of reality prevail over other people's definition of reality.

Dorothy Rowe, 1989: 16

For learning, power is a disability. Part of the explanation of persistent error lies in interpersonal power relations. Powerful professionals can impose their realities. For many years psychoanalysts sustained the belief that child sex abuse was a fantasy. Uppers' learning is impeded by personal dominance, distance, denial and blaming the victim. For their part, lowers defend themselves through what they select to show and tell, diplomacy, and deceit. Self-deception and mutual deception sustain myths.[1] Questionnaire surveys tend to confirm the realities of uppers, imposing their constructs and mirroring their realities. Uppers, especially senior males, patriarchs and academics, are vulnerable to being out-of-touch and out-of-date. Multiple channels of positive misinformation mislead the World Bank and the self-deceiving state. Believing becomes seeing. All power deceives, and exceptional power deceives exceptionally.

Power as disability

What sort of people we are and how we interact are fundamental to learning and action. Yet these are gaps in development studies. Development actions and inactions, policies, programmes, projects, research studies, evaluations, all these are decided on and acted through by people. If people acted differently, the outcomes would be different. To make such a self-evident point seems almost an insult.

Those most able to act are the powerful. In development, power is usually seen as an asset. It is a means to getting things done. Those who work their way up and become presidents, ministers, permanent and principal secretaries, directors-general and chief executives do, after all, have huge scope for changing things for the better. Many of the good things which have been achieved have been initiated through the guts, vision and commitment of one or a few people at the top.

But there is another side to the coin: power as disability. All who are powerful are by definition uppers, sometimes uppers many times over. Others relate to them as lowers. In their daily lives multiple uppers are vulnerable to acquiescence, deference, flattery, and placation. They are not easily contradicted or corrected: 'Their word goes'. It becomes easy and tempting for them, like Mr Gradgrind, to impose their realities and deny those of others. It becomes difficult for them to learn. The views of uppers are often privileged, supposed to be empirically true and morally right. But as we have seen in earlier chapters, the realities of socially dominant professionals are often neither true nor right. With apologies to Lord Acton, the question can then be posed: whether all power tends to deceive; and whether exceptional power deceives exceptionally.[2]

In exploring power relationships as a source of error, we can draw on the examples in Chapter 2. But we are concerned with a field much wider than development. There are insights from power and error in other settings, disciplines and professions. Since it is the interpersonal that has been so neglected in development, it is fitting to turn to a professional activity where interpersonal interactions are central, namely psychotherapy. We can ask whether there are examples there of interpersonal power generating and sustaining error, and whether there are lessons to be learnt from the experience.

Whose reality? Whose fantasy?

Among the most powerful professionals, at the personal level, are psychoanalysts. There are several reasons. They derive authority from their long training, as therapists concerned with the mind, and sometimes in addition as doctors concerned with the body. They are an organized and exclusive guild. They are believed to hold special insights into psychological disorders. Those who come to them as clients are defined as patients, people who are mentally disturbed. The patients are further isolated and weakened by the therapists' emotional distance and lack of eye contact. In classical psychoanalysis, the patient lies on a couch while the psychoanalyst sits in a chair. The patient is meant to free-associate, without defences. The psychoanalyst is meant to remain detached and not to reveal personal information. Professionally, personally and physically, the psychoanalyst is a multiple upper, exceptionally powerful and defended. The patient, a multiple lower, is exceptionally weak and vulnerable.

If power is a disability, one would then expect the psychoanalysts to be exceptionally open to error. This does indeed seem to be borne out. There is evidence (see e.g. Webster, 1995) that Freud and many psychoanalysts following him have held a belief that was wrong.

The belief, sustained from the turn of the century until the 1980s, was that the child sex abuse reported by patients was a fantasy.[3] Freud evolved the theory that young children were sexually attracted to their parents of the opposite sex. So women's accounts of incest came to be interpreted as fantasies of wish-fulfilment, not events which had happened. It seems now beyond reasonable doubt that Freud and his successor psychoanalysts were often wrong (see e.g. Rowe, 1989; Masson, 1989, 1992; Sanderson, 1990; Karle, 1992; Webster, 1995) and that child sex abuse, in the West at least, is both common and deeply damaging. Where a woman recounted the reality of incestuous abuse, the psychoanalysts were trained to deny that reality, interpreting it as a manifestation of her sexual desire for the abuser. They blamed the victim. In the words of Janet Radcliffe Richards (1992): 'If the therapists had actually conspired with the abusers to drive the victims to

77

madness and despair, it is hard to see how they could have done better'. The fantasy, it seems, was Freud's.

The important question is how such highly trained and intelligent professionals, the professed and acknowledged experts, could have been so wrong for so long; and whether the answer can help identify, explain and overcome errors embedded in development beliefs and practices. Among others, four possible explanations stand out:

(1) There was a sequence of conditioning and brainwashing and of the 'transfer of reality'. Psychoanalysts underwent prolonged professional training which required them to be psychoanalysed themselves, and so to internalize the beliefs, constructs, and system of interpretation of psychoanalysis. That system was then transferred to the patient.

(2) Dominance and distance were maintained by the social and professional detachment of the upper. The psychoanalyst sat while the patient lay on a couch. His (most were men)[4] authority was based on a mystique of difficult texts and esoteric jargon. Treatment was not subject to evaluation. Those who might have evaluated it, the patients, were powerless lowers: they were mostly women confronting a patriarchal power structure, deeply distressed, stigmatized as mad or mentally ill, isolated and unable to meet others and to organize, had no one to appeal to, and were anyway the last people to be regarded as credible or willing witnesses.

(3) The reality of the patient was rejected, denied and reframed to fit the beliefs of the psychoanalyst, who was thereby prevented from learning. The upper was assumed to be right, and the lower wrong.

(4) The upper blamed the victim. The lower was pretending to be a victim, denying the 'reality' of her sexual desire and blamed for continuing to be disturbed. The message was: 'You have misperceived reality', the psychotherapist says to the patient. You must try harder. "If you don't get better, it is your fault." ' (Rowe 1989: 14).

Combined, these factors can be seen as impediments to learning by the psychoanalyst, as well as to the therapeutic process for the patient. The psychoanalyst was also a victim – of training and conditioning, of being dominant and distant, of being able to reject, deny and reframe the patient's reality, and of being able to blame her. Together, these made it almost impossible for him to learn from her.

Uppers' impediments

The same impediments are found among development professionals reinforced by others from the examples of error in Chapter 2. Let us consider them in turn.

Conditioning

The vertical transfer of reality occurs with all development bureaucrats and professionals through their education, training and socialization; and many then seek to transfer their reality in turn to the poor and the weak. While the conditioning can rarely be as intrusive or radical as that of psychoanalytic training, the imprinting can be deep and strong, leading to the internalization and adoption of normal professional concepts, values, beliefs, methods and behaviours.

Dominance

Some dominance and superiority is biologically and socially pre-set (see p. 59), especially when derived from ethnic group and gender; people are born into races, castes, tribes and nationalities, with socially defined relative status and power; and in most societies men are defined as uppers and women as lowers, reinforced by socially embedded gender roles, by power structures and by the bottom line that men are taller and stronger and can shout louder.

Interpersonal dominance and superiority are also established, expressed and reinforced physically, socially and in behaviour in many combinations in the encounters between uppers and lowers, for example, between donors and recipients, seniors and juniors, officials and local people, and scientists and farmers. Some of its dimensions are:

○ *Speech.* Words are chosen to impress and mystify. A forester uses Latin names for indigenous plants, a scientist uses words he knows local people will not understand.[5] Outsiders in the presence of local people use a language associated with power and superiority, often English. Dominance is expressed through interrupting, monopolizing conversations, not listening, lecturing, shouting, disagreement, and many forms of disparagement and rudeness.

○ *Behaviour.* Non-verbal and spatial ways of expressing superiority and dominance are many: holding the stick, wagging the finger, frowning, looking down on people, sitting at a higher level, making lowers physically lower (sitting on mats or in classroom rows, or even prostrating themselves), impatience, looking at one's watch, sniffing, twitching the moustache, and simply keeping at a distance.

○ *Accessories.* Superiority and authority are expressed through dress (classically the jacket and tie for men), dark glasses, shoes, uniforms, briefcases, files, clipboards and notebooks, maps, papers and pens, guns, radios, vehicles, food and drink, and any physical technology which it is sought to transfer from upper to lower.

○ *Associates.* Superiority is also sought and strengthened through choice of whom to associate with. Uppers associate with lowers who are uppers in their own social contexts: men with men; the educated with the educated; English-speakers with English-speakers, French-speakers with French-speakers, Portuguese-speakers with Portuguese-speakers, Spanish-speakers with Spanish-speakers; high class or caste with high class or caste; extension agents with progressive farmers. The status of both parties is then mutually reinforced.

These points are so widespread and so well known in development practice that they have rarely been deemed worthy to note. I know of no book devoted mainly to the behaviour of development professionals.[6]

79

Distance

Distance for the psychoanalyst was largely social and professional. In development, distance takes several forms: isolation and remoteness, keeping at a distance, and avoidance.

(1) *Isolation and remoteness.* Many planners and economists are cocooned in comfortable (centrally heated, air-conditioned) offices, with their exposure to the world of ordinary people largely limited to commuting, shopping, bars, tourism and, for some, brief visits to a rural home. Their physical isolation is compounded by an illusion of instant contact through fax, e-mail, statistics and other proxies for people. The more powerful they are, so too the more centrally located they are, the further from the real experience of poor people, and the more vulnerable to delusion. Power, distance, isolation and ignorance correlate.

Given who they are, and where they are, it is understandable:
○ how macro-economists in Washington and other capitals so badly neglected the effects of structural adjustment policies on the poor – whom they had not met;
○ how policymakers and scientists the world over could have supposed that post-harvest losses at the village level were 30 to 40 per cent – when they had never been to villages and measured them;
○ how multi-purpose wheeled toolcarriers could have been supposed to be successful – when they were developed in the privileged isolation of laboratories and research stations, not with farmers in farmers' conditions;
○ how woodfuel forecasts could have been so wildly wrong – when those who made them were sitting at computers making assumptions uncomplicated by exposure to the complexities of how poor people actually cope;
○ how engineers in Delhi could have supposed that one system of water distribution under canal irrigation could be applied all over India – where they had not, and could not, have been.

For all these, out of sight was not just out of mind; out of sight was fantasized.

(2) *Keeping at a distance.* Distance can be deliberate. Relegating to a distance is a way to marginalize whatever is new or threatening.[7] When additional disciplines are recruited, far from their new insights and approaches being made central, they are often forced physically to the fringe. The first agricultural economist appointed to the Indian Council for Agricultural Research in Delhi was allocated an office at the furthest extreme of the headquarters building, and three months after arriving was still struggling to obtain basic office furniture. In the late 1980s, in the Ministry of Health in Khartoum, nutrition was not in the main building but outside in the last hut up against a wall (Richard Longhurst, pers. comm.).[8] Physically marginalized, it then becomes harder for new insights and disciplines to inform policy and practice, and past patterns (and often errors) are more likely to persist.

(3) *Avoidance.* Whatever threatens personally, with dangers to ego, comfort and self-esteem, can be avoided. This takes many forms: the place not visited, the people not met, the remarks not listened to, the telephone call not made, the report not read. Certainly I, and perhaps some readers too, try habitually to avoid conflict, unpleasantness and humiliation. Understandably, many uppers avoid situations and information which confront their power, or where they may be shamed. But the consequence is that they – we – lose opportunities to learn, and errors more plausibly persist. So those who are senior, central, well paid and powerful avoid contact with those who are junior, peripheral, poor and weak, except sometimes in specially controlled conditions.

Avoidance can prevent uncomfortable learning. Independent researchers were once invited to a workshop at the World Bank to present their findings from field research on a World Bank-supported project. These were negative, contradicting a mid-term review. One staff member from the review team listened, was convinced, and said he regretted his mistakes, but other staff members, also involved, did not even attend. If they were avoiding learning, it worked. By not being present, they did not have to know. Failure could be shut out; learning did not have to take place; past errors remained buried; and present error was sustained.

Denial

A common reaction of uppers to discordant information and to the realities presented by lowers is denial through rejection or reframing.

Rejection has been the fate of much new truth. Sometimes the new is wrong. But again and again, when right, it has been rejected. The long and honourable roll-call of those who have suffered persecution or vilification includes Copernicus and Galileo with the great reversal of the earth going round the sun, and Alfred Wegener with the theory of continental drift. Rupert Sheldrake's (1981) book *A New Science of Life*, which proposed conventional scientific testing of a new theory, provoked the editor of *Nature* to write an editorial 'A book for burning?' (ibid, second edition 1987: 225–7) The dismissive intolerance shown by many normal scientists towards those who research into extra-sensory perception, psychokinesis, precognition and other psychical phenomena is another example.[9] In 1996 a leading journal of development rejected an article (Satterthwaite, 1996) which found, contrary to common belief, a notable slow-down in the growth rate of many major cities and many nations' urban populations during the 1980s, and little evidence of unprecedented rates of urban change in the South when compared to historic or contemporary rates of urban change in Europe and North America. But as Thomas Henry Huxley wrote: 'It is the customary fate of new truths to begin as heresies and to end as superstitions'. One wonders how much of today's normal science and rhetoric will be seen by future scientists as superstition.

Rejection can take many forms, including discrediting those responsible, questioning the methods used, denying the evidence, citing contrary evidence, or simply asserting contrary knowledge. In Guinea, for example, authorities were so convinced of degradation in the forest-savannah transition zone that they had not compared aerial photographs and satellite images they had commissioned with those available from 1952. Leach and Fairhead (1994: 4) report that:

> The incredulous reactions of forestry staff when presented with 1952–90 air-photograph comparisons showing increased woody vegetation led them to a sceptical search for ways to render the comparison invalid (the photographs were taken in atypical years, or incomparable seasons . . .)

In other parts of West Africa, similarly surprising results have simply been disbelieved and dismissed, as with this statement: 'A comparison of the information from the two surveys gives an increase in woody biomass in the early 1980s. This is highly improbable, and is undoubtedly an artefact of different research methodologies . . .' (Price, 1992). In Thailand, when unexpected impacts from rhizobium inoculation of soya were encountered, 'these were at first simply not believed' (Hall and Clark, 1995: 1609).

There are subtleties here. What happens can be more nuanced than straight rejection or denial. In India, a consultants' report on a new approach to distributing irrigation water interpreted research results as showing marked benefits. These included higher and more uniform yields, and less time taken to irrigate. On analysing the same data, I found the conclusions unjustified.[10] A meeting was called with the consultants. My points were more or less accepted, but then the matter was consigned to an indeterminate limbo.[11] Nothing was done. Far from being rejected or modified, the consultants' conclusions were published unchanged (Chadha, 1981), and without reference to the criticisms. Perhaps there was too much at stake. The consultants knew that the World Bank, which had commissioned the study, was keen to justify the new approach. They knew what result was wanted. Supported by the consultants' unchanged report, the new approach was implemented on a large scale. So, even if bad news is reported, it may be avoided, rejected or finessed out of sight.

Reframing is also a form of denial. Diverse and discordant realities are given professional labels or fitted into stereotypes. Uppers' categories for the personal realities of lowers are often negative. Psychoanalysts reframed the realities of the victims of incestuous abuse as fantasy (see e.g. Sanderson, 1990: 24). Whether in psychiatry or development, labelling can disempower lowers and deny their complex and diverse reality. In the words of a psychiatric patient, the label for a disorder

> . . . does not help the professional or the individual to understand what is happening or what would assist the individual. It stops the individual from *owning* the experience and finding his/her *own* language and interpretation. Disempowerment of this kind drives people crazy . . . in categorizing the distress the distress itself is not acknowledged.
>
> (Pembroke, 1994: 42–3, emphasis in original)

So too in development, professional labels and categories – in fields as diverse as agriculture, engineering, forestry, medicine, and soil science –

Table 5.1: Acceptability of explanations of error and failure

Explanation	Prescription	Acceptability to uppers
Lowers' moral defects: lazy, stupid	Lowers reform themselves	High ↑
Lowers' ignorance	Uppers teach lowers	
Lack of resources	Increase resources	
Uppers' ignorance	Lowers teach uppers	
Uppers' moral defects: ego, greed, short-sight	Uppers reform themselves	↓ Low

can impose alien frames which distort and disempower. Pioneer farmers are squatters or encroachers; local remedies are superstitions; and a whole lexicon of adjectives (conservative, ignorant, indolent, irresponsible, lazy, primitive, short-sighted, stubborn and the like), when used for the poor, disparage, distort and so deny their reality.

Blaming the lower

To blame the victim is perhaps the most widespread and popular defence. It flatters uppers and flattens lowers. There is a hierarchy of acceptability to uppers of different explanations of error and failure (see Table 5.1).

Uppers usually prefer to blame lowers, and usually prefer explanations and prescriptions which require that lowers change rather than that they themselves or other uppers change. So Freud and the psychoanalysts blamed the female victims of sex abuse, requiring them to change, and rejected or did not entertain the idea that other uppers might have been responsible. One may wonder whether and how much something similar is found in development.

With environmental degradation, for example, as with psychoanalysis, the normal reflex is to blame the long-term victim, not the short-term exploiter. This blame is linked easily with what appears the proximate cause. The photograph on the dust cover of the green book shows a farmer in the foreground with a smoking, charred forest behind, burnt for shifting cultivation. But such farmers are often victims, moving in only after much of their forest has been destroyed. As Fairhead and Leach (1994: 11) observed for Guinea

> . . . the image of the rural farmer as environmental destroyer, and of the need for modernization of resource management and farming techniques, conforms to and helps to justify the self-distinction of urban intellectuals as relatively more 'civilized' of 'globalized'.

They conclude (Fairhead and Leach, forthcoming) that if their analysis is correct, the people living in the approximately 25 million hectares of the forest zone of West Africa which has been only mythically deforested during this century are owed an apology, for they have been blamed for damage they have not caused.

There is no photograph on the dust jacket of the green book of the global person, corpulent, male, middle-aged, suited and cigar-smoking, who grows wealthy on the huge hardwoods that were first cut out of the forest. (If there were, he might sue.) Fat contractors, corrupt politicians, international companies, and consumers of the North, like the child sex abusers, are hidden from sight. The abuse, whether sexual or environmental, by the upper, is an irreversible act which is hidden or passes out of sight. The damage to the victims is lasting and manifest, a stigma or loss for which they are then held responsible.

So agricultural researchers and extensionists blame farmers when they do not adopt packages of practices, instead of asking whether the packages are wrong; staff of multinational banks blame poor countries which resist policies of structural adjustment, instead of campaigning for the abolition of debts incurred through their own past lending policies. Who apologizes? Who sees even the cause for apology? Better to blame the victim than to bear the responsibility oneself.

Lowers' strategies

In power relations, vulnerable lowers have their own strategies. They can conform, and adopt and internalize the paradigms of uppers, accepting the transfer of reality. They can speak out, rebel and reject. Or they can follow a middle course of diplomacy and deceit. It is this middle course that most misleads.

Three main manifestations of this stand out: selective presentation; diplomacy; and deceit.

Selective presentation

Lowers select where uppers go, what they see and whom they meet. In the domain of development this takes two related forms:

(1) *Islands of salvation.* These are villages, areas, projects, schools, clinics or organizations which have received special treatment. Potemkin villages are the archetype. To an astonishing degree, a single village or project can be quoted and requoted at conferences and in papers without any analysis of its atypicality. One village, Ralegaon Shindi, in Maharashtra, has been repeatedly cited as a model for sustainable environmental management, although accounts agree that it has most exceptional and unusual leadership. The Mohini Water Cooperative Society, a canal irrigation cooperative and the recipient of extraordinarily privileged treatment from government, has been the source of a myth accepted by both the Planning Commission in India (GOI, 1985: 82) and authorities outside the country. To quote one, 'In Gujarat State in India, the irrigation agency sells water volumetrically in bulk to cooperatives, which distribute it and collect fees from their members' (Repetto, 1986: 33). Mohini was, in fact, probably almost alone in this respect. The myth of water co-operatives in Gujarat had a capacity to spread not shared at that time by the institution itself (Chambers,

1988b: 59–62). Or take the T&V system of agricultural extension. When T&V was pioneered in India in the Chambal Command Area, it achieved 'apparently astonishing success', but this could be attributed to the 'pilot project effect' – because the World Bank was intensively involved, staff were therefore motivated, and irrigation and input supplies arrived on time (Moore, 1984: 306–7). Nurtured and protected specially, islands of salvation systematically mislead.

(2) *Rural development tourism* (the brief rural visit by the urban-based outsider, often a senior person). This reinforces the island-of-salvation effect, being often directed to special places and people. Nationally renowned projects near capital cities are favourites for visits by VIPs. At a humbler level, local development staff have often had a special village, and special 'tame' people in that village, to solve the problem of how to give visitors a good impression. Visits by senior officers are usually planned and orchestrated by local staff to ensure carefully selected perception: in agricultural extension, farmers are rehearsed in the answers they are to give; in canal irrigation, an irrigation committee is mustered, though it exists only when visitors are around; and in watershed development, the area visited follows the road along the top of a ridge where erosion created by bad conservation works is not to be seen. Experienced staff package their tours; for example, in the Maheshwaram watershed near Hyderabad in India, they had both a 'two-hour', and a 'four-hour treatment' for visitors.

Rural development tourism has other built-in biases against the perception of poverty and meeting with poor people (Chambers, 1983: 10–25). The farmer visited is resource-rich (and known variously as a master, model, demonstration, progressive, or contact farmer) and can show the package of practices in the field before presenting the visitor's book to be signed. In India, the same poor person who has been provided with a milch buffalo is shown off to a succession of visitors to the village, and has been carefully coached and supported by staff to present an impression of dutiful success. Only the best is shown and seen. Worse, the more senior and influential the visitor, the more elaborate the preparations, and the more biased the impressions. The glowing words of the VIP or VVIP in the visitor's book then reflect not the wider reality, but the extent to which the visitor was misled, in turn a tribute to the skill and care with which the visit was arranged and managed.

Diplomacy

Top–down, North–South, centre–outwards patterns of administration and control give personal and financial reasons for conforming to professional and bureaucratic norms, and imposing these on others. This gives rise to a spectrum of distortion, from the mildest massaging of syntax to outright falsification of figures and bald lying. Many influences (bureaucratic, political, personal, commercial, corrupt, criminal) induce these deceptions, mediated through everything from the quiet word, and 'nudge-nudge, wink-wink', to outright bribery, blackmail, physical threats and murder. At one end of the spectrum is diplomatic discretion; at the other, downright deceit.

Diplomatic discretion takes many forms. Errors are not paraded. Failures are forgotten. Silence is kept on sensitive subjects. Bad news is not reported. Figures are chosen which show things in a favourable light. Confrontation is avoided. Uppers are flattered in subtle and not so subtle ways. Such discretion is common in three contexts: with foreign-funded projects, with private consultants and with local people.

National hosts for foreign-funded projects take care to be nice to the donors who fund them. They do not want to scare money away. The bigger the donor, the more marked the niceness. So it has been that the impression has been sustained that the T&V system (pp. 71–2) was working in countries where it seems it was not. Typical remarks have been: 'I can't talk about this in the office'; 'It is as much as my job is worth to criticize'; 'It is not working but I cannot say so'; 'To talk against T&V was next to treason'; 'There is what is in my report, and there is my opinion'.

For their part, consultants and commissioned researchers also often feel constrained to be prudent. Their livelihood security, after all, may depend on it. They do not want to bite the hand that feeds them. Self-censorship is common (and who is without guilt?) among those who write up research and consultancy reports. So reports are toned down, statistics selected and syntax softened, to smooth the sharp edges. Findings are interpreted in a favourable light. Similarly, bids for competitive contracts contain misleading claims: a consultant says: 'I do not believe in PRA [participatory rural appraisal], but they want it, so I have put it in'.

Local people, too, are often skilled in discretion. They know what to do when visitors come. A community has its experts who know how to handle outsiders and what to say and show. The first task is to find out what threats or opportunities visitors may be bringing. It is then a question of saying and showing whatever will minimize penalties and maximize gains. The priority needs of the community then coincide happily with what the visitor has to offer. From Namibia, the following exchange was reported (1995) between a villager and a visitor after a needs appraisal for a pre-set sectoral programme:

'If we had been different people, would you have said you had the same priority need?'
'Of course not. Do you think we are stupid?'

Deceit

Diplomatic discretion is in a continuum with the downright deceit of misreporting and lies. With internal bureaucratic reporting, there are interactions between:

○ time-bound target-setting imposed top-down;
○ performance judged on the reported achievement of targets;
○ a punitive style of management;
○ an overload of reporting (making exact reporting impossible);
○ corruption (with facts to conceal or figures to change); and
○ political influence.

Where any of these conditions exist, and more so when they combine, performance tends to be exaggerated, and targets reported achieved when they have not been. This can be ordered explicitly. In both Africa and Asia I have heard quite senior officials complain that their political masters had demanded that they falsify figures to give a better picture. There can also be tacit connivance between uppers and lowers. The remarks of a district agricultural officer to his subordinates in India in the early 1970s may reflect conditions which still persist: 'We have achieved all our targets. Do you understand? Make the necessary arrangements in your blocks'. The achievement of targets then becomes 'a largely book-keeping affair' (Mook, 1974: 143).

When, in this style of management, targets are raised annually, mis-reporting mounts. This occurred in India for the area under high-yielding varieties (HYV) of rice. For 1972–73, officially reported figures for the area under paddy HYVs in two *taluks* (administrative areas) in North Arcot District in Tamil Nadu were 39 and 48 per cent respectively, but a survey in 12 representative villages gave a figure of only 13 per cent (Chambers and Wickremanayake, 1977). In one of the villages, the survey showed less than 50 per cent adoption, but the reports of the hapless village-level worker had risen to 95 per cent, leaving him nowhere to go and the problem of how to conceal the truth from visiting senior officers. A growing divergence between report and reality places stress on the reporter, who is then driven to make up the appearances of reality cosmetically as well as numerically.

Where donors are involved, figures may be selected, misreported or invented in order to gain advantage. With post-harvest losses of grain at the village level, there was

> often the temptation to cite 'worst case' figures to dramatize the prob-
> lem. In some cases there is the temptation to exaggerate the figures of
> loss particularly if there is a prospect that high figures of loss will prompt
> aid or grants from some donor.
> (Bourne, 1977: 15, cited in Greeley, 1987: 11)

The power and patronage of money means that donors are often misled.

Where control-oriented bureaucracy and corruption combine, mis-reporting can flourish in advanced forms: parallel accounts are kept; lies are routine. Subsidized inputs or assets play a part, providing a surplus for rents; reporting must not, however, reveal this. Endemic corruption means endemic false reporting. Work is reported done which has not been done, and workers paid who have not been paid. Costs are inflated. In one case in India in 1989 this was by a factor of four: a forest department was account-ing a cost of Rs40 per running metre of protective stone walling, when an NGO working on the ground found the cost to be only Rs10. Or again, administrators receive figures which they know are already false, and are then ordered by politicians to falsify them further. In one technical depart-ment in India, the annual meeting of some 500 senior staff is said to have been confronted by their chief statistical officer who asked: 'Why do you all lie?' There was no reply. The question was repeated. There was still no reply. The reply might have been: corruption has to lie.

Self-sustaining myth

In crude terms, then, myth and error are generated and sustained by uppers' impediments of dominance, distance and denial and by blaming lowers, and by lowers' strategies of selective presentation, diplomacy and deceit. But what happens is interwoven with nuances and subtleties, and deserves a book on its own. For myth and error are further sustained through other modes of deception, both personal and interpersonal.

Self-deception

Personally, it is easy for uppers to deceive themselves through, for example, repetition and redefinition. Repetition is a broad and easy path to self-deception. Much of our learning and internalizing are through talking. We repeat and remember simple numbers which fit our beliefs. Repetition quickly converts spurious statistics into common credos. Certain figures are easy to remember – 30 per cent, 40 per cent and 10 million hectares, for example. So it was that post-harvest grain losses at the village level came to be so widely believed to be 30 to 40 per cent, and 10 million hectares to be believed the area waterlogged and saline as a result of canal irrigation in India.

Facts and figures are also redefined as they are repeated. As they are requoted, qualifications are omitted or altered to suit the social context or the speaker's predispositions. 'Possibly as many as' becomes 'no less than'. The upper or lower limit of a range is emphasized, and then repeated and reified as truth, while the other limit lapses into oblivion. Facts are fashioned to fit needs.

Self-deception can be insidious and unconscious. It is alarming how we tailor what we say to the context in which we say it, and how we come to believe what we say. I have noticed this in myself and my colleagues in showing slides of participatory rural appraisal (PRA). I select slides from a series of photographs I have taken and show them in order to make a point. The first time I show them I can remember much of what happened, and give qualifying detail. The second and third times I remember less and shorten what I say, qualify less, and fit my words more to the occasion. And after a time, what I present is a new reality, moulded to serve the purpose of showing the slide. I come then to believe that what happened was what I have repeatedly, but wrongly, said happened. My reality has been reconstructed for the social context in which it is presented. I have been shocked to discover old slides in a series which contradict what I find myself saying now and which I had believed to be the truth. With some slides I cannot even be sure what happened; all I know is that it is probably not what I now say it was.

Nor am I alone in this misdemeanour. I have heard a politically correct version of how women were excluded from a committee on the Mwea Irrigation Settlement in Kenya. This blamed the white, male expatriate manager. But the record is that it was he who tried to ensure their participation, and it was not he but male tenants who kept the women away. But I must question my memory even of this. For I have several times repeated this, and may by now have moulded it to meet my need for a neat example of such distortion.

The lessons are that what we say continuously redefines our personal realities and depends on social context; that we refashion facts to fit occasions; that, as all catechists know,[12] repeating words dispels doubts and embeds beliefs; that, in sum, our personal realities are a flux and mesh of personally and socially constructed approximations and distortions, and that these often acquire the character of self-sustaining myths to fit our needs and purposes.

Mutual deception

Mutual deception takes many forms. The ways it evolves and is maintained include reciprocity, distance and tacit deceit.

Reciprocity is where uppers and lowers support each other through a common myth, usually in a long-term relationship. The patients of psychoanalysts are usually uppers in society, since they have to be able to pay a lot. But they need to believe their big investments of time and money make sense, and that the therapy helps, not harms. The psychoanalyst needs the same belief. So the patient defines herself or himself as a lower, and the therapist as saviour, and comes to accept, for example, lying on a couch instead of sitting in a chair, a step which reassures the psychoanalyst. More broadly, lowers support and protect their uppers by internalizing their inferiority and blaming themselves: cases can be found with battered women and their men, harijans and caste Hindus, blacks and whites. Lowers' shame, guilt and belief in their inferiority protect uppers and maintain relationships. As evolving personal realities, lowers' beliefs in their incapacity are in part self-fulfilling and in part myths shared with uppers.[13]

Distance can maintain myth. When Starkey began his investigation of multi-purpose wheeled toolcarriers (pp. 21–2) he found correspondents believed that although they faced difficulties, there had been successes elsewhere. Optimistic public relations reports had contributed to this impression. He himself was taken in at first, and 'believed the apparent success of wheeled toolcarriers in India'. Only after eighteen months of correspondence and a literature review did it 'slowly become apparent that everyone contacted thought that these implements were indeed successful – but somewhere else!' (Starkey, 1988: 8, 121–6).

Mutual deception can be tacit deceit: those who deceive know that those they are deceiving know they are being deceived but also that they are willing to be deceived in a way that does not show that they know. Here is a conversation with an Indian Administrative Service Officer in 1992:

IAS Officer: 'I said to my BDOs [Block Development Officers] – you must each have a VIP circuit. It is part of the game.'

Question: 'Do the VIPs know that they are being given this treatment? Do they know they are not getting the truth?'

IAS Officer: 'They don't want to know. For them, it would only make trouble.'

Tacit deceit, where both uppers and lowers are aware, slides into delusion as the deceit comes to be taken as real. Distinctions blur. What begins as conscious connivance consolidates into convenient belief.

For many reasons, and in many ways, lowers reflect back to uppers what they believe uppers believe, or want to be told, or even want lowers to want. Illustrations can be drawn from Guinea, India and Denmark. In Guinea, as we have seen (pp. 26–7), development professionals, bureaucrats and donors all erroneously believed that people were causing deforestation and environmental degradation in the forest–savannah mosaic zone. In fact, people were planting and protecting trees; and more people tended to mean more trees. After their extensive and detailed fieldwork, Melissa Leach and James Fairhead wrote:

> Villagers, faced by questions about deforestation and environmental change, have learned to confirm what they know the questioners expect to hear. This is not only through politeness and awareness that the truth will be met with incredulity, but also through the desire to maintain good relations with authoritative outsiders who may bring as yet unknown benefits; a school, road or advantageous recognition of the village, for example.
>
> (Leach and Fairhead, 1994: 86)

For uppers, believing is being told what you believe.

In India, new villages were being planned after the Maharashtra earthquake of 1993 (M.K. Shah, 1996 and pers. comm.).[14] The homeless people were lowers: displaced, impoverished, weak and wanting houses soon. The planners were uppers: professionals, powerful and controlling the building of houses. The planners wanted a grid layout for the new villages. Given a choice between a grid and a cluster layout, people opted for the grid. The planners said the decision was participatory. They were pleased because this endorsed their plans. Both uppers and lowers agreed. Nevertheless, Meera Shah persisted with participatory approaches and methods, including mapping and modelling which clarified the choices and empowered the weak, and especially those who were older and non-literate.

Eventually it emerged that several factors had combined to induce choice of the grid layout: the planners had loaded their description in favour of the grid; the older people did not fully understand the choice; young men said the grid was modern, and ridiculed the older people for their doubts; the grid was known to be what the outsiders wanted to provide; and people believed they would get housing quicker if they agreed to the grid, since some other villages had already been constructed on those lines. However, when Meera Shah had empowered them in a PRA mode to conduct their own analysis, the older people opted for a more complex pattern which corresponded closer with their social realities and wishes.

The displaced people, concerned with self-esteem, not fully understanding and feeling unable to change things, had earlier acquiesced and said they wanted what they thought they were wanted to want and would be able to get. It took patient and resolute effort to reverse the dominant reality, and for the lowers to be able to define and express their wishes. It would seem that the planners had ventriloquized.

From Denmark comes Hans Andersen's (1984) fairy tale of the emperor's new clothes.[15] The emperor was deceived by two weavers into believing that he was wearing grand robes when he was naked. His courtiers did not disagree. When he went in public procession, nobody wished to appear foolish by saying what they saw until:

'But, Daddy, he's got nothing on!' piped up a small child.

'Heavens, listen to the voice of innocence!' said his father. And what the child said was whispered from one to another.

'He's nothing on! A little child said so. He's nothing on!'

At last, everybody who was there was shouting, 'He's nothing on!' And it gradually dawned upon the Emperor that they were probably right. But he thought to himself, 'I must carry on, or I shall ruin the procession'. So he held himself up even more proudly than before, and the Gentlemen of the Chamber walked along carrying a train that was most definitely not there.

The Emperor (an upper) was deceived by the weavers (lowers) and then trapped by the deception. He felt he had to keep up appearances which were not, so to speak, there to be kept up. One can ask how often uppers are deceived by lowers, and then lowers in turn are deceived; how often both uppers and lowers tacitly connive to keep up appearances, none wishing to appear ignorant or stupid or to offend the other; and how often both uppers and lowers lack little children to shout 'He's got nothing on!', or silence them if they do.

Sometimes it may be children alone who speak truth to power.

Out-of-touch, out-of-date and wrong

Patriarchal prisoners

Myths and errors are common and strong among powerful old men. In Chapter 3 we saw where normal successful careers lead. The heads and leaders of bureaucracies, political systems and institutions of learning are mostly male, old and isolated; and their field experience of peripheries and of poor people, if any, took place decades earlier. To be fair, some old males are wise and wonderful. But dominant old males can be a public menace; they suffer the double disadvantages of being out of date, and deceived by power. What they believe and say carries weight; and what they believe and say is liable to be wrong.

Old men in central places are among the most vulnerable to error because of their high scores as uppers and their delight in drawing on their past.[16] Out of deference, respect and fear, they may never be contradicted, at least to their faces. They do, indeed, have long experience, and have often made major contributions. Who would wish to gainsay Norman Borlaug, deservedly Nobel prize-winner for his part in the Green Revolution, after he has begun (1994):

I have been engaged in agricultural research and rural development in the Third World for almost 50 years, and have probably met with more farmers in more countries than any man alive?

There is a view which sees multiple uppers like old, male Nobel prize-winners as victims. They are open to temptation to pronounce with authority on many subjects, despite the limitations of their personal experience. Those who head large authoritarian hierarchies, whether religious or secular, would appear especially at risk. This interpretation could be illustrated by the Pope. Being not just old and male, but revered, impressively attired, empowered by ritual, expected to pronounce on doctrine, and head of a vast international male-dominated bureaucracy, he could be seen as an ultimate patriarch, an ultimate victim.

Readers may wish to make their own lists to illustrate the phenomenon of male uppership, isolation and vulnerability to error. It has many manifestations. Sadly and dangerously, old, male multiple uppers are denied the opportunities to interact, experience and learn which are open to more ordinary mortals. Did they not often do so much damage, they would deserve sympathy for their disabilities, and perhaps they deserve it anyway for they are prisoners of power. It is difficult for them to be in touch, up to date and right. Infallibility misleads.

Face-to-face mutual reinforcement between uppers sustains the errors of being out-of-date and out-of-touch. Clubs for élite old men and seminaries for the celibate are classic sites for the incestuous inbreeding of ignorance. I, too, have caught myself in the act. In the corridors of the World Bank, I met a former district agricultural officer of Nyeri District in Kenya. We had both worked there in the early 1960s. We spoke with enthusiasm about its agriculture. Then I realized that we were treating 1962, when we were both there, as though it were the present of the late 1980s, a generation later. Among many changes, the population had, in the meantime, probably doubled. But there we were, in a central place far from the field, mutually reinforcing our out-of-date reality.

Academic lags

The staff of universities and training institutes are similarly disadvantaged: age, often gender (most are usually men), education, status, and power (as those who set exams and questions, assess performance and give marks) all make them multiple uppers, with students and trainees as multiple lowers.

Academics and teachers often lag in their knowledge and understanding. They are vulnerable in several ways to being out-of-date and wrong. As uppers, they are relatively safe from being challenged. They are often confined to classrooms and libraries and so out of touch with developments in the field. To change teaching notes and syllabuses is tiresome. Whether through overwork, indolence, incapacity, or other priorities, staff tend to repeat rather than innovate. Textbooks are out of date, years, sometimes decades, behind the books and articles which present the cutting edge of disciplines. A manager of the English Language Books Society, which provided British-published textbooks at low prices to countries in the South, was embarrassed, in the 1980s, to receive a request from one country for a textbook published in the nineteenth century. So it is that through the teaching of lowers – the young, students, persons on courses – the normal professionalism, understandings and errors of the past are reproduced and sustained.

Academics can be among the slowest and last to learn. Social anthropological fieldwork takes years to process into a PhD thesis, which in turn takes years to process into a book, which then may take years before it is published, reviewed, placed in libraries and on bookshelves, and read, let alone acted upon. Certain research, like Hanger and Moris on women and the household economy (1973, based on 1967 fieldwork) is liable to be quoted and requoted for decades as though it was the contemporary reality. Large-scale questionnaire surveys delay learning because of the time taken for fieldwork, analysis and writing up. Government statistics are often not available until they are officially printed, years out of date. The prestigious and influential *Economic and Political Weekly* in India often publishes detailed statistical analyses of what have become historical data, ten or twenty years old, but which authors treat as contemporary material. Nor have I avoided that trap in this book. We are all vulnerable; all guilty.

Confirmation by questionnaire

Questionnaire surveys are still the most common method used for central uppers to learn about the lives and conditions of peripheral lowers. They are still widely regarded as objective. Like other learning, though, they entail interpersonal relationships of power, distort peripheral realities and fit them into centrally pre-set frameworks. This occurs in three stages.

Constructing the questionnaire

Typically, questions and categories are thought up in some central place, far removed from the field. A research funding body may even set conditions that make this mandatory. The form ESCOR 1 (revised 12/88) for applications for UK government funding for 'economic or social research for the benefit of developing countries' includes under 'method': 'Where a questionnaire survey is intended a draft version should be supplied with the application'. To my shame, in the early 1970s, I sat with colleagues in Cambridge (England) and drew up a questionnaire to be applied in Tamil Nadu and Sri Lanka. At the time it did not seem so wrong. Nor is this behaviour exceptional, even in the 1990s. In 1995 graduate students and a professor at a US university drew up, in the United States, a 22-page questionnaire which was then sent to two historically black universities in South Africa for them to administer (pers. comm., Anne Vaughan).The lowers (collaborating universities and institutes in the South) need the resources, are co-opted and submit; the uppers (institutes of superior and international status in the North) are trusted by the funders, and the money they raise reinforces their power and patronage. In these two instances, the high status of Cambridge in the first case, and the low status of the historically black universities in the second, served to sustain the North–South pattern of dominance.

The concerns, concepts, categories and questions are then those of the 'North', of the uppers, not those of the 'South', the lowers.

In questionnaire interviewing, power and initiative lie with the interviewer. Questionnaires are 'administered', like oaths or drugs; they are something that is done to people, the person interviewed. The interviewee is a 're-spondent', a person who replies or reacts. The Latin *respondere* means to return like with like. The questions and categories are those of the inter-viewer, who also records the 'response'.

Upper–lower dominance is built into interviews. Interviewers in the South are more often men than women. The status of the interviewer is shown by clipboard and paper, and often by clothing. What is recorded results from, and suffers the distortions of, an upper-lower interaction which is verbal and often eye-to-eye. Respondents are sometimes intimidated, fearful and defer-ential. What is said is a social artefact of upper–lower interaction.

Prudence and presentation of the self can then lead to lies and evasions. Respondents often know or sense the replies they are meant to give, and interviewers know what their superiors hope to find. In a questionnaire survey in India, only one farmer among 272 (0.4 per cent) was recorded as crossploughing, a practice officially frowned upon, but after group discus-sions the figure jumped to 28 per cent (pers. comm., Sitapathi Rao). Notori-ously, farmers are recorded as having been visited by extension staff far more than in fact they have (see e.g. Chambers and Wickremanayake, 1977: 158–9). In a devastating review of evaluation surveys of beneficiaries of the Integrated Rural Development Programme in India, Jean Dreze (1990) has shown how favourable biases were built into the questionnaire process to generate an illusion contradicted by a mass of micro-evidence.

Interviewers, as uppers, play a part in constructing the reality. What is written down may be influenced by what they know their superiors hope to find, and also by habits they develop. Especially where schedules are long, the temptation to abbreviate replies is strong, and the item 'Other' rarely filled in. Where completed schedules are compositions, filled in without the inconvenience of an interview, the reality invented will be what the com-poser believes her or his superior will accept and not question; clearer correlations are likely to result, pleasing all. Those who process completed forms also prefer them neat. In the words of Baburao Baviskar (pers. comm.): 'A professional investigator's forms are much better for the com-puter than those of an honest investigator'.

The realities so constructed by interviewers differ by person. I have had to tear up a paper on agricultural extension on finding that the individual investigator was a powerful independent variable. On the same lines, Gerard Gill (1993a: 9) records that:

A colleague once informed me that in a . . . situation where the coeffi-cients were 'all over the place', he ran an analysis of variance on a randomly selected subset of the data, using the enumerators' identifica-tion numbers as the independent variable. He was alarmed, if not totally surprised, to find that the values of the F statistics were consistently so high as to be 'off the end of the scale'! He did not, for some reason, try to publish his findings.

A very large survey organization has been challenged three times to analyse its data for investigator bias. Perhaps it would be too damaging, and destroy investigators' livelihoods. Who am I to speak? I never published the paper 'Up the Garden Path' which analysed investigator bias in my study of agricultural extension. I did not want to upset and undermine my colleagues. I have been party to the conspiracy of silence. To this day, the extent to which survey results are socially and personally constructed remains under-researched, under-reported and under-recognized.

Analysing the results

Analysis has, then, a tendency to reassure and to reinforce preconceived reality. This is in four respects. The realities portrayed in the final analyses can be expected to be:

o *Selective.* The greater the volume of data (and they are often voluminous) the more analysts are forced and inclined to select. Selection necessarily reflects their priorities and predispositions, which are then reinforced.

Data are limited to what was asked. They fit and, by definition, do not challenge uppers' categories in the first place. Mary Tiffen (1994: 7–8) has noted that capital has become unfashionable (among uppers – development professionals, not among lowers – practising farmers) as a subject in peasant agriculture. She and her colleagues found for Machakos District in Kenya that farm incomes depend crucially on capital investment. Yet of 20 different farm studies made between 1963 and 1983 none gave information on trees planted, terraces constructed, dams, ponds or fencing. What is not asked about is not found out about and cannot be part of the analysis. Nor is it asked about the next time. The circular process sustains the errors of ignorance.

o *Simplified.* Long schedules take time, are tedious, and generate poor data. But short questionnaires miss much. In the context of work and employment:

> The concise questionnaire necessary to guarantee a reasonably reliable survey cannot do justice to the complexity of the actual employment pattern. For example, by pressing respondents to state only the principal source of external earnings over the preceding year, the individual variation in, or even combination of, occupations is concealed.
>
> (Breman, 1985: 300, quoted in Harriss, 1989: 144)

Polly Hill recounts (1986: 32) that FAO's instructions for the 1980s World Census of Agriculture were to ignore crop mixtures: crops had to be recorded as monocultures. The local reality of crop mixes, so common in the tropics, was too complex to be captured. (The resulting undercounting of agricultural production is mind-boggling.) Perhaps most commonly, investigators' life is easier the fewer probing questions they ask, the fewer boxes they tick, and the less they make entries in the box marked 'Other'. Convenience simplifies complexity.

95

○ *Overfavourable.* As we have seen, overfavourable results are generated by the interview interaction, and the prudence and deference of respondents and interviewers alike. Then, in Polly Hill's (1986: 33) words:

> . . . at later stages, the field material is commonly fudged, cooked and manipulated by officials at higher levels, the main purpose being to ensure that the trends will be found satisfactory and convincing by those with still greater authority.

○ *Reconfirming.* Questionnaires tend to reconfirm the beliefs of those who design them. They reflect the same concerns, concepts and categories, following the principle of GOWYPI (get out what you put in). Two examples suggest how their structure and application then tend to confirm diagnoses and beliefs.

(1) Bernadas (1991) reports from the Philippines: 'Highly structured interviews using a questionnaire were employed in the gathering of data. Based on the information gathered during these formal surveys, low income due to declining soil fertility was found out to be the most pressing problem of the farmers'. In response, staff went direct for soil fertility through a rotation. They met no success for two years. But the actual problem of the farmers turned out to be the cogon weed plus soil fertility. The weed meant that a long fallow was required, until bushes had shaded out the weed. The fallow did not, however, adequately restore soil fertility. Bernadas concludes:

> The staff themselves had formulated the questions on the basis of what they felt to be the priorities. The problem areas considered were predetermined, based on the outsiders' point of view. The data gathered, although not incorrect, was incomplete and therefore misleading. Many social and economic, as well as technical aspects which would determine appropriate solutions remained unknown. (Ibid: 11)

(2) In Tamil Nadu questionnaire surveys led repeatedly to the conclusion that farmers' priority was white rice. Only when farmers conducted their own analysis with matrix scoring, and without a questionnaire, did scientists learn that red rice was preferred (Manoharan *et al.*, 1993). Through whatever combination of deference, suggestion, question structure or other distortion, the questionnaire had generated the higher-status, more urban, and middle-class response, which would also have been that of the scientists.

Despite, and in part because of, these shortcomings, questionnaire surveys are sustainable. For uppers, they are convenient, congenial and reassuring:

○ For all uppers, questionnaires bolster self-esteem and status. They 'lower lowers' as respondents. Questions asked badly, or not understood, or using alien concepts or words, lead to 'Don't know', or 'No response' which imply ignorance. By under-reporting or missing complexities of livelihood, farming system, season and society, and consequently by making poor people's lives and conditions appear simpler than they are, they confirm uppers in their prejudices. They tend to make respondents appear simple, ignorant and stupid.

o For teachers and trainers questionnaire surveys provide a syllabus of well-defined steps and practices (see e.g. Moser and Kalton, 1971), a Model-T method whose teaching will last for life. For students, they present the security of set learning, and mass-produced cheap textbooks which, though dog-eared, grubby, underlined and stuck with Sellotape, can be sold on to the next batch.

o For academics, consultants and bureaucrats, they reliably (even if usually late) generate numerical data for analysis.

o For donors, government departments, NGOs and those responsible for projects and programmes they provide over-favourable evaluations.

o For research institutes they provide steady income and stable employment for fieldworkers.

o To all development professionals they are reassuring, portraying poor people as less knowledgeable and their lives and conditions as simpler and more standardized than they really are. Professionals' sense of superiority is then reinforced. Their constructs and beliefs are reaffirmed. New knowledge may be generated but is unlikely to challenge the categories, constructs and beliefs which are centrally held. So questionnaire surveys tend to confirm the realities of uppers, not contradict them, and so may sustain myth and error more than dispel them.

World Bank and self-deceiving state[17]

The factors which mislead combine where power is concentrated. In development, two types of power centres stand out: national governments in the South, at the head of hierarchical bureaucracies; and the Bretton Woods institutions, notably the World Bank and the IMF in Washington, at the centre of global networks of influence. In development policy and practice, these two sorts of centre work together, with the Bretton Woods institutions as uppers and national governments as lowers.

Anyone seeking to understand the genesis of errors in development policy would do well to start in Washington. For it is there that power to propagate economic and social policies in countries of the South has become increasingly located, in the Government of the United States, the IMF and the World Bank. It does not help to condemn the World Bank for existing; if it did not exist, something like it would probably have to be invented. Nor should one underestimate the intelligence, professional qualifications, hard work and intensity of interaction of those who work there. Its form and actions are, though, frightening. It comprises the greatest single mass of development professionals in the world. It is an extraordinary concentration of clever people connected with each other through computer networking, and through e-mail, fax and telephone with those parts of the world that have e-mail, fax and telephone. Seen in reverse, from the periphery, the World Bank is a citadel – remote, cut off, insulated in high buildings, isolated from peripheral realities which are perceived from a distance, bent through upper–lower prisms of power.

Though often differing on macro-policies, the Bank and the governments of the South with which it works have common interests in projects. Rewards have come from committing and spending loans. Top-down drives for rapid expenditure and implementation have generated targets and Model-T programmes and projects which have misfitted local conditions and deterred participation. The transfer and imposition of reality, whether through infrastructure or procedures, has had to be fast and widespread. There has been scope for uppers' dominance, distance, denial and blaming the victim to come into play, supported by lowers' selective presentation through development tourism, prudent diplomacy both within the host government bureaucracy, and between its bureaucrats and those of the Bank, and the deceit of misleading reporting.

In practice, flows of misinformation have had many channels: senior officials who negotiate with the Bank are near the end of their service and hope for Bank consultancies after retirement; other host-government officials who seek to give a good impression; progress reports which rarely damn; the single universal solution which is seen on rural visits only at its most special and successful; independent evaluations which confirm positive impressions; prudent respondents, researchers, evaluators and consultants who refrain from brutal honesty. A consultant who bears bad news may soon be looking for other employment; and when bad news does get through, it may be rejected. The flow of loans and disbursements must be sustained.[18] So though local conditions differ, evidence of misfits is filtered out. The standard blueprint makes it easier to spend money, and then seems sound: the HYV package for all farmers; warabandi for all canal-irrigation systems; Vetiver grass for most or all watershed development; milch buffaloes for IRDP loanees in India; teacher training colleges or secondary schools all over Indonesia; the Sasakawa Global 2000 mass-produced Model-T packages of high-input agriculture in Africa. Positive misinformation reinforces top-down reflexes and props up standard programmes. False feedback defends against dissonance. There is a danger of delusionary symbiosis between the self-deceiving state and the self-deceiving Bank (Chambers, 1992). Both have an interest in appearing successful. At worst, they combine in a *folie à deux*.

In understanding how and how much this happens, a key phenomenon, little studied, is the frenetic country visit by the harassed World Bank staff member.[19] This has often required the rapid identification of a large project or a large-scale programme, or a rapid evaluation. There is little scope for diversity and equally little time for listening. Urgency demands dominance. An aid agency staff member came on a field visit in India with a pre-set solution to problems of irrigation. He interviewed farmers who were patently eager to please in such a manner that within a few minutes invariably they agreed that they needed *warabandi* (see pp. 72–3), regular timed rotation of water. But in a meeting, one farmer stood up and challenged this. He said that the priority was getting water from the system in the first place. They could only talk about how to distribute water when they had water to distribute. 'Sit down!' he was told, 'sit down!' And when he continued to protest, he was not listened to but told again to 'Sit down! Sit down!'[20] Gradgrind (see page 75) would have done the same.

A tragic and well-known illustration of this dominance is to be found in the policies of structural adjustment forced on many nations in the South. The radical cut-backs which were demanded on recurrent government expenditure led usually to a sharp decline in services, especially for education and health. These policies penalized the poor. Yet it took a long time for policymakers in Washington to understand and accept this. The reality of their economic dogmas was more immediate and mattered more than the reality of poor people at the peripheries.

Being clever, centrally placed, served by instant communications of unprecedented quality, and powerful does not, then, ensure being right or doing good. To the contrary, these factors are an impediment. It is difficult for the staff of the Bank to get things right, combining as they do awesome responsibility and power with physical, cultural and cognitive distance from the peripheries and poor people of the South. With the cards so stacked against them, it is an achievement that they have not got things wrong even more than they have.

In offsetting these negative factors, two developments in the World Bank have been significant. The first is participation. A Bank-wide Learning Group on Participatory Development was launched in December 1990. A small and determined group with high-level support managed and extended a process of consultation, research and workshops which led to a policy statement (World Bank, 1994) and a series of publications, including a sourcebook (World Bank 1995). In consequence, special funds are available for participation in project preparation. It can be a plus mark for a task manager, responsible for the development of a project, to show that participatory approaches have been used, and Participatory Poverty Assessments (e.g. World Bank, 1994; Norton and Stephens, 1995) have begun to represent the realities of the poor in national policymaking.

The second is transparency. The World Bank is outstanding among development agencies for its capacity for transparent self-criticism (e.g. Morse and Berger, 1992; World Bank, 1992 (Wapenhans Report)). Open criticism is a means to continuous correction. The Bank is an easy and politically correct target for negative radicals. It has, though, shown an increasing openness, rare among national and international bureaucracies, in commissioning and publishing critical evaluations. The Independent Review of the Sardar Sarovar Project in India (Morse and Berger, 1992) is impressively outspoken. It concludes 'that the Sardar Sarovar Projects as they stand are flawed, that resettlement and rehabilitation of all those displaced by the projects is not possible under prevailing circumstances, and that the environmental impacts of the projects have not been properly considered or adequately addressed' (ibid: xii). The Bank subsequently withdrew support from the scheme. The NGOs, which so roundly criticize the Bank and influence decisions like this, do not dare to be so frank about their own performance. The NGO and bilateral courtiers and critics feel compelled to keep their privates covered. Only the Emperor dares go naked.

Participation, transparency and learning come together in the public sharing of experience, as in this part of a Bank task manager's account of an OOPP (ZOPP) process in Chad:[21]

99

At one point, a Chadian participant said to one of us from the Bank: 'I am telling you that I have a headache, and you keep telling me that I have a footache and you want to force me to take a medicine for that'. Hearing that made us from the Bank think twice about our own feeling that we were really just part of the group.

(Ndao, 1995: 30)

Sharing experiences like this sets an example which helps all to learn.

As a learning institution, though, the Bank remains a victim of its power and isolation, disadvantaged from the start in trying to learn the realities of the poorest and weakest whom it says it seeks to serve. If all power deceives, the exceptional power of the World Bank deceives exceptionally. But all is not hopeless. For as the participatory learning process and the transparent self-criticism have begun to show, exceptional power and error present exceptional opportunities for doing better.

Whose reality counts?

Much has been done that is good. But so much has been done so badly that to dispel and correct myth and error remains hugely important. The fantasies of Freud and of many of his successors, perpetuated through personal and professional dominance, are a warning to all who hold power in the domains of development. One can ask how much more hurt has been done and will be done on a vast scale by the normal professionals of the IMF, the World Bank, the EU and other centres of power, to countries and people who are variously too weak, vulnerable, distant, prudent and polite to answer back or be heard. Myths have led to massive misallocations of funds and human resources, to misguided programmes, to missed opportunities and, among professionals, to deception, cynicism and loss of commitment.

In seeking to do better, criticism is easy. To be constructive is harder. Taking responsibility and accepting risk by actually doing something is hardest of all. But much of the best learning is through self-critical commitment to action, to engagement with the world, to learning by doing.

Self-critical commitment demands personal insight and reflection. If believing is seeing, we have to question belief in order to see well. Learning is then through doubt, self-examination and willingness to change, seeking self-correcting engagement with dynamic realities and making learning a way of life. In a phrase, this is epistemological awareness, awareness of how we learn, how that affects what we think we know, and how we perceive and distort the realities of others.

According to Ralph Waldo Emerson: 'People only see what they are prepared to see'. I have argued that what we do is more active: we create what we want to see; and the more powerful we are, the more we do this, and the more it is done for us. At the cost of their reality, and of pluralism, diversity and truth, others reflect our reality back to us. For uppers, believing is being shown and told.

> All powerful uppers think they know
> What's right and real for those below

At least each upper so believes
But all are wrong; all power deceives.

So we can ask: how much is the reality we perceive our own creation as uppers? What are the realities of lowers and how can they be expressed?

Whose knowledge counts?
Whose values?
Whose criteria and preferences?
Whose appraisal, analysis and planning?
Whose action?
Whose monitoring and evaluation?
Whose learning?
Whose empowerment?

Whose *reality* counts?

'Ours' or 'Theirs'?

What can and should we, as uppers, do to make our realities count less, and the realities of lowers – the poor, weak and vulnerable – count more?

6

Learning to Learn

It's the best possible time to be alive, when almost everything you thought you knew is wrong.
Valentine, in Tom Stoppard's play *Arcadia*, quoted in
John Carey, *The Faber Book of Science*, p. 503

As professionals have become more aware of errors and myths, and of the misfit between the reality they construct and the reality others experience, some have sought and developed new approaches and methods in their work. Insights and developments in action–reflection research, agro-ecosystem analysis, applied social anthropology, farming-systems research, and rapid rural appraisal (RRA) have contributed to the evolution of participatory approaches to learning and action, including participatory rural appraisal (PRA). PRA is a growing family of approaches and methods to enable local people to share, enhance and analyse their knowledge of life and conditions, and to plan, act, monitor and evaluate. Its extensive and growing menu of methods includes visuals such as mapping and diagramming. Practical applications have proliferated, especially in natural resources management, agriculture, health and nutrition, poverty and livelihood programmes, and urban contexts. PRA approaches and methods present alternatives to questionnaire surveys in appraisal and research, and generate insights of policy relevance. Past dominant behaviour by outsiders goes far to explain why it is only in the 1990s that these participatory approaches and methods have come together and spread.

The challenges

The challenges presented in the preceding chapters of this book are personal, professional and institutional. The evidence, arguments and conclusions may be modified or rejected. If they are substantially accepted, 'more of the same' will not do. Radical change is required on a wide front. The chapter themes and challenges are:

Chapter 1   *Theme*: accelerating change, polarization into overclass and underclass, and an emerging consensus of concepts and values – well-being, livelihood, capabilities, equity and sustainability.
Challenge: to be alert, nimble and in touch, reducing inequities, and adopting, developing and applying the concepts and values of the emerging consensus.
Chapter 2   *Theme*: potential huge gains from avoiding normal error.
Challenge: to learn continuously, embracing, correcting and avoiding error.
Chapter 3   *Theme*: professional realities present much of the problem, valuing things over people, measurement over judgement, reductionism

over holism, with a dominant cult and culture of economics, all combining to create a professional prison.

Challenge: to reverse values and break out of professional prisons.

Chapter 4   *Theme*: powerful professionals transfer their reality, through teaching, centralized bureaucracy and career patterns, with tendencies to simple, standardized packages transferred top–down, and misfitting local realities and needs.

Challenge: to reverse upper-lower dominance, and top-down, centre-outwards standardization and control.

Chapter 5   *Theme*: the powerful are systemically deceived through their upper–lower relationships in which they assert their reality and lowers sustain uppers' delusions.

Challenge: to enable the poor, weak and vulnerable to express their realities, to plan and to act.

In a spirit of pluralism, each person, profession and institution can find an individual pathway for meeting these challenges. This chapter introduces a family of approaches and methods which provides one starting point. Participatory rural appraisal (PRA) is not a panacea, and will not solve all the problems of the world; but it does open up some ways of trying to tackle these challenges. Its development and spread in the first half of the 1990s have been so rapid that it is timely to stand back, as this chapter tries to do, and review its origins, evolution, methods and applications, and to ask why it has taken so long to come about.

PRA has often astonished facilitators and surprised local people who have found themselves doing things they did not know they could. The essence of PRA is changes and reversals – of role, behaviour, relationship and learning. Outsiders do not dominate and lecture; they facilitate, sit down, listen and learn. Outsiders do not transfer technology; they share methods which local people can use for their own appraisal, analysis, planning, action, monitoring and evaluation. Outsiders do not impose their reality; they encourage and enable local people to express their own.

Readers who are not thrilled by history may wish to skip lightly, perhaps dipping into the methods and applications (pp. 116–22) to gain a sense of the range of PRA, and then move on to Chapter 7 for a sense of the excitement of the 'discoveries' of PRA, and attempts to understand its elements and principles.

This chapter also complements the final three chapters: Chapter 8 which explores the local, complex, diverse, dynamic and unpredictable (lcddu) realities of people, the poor, peripheries, farming systems and livelihood systems as they have been and can be revealed through PRA; Chapter 9 which explores its wider paradigmatic significance; and Chapter 10 which examines problems and bad practice, and the challenges – personal, professional and institutional – of reversals to put the first last.

Streams of change

Confronted with the formidable challenge of reversals necessary to empower lowers and to reveal local realities, professionals in the natural and social sciences, and practitioners in the field, have evolved new approaches and combinations of methods. As an intermittent participant/observer in this process, I cannot avoid a partial view. However much I try to present a balanced and multiple perspective, I cannot escape from presenting a reality which is personal and fallible. At best, then, what follows can be taken as a personal interpretation of what has happened.

Participatory approaches are always half hidden. The ways of learning that are most visible to the world élite have been generated by the new hardware and software of the cores. It is computers and their programs which attract most attention, with their new magazines and their full-page advertisements in the newspapers of the North. It is these which have captivated many of a generation of affluent, mainly male, adolescents in the North with the new worlds of computer games. Computers, games and programs have been subject to frenetic competition and almost instant obsolescence. And it is these which have generated the new proxy realities of GIS (Geographic Information Systems) on their screens, and the new adventures of surfing in cyberspace on the Internet, for those uppers who have access.

Less conspicuous, quieter, more dispersed, but significant for human fulfilment and well-being, have been streams and confluences of development approaches and methods in the peripheries of the South, flowing out to cover new ground. These have been many. Some have made striking contributions to understanding and modes of learning. These, as its precursors and now cousins, have led on to and contributed to PRA and its siblings PALM (participatory learning methods), DRP (*diagnostico rurale participativo*) and MARP (*méthode accélerée de recherche participative)*; and all are currently sharing and exchanging experiences and methods.

PRA has evolved so fast, and continues to evolve so differently, that no final description can serve. At one stage PRA was called 'an approach and methods for learning about rural life and conditions from, with and by rural people', with the emphasis on learning by outsiders. The prepositions were then reversed to read 'by, with and from', as the analysis and learning shifted from 'us' to 'them'. Then the term PRA came to cover more than just learning. It extended into analysis, planning, action, monitoring and evaluation. It was also used to describe a variety of approaches as they evolved in different countries, contexts and organizations. To cover these, it was described in May 1994 as: 'a family of approaches and methods to enable rural people to share, enhance, and analyse their knowledge of life and conditions, to plan and to act' (Absalom *et al.*, 1995). To this can now be added 'and to monitor and evaluate'. For some, too, it is now a philosophy and a way of life which stresses self-critical awareness and commitment to the poor, weak and vulnerable.

The essence of PRA has been induced from practice and what has been found to work, not deduced from a priori principles. It has three foundations or pillars (Mascarenhas *et al.*, 1991; and Figure 6.1):

○ the behaviour and attitudes of outsiders, who facilitate, not dominate;
○ the methods, which shift the normal balance from closed to open, from individual to group, from verbal to visual, and from measuring to comparing; and

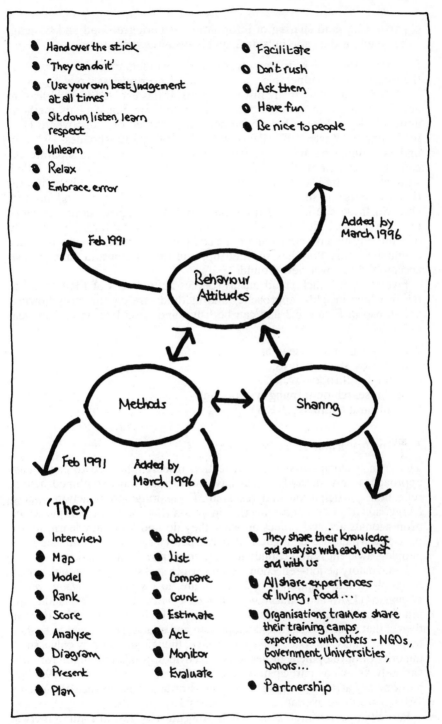

Figure 6.1: The three pillars of PRA

105

○ partnership and sharing of information, experience, food and training, between insiders and outsiders, and between organizations.

For many, PRA seeks to empower lowers – women, minorities, the poor, the weak and the vulnerable – and to make power reversals real.

PRA has currently many historical roots. It has evolved from, draws on and resonates with several sources and traditions. Some of its methods appear new; and some have been adopted, adapted or rediscovered (see, for example, Whyte, 1977; Pelto and Pelto, 1978; and Rhoades, 1990). In understanding what has happened, it makes no sense to try to separate out causes, effects, innovations, influences and diffusion as though these follow straight lines. In a world of continuously quicker and closer communication, transfers and sharing have become more and more rapid and untraceable. So these sources and traditions have intermingled more and more over the past decade, and each also continues in several forms; but directly or indirectly all have contributed to a confluence in PRA; and as with other confluences, the flow has speeded up, and innovation and change have accelerated to cover new ground.

Five streams which stand out as sources and cousins of PRA, and between which insights, approaches and methods are continuously flowing, are shown in Figure 6.2 and can be listed and described, in alphabetical order, as:

○ action–reflection research;
○ agro-ecosystem analysis;
○ applied anthropology;
○ field research on farming systems; and
○ rapid rural appraisal (RRA).

Participatory action–reflection research

The term 'participatory action–reflection research' is used to encompass approaches and methods which have in various ways combined action, reflection, participation and research. These range from action science (Argyris *et al.*, 1985) and reflection-in-action (Schon, 1983, 1987) in which professionals act and reflect on what they do and how they learn, to approaches which use dialogue and participatory research to enhance local people's awareness and confidence, and to empower their action.

Participatory action–reflection research which seeks to empower owes much to the work and inspiration of Paulo Freire, to his books *Pedagogy of the Oppressed* (1970) and *Education for Critical Consciousness* (1974), and to the practice and experience of conscientization in Latin America. The Freirian theme, that poor and exploited people can and should be enabled to analyse their own reality, has been widely influential, though practiced by only a small minority of development professionals. Activities in this tradition have been variously known as participatory research (Cornwall and Jewkes, 1995) and participatory action research (PAR) (Fals-Borda and Rahman, 1991; Whyte, 1991). Since these overlap, they can be considered together.

Participatory research and PAR have been strongest in Latin America. They have long been associated with the adult education movement

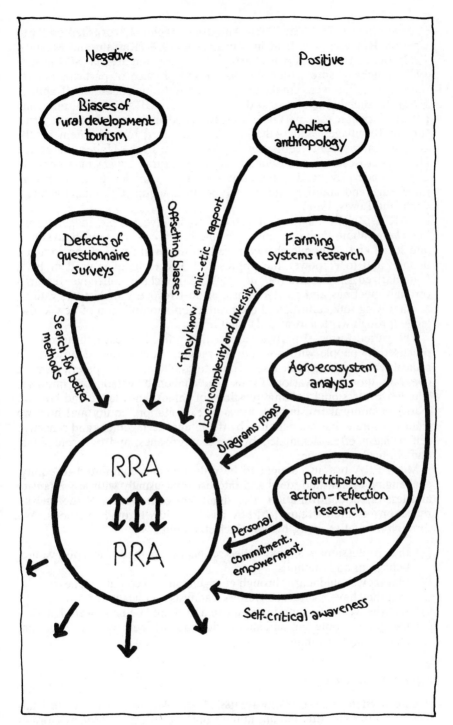

Figure 6.2: Some sources and relatives of RRA and PRA

107

(*Convergence*, 1975; 1981; 1988). An African regional Workshop on Participatory Research was held in Tanzania in 1979 (Kassam and Mustafa, 1982). In India, the Society for Participatory Research in Asia (SPR in Asia 1982) sought to spread the philosophy and practice of participatory research. Activities were conducted in widely differing conditions (Rahman, 1984). In Bangladesh, as recorded in *The Net* (BRAC, 1983), poor and powerless people took part in investigation and analysis of the power structure in 10 villages, and of how benefits directed towards them by the government were intercepted by the local élite. In the United States, the Highlander Research and Education Center in rural Appalachia worked to enable underprivileged communities to gain confidence in their own knowledge and abilities, and to take political action (Gaventa, 1980; Gaventa and Lewis, 1991).

PAR especially has sought actively to involve people in generating knowledge about their own condition and how it can be changed, to stimulate social and economic change based on the awakening of the common people, and to empower the oppressed.[1] The techniques used in PAR (summarized in Cornwall *et al.*, 1993: 25) include collective research through meetings and socio-dramas, critical recovery of history, valuing and applying folk culture, and the production and diffusion of new knowledge through written, oral and visual forms.

The varied forms of participatory action-reflection research have been practised by people with orientations ranging from scientific curiosity to radical zeal, and from critical self-doubt to confident crypto-paternalism. In common, though, its various forms have challenged established interests, whether professional (raising questions of values, knowledge and how we learn) or political (raising questions of exploitation, equity and how we change). Spread has been limited by the intense engagement and reflective self-criticism often demanded by these approaches, and by professional and political opposition.

Much PRA has also sought to be reflective and committed to equity, challenging established ideas and interests, but usually with less intensity and less direct confrontation. The significant contribution of the action–reflection research stream to PRA has been less through methods than through normative ideas, five of which stand out:

(1) that professionals should reflect critically on their concepts, values, behaviour and methods;
(2) that they should learn through engagement and committed action;
(3) that they have roles as convenors, catalysts and facilitators;
(4) that the weak and marginalized can and should be empowered; and
(5) that poor people can and should do much of their own investigation, analysis and planning.

Agro-ecosystem analysis

Agro-ecosystem analysis (Conway, 1985, 1986, 1987) was developed in Thailand from 1978 onwards, initially at the University of Chiang Mai, by Gordon Conway and his colleagues (Gypmantasiri *et al.*, 1980). It spread first through

Southeast Asia and later elsewhere. Drawing on systems and ecological thinking, it combines analysis of systems and system properties (productivity, stability, sustainability and equitability) with pattern analysis of space (maps and transects), time (seasonal calendars and long-term trends), flows and relationships (flow, causal, Venn and other diagrams), relative values (bar diagrams of relative sources of income etc.), and decisions (decision trees and other decision diagrams). The approach was further developed by Conway and others with the Aga Khan Rural Support Programme (Pakistan) for application in villages in Northern Pakistan, where it took a form which led to identification and assessment of practical hypotheses for action.

Agro-ecosystem analysis was so powerful and practical that it quickly overlapped with and contributed to much rapid rural appraisal (RRA) (see below). In some cases, either or both labels could be used to describe what was done. Some of the major contributions of agro-ecosystem analysis to current RRA and PRA have been:

○ visual representations and analysis;
○ transects (systematic walks and observation);
○ informal mapping (sketch maps drawn on site);
○ diagramming (seasonal calendars, flow and causal diagrams, bar charts, Venn or *chapati* diagrams); and
○ innovation assessment (scoring and ranking different actions).

Applied anthropology

Social anthropology in its classical forms has been concerned more with understanding than with changing. In the 1970s and 1980s, however, applied anthropology and development anthropology gained professional legitimacy. In the USA, the Institute for Development Anthropology established a network and a regular bulletin. A very few social anthropologists found their way into the International Agricultural Research Centres, where they had an influence disproportionate to their tiny numbers, and the social anthropologists in aid agencies rose in numbers and status, though they were still few. Social anthropologists helped other development professionals to appreciate better the richness and validity of rural people's knowledge and to distinguish the etic (the outsider's mental frame, categories and world view) and the emic (those of the local insider).

So in agriculture, *The Art of the Informal Agricultural Survey* (1982), by Robert Rhoades, a social anthropologist at the International Potato Center in Peru, was an example, widely read and influential far beyond the informal form of its publication; and in health and nutrition, the approaches of social anthropology were adopted in rapid assessment procedures (RAP) (Scrimshaw and Hurtado, 1987; Scrimshaw and Gleason, 1992) and in rapid ethnographic assessment (REA) (Bentley *et al.*, 1988), which used conversations, observation, informal interviews and focus groups, and reduced the time required for fieldwork.

PRA represents an extension and application of social-anthropological insights, approaches and methods, cross-fertilized with others. Some of those coming from and shared with social anthropology have been:

o the idea of field learning as flexible art rather than rigid science;
o the value of field residence, unhurried participant observation, and conversations;
o the importance of attitudes, behaviour and rapport;
o the emic–etic distinction; and
o the richness and validity of indigenous technical knowledge.

Field research on farming systems

Field research on farming systems, whether by social anthropologists, geographers, agricultural economists or biological scientists, has revealed the complexity, diversity and rationality of much apparently untidy and unsystematic farming practice. Among those who showed its good sense were, in the 1960s D.G.R. Belshaw at Makerere University in Uganda, and in the 1970s David Norman and his colleagues at Ahmadu Bello University in Northern Nigeria (see e.g. Norman (1975) for the value of mixed cropping), Michael Collinson in Tanzania, Richard Harwood in Thailand (Harwood, 1979) and Peter Hildebrand in Guatemala. Farming-systems research (Gilbert et al., 1980; Shaner et al., 1982; FSSP, 1987) systematized methods for investigating, understanding and prescribing for farming-system complexity, but these sometimes got bogged down in ponderous surveys and data overload.

A parallel stream of research drew attention to farmers' capabilities. Stephen Biggs, in describing 'informal R and D' (1980), Paul Richards in his classic *Indigenous Agricultural Revolution* (1985), and Roland Bunch in *Two Ears of Corn* (1985) were among those who showed and recognized that farmers were experimenters. Farmers' participation in agricultural research became a focus (e.g. Farrington, 1988; Farrington and Martin, 1988; Chambers, Pacey and Thrupp, 1989; Ashby, 1990). Clive Lightfoot and his colleagues pioneered analytical and flow diagramming by farmers (e.g. Lightfoot et al., 1991; Lightfoot and Minnick, 1991; Lightfoot and Noble, 1993) and Jacqueline Ashby at CIAT in Colombia and Michel Pimbert at ICRISAT in India showed through widely influential videos how farmers (women and men) were capable of conducting their own trials, assessments and analysis. In the later 1980s and early 1990s it was increasingly recognized that farmers should and could play a much greater part in agricultural research.

Field research on farming systems contributed especially to the appreciation and understanding of:

o the complexity, diversity and risk-proneness of many farming systems;
o the knowledge, professionalism and rationality of small and poor farmers;
o their experimental mindset and behaviour; and
o their ability to conduct their own analyses.

Rapid rural appraisal

The philosophy, approaches and methods known as rapid rural appraisal (RRA)[2] began to emerge in the late 1970s. Workshops held at the Institute of Development Studies at the University of Sussex in the UK on rural development tourism (1977), indigenous technical knowledge (1978), the RRA itself (1978, 1979) were only some among the parallel moves in different parts of the world in search of better ways for outsiders to learn about rural life and conditions. RRA had three main origins.

(1) Dissatisfaction with the biases, especially the anti-poverty biases, of rural development tourism (Chambers, 1983: 13–23), the phenomenon of the brief rural visit by the urban-based professional. These biases were recognized as: spatial (visits near cities, on roadsides and to the centres of villages, to the neglect of peripheries); project (where projects were being undertaken, often with special official attention and support); person (meeting men more than women, élites more than the poor, the users more than the non-users of services, and so on); seasonal (going in the dry and cool rather than hot and wet seasons which are often worse for poor rural people); and diplomatic (where the outsider does not wish to cause offence by asking to meet poor people or see bad conditions). All these could combine to hide the worst poverty and deprivation.

(2) Disillusion with the normal processes of questionnaire surveys and their results. Again and again, over many years and in many places (see e.g. Moris, 1970: Campbell *et al.*, 1979), the experience had been that questionnaire surveys tended to be long-winded, tedious, a headache to administer, a nightmare to process and write up, inaccurate and unreliable in data obtained, leading to reports, if any, which were long, late, boring, misleading, difficult to use, and ignored.

(3) More cost-effective methods of learning were sought. This was helped by the growing recognition by development professionals of the painfully obvious fact that rural people were themselves knowledgeable on many subjects which touched their lives. What became known as indigenous technical knowledge (ITK) (IDS, 1979; Brokensha *et al.*, 1980) was then increasingly seen to have richness and value for practical purposes. One major question, as it seemed then, was how more effectively to tap ITK as a source of information for analysis and use by outsider professionals.

In the late 1970s, though, most of those professionals who were inventing and using methods which were quicker and more cost-effective than 're-spectable' questionnaire surveys, were reluctant to write about what they did, fearing for their professional credibility. They felt compelled to conform to standard statistical norms, however costly and crude their applications, and obliged in their reports and publications to use conventional methods, categories and measures. In a classic statement, Michael Collinson (1981) described how he would take only a week to conduct an exploratory survey to identify agricultural research priorities, but would then feel obliged to follow this with a formal verification survey which represented the major commitment of professional time and funds. This more costly exercise had always confirmed the exploratory survey but 'the numbers which this formal survey provides are the only hard evidence produced by the diagnostic process. This is extremely important in convincing 'the

Establishment' . . .' (ibid: 444). To be convincing, the researcher had to be conservative, but the process was costly, and decisions and actions were delayed.

During the 1980s, in some places this situation was transformed, and RRA gained increasing acceptance. It began to be seen that it had its own principles and rigour (Belshaw, 1981; Carruthers and Chambers, 1981; Chambers 1981). In the early years of the decade, RRA was argued to be cost-effective, especially for gaining timely information, but still with some sense that it might only be a second-best. By the mid-1980s, however, its approaches and methods, when properly conducted, were increasingly eliciting a range and quality of information and insights inaccessible through more traditional methods. Except when rushed and unself-critical, RRA came out better by criteria of cost-effectiveness, validity and reliability when it was compared with more conventional methods. In many contexts and for many purposes, RRA, when well done, showed itself to be not a second-best but a best.

Many people and institutions took part in establishing the methods and principles of RRA. No account can do justice to them, and with imperfect knowledge there is no avoiding significant omissions. An earlier attempt to list countries where RRA had been developed identified 12 in Africa, 8 in South and Southeast Asia, 3 in Latin America, 3 in Australasia and the Pacific, and one in Europe. Perhaps more than any other movement, agro-ecosystem analysis in Southeast Asia introduced new methods and established new credibility. In the mid-1980s, the University of Khon Kaen in Thailand was world leader in developing theory and methods, especially for multidisciplinary teams, and in institutionalizing RRA as a part of professional training. The International Conference on Rapid Rural Appraisal held at the University of Khon Kaen in 1985, and the published volume of papers which resulted (KKU, 1987), were landmarks. The practical value of RRA was confirmed, and its underlying theory outlined (Beebe, 1987; Gibbs, 1987; Grandstaff *et al.*, 1987a; Jamieson, 1987). In the latter 1980s, RRA continued to spread, and was adopted not only in tropical countries but also in Australia (Ampt and Ison, 1989; Dunn and McMillan, 1991). It was further developed and disseminated through extensive training by the International Institute for Environment and Development (IIED) based in London, working with colleagues mainly in Africa and Asia, and through its publications, especially the informal periodical *RRA Notes* (1988–   ).

In specialized fields, too, there were parallel and overlapping developments. In health and nutrition, for example, RAP (Scrimshaw and Hurtado, 1987) was practised in at least 20 countries; in agriculture, some practitioners of farming-systems research and extension innovated with lighter, quicker methods in an RRA style; and in irrigation, a small literature was built up (e.g. Potten, 1985; Groenfeldt, 1989); and 'hard' journals began to publish papers.

RRA began and continues as a better way for outsiders to learn. In answering the question 'Whose knowledge counts?' it sought, and continues to seek, to enable outsiders to gain information and insight from rural people and about rural conditions, and to do this in a more cost-effective and timely manner. It was, and remains, less exploitative than extractive questionnaire surveys where much is taken by the outsider, and little or nothing given back. All the same, like most past farming-systems research, its normal mode entails outsiders obtaining information, taking it away and analysing it. This is a valid and useful activity which has and will continue to have its place. Depending on one's point of view and the context, the normal practice of non-participatory RRA can be described as extractive, or, more neutrally, elicitive.

PRA: confluence and spread

In the mid-1980s, the words 'participation' and 'participatory' entered the RRA vocabulary. They had already a long history in rural development. To take but two examples, for some years in the 1970s and early 1980s, under the leadership of Normal Uphoff and others, Cornell University published the *Rural Development Participation Review*, until USAID, with curious crassness, terminated its support; and participation was a recurrent theme in the contributions to Michael Cernea's book, edited for the World Bank, *Putting People First* (1985) which drew on experience from earlier years. It was at the 1985 Khon Kaen International Conference that participation began to be used in connection with RRA. Discussions at the conference generated a typology of seven types of RRA (KKU, 1987: 17) of which 'participatory RRA' was one. For this, the dominant purpose was seen at that stage as stimulating community awareness, with the outsider's role as catalyst. Later, in 1988, participatory RRAs were listed by the IIED team as one of four classes of RRA methodologies, the others being exploratory RRAs, topical RRAs, and monitoring RRAs (McCracken *et al.*, 1988).

In 1988, there were parallel developments in Kenya and India. In Kenya, the National Environment Secretariat, in association with Clark University, conducted an RRA in Mbusanyi, a community in Machakos District, which led to the adoption in September of a Village Resource Management Plan (Kabutha and Ford, 1988). This was subsequently described as a participatory rural appraisal, and the method outlined in two Handbooks (PID and NES, 1989; NES, 1990). Around the same time in 1988, the Aga Khan Rural Support Programme (India) was interested in developing participatory RRA, and invited IIED to help. In September and October 1988 Jennifer McCracken from IIED, and AKRSP staff including Meera Kaul Shah and Parmesh Shah, facilitated participatory rapid rural appraisals with villagers in Gujarat (McCracken, 1988). The Kenya and Indian experiences were seminal for the development of PRA.

Subsequently, there was an explosion of innovation in India (for which see *RRA Notes* 13) mainly in the NGO sector but also increasingly in government organizations.[3] MYRADA, based in Bangalore, trained its senior staff in PRA in early 1990 (Ramachandran, 1990), and came to play a major role in training for other NGOs and for government. Those who pioneered and evolved new methods and applications were many, including John Devavaram, Sheelu Francis, Ravi Jayakaran, Sam Joseph, Kamal Kar, James Mascarenhas, Neela Mukherjee, P.D. Premkumar, Anil Shah, Meera Kaul Shah and Parmesh Shah, all of whom subsequently conducted

PRA training for others in other countries and continents, while Somesh Kumar was one of those who early trained government staff. AKRSP continued to innovate and broke new ground in showing how well village volunteers could themselves be facilitators of PRA, while ActionAid, Bangalore undertook a networking role.

At the same time, cross-fertilization and spread took place internationally.[4] The small group in the Sustainable Agriculture Programme at IIED – Irene Guijt, Jules Pretty, Ian Scoones and John Thompson, with support from the Ford Foundation and SIDA – were decisively influential through their activities in Africa and Asia, and contributed to the spread and evolution of PRA and its methods through 30 substantial field-based training workshops in 15 countries and through publications and papers, especially *RRA Notes*. Source books, manuals and books also contributed to the dissemination of PRA (e.g. McCracken *et al.*, 1988; Gueye and Freudenberger, 1990, 1991; Theis and Grady, 1991; *RRA Notes 13*, 1991; Mukherjee, 1993).

Much of the spread was South–South, through sharing field experiences and training. PRA methods were introduced from India to Nepal on the initiative of Winrock International and to Sri Lanka on the initiative of Intercooperation. Trainers from India, and later from Kenya, Zimbabwe and other countries, conducted training in other countries and continents. James Mascarenhas in South Africa and Kamal Kar in Indonesia facilitated training workshops which were seminal, leading to rapid adoption and spread. The World Resources Institute was active in Latin America. A series of international field workshops was held, hosted in India by ActionAid, AKRSP, MYRADA and subsequently by OUTREACH (Bangalore), and in the Philippines by the International Institute for Rural Reconstruction and Helvetas. PRA approaches and methods also spread from South to North, to the industrialized world, with trainers from the South helping to initiate Northerners into PRA in Canada, Finland, Norway, Sweden, Switzerland and the United Kingdom.

By mid-1996, activities described as PRA were being practised in perhaps 100 countries and there were over 30, mainly national, PRA-related networks.[5] Several countries had held national PRA conferences (see e.g. Assefa and Konde (1996) for Ethiopia). Applications had become legion, in almost every sector of field-level development. Not only NGOs and government departments but also training institutes and universities were increasingly using PRA methods and approaches.

PRA has also shifted and spread in other dimensions:

○ in emphasis, from stressing methods to stressing behaviour and attitudes;
○ in impact, from methods to professional change, from behaviour and attitudes to personal change, and from field applications to changes in organizational procedures and cultures;
○ in focus, from appraisal to analysis, planning, action and monitoring and evaluation;
○ in location, from rural to include urban; and
○ in analysis, from practice to theory, finding what works, and then asking why.

The sudden popularity of PRA has generated huge problems and wide-spread bad practice (see pp. 211–14). Quality assurance has become a massive concern. Nevertheless, PRA or PRA-type activities continue to evolve and spread on an astonishing scale. In some countries and regions, such as Nepal and Andhra Pradesh, the question is reportedly less whether to use PRA processes or methods, and more how well or badly they will be used.

RRA and PRA compared

Many practitioners consider it important to distinguish PRA from RRA. A summary comparison is given in Table 6.1.

Table 6.1: RRA and PRA compared

	RRA	PRA
Major development	late 1970s, 1980s	late 1980s, 1990s
Major innovators in	Universities	NGOs
Main users	Aid agencies, Universities	NGOs, Government field organizations
Key resource earlier overlooked	Local people's knowledge	Local people's capabilities
Main innovation	Methods	Behaviour
Outsiders' mode	Eliciting	Facilitating
Objectives	Data collection	Empowerment
Main actors	Outsiders	Local people
Longer-term outcomes	Plans, projects, publications	Sustainable local action and institutions

In practice RRA and PRA present a continuum, as in Table 6.2.

Table 6.2: The RRA–PRA continuum

Nature of process	RRA ←—————————→ PRA
Mode	finding out–elicitive ←→ facilitating–empowering
Outsiders' role	investigator ←—————→ facilitator
Information owned, analysed and used by	outsiders ←————→ local people
Methods mainly used	'RRA methods' ←————→ 'PRA methods'

RRA and PRA have been distinguished as approaches rather than methods. Many practitioners consider that the term RRA should be used for data-collecting activities, while PRA should be reserved for an on-going empowering process. RRA should not be considered a second-best, but simply a different activity with different objectives and justifications.

115

It helps to recognize that there is an overlap of methods: a participatory or PRA method can be used as part of an RRA (finding out–elicitive) approach, and an RRA method can be used as part of a PRA (facilitating–empowering) approach.

A menu for RRA and PRA

In its early days, RRA seemed to be largely organized commonsense. During the 1980s, though, creative ingenuity was applied and more methods were borrowed, adapted and invented, many with a more participatory mode. Some of these were codified and written up in guidelines and manuals.

One view is that manuals should be avoided; that the PRA principle of 'use your own best judgement at all times' permits and encourages creativity; that manuals encourage teaching and learning by rote, the ritual performance of methods for their own sake, the imposition of methods on local people, and a loss of creativity and flexibility. In this view, very basic descriptions of methods are enough. Others consider sourcebooks useful as introductions and for sharing experiences and ideas. A balance between these two views seems best.

RRA and PRA methods have been classified as visualized analyses; methods for interviewing and sampling; and methods for group and team dynamics (Cornwall *et al.*, 1993: 22). Here they will be separated into those which are more typical of an RRA mode and those more typical of a PRA mode, remembering that all can be used in either mode.

RRA has tended to stress the use of secondary sources, observation and verbal interaction. Semi-structured interviewing and focus groups have been stressed. These, then, can be described as typically 'RRA methods and approaches'. PRA, on the other hand, has been distinguished especially by shared visual representations and analysis by local people, such as: mapping or modelling on the ground or paper; listing, sequencing and card sorting; estimating, comparing, scoring and ranking with seeds, stones, sticks or shapes; Venn diagramming; linkage diagramming; and group and community presentations for checking and validation. These are often what are described as PRA methods and approaches. The list is indicative not comprehensive.[6]

Some originally RRA methods and approaches

○ *Secondary data*: such as files, reports, maps, aerial photographs, satellite imagery, articles and books. These can help a lot especially in the earlier stages, e.g. deciding where to go, and where gaps or contradictions in understanding exist.

○ *Offsetting biases*: being self-critically aware of biases in our behaviour and learning, and deliberately offsetting them. These include biases of place: where we go; person: whom we meet, especially élite and gender biases; and season and time of day: when we go.

○ *Observing directly* (see for yourself): this can be most effective if combined with self-critical awareness of what we tend to see and not see, resulting from our own specialized education and interests, and consciously trying to correct for these.

○ *Semi-structured interviewing*: this has been regarded as the core of good RRA (Grandstaff and Grandstaff, 1987a). It can entail having a mental or written checklist, but being open-ended and following up on the unexpected. Increasingly it is using participatory visual as well as traditional verbal methods, and eliciting local people's checklists in place of those of outsiders.

○ *Seeking out the experts*: asking who are the experts on specific topics. This is obvious, yet often overlooked, perhaps because outsiders assume that experts do not exist. Who, in a community, knows most about medicinal plants, water supplies, changes in sources and types of fuel, agro-ecological history, what goes on in school, changing values and customs, who is pregnant, fodder grasses, animal diseases, home gardens, markets and prices? Who in the community is experienced and accepted in conflict resolution? Sometimes the experts are identified through participatory social mapping.

○ *Key probes*: questions that can lead directly into key issues, for example 'What new practices have you or others tried out in recent years?' or 'What happens when someone's house burns down?', followed by probing actual practice and experience.

○ *Case studies and stories*: a household history and profile, a farm and farming system, how a crisis was coped with, how a conflict was resolved.

○ *Transect walks*: systematically walking with local guides and analysts through an area, observing, asking, listening, discussing, learning about different zones, soils, land uses, vegetation, crops, livestock, local technologies, introduced technologies, seeking problems, solutions and opportunities; and mapping and diagramming the zones, resources and findings (Mascarenhas, 1990). Transects take many forms: vertical, loop, combing, along a watercourse, and even sea-bottom.

○ *Groups* of various kinds (casual or random encounter; focus; representative or structured for diversity; community, neighbourhood or socially specific; or formal, such as a committee). Group interviews and activities can present problems especially if time is short (e.g. Pottier and Orone, 1995) but when well-managed are often powerful and efficient. They have been relatively neglected, perhaps because of the habit of individual questionnaires to generate statistics.

Some typical PRA methods and approaches

○ *'Handing over the stick' and they do it*: basic to PRA is facilitating, handing over the stick, chalk or pen, enabling local people to be the analysts, mappers, diagrammers, observers, researchers, historians, planners and actors, presenters of their analysis, and then in turn facilitators: women, men, poor, non-poor, children, parents, schoolteachers, farmers, local specialists.

○ *Do-it-yourself*: roles of expertise are reversed, with local people as experts and teachers, and outsiders as novices. Local people supervise and teach skills: to transplant, weed, plough, level a field, mud a hut, draw and carry water, fetch firewood, wash clothes, cook a meal, stitch, thatch.

○ *Local analysis of secondary sources*: most commonly the analysis of aerial photographs (often best at 1:5000) to identify soil type, land conditions, land tenure etc. (Dewees, 1989a; Mearns, 1989; Sandford, 1989). Satellite imagery has also been used (pers. comm. Sam Joseph).

○ *Mapping and modelling*: people's mapping, drawing and colouring with chalks, sticks, seeds, powders, pens etc. on the ground, floor or (often later) paper to make social, health or demographic maps, resource maps of village lands and forests, maps of fields, farms and home gardens, thematic or topic maps (for water, soils, trees, the incidence of pests etc.) (P. Shah, 1995), service or opportunity maps, maps of the location of anti-personnel mines (pers. comm. Michele Barron for Mozambique), three-dimensional models of watersheds, etc. (Hahn, 1991; Mascarenhas and Kumar, 1991). These methods have been among the most widely used and can lead into household listing and well-being ranking, transects, and linkage diagrams.

○ *Time lines and trend and change analysis*: chronologies of events, listing major local events with approximate dates; people's accounts of the past, of how customs, practices and things close to them have changed; ethno-biography – a local history of a crop, an animal, a tree, a pest, a weed . . . diagrams, maps (see Sadomba, 1996 for retrospective community mapping) and matrices (Freudenberger, 1995) showing ecological histories, changes in land use and cropping patterns, population, migration, fuel uses, education, health, credit . . . and the causes of changes and trends, often with estimates of relative magnitudes.

○ *Seasonal calendars*: by major season or more usually by month to show: distribution of days of rain, amount of rain or soil moisture; crop cycles; women's, men's and children's work, including agricultural and non-agricultural labour; diet and food consumption; illnesses; prices; animal fodder; fuel; migration; sources of income; expenditure; debt etc.

○ *Daily time-use analysis:* indicating relative amounts of time, degrees of drudgery etc. of activities, and sometimes seasonal variations in these.

○ *Institutional or Venn diagramming*: identifying individuals and institutions important in and for a community or group, or within an organization, and their relationships (for examples, see Guijt and Pretty, 1992).

○ *Linkage diagrams*: of flows, connections and causality. These versatile diagrams have been used for the analysis of sequences, marketing, nutrient flows on farms, migration, social contact, and impacts of interventions and trends, and for income and expenditure trees (Archer and Cottingham, 1996b: 135).

○ *Well-being (or wealth) grouping (or ranking)*: card sorting into groups or rankings of households according to local criteria, including those considered poorest, worst off and most deprived, often expressing key local indicators of well-being and ill-being. A good lead into livelihoods of the poor and how they cope (Grandin, 1988;[7] Swift and Umar, 1991; Mearns *et al.*, 1992; *RRA Notes* 15: *passim*; Turk, 1995; Booth *et al.*, 1995).

○ *Analysis of difference*: especially by gender, social group, wealth/poverty, occupation and age. Identifying differences between groups, including their problems and preferences (Welbourn, 1991). This includes contrast comparisons: asking one group why another is different or does something different, and vice versa (pers. comm. Meena Bilgi).

o *Matrix scoring and ranking*: using matrices and counters (usually seeds or stones) to compare through scoring, for example different trees, or soils, or methods of soil and water conservation, or varieties of a crop or animal, fields on a farm, fish, weeds, conditions at different times, and to express preferences (see e.g. Drinkwater, 1993; Manoharan *et al.*, 1993; Posadas, 1995; Maxwell and Duff, 1995).

o *Team contracts and interactions*: contracts drawn up by teams with agreed norms of behaviour; modes of interaction within teams, including changing pairs, evening discussions, mutual criticism and help; how to behave in the field etc. (The team may consist of outsiders only, of local people and outsiders together, or of local people only).

o *Shared presentations and analysis*: where maps, models, diagrams and findings are presented by local people, and/or by outsiders, especially at community meetings, and checked, corrected and discussed. But who talks? Who talks how much? Who interrupts whom? Whose ideas dominate?

o *Participatory planning, budgeting, implementation and monitoring*, in which local people prepare their own plans, budgets and schedules, take action, and monitor and evaluate progress.

o *Drama and participatory video-making*: on key issues, to enable people to discover how they see things, and what matters to them, and to influence those in power.

o *Short standard schedules or protocols* as alternatives to questionnaires to record data (e.g. census or similar information from social mapping) in a standard and commensurable manner.

o *Immediate report writing*, either in the field before returning to office or headquarters, or by one or more people who are designated in advance to do this immediately on completion of fieldwork.

Specific methods have also been improvised and invented. Some of these can be found in recent sourcebooks (e.g. Schonhuth and Kievelitz, 1994; Kane, 1995; Mikkelsen, 1995; Welbourn, 1996; Archer and Cottingham, 1996b), and more can be expected.

Practical applications

Applications of RRA and PRA approaches and methods have proliferated and continue to multiply. The inventory which follows will be quickly outdated;[8] but it can indicate some of the range.

Most of the applications have one of three purposes: (i) topic investigations and research (mainly RRA);[9] (ii) training and orientation for outsiders and local people (generating much of the literature e.g. *RRA Notes* 19 Special Issue on Training; Pretty *et al.*, 1995); and (iii) PRA proper, as an empowering process of appraisal, analysis, planning, action, monitoring and evaluation (under-reported, especially the later stages of the process).

Applications have been initially in five main sectors:

119

1. Natural resources management

o *Watersheds, and soil and water conservation*: e.g. participatory watershed planning and management (Pretty, 1990; Kerr, 1991; Devavaram *et al.*, 1991; Neefjes *et al.*, 1993; Shah, P. 1993; GOI, 1994; Hinchcliffe *et al.*, 1995; Mascarenhas, 1996).

o *Land tenure and policy* (Johansson and Hoben, 1992; TriPARRD, 1993; Freudenberger, 1994, 1996; Denniston with Leake, 1995).

o *Forestry*, including: social and community forestry; degraded forest assessment, protection, nurseries and planting; identification of tree uses; and uses and marketing of forest and woodland products (Case, 1990; Inglis, 1991; Freudenthal and Narrowe, 1991; SPWD, 1992; Freudenberger, 1994; HSWG, 1995; M.K. Shah, 1995a; Vochten and Mulyana, 1995; Inglis and Guy, 1996).

o *Coastal resources and fisheries* (McCracken, 1990; Mascarenhas and Hildalgo, 1992; Colaco and Bostock, 1993; Pido, 1995; IDS Coastal and Fisheries, 1996).

o *People, parks and biodiversity* (Kar, 1993; Wild, 1994; Mason and Danso, 1995; Pocknell and Annaly, 1995; BSCRM and WWF-International, 1995; Denniston with Leake, 1995; Pimbert *et al.*, 1996; Gujja *et al.*, 1996; IDS People and Parks, 1996).

o *Community plans*: preparing Village Resource Management Plans (PID and NES, 1989); Participatory Rural Appraisal and Planning, as developed by AKRSP (Shah *et al.*, 1991).

2. Agriculture

o *Farmer participatory research*, farming-systems research and problem identification and analysis by farmers (Ampt and Ison, 1989; Dunn and Macmillan, 1991; FSRU, 1991; Lightfoot *et al.*, 1991; Guijt and Pretty, 1992; Chambers, 1993b; Drinkwater, 1993; Lightfoot and Noble, 1993; Manoharan *et al.*, 1993; ODA, 1995; Posadas, 1995; IDS Agriculture, 1996).

o *Livestock and animal husbandry* (Leyland, 1993; Maranga, 1993; Sonaiya, 1993; Young, 1993; *RRA Notes* 20, 1994: Special Issue on Livestock; Waters-Bayer and Bayer, 1994).

o *Irrigation*, including rehabilitation of small-scale gravity-flow irrigation systems and irrigation management research (Potten, 1985; Groenfeldt, 1989; Kasivelu *et al.*, 1995; Gosselink and Strosser, 1995).

o *Integrated pest management* especially in Indonesia (Kingsley and Musante, 1996; see also Omolo *et al.*, 1995).

3. People, poverty and livelihood

o *Women and gender*: participatory appraisal of problems and opportunities, and research into the conditions and lives of women (Welbourn, 1991; Grady *et al.*, 1991; Women of Sangams, Pastapur etc. and Pimbert, 1991; Tolley and Bentley, 1992; pers. comm. Meena Bilgi; Robinson

(Eva), 1993; Welbourn, 1993; Guijt, 1994; M. Shah and Bourarach, 1995; Dent, 1996; IDS Gender, 1996; Guijt and Shah, forthcoming).

o *Selection*: finding and selecting poor people for a new programme, de-selecting the less poor from an old one (e.g. Chandramouli, 1991; *RRA Notes* 15: *passim*; Pretty *et al.*, 1995; Turk, 1995).

o *Livelihood analysis*: means and economics of livelihoods, (e.g. Bishop and Scoones, 1994), the identification of non-agricultural income-earning opportunities, seasonality, credit etc. (Colaco and Gururaja, 1993: 18–26; Appleton, 1995; Murphy, 1995).

o *Participatory poverty assessments* as part of the World Bank-supported Country Poverty Assessments in Ghana, Kenya, Tanzania, Zambia, South Africa and Mozambique (see below pp. 127–8).

4. Health and nutrition

o *Health (general)* For collections of papers, see *RRA Notes* 16; de Koning and Martin, 1996; IDS Health, 1996. For applications, see also e.g. Francis *et al.*, 1992; Joseph, 1992; Welbourn, 1992; Vigoda, 1994.

o *Food security and nutrition assessment and monitoring* (Maxwell, 1990; Appleton, 1992; Buchanan-Smith *et al.*, 1993).

o *Water and sanitation assessment, planning and location* (Narayan, 1993; Joseph, 1994; Okumu, 1994; RDWSSP, 1994).

o *Sexual and reproductive health*: (Tolley and Bentley, 1992; Cornwall, 1992; IDS Sexual and Reproductive Health, 1996. For HIV/AIDS awareness and action see Welbourn (ed.), *PLA Notes* 23: 57–81, special section; Duangsa, 1995; Welbourn, 1996).

5. Urban (RRA Notes 21, special issue on Participatory Tools and Methods in Urban Areas, 1994)

o *Needs assessment* (Drinkwater, 1994; Ward *et al.*, 1995; Jayaratne and de Silva, 1995).

o *Community participation* (Reusen and Johnson, 1994).

o *Urban poverty and violence* (M.K. Shah, 1995b; Moser and Holland, 1995, 1996).

Beyond these five sectors, other applications of PRA and PRA methods have multiplied. An illustrative but surely incomplete list is:

o *Adult literacy*, with the REFLECT (Regenerated Freirean Literacy through Empowering Community Techniques) approach pioneered by ActionAid in Bangladesh, El Salvador and Uganda (EA, 1994– ; Archer, 1995; Archer and Cottingham, 1996a and b) and being spread to other countries.

o *Children* (Johnson *et al.*, 1995; Teixeira and Chambers, 1995; Guijt, 1995; *PLA Notes* 25 which includes special issue on children's participation, 1996).

o *Education* (Kane, 1995; Booth *et al.*, 1995; Kane *et al.*, 1996).

○ *Emergencies and refugees* (Slim and Mitchell, 1992; Hinton, 1995; Hudock, 1996; M.K. Shah, 1996; IDS Emergencies, 1996).
○ *Organizational analysis* (Kievelitz and Reineke, 1993; Howes and Roche, 1995).
○ *Participatory monitoring and evaluation* (P. Shah *et al.*, 1991; McPherson, 1995).

Crosscutting all these, PRA approaches and methods have had two other practical applications: as alternatives to questionnaire surveys; and for policy appraisal and insights.

Participatory alternatives to questionnaire surveys

One consequence of the evolution of participatory methods has been the discovery of alternatives to many of the normal applications of questionnaire surveys (Mukherjee, 1995). The reliability, validity and trustworthiness of these methods are assessed in Chapter 7 (pp. 141–5).

Possibly some questionnaire surveys will always be justified, notably some time-series and national-sample surveys. The evidence about many larger and one-off surveys is, though, so damning (see e.g. Moris, 1970; Campbell *et al.*, 1979; Hill, 1986; Bleek, 1987; Daane, 1987; Inglis, 1991, 1992; Gill, 1993a) that almost any alternative would be welcome – for their costs are high: in time and money; in delays in learning; in resources diverted from other means of learning; in information which is misleading or not used; in reconfirming the realities of uppers (pp. 93–7); and in discrediting the social sciences. Apart from providing employment for enumerators, evidence of benefits from such surveys is often slender.

Questionnaire surveys have, though, proven robustly sustainable as a rural and urban industry. For some professionals, rural research *is* questionnaire surveys. The fixation is illustrated by Poate and Daplyn's 1993 textbook *Data for Agrarian Development*, promoted as 'a comprehensive guide to collecting and managing agricultural data in developing countries'. The authors say that the surveyor must match the approach to the purpose, and that the reader should seek out accounts from as wide a range of studies as possible (1993: 3 and 207). But they themselves give just one paragraph each to aerial survey, case study, rapid methods and experimentation, and dedicate most of the other 365 pages of text to the planning, execution, analysis and writing up of questionnaire or measurement surveys.

A major source of sustainability has been the demand of donor agencies and governments for surveys for four purposes: to gain insights, including for project formulation; to identify social and economic differences; to provide baselines and means for monitoring and evaluation; and to generate statistics. For each of these there now exist participatory alternatives.

(1) *Insights.* Questionnaire surveys used to gain insights, especially for project formulation, select and simplify reality, often mislead, and reconfirm the realities of uppers, missing local complexity and diversity. In contrast, PRA methods usually engage the commitment and

analysis of local people, enable the expression and sharing of their diverse and complex realities, give insights into their values, needs and priorities, and can also lead on into participatory action. PRA methods such as mapping, seasonal calendars, trend and change analysis, well-being ranking, matrix scoring, Venn diagramming, and linkage diagramming have enabled local people to express their knowledge, categories, criteria and preferences. Local analysts are also often committed to ensuring information is complete and accurate. No methods are foolproof, but these are a plurality, not just one, and permit triangulation, cross-checking and analysis from emic perspectives.

(2) *Identifying social and economic differences.* Participatory methods have been used increasingly instead of questionnaires to identify so-called target groups: well-being ranking has been used for this purpose in Ethiopia, India, Pakistan, Sri Lanka and Vietnam, and probably in many other countries; in India MYRADA and ActionAid have used it to identify the poorer with whom they seek to work; in Pakistan, ActionAid staff have facilitated the ranking of 38,000 people for the same purpose (pers. comm. Humera Malik); in Bangladesh, BRAC has tested participatory mapping as an alternative way to identify target groups for a non-formal education programme; and in Pakistan, listing and card sorting have been used to enable local people to categorize types of potato farmers (Guijt and Pretty, 1992).

(3) *Monitoring and evaluation.* For project baselines and later impact assessments, questionnaire surveys pose horrendous problems: of comparability of sample; of assessing what would have happened anyway; of finding comparable control areas; and of disentangling multiple causality and knowing what caused what. In consequence, conventional baseline surveys are virtually useless for impact assessments.

The question now is how widely local people can be enabled to identify their own indicators, establish their own participatory baselines, monitor change, and evaluate causality, for example through causal linkage diagramming of observed phenomena which touch their personal experience over seasons and years.

These frontiers have begun to be explored. In Bangladesh, participatory mapping has been facilitated by CARE to enable women to present and assess changes resulting from a Women's Development Project (Vigoda, 1994). In Bolivia, a participatory baseline study (Vigoda *et al.*, 1994) for the Central Chuquisaca Renewable Natural Resources Project was facilitated in 23 communities. Among other activities, 55 maps were made by groups. Through participatory analysis, the study was more than a baseline; it helped local people to identify their problems and priority interests, and to define the project's interventions. In India, in some AKRSP villages in Gujarat, village volunteers retained the maps made by villagers and used them for monitoring soil and water-conservation measures and yields (Shah *et al.*, 1991). In Nepal, in September 1991, ActionAid staff facilitated participatory mapping as a basic method for a utilization survey for services. Participatory maps were made in about 130 villages, giving information covering the total population of each. This presented a differentiated census, and a range of information, including utilization of services for education and health, the use of pit latrines, adoption of various agricultural practices, and participation in group activities. The information was collated by the ActionAid teams and presented in conventional tables (ActionAid-Nepal, 1992).

(4) *Statistics.* Participatory approaches have been equated, misleadingly, with only qualitative data. But whether literate or not, almost all people can count, and counting can be shared and cross-checked visually. As in the Nepal utilization survey, statistics can be generated by participatory methods, especially mapping followed by listing and counting.

Examples have been documented in countries as diverse as Bolivia (Vigoda *et al.*, 1994), India (NCAER, 1993), Nepal (ActionAid-Nepal, 1992) and Zimbabwe (Marindo-Ranganai, 1995), and personal communications supply other examples from Nigeria, Pakistan and the Philippines. From its research project to compare RRA/PRA methods with questionnaire sample surveys, the National Council of Applied Economic Research in India found that participatory methods could generate valid statistical data at the village level, as well as unexpected insights (NCAER, 1993). Participatory maps can be used to present demographic data (Marindo-Ranganai, 1995), with different seeds, colours, stones, vegetables or other symbols representing different sorts of people and conditions. In India, local people, non-literate as well as literate, have used marks and symbols on cards to record household information, including assets.

Two methodological aspects deserve comment: (i) participatory mapping and listing avoids laborious sampling and sampling errors, since all people are included; sampling focuses on the choice of communities, not choice within them; (ii) comparability can be sought through protocols or schedules. Parmesh Shah (1993) has developed this approach with a 'visual interactive questionnaire'. In India, IFPRI and ICRISAT developed and tested procedures, schedules and routines for facilitating and recording visual analyses by villagers, using mapping, charts for food and women's time and energy-use.

The potential of RRA and PRA methods can be sensed from an account by the late Selina Adjebeng-Asem (pers. comm. July 1992) of Obafemi Awolowo University, Ife-Ife, Nigeria, of monitoring a soyabean project in Nigeria:

I trained the . . . soyabean project group in the use of PRA for monitoring of the project impact in five states of the Federation i.e. Kaduna, Niger, Enugu, Anambra and Oyo States . . . The group of 16 researchers were amazed about how much easier it is to obtain indepth information through participatory mapping in addition to other RRA techniques they have already known. We were able through mapping to obtain all relevant socio-demographic information we required for the project; for example, the number of households in a village, households involved in

124

soyabean production, gender issues in soyabean production, utilization of soyabean, and preference rankings of various soyabean diets . . . We gathered an incredible amount of information within an hour and a half visit to the village . . . The researchers have been begging me to give more training in PRA . . .

In cases such as this, PRA methods, used well, can be not only more cost-effective than questionnaire surveys; they are also more popular with researchers and local people alike, all of whom learn from the process. After using PRA methods, a villager in Zimbabwe had this to say: 'We did not know we had all this information' (Marindo-Ranganai, 1995: 61); and an NGO worker in Sri Lanka said: 'I shall never go back to questionnaires'.

In the mid-1990s, the use of PRA methods in place of questionnaire surveys has already occurred on a large scale, but has passed largely un-noticed and unresearched. Issues now include the feasibility and cost of training fieldworkers in PRA methods, the trade-offs between participa-tion and standardization, the ethics of people's time taken and expectations raised, and how far local people can own the data they generate and use it for their own censuses, appraisal, baseline indicators, monitoring and evaluation.

Insights for policy

RRA and PRA approaches and methods have generated policy-relevant understandings of local realities. Explorations have taken two forms: thematic and general.

Thematic explorations

These have been numerous, and have typically led to insights which modify or add to the beliefs and knowledge of policymakers:

○ In Chad in 1991, 13 survey facilitators worked in 55 representative vil-lages with a checklist as guide for group interviews, to learn people's perceptions of food-security problems, and what solutions they pro-posed. The study found three categories of administrative area, each with a distinctive household food-security strategy. It challenged con-ventional policy thinking that promoting free-market systems was the key to raising production. The constraints, rather, were lack of credit for ploughs, oxen, improved seeds and more efficient irrigation (Buchanan-Smith, *et al.*, 1993).

○ In Zimbabwe in November 1991, RRA with PRA methods were used to investigate the effects on agriculture of structural adjustment policies. RRAs were conducted by a team of researchers over two weeks in two communal areas. The report (FSRU, 1991) was completed immediately after the fieldwork. Its findings and recommendations covered market-ing, transport, input supply, prices, food security, and farmers' attitudes towards agricultural structural-adjustment policies.

125

o In Tanzania (Mohamed Idris, pers. comm; Johansson and Hoben, 1992), RRAs were conducted to find out about land tenure. Four teams of mid-level policymakers stayed five days in four villages, each chosen to represent different conditions. They found that communities and people were already doing land-use planning; that imposing a land-use map was misguided; that the government's top-down approach was wrong; and that new participatory approaches were needed.

o In Honduras and Panama, mapping has been used by indigenous Indians to defend their land (Denniston with Leake, 1995). Indigenous 'surveyors' visited zones and hand-drew maps, showing land use. The maps showed an almost perfect overlap between the remaining forest, savannah and wetland with the Indian territories. A consolidated master map served as the basis for presentations to government ministers, other indigenous peoples, conservationists and NGO groups at two-day conferences in the two capitals, Tegucigalpa and Panama City. The maps provided a graphic and credible base for political campaigns to legalize communal homelands and stem incursions by settlers and development by multinational companies. The Panamanian Minister for Government and Justice gave public support for legal recognition of Indian homelands in Darien. Two Miskito Indians from Nicaragua asked the Indian co-ordinators to help them with a mapping effort of their own.

o In the Gambia, Zambia, and the Philippines,[10] participatory seasonal calendars revealed school fees and expenses falling due at bad times of the year. This is during the rains, when food and cash are shortest, disease at a peak, and the need to work intense, aggravated further in Zambia by the high costs of Christmas. In consequence, the Zambian Government was in 1995 considering changing the dates of payment. The Gambian Government, within a few months of the finding, re-scheduled school fees for a time of year better for parents. Subsequently, more girls were going to school (pers. comms Eileen Kane (1994) and Haddy Sey (1995); Colletta and Perkins, 1995).

o In Nepal in 1992 the Tarai Research Network was established to improve the timeliness, accuracy and relevance of information flows between lowland farmers and agricultural policymakers. Seventeen network members were recruited, including academics, agricultural researchers and extensionists, to be available when needed. They were trained in PRA philosophy, behaviour and attitudes, and techniques. Three rounds of disaster assessments following flood, drought and hail damage helped focus and target relief and rehabilitation. A study in 44 villages solved the mystery of aggregate statistics showing slowly-rising yields while detailed field reports showed them declining: agricultural productivity jumped when irrigation or high-yielding varieties were introduced, after which long-term decline followed (Winrock International, 1995; Gill, 1996a and b).

Other recent policy-relevant findings from RRA and PRA illustrate a range of applications and insights:

o The position and lives of women in Morocco (Shah and Bourrarach, 1995): 'Women's problems and priorities vary sharply, between those

126

communities with access to basic services and infrastructure and those without, and between women of different social groups in the same community; and often differ from those of men.'

o Urban violence in Jamaica (Moser and Holland, 1996): 'Area stigma, from living in an area with a bad reputation for violence, makes it difficult to get employment.'

o Girls' education in The Gambia (Kane *et al.*, 1996): 'Girls denied access to primary education are bitter, and about a quarter of girls of school age have been "invisible", not considered eligible because they were about to be married.'

o Conservation management of two parks, in India and Pakistan (Gujja *et al.*, 1996): 'Local people are able to define wise [land] use and conservation for themselves in a responsible manner.'

o Land tenure in Guinea (Freudenberger, 1996): 'The belief of officials that customary tenure systems no longer existed was wrong: tenure systems persisted, were immensely diverse, and had to be taken into account in formulating policy.'

o Forest policy in the UK (Inglis and Guy, 1996): 'Village people in Scotland are interested in forests as a means of generating local livelihoods.'

General explorations

To date, these have taken mainly the form of participatory poverty assessments (PPAs). These have been part of some of the country poverty assessments sponsored by the World Bank. PRA methods were first used for PPAs in Ghana, and then in Zambia, Kenya, Tanzania, South Africa and Mozambique.[11] National teams were trained first in PRA. They then facilitated local people's own appraisal and analysis. The objectives were to explore local conceptions of poverty, vulnerability and relative well-being in poor urban and rural communities, to assess what poor people themselves saw as the most effective actions for poverty reduction, and to learn how their concerns and problems had changed and their perceptions of the effects of policy changes.

Approaches differed. In Ghana and Zambia, a trained team worked in more depth in fewer communities. In Kenya and Tanzania, multiple teams worked in more communities in a more standardized manner. In South Africa, 14 local organizations conducted thematic studies, 8 of them using PRA approaches and methods.

The Zambian PPA showed the policy potential. The rural part of the Zambian PPA was conducted in six representative villages, and the urban part in two communities. Two examples of specific insights were first, that rural women needed maize grinders, as until the urban subsidy on mealie meal was removed, they had been buying subsidized urban maize meal, not grinding their own as had been supposed; and second, how much remote rural people valued all-weather roads for access to markets and to medical treatment during the rains. More generally, the World Bank task manager found that the PPA provided 'extremely valuable insights when addressing issues of cross-sectoral balance . . . consistent messages were generated from these exercises which created a convincing composite picture of the priorities of the rural and urban poor in relation to public policy' (in Norton and Stephens, 1995: 15).

The Zambia PPA led to thematic explorations. The PPA found that health services were generally given higher priority than education. Wealth and well-being ranking in a study of the impact of user fees in health in Zambia presented clearly to policymakers the realities of how sharply the introduction of user fees had deterred and debarred the very poor from access to health services and schools. There was a wide gap between policy-in-principle and policy-in-practice regarding exemptions from charges for the destitute and those with infectious or chronic diseases (Booth, 1995; Booth et al., 1995; Milimo, 1996). The PPA also led to action. Its finding that hostile behaviour by health staff deterred poor people from seeking medical treatment was addressed by a programme of training launched by the Ministry of Health (Norton and Stephens, 1995: 14).

These thematic and general explorations indicate a potential. Well-trained and motivated teams can use mixes of participatory methods to generate up-to-date and valid policy-relevant insights. The realities of lowers – the poor, the marginalized, women, the remote – can then be presented credibly to uppers. Some policy changes, like the timing of school fees, can bring early gains to the poor for low cost. Others, like land-tenure and rights, are harder and need longer commitment. With this new repertoire of approaches and methods, the way is open for the state to be less self-deceiving (pp. 97–100), for central and powerful policymakers to be more up-to-date and more in touch (pp. 63–4), and for policy to fit and serve better the varied needs of the poor.

But credible knowledge does not ensure change. The crunch is whether, in both policy-in-theory and policy-in-practice, changes actually occur. Vested interests, inertia, transfers, the short-time horizons of politicians and bureaucrats all maintain the *status quo*. It is usually easier to delay and do nothing. Against such obstacles, many tactics can be used (Johnson, 1995; A. Shah, 1996). Experience points to the importance of patience and alertness, and to the personal understanding and commitment both of policymakers and of those who seek to change policy.

Why did it take us so long?

Faced with these many applications, experiences and potentials, the mystery is why we have not known about them earlier. If PRA approaches and methods are so powerful and popular, the puzzle is why it has taken until the 1990s for them to emerge: for different methodological streams to converge, coalesce and take off; for the menu of methods to be variously brought together, invented and evolved, leading to what appears to be self-sustaining cross-fertilization and growth; for so many applications to become evident. At a personal level, others like me in middle-age can wonder how for decades we have been working in rural development without knowing about all this. More generally, it is astonishing that it has taken so long, despite earlier pioneers, for the development community as a whole to discover not just the richness of the knowledge of local people, but more crucially their creative and analytical abilities.

Much of the mystery disappears if we look for explanation not in local people, but in ourselves, as outsider professionals. Our personal and professional concepts, values, methods and behaviour have prevented our learning. Our beliefs, behaviour and attitudes have been similar all over the world. Agricultural scientists, medical staff, teachers, officials, extension agents and others have believed their knowledge to be superior and that of farmers and rural people to be inferior; and even when the richness and validity of much local knowledge began to be recognized, we still believed that we had to be the ones who did the analysis.

So as outsiders most of us dominated. We lectured, holding sticks and wagging fingers; we interviewed impatiently, firing rapid questions; we interrupted, and did not listen; we 'put down' the poor and weak. Our reality blanketed that of local people. Our beliefs, demeanour, behaviour and attitudes were then self-validating. Treated as incapable, poor people behaved as incapable. They reflected the beliefs of the powerful. Their capabilities were hidden even from themselves. Nor did many outsider professionals know how to enable local people to express, share and extend their knowledge. The ignorance and inabilities of local people were then not just an illusion; they were an artefact of outsiders' behaviour and attitudes, of arrogant and ignorant manners of interacting.

For PRA to take off, different conditions had also to come together: recognition of past error and inadequacy; greater confidence, professionalism and inventiveness among NGOs; new approaches and methods, like those of agro-ecosystem analysis, still less than two decades old; an international community of communication; and a critical mass and momentum in which approaches and methods could be shared between disciplines, countries, and organizations.[12]

Most important of all has been learning that to facilitate PRA our behaviour and attitudes matter more than the methods. Perhaps then it is understandable that it has taken until now for new participatory approaches and methods, in their many forms and with their many labels, to cluster and coalesce, and to spread, as philosophy, repertoire and practice. Done well, they are still a small proportion of all rural and urban development activity. But they have spread and evolved, and continue to do so. We can ask ourselves whether, in the mid-1990s, their time has come; and whether they are one good reason for hope for the twenty-first century.

7

What Works and Why

This is just astonishing. We know each of these pieces because they are parts of our existence. But we have never thought of it all put together like this. This is our life and our history.
Villager in Sinthiane, Senegal, after completing a historical matrix, quoted in K. and M. Schoonmaker Freudenberger, 1994: 148

And we thought we were so foolish because we could not write. Yet look, we had all this information inside us.
A Tembomvura woman, Zimbabwe, to Ravai Marindo-Ranganai (1996: 188) after PRA modelling and diagramming

The PRA experience has led to insights and discoveries: that local people have largely unexpected capabilities for appraisal, analysis and planning; that the behaviour and attitudes of outsiders are critical in facilitation; that diagramming and visual sharing are popular and powerful in expressing and analysing complexity; and that sequences of PRA methods can be strong. The validity and reliability of information shared through PRA approaches and methods have usually been high. Explanations include the reversals and shifts inherent in PRA: from closed to open, and from etic to emic; from measuring to comparing; from individual to group; from verbal to visual; from higher to lower; from reserve to rapport; and from frustration to fun. Done well, these shifts and reversals reinforce a shift of power, from extracting to empowering. Local analysts then own the outputs in a process leading to planning and action.

The principles of RRA and PRA can be induced from experience: those shared by RRA and PRA are primarily epistemological – reversals of learning; optimal ignorance; triangulation; and seeking diversity. The principles additional in PRA are primarily personal and behavioural; handing over the stick; self-critical awareness; personal responsibility; and sharing. These contribute to quality through a rigour of trustworthiness based on judgement and of relevance based on context. The principles, methods and applications present practical means to enable local people to express and analyse their realities.

Insights from the PRA experience

Most historians believe that there is little new under the sun. What appear to be methodological 'discoveries' are often only rediscoveries (as pointed out in Rhoades, 1992). But some of the methods and sequences of PRA, and many of its applications, do appear new, in both their form and combinations. Practitioners of PRA are true to their own experience in sensing that they are on fresh ground. They are often surprised at first by what happens. The presentation and analysis of detailed knowledge in maps, models, matrices, diagrams and the like by local people can impress in a personal way which challenges preconceptions, and affects beliefs and behaviour. Some facilitators of PRA have been exhilarated by a sense of liberation and discovery. The reality of their experience demands respect; at the same time, there is a case for careful and critical analysis, and for evaluating and understanding what happens. To understand what is new, let us contrast traditional research and RRA on the one hand, and on the other participatory research and PRA.

Major differences between the more extractive data-gathering of traditional research and RRA, and the more participatory data-sharing, presentation and analysis of PRA, are evident in roles and in behaviour and attitudes. In data-gathering the outsiders dominate. 'We' determine the agenda, obtain and take possession of information, remove it, organize and analyse it, and plan and write papers and reports. We appropriate and come to own the information. We hunt, gather, amass, compile and process, and produce outputs. In PRA, in contrast, we encourage and allow 'them' to take the lead, to determine much of the agenda, to gather, express and analyse information, and to plan. We are facilitators, learners and consultants. Our activities are to establish rapport, to convene and catalyse, to enquire, to help in the use of methods, and to encourage local people to choose and improvise methods for themselves. We watch, listen and learn. Metaphorically, and sometimes actually, we 'hand over the stick' of authority. Local people then do many of the things outsiders formerly believed only they themselves could do.

The participatory orientation of PRA has given new impetus to the development of methods. Gifted facilitators have delighted in the lack of a blueprint. Participation has then generated diversity; local people play a part in interpreting, applying, and sometimes inventing methods themselves. Local people and outsiders alike are encouraged to improvise in a spirit of play. What is done is different each time, the outcome of a creative interaction. This helps to explain the explosion of inventions and insights of the early 1990s, among which five salient factors stand out. These describe some of what appears different and new about PRA: local people's capabilities; the value of relaxed rapport; diagramming and visual sharing; the expression and analysis of local complexity; and the power of sequences of methods.

Capabilities: they can do it

The discovery here has been that local people have capabilities of which outsiders have been largely, or totally, unaware. In learning what local people could do, it is as though a succession of dominoes has fallen.

First, local people have shown a far greater ability to map, model, observe, list, count, estimate, compare, rank, score and diagram than most outsiders had supposed. Much of this is through visualization, the physical expression and sharing of knowledge, judgement and analysis: people make maps, models, lists, matrices and diagrams; they walk transects and observe; they investigate and interview; they present information; they analyse and plan. In consequence, they are more in command of the process, they own and retain more of the information, and they are better placed to identify their priorities for action, and to determine and control that action.

Participatory mapping and modelling (Mascarenhas and Kumar, 1991) was a striking finding. An earlier work on mental maps (Gould and White, 1974) did not reveal fully the richness of detail and discrimination expressed later by rural people in countries of the South. Since at least the early 1980s (Kenyon, 1983), the power and popularity of participatory mapping had been known. Rural people in the South seem to have more extensive and detailed mental maps than the urban people in the North who earlier were the main source of insight; and given the right conditions and materials, they can express them visibly on the ground or on paper, either as maps or as three-dimensional models (for example, of watersheds). These have shown the huts, houses and people in a village (social, census and health maps), the surrounding village area (resource maps and models), or specialized information (topic maps). By the mid-1990s tens of thousands of such maps and models had been created in at least 50 countries. As with mapping, so with listing, counting, estimating, comparing, ranking, scoring and diagramming, people showed themselves capable of expressing and sharing their knowledge far beyond normal professional expectations.

Analysis and planning followed. Local people analysed, ranked and scored problems and opportunities as they perceived them. They worked out their preferences – for improving their farming systems, for managing and using common property resources, for better livelihoods, for health interventions, for species mixes in tree nurseries, for the qualities of new varieties of a crop, for amenities and their location, for development actions in their communities, and so on. It became common in PRA to refer not to respondents or informants, but to mappers, analysts and planners. And it became a rule in good practice to acknowledge their names in writing on maps and diagrams.

Monitoring, evaluation and research were other dominoes to fall. In Indonesia 1500 farmers' groups were reported to be using their own maps to monitor pest infestations and plan action (pers. comm. Russ Dilts, 1995). In Bangladesh and elsewhere, farmers used the maps they had drawn of their farms to monitor yields. Many applications have been found in participatory monitoring and evaluation (McPherson, 1995). Having learnt that they could use the tools of mapping, matrices, scoring and so on, local people have sometimes adopted these for their own purposes. In Tamil Nadu, Sheelu Francis (pers. comm.) found women making maps locating violence against women in order to identify patterns and to plan action. In Wajir District, Kenya, groups of pastoralists use matrices to analyse conditions, including conflict, for their own early warning systems, monitoring indicators which they judge to be relevant month by month (pers. comm. Matthew Law, 1996).

Facilitation came in parallel. Local people already familiar with a PRA approach and methods have proved good facilitators (P. Shah *et al.*, 1991; Shah, 1995: 93–4), and often better than outsiders. The Aga Khan Rural

Support Programme (AKRSP) (India) found that village volunteers were invited by other villages to come as facilitator/consultants (pers. comm. Parmesh Shah). A village volunteer wrote to AKRSP staff that they were going to carry out a PRA but 'you do not need to come' (pers. comm. Apoorva Oza). In the Gambia, teenage girls were trained in PRA methods for use with their peers in an enquiry into girls' education (Colletta and Perkins, 1995). In Kenya, villagers who had taken part in PRA processes have been found to make 'excellent facilitators for PRA work in other sub-locations' (Adriance, 1995: 44).

A further domino to fall has been providing learning experiences and training for outsiders.[1] In urban centres, local people have presented their realities and priorities to policymakers and urban élites: in Colombo, Dhaka and Gaborone they have recreated and presented their visual analyses. In their villages, they have become trainers, providing field-learning experience for outsiders; in Western Kenya, traditional herbalists held a workshop on attitudes and practices relating to sexually transmitted diseases and condom use, for the benefit of a team applying PRA to HIV/AIDS (pers. comm. Tilly Sellers); in Uttar Pradesh and Karnataka in India, Sam Joseph of ActionAid has pioneered approaches to field exposure for outsiders such as the staff of international NGOs and aid agencies. The trainers are farmers; it is they who manage the process. They receive a fee and decide how to use it. The visitors are hosted overnight in the villages, take part in local activities, and watch and listen while the farmer–trainers demonstrate PRA methods and analysis (PIA, 1995). In all this, both the participatory methods and familiar local materials have helped in enabling local people to express and analyse their knowledge and preferences, and to take command of the process.

To enable these capabilities to be expressed, the practical principle has been to assume that people can do something until proved otherwise, and to encourage them by example. A Zimbabwean villager said:

> At first we thought you were crazy, playing with mud and stones and we did what we could to humour you, but later especially after the area modelling exercise it was exciting to see one's village on the ground. (Marindo-Ranganai, 1995: 61)

Once they have started, local people often surprise themselves, and then are proud and empowered. The PRA video made by the Self-Help Support Programme in Sri Lanka has as its title a villager's remark: 'We could do what we never thought we could'.

Behaviour and rapport

The second insight here has been the importance of outsiders' behaviour and of relaxed rapport established early in the process.

Rapport is a key to facilitating participation. Relaxed rapport between outsiders and local people, and some measure of trust, are minimum conditions for PRA. In the past, two extreme types of interaction between the two groups have missed major opportunities: the rushed and unself-critical rural development tourist has lacked the time and sensitivity to get far beyond formal mutual misunderstanding; and the fastidious social anthropologist has allowed so much time and shown such sensitivity that she or he has come to believe that only through prolonged residence can good rapport and helpful insights be gained. The two contrasting and conflicting cultures – of rushed visitor, and of resident participant-observer – have concealed the scope for gaining rapport early and well, and early enough and well enough for the honest and accurate sharing of detailed knowledge and values. To a hardened old hand at rural development tourism (the senior official: 'I was born and brought up in a village', 'I am a farmer myself', 'You can't pull the wool over my eyes') this might seem unnecessary: he (most are men) knows it all and assumes he has an automatic good rapport with all local people. To a seasoned social anthropologist (the university professor: 'It took a year before they would tell me that . . ') this might seem an affront: it would be unfair if others in a short time could achieve much of what had taken her (relatively more are women) so long.[2] For anyone who has endured and struggled through months of residence and participant-observation to achieve rapport and insight, learning a new language and living a new life, it could seem unlikely and even unwelcome that other outsiders should find ways to facilitate analysis and gain understanding so quickly, and often with pleasure, participation and fun.

Empirically, though, the recurrent finding with PRA has been that if the initial behaviour and attitudes of outsiders are relaxed and right, and if the process can start, the methods of PRA themselves foster further rapport. Early actions by outsiders can include transparent honesty about who they are and what they are doing; and participation in local activities, especially being taught and performing local tasks. Personal demeanour counts, showing humility, respect, patience and interest in what people have to say and show; wandering around and not rushing; and paying attention, listening, watching and not interrupting. Having confidence that 'they can do it', and transmitting that confidence, again and again enables local people to get started with activities like participatory mapping, diagramming or matrix scoring. Then they quickly lose themselves in the activity and are often pleased and proud of what they find they know and can do. In contrast to questionnaires, they are not simply responding, giving answers to be recorded and removed. The information is theirs. They express it and own it, but share it. They often enjoy the creativity of what they are doing, and what they see and learn through their presentation and analysis. The pleasure, fun and utility of what they have been helped to undertake express themselves in rapport. By reinforcing rapport, PRA methods thus sustain and strengthen the participatory process of which they are a part.

Diagramming and visual sharing

The third discovery here is the popularity and power of participatory diagramming and visual sharing.

Diagramming and visual sharing are common elements in much PRA. With a questionnaire survey, information is transferred from the words of the person interviewed to the paper of the questionnaire schedule. The learning is one-off. The information becomes personal and private, unverified, and processed and appropriated by the interviewer. In contrast, with visual sharing of a map, model, diagram, or units (stones, seeds, small fruits etc.) or lengths (sticks etc.) used for counting, estimating, ranking, scoring, and comparing, it is open to all who are present to participate. Different people add details, and crosscheck and correct each other. The learning is progressive. The information is visible, semi-permanent, and public to the group, and can be checked, verified, amended, added to, and owned, by the participants.

For example, in participatory mapping and modelling, villagers draw and model their villages and resources, deciding what to include, and debating, adding and modifying detail. Everyone can see what is being 'said' because it is being 'shown'. In shared diagramming, information is diagrammed to represent, for example, seasonal changes in dimensions such as rainfall, agricultural labour, income, indebtedness, food supply and migration. Paper can be used for diagrams, but the ground and other local materials have the advantage of being 'theirs', media which villagers, whether literate or non-literate, can command and alter with confidence. The diagram also builds up a visible local checklist or agenda.

Expressing and analysing complexity

The fourth discovery is that visual arrangements, tools and materials can be combined in many ways and so applied in many forms. The arrangements, tools and materials include maps, models, cards, lists, symbols, diagrams, matrices, counters, the ground, chalk, paper, pens. New combinations and applications are continuously being improvised and invented. Analysing this in terms of what people do, six main activities stand out: mapping and modelling; listing; sequencing; sorting and ranking; using numbers to count, estimate and score; and linking and relating (see Table 7.1).

Table 7.1: Dimensions, activities, forms and materials

Dimension/character	Activities	Forms and materials
Spatial	Mapping and modelling	maps on the ground or paper, chalk, pens, symbols
Nominal	Collecting, naming, listing	collections, cards, symbols, lists
Temporal	Sequencing	ground, paper, cards, . symbols
Ordinal[3]	Sorting, comparing, ranking	cards, symbols, matrices
Numerical	Counting, estimating comparing, scoring	seeds, stones, sticks, matrices
Relational	Linking, relating	Venns, cards, symbols, lines

These activities can be combined in many ways. Combinations in sequence enable the expression and analysis of local complexity and diversity, for example:

o *Naming, listing, sequencing, comparing and scoring.* A group of villagers in Senegal named and sequenced six times of crisis, listed 18 coping strategies, made a matrix, and scored the boxes for the prevalence of each strategy in each crisis (Figure 7.1).

o *Listing and linking.* As part of the Zambia Participatory Poverty Assessment, a group of women first listed problems faced by people in their area, and then showed these in a causal flow diagram (Figure 7.2).

o *Mapping, linking, comparing and estimating.* Farmers in Kenya made maps of their farms, and then drew linkage lines for nutrient flows to and from their compost pits and cattle pens. They then placed seeds on the lines to indicate the volume and importance of each flow, counted these and wrote in the numbers (Figure 7.3).

o *Listing, linking, comparing, estimating.* A villager in Vietnam listed on cards the causes and effects of deforestation, and then diagrammed these with chalk on the ground, and scored each card for significance with seeds.

o *Naming and listing, comparing and scoring.* Street children in Kathmandu, Nepal, listed illnesses and hurts to which they were subject, and their characteristics, and then scored these and indicated where or from whom they sought treatment (Table 7.2).

o *Naming and listing, sequencing* (before and after), *comparing and scoring.* A group of herders in Somaliland named 25 water supplies which had been improved, listed 45 criteria for assessing their quality and utility, and then scored each box in the resulting matrix twice out of ten, once for before improvement and once for after (Joseph, 1994).

With visualizations, people need materials to express diversity and differentiation. A purist school leans towards always asking local people to choose and use their own materials. This makes for control, ownership and creativity. Suitable local materials may, however, be lacking, or they may be difficult to use or see. In that case, providing different seeds, colours of chalk, powders, crayons, pencils or pens, or other symbols or materials, can help.

Sequences

Sequences of participatory methods are both powerful and popular (see e.g. P. Shah *et al.* 1991). To take some examples:

o with participatory mapping, villagers draw not one, but several maps, which become successively more detailed and useful, or which present new and complementary information. The map is then used as a reference for other planning, and is retained by villagers for their own monitoring and evaluation (as with integrated pest management);

o social mapping shows people, social groups, health and other household characteristics, leading on to identification of key informants, and then to discussions with them and analysis by them;[4]

Strategy \ Crisis	WWII 39/45	Locust invasion 1950	Fire in village 1967	Drought 1973	Rat invasion 1976	2nd locust invasion 1988
Eat nëow tree fruit	•• ••	•• ••	••	•• ••	•• ••	•
Eat wild leaves	••• •••	••• •••	•	•	•	
Eat manioc	••••••	•••••••				
Eat dugoor tree fruit	••					
Food aid	•• ••	•• ••	•••	•• ••	•• •	•
Cultivate and weave cotton	•• ••		•••			
Eat millet bran	•• ••		•••			
Hunting	••• •••	••• •	••		••• ••	
Eat cowpeas	••• •••	••• •••	•• ••	••	••	•••
Dig trenches against locusts	••• •	••• ••				
Trade nëow fruit for millet	••• ••	••• ••	••	••	•	
Sell chickens	••• •••	••• •••	••• •••	••• •••	••• •••	••• •••
Rural → rural Rural → urban migration				••• •••	••• •••	••• ••
International migration				•••• ••••	•••• ••••	••••••
Sell weak animals to buy food for strong			••• •	••• •••	••• •	••• •
Buy flour				••• ••		
Cut branches for animal feed				••• ••		
Eat own animals	••• ••			••• •••		

Figure 7.1: Historical matrix: coping strategies in times of crisis.
Source: Fields, Fallow and Flexibility: Natural Resource Management in Ndam Mor Fademba, Senegal. IIED, London, 1993, reproduced in K. and M. Schoonmaker Freudenberger, 1994.

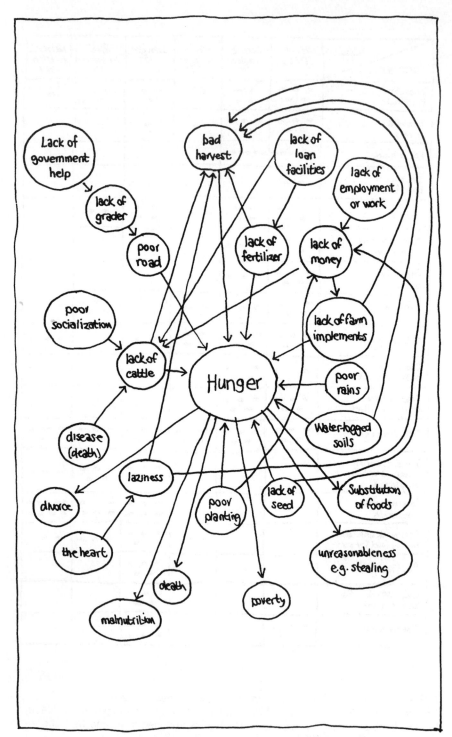

Figure 7.2: Flow diagram of causes of hunger by 22 women, Hamaumbwe Village, Monze, Zambia, 15 October 1993. Source: World Bank 1994: 32

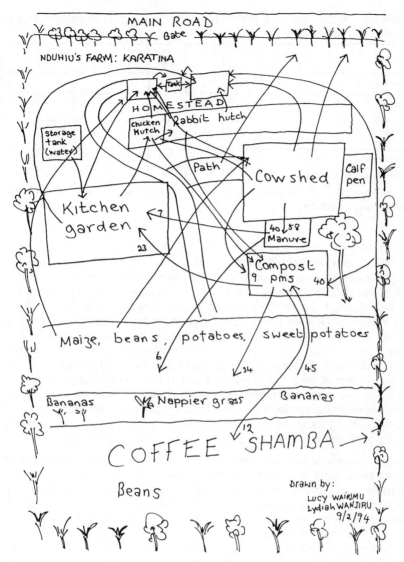

Figure 7.3: A farmer's nutrient flow diagramming on her farm map, Karatina, Kenya, 1994

○ a participatory resource map leads to planning transect walks in which villagers who made the map act as guides for outsiders. The transects in turn lead to the identification and discussion of problems and opportunities, which then lead to listing and ranking options or 'best bets';

○ matrix scoring or ranking elicits villagers' criteria of value for a class of items (trees, vegetables, fodder grasses, varieties of a crop or animal, sources of credit, market outlets, fuel types etc.) which leads into discussion of preferences and actions.

Table 7.2: Matrix made by street children in Kathmandu showing impact of illnesses and action taken

Illness	Boil	Dog bite	Wound	Scabies	Diarrhoea	Hit by vehicle	Cold	Fracture	Hunger	Fever
Frequency	4	5	5	3	5	2	5	3	5	3
Degree of pain	5	4	3	3	3	5	2	4	5	5
Effect on earning	5	3	1	0	5	3	2	5	2	5
Treatment sought at/ with	Free homeo-pathic clinic	NGO clinic/state hospital	NGO clinic	None – friends	None – friends	NGO clinic/junk-yard owner	None	NGO clinic/state hospital	Friends/ junk-yard owner	Homeo-pathic clinic

Source: Baker, 1996: 58.

○ a participatory resource map of an area of degraded forest, and a root-stock census of quadrats in the forest carried out by villagers, leads to a calculation of numbers of trees to be planted; and debate and analysis leads to people's decisions about the proportions of different trees to be planted, and the numbers required in tree nurseries (M.K. Shah, 1995a);
○ a village social map provides an up-to-date household listing which is then used for well-being or wealth ranking of households which leads in turn to focus groups with different categories of people who then express their different preferences, resulting in discussion, negotiation and re-conciliation of priorities (Swift and Umar, 1991; Mukherjee, 1992);
○ village role-plays separately by women, men and boys to illustrate the values of woodland lead to a listing of values which are then drawn on cards. The cards are then scored separately by the women, men and boys, each with 100 seeds to allocate between the cards (HSWG, 1995: 57–9).[5]

Longer sequences have been devised and used in fuller PRA activities. In Kenya these have been part of a stepwise sequence (PID and NES 1989). In India, for example with the AKRSP, the sequences have been less codified and more in a style of systematic improvisation, though with specialized sequences for appraisal, planning and action with degraded forests as above, or with identifying and working with the poorest.

The power of such sequences is fourfold: (i) the commitment of participants increases, making further action more likely, more spontaneous and more sustainable; (ii) sequences cross-check and reveal errors or omissions in earlier presentations; (iii) the different activities interact cumulatively, each activity adding a dimension and details which qualify and enrich others, so that taken together the whole becomes more than the sum of the parts; and (iv) all concerned learn through the process, through local people sharing what they know, through observation and through analysis.

In ways such as these, participatory methods fit well with a flexible learning-process approach which is more open-ended and adaptable than some earlier RRA; they also have the advantage that they generally enable local people to use their own categories and criteria, to generate their own agenda, and to assess and indicate their own priorities.

Validity and reliability

These five insights or discoveries illustrate how PRA approaches and methods present a new repertoire for participatory learning and action. As with all new developments, strengths and weaknesses must be assessed. Evaluation can have many criteria. Some are the scale and quality of contributions to the ends and means of the new consensus – responsible well-being, enhanced capabilities, livelihood security, equity, and sustainability, especially empowering lowers, enabling them to express and analyse their realities. Others concern credibility. But first, let us start with the conventional scientific criteria. These are the validity and reliability of information shared.

Validity here refers to the closeness of a finding to a physical reality, and reliability refers to the constancy of findings. Highly valid findings are also highly reliable. Through a systematic bias, however, reliability can be high but validity low. Validity and reliability are not absolute values. There can be trade-offs where lower validity and reliability are more cost-effective through lower cost, greater relevance, more timely availability, and/or offsetting gains through participation, local learning and ownership of data, sustainability and quality of process. But here let us apply conventional tests. These can be applied to accuracy and detail where something can be counted, measured or estimated, comparing RRA and PRA approaches with others.

The four main areas where RRA and PRA have generated numerical data or insights which can be compared with those from questionnaire surveys or other conventional sources are: farm and household surveys; wealth and well-being ranking; participatory mapping and village censuses; and rainfall.

Farm and household surveys

In three cases comparisons have been made between the findings of an RRA approach and a conventional questionnaire survey.

○ Michael Collinson's (1981) exploratory survey of a farming system, involving some 20 professional person-days, was never contradicted in any major way by the subsequent longer-drawn-out and more expensive verification survey which represented the major commitment of professional time and funds.

○ Diane Rocheleau and her team (Rocheleau *et al.*, 1989) working on agroforestry in Kenya used a chain of informal in-depth interviews, and group interviews, and compared the results with a survey of a formal randomized sample of 63 households. They found that 'the formal survey took three times as long and reproduced the same results as the group interviews and chain of interviews, with less detail and coherence' (ibid: 21).

○ Andy Inglis (1990, 1991) led a team which used a repertoire of RRA techniques to gather local forestry knowledge in Sierra Leone in an area where a lengthy questionnaire with 278 questions had already been applied. The RRA results were presented four days after the last location was surveyed, but the questionnaire report was still not available six months after the completion of fieldwork. Comparisons of the questionnaire survey and RRA data showed sharp discrepancies in two localities

141

where the questionnaire survey's findings were implausible and suspect. As Inglis points out:

> if information is wrong to begin with, no amount of statistical manipulation will enable it to help the project staff make good decisions . .
> In contrast, the RRA survey was completed in a much shorter time, the results have been produced in specific locational reports that can be individually used as discussion papers in the field in follow-up surveys. As research biases, mistakes and omissions are admitted and not lost in a mass of questionnaire codes, the decision maker can see how the information was generated, how important factors were revealed, and how the best bets were arrived at. (Inglis 1990: 107)

In these three cases, with good practice, the outcomes of the RRA approach, compared with the more formal questionnaire, were variously more valid, less costly, more timely and more useful.

Bad practice is also common. A cautionary counter-example can serve as a warning. Johan Pottier (1992) analysed a one-week survey through interviews with 30 farmers in Northern Zambia, described by the researcher as an RRA. Pottier argues persuasively that in such hurried interviews an insensitivity to the context, to who is being met, to what is being said, and why, can lead to misleading conclusions, in this case that food security had been enhanced by growing maize. The investigation was, it seems, rushed and wrong. Hectic one-off individual interviews are bad practice whatever the label attached to them; and the findings can mislead by being reliable but invalid, and so maintaining myths.

Wealth and well-being ranking

Ranking and scoring for social characteristics have long been part of the repertoire of social anthropologists. People in communities rank other individuals or households for characteristics as varied as aggressiveness, drunkenness, industriousness, or more commonly some concept of respect, honour, wealth or well-being (Pelto and Pelto, 1978: 82–7; *RRA Notes* 15, 1992).

The most common method is sorting cards into piles, carried out either by local individuals in private, or by groups. Different informants often use different numbers of piles for the same community, but evidence is consistent in finding close correlations in rank orders between different informants. Sydel Silverman (1966: 905) found that 'there was high agreement in the relative rank of most persons' when three informants in an Italian community card-sorted households according to their criterion of *rispetto* (prestige). This has been borne out by much subsequent wealth or well-being ranking, including the original studies by Barbara Grandin among Maasai in Kenya.[6]

Silverman and Grandin as social anthropologists can be expected to have developed good rapport before the exercise. The test is whether without a social anthropological training and relationship, the method can also be reliable and valid. Those who have facilitated such ranking exercises have usually found them easier than expected (see *RRA Notes* 15) and usually

report high correlations between the rankings given by different informants or groups.

Well-being or wealth ranking has now come commonly to incorporate
cross-checking. Earlier, Polly Hill's three informants in Nigeria thrashed out
discrepancies between themselves (Hill, 1972: 59). In a PRA mode, on similar lines, MYRADA in South India evolved a method of successive approximation in which separate groups rank households, and then meet to
reconcile differences (pers. comm. Vidya Ramachandran), a procedure now
used in selecting households for anti-poverty programmes in many countries.

Comparisons with questionnaire surveys have shown that wealth ranking
takes less time and generates more complex and nuanced findings. Ian
Scoones' (1995a) comparison of questionnaire survey and wealth-ranking
data from fieldwork in Zimbabwe in the latter half of the 1980s led him to
question the conventional assumption that surveys always provided better
data. A team from the Christian Medical College, Vellore, South India has
compared a formal questionnaire survey with wealth ranking for identifying
the rural poor. The researchers concluded that questionnaire survey using an
outsiders' 'professional' classification was only 57 per cent accurate while the
community classification was 97 per cent accurate in identifying the economic levels of households: 'This confirms that community classification by
wealth ranking is accurate. Also it highlights the limitation of the professional classification specially when it deals with economic level' (Rajaratnam
et al., 1993: passim, 17 and 22, and pers. comm. Abel Rajaratnam).[7]

Ranking exercises do not always converge on consensus. There can be
significant differences between the values, scores and ranks of women and
men, and of different groups. These are, however, not weaknesses of the
method, but expressions of different realities.

Distortions can occur. In a group, one person may dominate and over-
rule others. With well-being ranking some analysts have been reluctant or
unreliable in ranking themselves, their near relatives or their close friends.
Shared concepts are also needed for consistent rankings. In general though,
as most of the examples cited suggest, close correlations are found between
the rankings given by different local analysts. This appears to be where
four conditions obtain: where information is common knowledge; where
criteria are commonly held and well understood; where what is ranked is a
matter of intense interest; and where analysts do not perceive advantages
in giving false or misleading judgements.[8] These conditions have, to date,
quite commonly prevailed.

Participatory mapping and censuses

Participatory mapping, in which local people make their own maps, is
probably the most widespread PRA method. In participatory resource
mapping, local people present their view of their natural resources. In
Honduras, cartographers were surprised to find that resource maps hand-
drawn by Indians were often accurate in their proportions, and that existing government maps were just as often inaccurate. Cartographers from
both the Honduran and Panamanian National Institutes of Geography said
that the Indian map of the Mosquitia was superior to any maps they could

143

have done (Denniston, 1995: 37, 39). In Nepal, resource maps have been found to be 'far more accurate than the sketch maps produced by field workers in isolation from local forest users' and to provide 'a more reliable and cost-effective way to collect, store and display information than methods and formats that were previously used' (Jackson *et al.*, 1994: 8).

In participatory social mapping, local people show the location of households. In India in 1991 this was extended by Sheelu Francis and others into participatory censuses. Census maps have shown social details, representing people and household characteristics with local materials such as different seeds, stones and vegetables, or markers such as *bindis* (the small spots Indian women place on their foreheads). A practice developed by Anusuya and Perumal Naicker of Kethanayakanpatti village near Madurai in Tamil Nadu is to have a card for each household and mark details with symbols on the card. These have been placed on the ground on the maps or models, indicating for each household the numbers of men, women and children, assets owned, wealth/poverty, the handicapped, immunization status, education and other information. With an informed group or person, a participatory census of a small village has been conducted in less than an hour, and then other information added by 'interviewing the map'.

The propensity of questionnaire surveys to generate misleading census data is well known. There can be many reasons for over or under reporting and recording in a face-to-face verbal interview, and it is easy to miss households and people. Campbell *et al.*, (1979: 36), in three villages in Nepal, compared results from a questionnaire survey conducted by experienced investigators, with those from their own participant observation. They found discrepancies in 12 per cent of the households. These averaged 3 persons per household.

The evidence from participatory social mapping presents a contrast. Seven examples are known where comparisons or cross-checking have occurred:

○ In May 1991, in Ramasamypatti village, near Tiruchuli, in Tamil Nadu, a triangulation of censuses took place. In a PRA training organized by SPEECH, an NGO, four groups of between approximately 5 and 15 villagers used different methods of analysis and presentation: two did social mapping direct on to paper; one made a ground model of the village with a card for each household; and one did a seed census on to a map drawn on a floor. Each group independently generated a figure for the total population of the village. The four estimates were the same – 355. A few discrepancies concerning occupations were quickly resolved in a village meeting.
○ In 1992, the National Council for Applied Economic Research undertook research to compare the costs, accuracy and reliability of a sample survey using questionnaires and RRA/PRA methods. The demographic data derived from the participatory mapping were much closer to the recent national census than those derived from the normal questionnaire survey. The study (NCAER, 1993: 91) reported that: 'The overall conclusion . . . supports the claim of RRA/PRA adherents that it provides a highly reliable village-level database on quantitative as well as qualitative variables'.
○ Also in 1992, a health-research team facilitated social mapping in a remote village, Mavatpura, in Sabarkantha District in Gujarat, giving a

total population of 598 persons. A random 10 per cent sample house-to-house check matched exactly with the participatory census, and no major discrepancy was found during a cross-check of the map with a different group of villagers four months later. Exact numbers of births and deaths by household over the previous year, including the age at death and the causes in local terms were also given, and confirmed with the same women on a second visit (SEWA-Rural Research Team, 1996: 91–2).

○ In August 1993, in the village of San Mauricio, Samar Island, the Philippines, about 20 villagers took part in census mapping (including information on education, land size and tenurial status of land as well as people) for their village of over 60 households. The Barangay captain and secretary said this was unnecessary as they had data on numbers of males and females and their ages from their own 1992 census and partially completed 1993 census. But as the participatory mapping proceeded, they noticed discrepancies and corrected what they found to be errors in their own data, in the end taking all their census data from the participatory process (pers. comm. Ditdit Pelegrina, 1993).

○ In 1994, in Kabera village in Uganda, general counts by two groups of villagers both gave the same figure of 382, confirmed again through a breakdown by both groups which in each case gave 66 men, 94 women and 222 children (Osuga and Mutayisa, 1994: 5).

○ In 1994 in Kottam village, near Paraikulum in Tamil Nadu, four social maps were made in parallel and then transferred to paper in the village. This gave populations of 239, 239, 242 and 247 respectively. On checking it was found that the 242 map included three cases of double-counting of relatives, and the 247 map, made by a small group on the edge of the village, included a household, omitted by all the others, that was in dispute with the rest of the village (pers. comm. Jules Pretty). Through cross-checking, accuracy was refined to converge on a single agreed figure.

○ In the Gambia, PRA methods including participatory social-educational mapping found that one quarter of school-age girls (those who were pregnant, married or about to be married) had been missed by enrolment statistics since they had not been counted by villagers in the initial census (Colletta and Perkins, 1995).

In assessing these findings, care is needed: we have to ask whether there is a bias towards reporting bad news about questionnaires, and good news about PRA methods. PRA methods can be done badly. They have been known at first to omit people such as minority groups, migrants, outcastes, those who live on the fringes or outside villages, and even those with only thatch on their huts. The evidence suggests, however, that where there is common knowledge about people in a community, where a group of people is trying to 'get it right', and where care is taken to ask about people who may have been left out, participatory social mapping is accurate.

Rainfall data

Farmers will often readily estimate days and amount of rainfall by month. In 1988 two farmers in Wollo in Ethiopia estimated numbers of days of rainfall by month for the previous five years, and also indicated the pattern they remembered from their childhood (Conway, 1988; ERCS, 1988: 50–52). A common method now is for local analysts to arrange a line of 12 stones for the months of the local calendar and then estimate rainfall using either seeds for numbers of days of rain by month or broken sticks for relative volume, or both. Some farmers in India have preferred to indicate depth of soil moisture by month as being more relevant for agricultural purposes (pers. comms. J. Mascarenhas for Karnataka and Sam Joseph for Rajasthan). A refinement, invented by women in Galkada village, Badulla District, Sri Lanka in January 1992, is to space the seeds to indicate the distribution of days of rain within each month.

The question is how valid such data are. Farmers' data on rainfall have several times been found to differ from those of nearby rainfall stations. At Nugu Dam in H.D. Kote, Karnataka, in August 1990, a discrepancy was found but not analysed further. In rapid-catchment analysis in Kenya (Pretty, 1990), when farmers' patterns of rainfall differed in six different catchments and also differed from the 'real' data from a nearby rainfall station, this was judged to reflect spatial heterogeneity, without ruling out the possibility that the farmers were wrong (pers. comm. J. Pretty).

The only detailed analysis of comparisons to date comes from Nepal. It was there in May 1990 near Lumle that farmers in Maramche village for the first time indicated volume and numbers of days of rainfall per month using seeds for days and sticks for volume. In 45 minutes, they presented first a normal year and then a pattern which they said occurred one year in five. Gerard Gill's (1991b) painstaking analysis of their perceptions compared with 20 years of daily rainfall data at the nearby rainfall station shows that what initially appeared as discrepancies where the farmers were 'wrong' turned out on closer examination to show respects in which the farmers' judgements were superior to that of the averaged met-station data. Gill's title 'But How Does It Compare with the REAL Data?' captures the irony of the assumption that 'scientifically' measured data are necessarily superior. More balanced conclusions are that there are different realities, that farmers' realities are likely to be linked to agricultural utility and weighted by recent experience, and that the issue is whose reality counts, in what contexts, and for what purposes.

These four sets of evidence from measurements and numbers all indicate high validity and reliability for data generated by RRA and PRA approaches and methods. There has, though, been much bad practice (see Chapter 10, pp. 211–14). Continuous critical assessment, recognizing and learning from negative cases, remains vital.

Reversals and reality

Most of those who have innovated in developing PRA have been practitioners, concerned with what works and what will work better, not academic theorists concerned with why it works. They have been searching not for new theories or principles but for new and better ways of learning and of relating to local people. For them, the power and utility of RRA and PRA, undertaken with rapport and self-critical rigour, are common experience and empirical facts: they know that they work, and that done well they can lead to better local development. But the why? questions remain, leaving issues of explanation. There is now enough experience to suggest some answers.

At the practical level, much of the explanation can be found in reversals, with shifts of orientation, activity and relationships away from past normal professional practice. Six stand out: from closed to open; from individual to group; from verbal to visual; from measuring to comparing; from higher to lower; and from reserve and frustration to rapport and fun.

From closed to open

The pervasive shift or reversal is from closed to open. This can be expressed as from etic to emic, from the knowledge, categories and values of outsider professionals to those of insider local people. The reversal is like a turning inside out, an expression and presentation of inner personal, family, community and local realities to outsiders and the outside world. These are not knowable by outsiders in advance. In contrast with questionnaire interviews, semi-structured interviews (Grandstaff and Grandstaff, 1987b) are more open, conversations (Scrimshaw and Hurtado, 1987) more so, and PRA mapping and diagramming often most open of all. In a semi-structured interview there can be a checklist for reference, but not a pre-set sequence of questions; and a value can be set on probing, on pursuing leads, on serendipity. In conversations, there can be greater freedom and equality. In PRA methods such as participatory mapping and modelling, matrix ranking and scoring, Venn or chapati diagramming and well-being ranking, insiders can be in charge of the agenda and detail, not only free to express their knowledge and values but encouraged and enabled to do so. The shift is from pre-set and closed to participatory and open.

From measuring to comparing

Normal professional training is to make absolute measurements. So if trends or changes are to be identified, or conditions compared between households or between places, measurements are made either at different times, of different things or in different places. Schoolteachers often value correct measurement more than independent judgement in their pupils. Our preoccupation with numbers drives us to ask 'how much?' For sensitive subjects like income, such questions commonly sow suspicion, wreck rapport, and generate misleading data.

Often, though, all that is needed for practical purposes is values which are relative, not absolute. Comparisons without measurements have advantages: involving reflection and judgement, they are easier and quicker to express; they can be elicited for trends and changes without formal baseline data; and they are less sensitive, as has been shown by wealth and well-being ranking, and by seasonal analysis – how income compares between months is easier to gauge and less threatening to reveal than are absolute figures. Comparisons, as with matrix ranking and scoring, can in a short time elicit complex and detailed information and judgements of value inaccessible by other methods without great labour. Moreover, trends, comparisons and weightings lend themselves to visual sharing, with all its potential gains in participation, cross-checking and progressive approximation and learning. Comparing is usually easier, quicker, cheaper and less sensitive than measuring.

From individual to group

Normal investigations stress individual interviews. Professionals' need for numbers is met by questionnaire surveys: individual or household schedules generate commensurable statistical data. In PRA, discussions with individuals can and do take place, but there is relatively more attention to groups and participatory analysis by groups.

Group dynamics can present problems, such as dominance by one person or an influential lineage, faction or ethnic group, or by men (Mosse, 1993 and 1995). Facilitators do, though, have a repertoire of ways of handling this: 'sacrificing' one of themselves, who draws a dominant person out of the group by requesting a separate discussion; social mapping and diagramming to learn about social groups; and sequences of meetings with separate groups, often women. Personal commitment and sensitivity on the part of facilitators are the key. How best to convene and facilitate groups remains an area for learning and invention.

At the same time, the advantages of groups have been undervalued. Typically, group members have an overlapping spread of knowledge which covers a wider field than that of any single person. Groups can also generate numbers with observable mutual checking through self-surveys, whether verbal or visual.

Contrary to many outsiders' beliefs, sensitive subjects are sometimes more freely discussed in groups, for example topics individuals would not wish to discuss alone with a stranger. Several sources have indicated that village women in parts of India will freely discuss intimate sexual matters in groups. Among Bhutanese refugees in Nepal, Rachel Hinton (pers. comm. and 1995: 24) found as a social anthropologist that with participatory methods in groups refugees shared sensitive information about illegal activities more willingly and accurately than in the conventional context of participant-observation and semi-structured interviewing.

From verbal to visual

With traditional questionnaire surveys and semi-structured interviewing, most of the transfer or exchange of information is verbal, and often one-to-one. This contrasts with participatory mapping and diagramming where the information shared is visual, and often created as a group activity.

With visual analysis, relationships and process change. The topic and method may be determined, or at least suggested, by the outsider, but the outsider's role is not to extract through questions but to initiate a process. The outsider is a convenor and facilitator, the insiders are actors and analysts. The outsider hands over control, and insiders determine the agenda, categories and details. Information is built up cumulatively, and cross-checking is often spontaneous. Knowledge overlaps. If a dozen women diagram a census map of their small community, showing women, men, children, handicapped persons and so on, not everything may be known by any one woman, but each item may be known by several of them. Groups often build up collective and creative enthusiasm, fill in gaps left by others, and add and correct detail. Debate can be lively because everyone can see what is being said. The visuals then present an agenda for discussion, and it is the visuals rather than the people that are interviewed.

Visual methods can also be empowering for those who are weak, disadvantaged and not alphabetically literate (Robinson-Pant, 1995). Taking literacy to mean the ability to create and understand symbols, three types stand out: alphabetical literacy, meaning reading and writing; visual literacy, meaning (following Bradley, 1995: 1) the way people understand pictures; and diagram literacy, meaning the ability to understand maps and diagrams. Many local people may not understand the written word, and have difficulty with pictures, maps and diagrams brought from outside.[9] But almost all local people can map and diagram for themselves. In the words of a Zimbabwean villager: 'One does not need to be able to write in order to be able to translate thoughts into concrete actions' (Marindo-Ranganai, 1995: 61). The faculty of being able to map and diagram may include all except some of the handicapped in a community, without privileging those who are alphabetically literate. So it is easier for almost all to take part, and they more or less by definition understand maps and diagrams which they have made themselves.

Visual diagramming can then be an equalizer. All who participate – children, women, men, poor, rich, illiterate, literate – can similarly understand what is being shown. Those who talk a lot dominate less. Describing the experience of the Neighbourhood Initiatives Foundation (NIF) in the UK, Tony Gibson (1992) has pointed out that in conventional processes 'the talkers nearly always win'. But with a physical model of their neighbourhood to play with, timid people can physically put down their ideas. Often 'people who put down an idea wait for others to talk first about it, and then say themselves: "I agree with you" ' (ibid.). The unobtrusiveness of the process is particularly important to 'those in the community who get brushed aside because they're too young or too old, or the wrong colour, or the wrong gender' (Gibson, 1995). Similarly participatory mapping and matrices by a marginalized group, often women, can enable them to express their preferences and priorities in a physical form which does not entail personal confrontation with those normally dominant, often men.

Relations with outsiders are also changed. Good facilitation of participatory mapping and modelling often requires that the facilitator 'hand over the stick'. The action is with those who map and diagram. After the early stages, outsiders have to keep quiet, observe process, and not interrupt. In the NIF experience, roles are reversed. Instead of professionals presenting their plans for residents' comments:

the residents are consulting the professionals to establish the range of options, the limitations, the possibilities – so that they can reach their own informed conclusions. *The experts are on tap, not on top.* (Gibson, 1995: 44, author's emphasis).

149

Table 7.3: Verbal and visual compared

	Verbal (interview, conversation . . .)	Visual (map, model, matrix, diagram . . .)
Outsider's mode and role	Probing investigator	Facilitating initiator and catalyst
Insider's mode and style	Reactive respondent	Creative analyst and presenter
Investigative style	Extractive	Performative
Insider's awareness of outsider	High	Low
Eye contact	High	Low
The medium and materials are those of:	Outsider	Insider
Detail influenced by:	Etic categories	Emic categories
Information flow	Sequential	Cumulative
Accessibility of information to others	Low Transient	High Semi-permanent
Initiative for cross-checking	Outsider	Insider
Ownership of information	Appropriated by outsider	Shared; can be owned by insider
Utility for complex analysis	Low	High

Some contrasts between verbal and visual modes are presented in Table 7.3.

The shift from verbal to visual is one of emphasis in PRA. Maps and diagrams are part of the repertoire. They can be facilitated on their own early in interactions. They can also be part of semi-structured interviews or conversations, introduced as a means for local people to express, share and analyse their knowledge. They then present an agenda for discussion: 'Interviewing the map', 'interviewing the matrix', and 'interviewing the diagram' have proved often the most fruitful, but also the most neglected, stages of a discussion and diagramming process. With the visual, 'a whole new set of questions and discussion arises which does not in the verbal' (pers. comm. James Mascarenhas). The verbal, as shown for example with oral histories (Slim and Thompson, 1993), will always remain important. But PRA experience suggests that combinations of visual and verbal, with early primacy to the visual, can help to bring in those normally marginalized, and can express much of the complexity and diversity of local realities, and that verbal and visual combined express more than either on its own.

From higher to lower

In both medium of expression, and in physical position, there is a shift from higher to lower. In medium of expression, practitioners of PRA have much debated the relative advantages of paper or ground for participatory visual analysis. One view has been that in mainly literate cultures, as in China, Jamaica, Sri Lanka and the UK, it is appropriate for diagramming and analysis from the beginning to be on paper. Some have argued, before the experience, that the ground is an insult to people who are educated, and that it is patronizing for a facilitator to encourage use of the ground. Cultures and conditions vary but to date these reservations have proven unfounded. Ground and paper both have pros and cons, summarized in Table 7.4.

Table 7.4: The advantages of ground and of paper

Ground	Paper
Democratic, less eye contact and dominance	Permanent
	Portable
Inclusive, more can take part	
	Easy to copy
Friendly for marginalized people – non-literates, women etc	Easy to display
Easy to alter and add to	Updatable
Size less limited	Usable for participatory monitoring and evaluation
Wide range of materials	
	More authoritative (with officials, policy-makers etc.)
Can be 3-dimensional	
Fun and creative	
Local ownership	

Note: Advantages only are given, as the advantages of one are disadvantages of the other.

Perhaps most important, the ground is an equalizer. The media and materials are often those of insiders – soil, stones, sand, seeds as counters, sticks as measures, vegetation and so on. Eye contact, and insider's aware-ness of the outsider, are low. Paper often inhibits: it is élitist, valuable and linked with literacy, and pen marks are permanent. All the same, the non-literate can use paper and pens to map and diagram. In Kiteto District in Tanzania, in June 1992, a non-literate Maasai young man, though mocked by his literate colleagues, took a sheet of paper, and went off and quietly drew a detailed map of a large village area and its settlements. In Pakistan, in March 1992, several non-literate women drew systems diagrams of their farms and households with internal and external flows and linkages (pers. comm. Jules Pretty). For people who do not read and write, though, the

151

ground is usually better. It invites: it belongs to all and is costless, familiar, fun and easy to alter. With the ground, more can take part and take part more easily. Passers-by stop and become involved. Paper is private; the ground is public. Paper empowers those who hold the pen; the ground empowers those who are weak, marginalized and illiterate. There is a democracy of the ground.

In terms of physical position, personal relationships differ when analysis takes place on a wall, a table or the floor. In the VIPP (visualization in participatory programmes) (Tillmann, 1993) approach, much of the participation is through writing on cards. These are grouped and ordered, usually pinned or stuck on a board or wall. The wall has advantages of visibility and items on it have some permanence. But with analysis on a wall, there is a tendency for one person to take over, slowing the process and limiting participation. The process can even become tedious.

In contrast, the ground is freer and faster. When cards are placed on the floor, they are easier to rearrange and more accessible to all.[10] Sitting, squatting or lying on the floor brings people down to the same level. The physically lower the visualization, the less participants have eye contact and the easier it is for all to intervene, by word or action, to express their reality, with the flexibility of moving items without having to fix them. Participants tend to think much more about what is being expressed than about who is expressing it.

Sequences are often the key. In terms of medium, the advantages of both ground and paper can often be captured by starting on the ground and then redrawing on paper. In terms of position, the advantages of both the floor and the wall can be captured by starting on the floor, and then moving to the wall. So a ground map can be redrawn on paper, and cards can be sorted and ordered on the ground. Then maps and cards alike can be stuck up and displayed more visibly on a wall. As with other reversals, it is less a question of either–or, and more a question of weighting and of where to start and what sequence to follow.

From reserve to rapport, and frustration to fun

The shifts and reversals outlined so far generate and reinforce a further reversal, that of relations: from suspicion and reserve to confidence and rapport, and often from frustration to fun.

With outsider–insider interactions, there is a scale of formality–informality, from the short-term structured interview with questionnaire, through the semi-structured interview with checklist of subtopics to the open-ended conversation. With interviews, and sometimes also conversations, outsiders ask questions and probe. The outsider maintains control, and largely determines agenda and the categories. Eye contact is common. The interviewee responds, conscious of an interaction with a person who is seeking information.

RRA and more so PRA stress the process of gaining rapport. An initial reserve of local people towards outsiders is a commonplace. Their responses are often prudent in order to avoid loss and hopefully gain benefits. Some social anthropologists have expressed scepticism about the relative speed with which rapport can be established. For their deeper and more fully emic understanding, there is a case for more lengthy immersion. But the experience with both RRA and PRA is that when outsiders behave well and methods are participatory, good rapport can come quickly. This is paradoxically through outsiders taking time, not rushing, showing respect, explaining who they are, answering questions, being honest and interested, and asking to be taught, being taught, and learning.

In the classical view, much good fieldwork is painful. It entails long hours of collecting and checking data. Moser and Kalton (1971: 296) observe of questionnaire surveys: 'An interviewer's interest is bound to flag after a time . . ' Pelto and Pelto (1978: 194–5) cite the case of an anthropologist, Kobben, who had to make 'a great sacrifice of time, during a year of field work, to collect . . . quantified data on a mere 176 persons' and even then he felt rather unsure of the validity of some of this material. The same authors go on to consider how extensive survey data from questionnaires need to be checked and qualified by other methods, and conclude:

Clearly, the quantified data of survey research or other standardized interviewing require close support from participant observation and general informal interviewing. But the converse is equally true. The lesson in all this, as Kobben made clear, is that field research entails a great amount of tedious, time-consuming work – both qualitative and numerical. (Ibid: 194–5)

Some earlier participatory research also suffered from being long-drawn out. The pilot project in appropriate technology for grain storage in Bwakira Chini village in Tanzania involved an outside team living in the village for eight weeks. This was considered a 'short period of dialogue', but even so the application of the dialogical methodology was 'time-consuming and tiresome' (Mduma, 1982: 203, 213).

The contrast with RRA is sharp. Professional conversations are mutually stimulating and interesting. Of cattlekeepers in Nigeria who ranked browse plants, Wolfgang Bayer (1988: 8) wrote that: 'Pastoralists were very willing to share their knowledge about browse plants with us and appeared to enjoy the interviews as much as we did'. Reflecting on the comparison between a topic RRA and a questionnaire survey on forestry and fuelwood in Sierra Leone, Andy Inglis (1991: 40) wrote that the RRA approach enabled respondents 'to enjoy a professional chat about their livelihood or kitchen habits, instead of being subjected to an intrusive 278 question questionnaire by bored enumerators'.

With PRA approaches and methods, the contrast is usually even sharper. Data are not collected by outsiders, but expressed and analysed by insiders. For outsiders, in John Devavaram's words (*RRA Notes* 13: 10), 'One doesn't get bored repeating field work. It is always interesting'. What is shared is often unexpected and at times fascinating. For insiders, the creative act of presentation and analysis is usually a pleasure, and a process too of thinking through, learning and expressing what they know and want. In matrix scoring for trees or varieties of a crop, using the ground and seeds, it is a common experience for the outsider to become redundant as the process takes off. People debate and score on their own, oblivious of the outsiders.

The process is often enjoyed, and found interesting and useful. After village participants had made and analysed models (*maquettes*) of their environment in Burkina Faso, 'All . . . expressed the strong desire to continue the work and to take it deeper' (Hahn, 1991: 3).[11] Quite often, dissatisfied with their first attempt at a map, local people scrub it out and start again with concentrated enthusiasm. Again and again, villagers in India have lost themselves in mapping and modelling, and outsiders have had to learn not to interview, not to interrupt, not to disturb their creativity. There is pride in what has been made, and pleasure in presenting it to others. In the words of a postcard from Pakistan, received as this is written: 'When PRA works well it seems to be a good experience for everyone' (pers. comm. J. Pointing). Fun is often part of PRA.[12]

Reversals of power: from extracting to empowering

PRA seeks and stresses power reversals between uppers and lowers. Initiative and control are passed to local people, using the metaphor (and sometimes reality) of 'handing over the stick' (or chalk, or pen). The shifts have built-in tendencies towards reversals of power from outsiders as uppers to local people as lowers:

○ *from closed to open* restrains the normal dominance of the etic, and encourages expression of emic reality;
○ *from measuring to comparing* enables the expression and analysis by people of realities and preferences which are otherwise inaccessible (because not measured or measurable) or sensitive (when expressed in absolute rather than relative terms);
○ *from individual to group* shifts the balance of power, with a lower ratio of outsiders to insiders;
○ *from verbal to visual* empowers local people, and lowers within a community, to express their reality – those who do not speak up, the marginalized, those who do not read or write, women, children, those of low social status;
○ *from paper, table and wall to ground* reduces the dominance of the few who hold pens, sit at tables, or stand at the wall, and encourages and enables more to participate, including those who speak less and who are less literate. The ground empowers the weak, and brings the strong down to the same level. There is less eye contact, less use of words, and greater ease of action;
○ *from reserve to rapport and from frustration to fun* help outsiders facilitate analysis by insiders and release social energy.

These then can be combined in PRA to reinforce reversals of power, knowledge and ownership. In this, PRA contrasts with the more extractive data-collecting nature of traditional methods of inquiry.

With questionnaires, the professional concern is less with people – the respondents, and more with what they provide – the responses. In their textbook *Survey Methods in Social Investigation* (1971) Moser and Kalton have only two entries for 'respondent', but 32 for 'response'. The responses matter more, for they are the raw material to be mined, packaged, transported and processed, the commensurable output to be collected, categorized, coded, counted and correlated.

In classical social anthropological investigation, too, the ultimate aim has been to obtain data which are then analysed and written up away from the field. Development anthropologists now aim to be useful through their work in more direct manner; and many anthropologists intervene in their field for ethical reasons. Often, though, the motivation is that of a researcher. However useful and justified the research may be, the crowning consummation tends to be data and insights processed into a PhD thesis, articles or a book.[13]

The contrasting thrust of many PRA practitioners is to empower more than extract, to start a process more than to gather data. Approaches and methods tend to be what Scoones and Thompson (1994: 22) call 'performative' (as also with folk theatre, stories, proverbs, songs and the like) through visualizations which break down the distinction between data and analysis. The initiative is passed to 'them'. The stick is handed over. The prime actors are the people. The outsider is less extractor, and more convenor, facilitator and catalyst. Four linked practical and ethical issues then arise:

(1) *Modes of facilitation.* It is difficult for a facilitator to avoid influencing outcomes. The transfer of reality can take place unintended. There is no complete escape from this trap, but solutions are sought in personal behaviour – transparent honesty, respect, sitting down, encouraging, listening, not interrupting . . .

(2) *Who is empowered.* The easy, normal tendency is for those local people who participate and who are empowered to be those who are already more powerful – the better-off, élites, officials, local leaders, men, adults and the healthy, rather than the worse-off, the underclasses, the vulnerable, lay people, women, children and the sick. When this occurs, the weak and poor may end up even worse off. With women, the problem is compounded by their many tasks which make it hard for them to find blocks of undisturbed time long enough for some participatory modes of analysis. Deliberate steps have been needed repeatedly to offset such biases, identifying different groups in a community, finding out the times most convenient for them (Euler, 1995) (especially women), and encouraging and enabling them to conduct their own analysis and express their own priorities (Welbourn, 1991).

(3) *Who owns the information* – the map or model, the diagram, the chart – *and what it is used for.* The unselfconscious sharing of information by local people through participatory methods is open to abuse by outsiders. PRA methods could be a clever trick for luring unsuspecting local people into parting with their knowledge. I do not yet know examples, but expect them. There is also the issue of who owns the physical output of the analysis. Many PRA practitioners have a strict code that the outputs belong to those who created them; and that only exceptionally, if at all, can outputs be borrowed.[14]

155

(4) *Empowerment and process.* The ideal sought by some PRA practitioners is a process in which people, and especially the weaker and poorer, are enabled not just to express and analyse their reality, but to plan and to act. This happens, for example, through participatory mapping of a watershed where the map is used by villagers to plot current conditions and plan actions, and is retained by them for monitoring action taken and changes made; through mapping and surveying degraded forest, deciding how to protect it and what to plant, and then managing the resource; through matrix scoring for varieties of a crop specifying and weighting characteristics of a 'wish' variety; through organization, bargaining and negotiation; or through preparing a proposal in a form that fits the norms of an NGO or government organization. The outputs of the process are enhanced knowledge and capability, an ability to make demands, and action and change.

All this fits together through the popularity and power of PRA. Conditions are not always right. But when they are, local people, and especially the poorer, enjoy the creative learning that comes from presenting their knowledge and their reality. They gain confidence, finding that they can do things they did not know they could, showing and analysing their complex realities. Things are then seen together and differently. It is not just that local people share knowledge with outsiders. They themselves learn more of what they know, and together present and build up more than anyone knew alone. It is not the reality of the outsider which is transferred and imposed, but theirs which is expressed, built up, and shared, and their confidence and capabilities which are strengthened. In a practical way, it is the reality of local people that comes to count.

Principles for participatory learning and analysis

The experience with both RRA and PRA has been that good performance requires practitioners and facilitators to follow basic principles. Some are shared by RRA and PRA, and some have additionally evolved and been emphasized in PRA.

The principles have been induced more than deduced. They have been found through experience, by trying out practices, finding what works and what does not, and most often only then asking why. Although different practitioners would list different principles and these have evolved over time (see e.g. Grandstaff *et al.*, 1987: 9–13; Grandstaff and Grandstaff, 1987a; McCracken *et al.*, 1988: 12–13; Gueye and Freudenberger, 1990: 10–19; *RRA Notes* 1–26), most would include those that follow, or something like them.

Principles primarily of RRA (also shared by PRA)

○ *A reversal of learning*: to learn from local people, directly, on the site, and face-to-face, gaining insight from their local physical, technical and social knowledge;

o *learning rapidly and progressively*: with conscious exploration, flexible use of methods, opportunism, improvisation, iteration, and cross-checking, not following a blueprint programme but being adaptable in a learning process;

o *offsetting biases*: especially those of rural development tourism, by relax-ing not rushing, listening not lecturing, probing instead of passing on, being unimposing instead of important, and seeking out those who are marginalized – the poorer people, women, ethnic minorities, children, those who are isolated and remote – and learning their concerns and priorities;

o *optimizing trade-offs*: relating the costs of learning to usefulness, with trade-offs between quantity, relevance, accuracy and timeliness. This includes the principles of optimal ignorance – not learning more than necessary, and of appropriate imprecision – not measuring what need not be measured, or more accurately than needed;

o *triangulating*: (Grandstaff *et al.*, 1987: 9–10; Gueye and Freudenberger, 1991: 14–16), meaning learning from several, quite often three, methods, disciplines, individuals or groups, locations, types of information, items, and/or points in a distribution, to cross-check, compare, gain insights and successively approximate;

o *complexity and diversity*: seeking and enabling the expression and ana-lysis of complex and diverse information and judgements. This includes looking for and learning from exceptions, oddities, dissenters and out-liers in any distribution. This has been expressed in terms of seeking variability rather than averages (Beebe, 1987: 53–54), and has been de-scribed in Australia as the principle of maximum diversity, or 'maximis-ing the diversity and richness of information' (Dunn and McMillan, 1991: 5,8). This can involve purposive sampling in a non-statistical sense. It goes beyond the cross-checking of triangulation; for defined broadly it deliberately looks for, notices and investigates contradictions, anomalies and differentness.

Principles primarily of PRA (but also applicable in RRA)

o *handing over the stick (or pen or chalk)*: facilitating investigation, ana-lysis, presentation and learning by local people themselves, so that they generate and own the outcomes, and also learn. This requires confidence that 'they can do it', that local people are able to map, model, rank, score, diagram, analyse, plan and act. Often the facilitator initiates a process of presentation and analysis, and then sits back and keeps quiet;

o *self-critical awareness*: meaning that facilitators continuously and crit-ically examine their own behaviour. This includes embracing error – welcoming it as an opportunity to learn; facing failure positively – 'failing forwards'; correcting dominant behaviour; and being critically aware of what is seen and not seen, shown and not shown, said and not said, and how what is shared and learnt is shaped and selected by the context and the social process of interaction;

o *personal responsibility*: PRA practitioners tend to take personal respons-ibility for what is done rather than relying on the authority of manuals

157

or on rigid rules, in the spirit of the one sentence (Peters, 1989: 378; KGVK, 1991): 'Use your own best judgement at all times'.

o *sharing*: of information and ideas between local people, between them and outsider facilitators, and between different facilitators, encouraging photocopying and translations, and sharing field camps, training and experiences between different organizations, regions and countries.

The principles of RRA are mainly epistemological, to do with obtaining information and gaining knowledge. The additional principles of PRA are mainly personal, to do with behaviour, attitudes and self-awareness. This contrast indicates the emphasis in PRA on how outsiders interact with local people.

A rigour of trustworthiness and relevance

The purpose of rigour is to assure quality. Positivist rigour seeks accuracy to achieve a close correspondence between data and physical or social reality, minimizing personal judgement. As traditionally conceived in the social and natural sciences, rigour is linked with measurements, statistical tests and replicability. These are often necessarily reductionist, since most realities, other than discrete units which can be counted (like people or animals), have to be examined as parts if they are to be measured. That this does not work well in the social sciences is only too evident from the widespread mistrust of the findings of questionnaire surveys. The simplifications which result, even if the measurements are accurate, miss or misrepresent much of the complexity, diversity and dynamism of system inter-relationships. In consequence, they are often not useful. As Uphoff puts it:

> Unfortunately, there appears to be an inverse relationship between rigor and relevance in most social science work. This may be because rigor always requires some reductionism, since certain aspects of phenomena are necessarily excluded by any classification and measurement. Moreover, their changing nature tends to be ignored because taking this into account greatly complicates analysis. (Uphoff, 1992: 295).

Reflection on PRA experience suggests a rigour based on two sets of criteria: trustworthiness and relevance. Trustworthiness is the quality of being believable as a representation of a reality; relevance refers to practical utility for learning and action.

Trustworthiness[15]

Trustworthiness can be sought and enhanced through applying the principles of RRA and PRA listed above, and through action, observation and reflective and self-critical judgement.

(1) The *action* of outsiders concerns behaviour. Trustworthiness here depends on quality: of interaction between outsiders and local people; of the convening and facilitation of group analyses; of the management and moderation of upper–lower distortions; of the processes of enabling and empowerment; of offsetting biases and applying the other principles of RRA and PRA.

158

Iterative process with successive approximation can enhance trustworthiness. In Nepal, two groups of outsiders found discrepancies in the information on seasonality and trends in agriculture which villagers had shared with them:

> The response was for both groups to go back to their village the next day and reconcile the information, with their respective groups of informants forming one combined group, and with the statement 'We got the information from you yesterday and there seems to be some difference. Can you help us?' And of course they did. Information flowed, arguments and discussions took place among the villagers, among the outsiders and between both villagers and outsiders . . . Explanations were given, corrections made, and it was a much more satisfied group of researchers that returned to the base camp that night. (pers. comm. James Mascarenhas)

(2) Rigour can be sought through *observation*, and especially observed process. Outsiders initiate, facilitate and then critically observe the process of analysis, especially with visual analysis by groups. In contrast with most questionnaire surveys, this group visual analysis gives the observer time and freedom to watch interactions, to see how much cross-checking and correction take place, to assess commitment to presenting complete and accurate information, and to judge whether information is being distorted or withheld. A group-visual synergy often develops (Figure 7.4) with cumulative group enthusiasm, adding and amending detail in order to create a complete and accurate picture.

(3) There is rigour from reflective *judgement*. Personal self-critical scepticism and awareness can be powerful, but are open to the old traps of self-deception, or of convenient omission of awkward questions.

Two of the cases described above are warnings. When the four groups at Ramasamypatti all came up with 355 as the population of the village (p. 144) I was excited. I collected the reporting maps and diagrams, and labelled, arranged and photographed them. This positive evidence has since been disseminated through copies of the slides. Only later did I think to ask whether there had been any exchanges of information or of figures between the groups. In fact I believe there was none. But had the groups come up with figures which differed, the question is whether my reaction too would have differed. The danger is selective recording and dissemination of the positive.

Similarly with rainfall, the Nepal case (p. 146) was meticulously analysed by Gill and published. But this was not done in the Kenya and Karnataka cases. We do not know what they would have revealed about farmers' judgements. Rigour requires consistency in probing inquiry into the whole range of types of case.

The surest safeguard is sharing with peers and local people, and inviting their analysis and critical review. The reversal implied covers action and observation as well as judgement. Trustworthiness then grows out of iterative processes of interaction, observation, analysis and judgement in which the actors are local people, outsiders, and outsiders' peers.

159

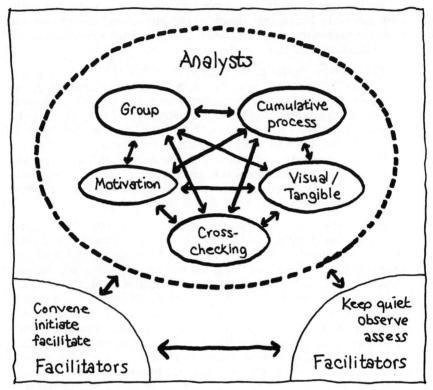

Figure 7.4: Group-visual synergy

To enhance trustworthiness, nine practical questions can be asked about process (for a longer relevant list, see Pretty, 1995b: 1256):

(1) Were biases recognized and offset?
(2) Was the stick handed over?
(3) Were relevant lowers freely involved, and were different points of view expressed and reconciled freely?
(4) Were upper–lower distortions recognized yet minimized?
(5) Were group (especially group-visual) synergies observed?
(6) Was there triangulation in its various forms?
(7) Were diverse and negative cases and exceptions identified, examined and analysed?
(8) Were actors, especially outsiders, self-critical, noting, embracing and learning from errors?
(9) Was learning progressive and iterative, between groups and actors, with feedback checks and successive approximation?

Relevance

The rigour of relevance has two dimensions:

160

1. Combining optimal ignorance and personal responsibility. This means that methods or processes are not facilitated for their own sake, but only if they make sense in the context. Judgement here is not simple. Facilitators often do not know what they do not know: the routine facilitation of a method may turn up a significant surprise. Participation in a method can be relevant to process by building confidence in a local person or group even if its direct output is irrelevant. What will be relevant may also be knowable only after the event, when priorities have been identified and actions planned. Good judgement may for these reasons mean facilitating a wide range of analysis in the early stages.

2. Commitment to 'getting it right'. It is not unknown for local people who see no point in an exercise, or are tired, short of time or simply playful, to make up visual information. Another risk is that they will bias what they present to fit what they perceive as their interests in the context. But usually, with visualization, they lose themselves in the activity. Commitment to completeness and accuracy are then generated by the process itself, as a creative and collective act of representation and judgement. Completeness and accuracy are also enhanced by a sense of relevance to purpose. If people see what they are doing as part of a practical process leading to analysis of priorities, planning and action, they are more likely to strive to 'get it right'.

The rigour of relevance, then, requires continuous reflection on the potential utility of process and analysis. It is supported by local focus and participatory process. The modes of analysis accommodate and express complexity, diversity and change. People experience the process as creative, fulfilling and often fun. Social energy, to use Uphoff's phrase, is released. The momentum of participation homes in on, and can be channelled towards, practical relevance in identifying options, expressing preferences, planning and action. This practical relevance in turn generates more social energy and commitment. So the rigour of relevance is sustained by virtuous circles of social energy. People do it, and do it well, because they enjoy it and see a point in it.

Concluding

The potentials of PRA and PRA-related approaches and methods continue to unfold. There is much abuse and much bad practice (see Chapter 10 pp. 211–14). This has been strongly criticized, especially by PRA practitioners themselves. But soberly assessed, the evidence to date is that the new repertoire is both powerful and popular. This chapter has explored PRA's underpinning of principles and rigour. Their application presents a practical means to mitigate some of the problems of the past. This can be especially through commitment to empower local people and whoever is vulnerable and marginalized. For the principles and means are now better understood to enable such groups and individuals to express, share and analyse the complex and diverse realities of their conditions and lives, to gain confidence, to plan and to act.

8

Poor People's Realities: Local, Complex, Diverse, Dynamic and Unpredictable

It is always the same, when I plant in straight lines, if there are mice, they start eating at one end and move on swiftly straight down the line, and I quickly lose the whole crop. I always replant randomly because there is a greater chance that less seeds will be found by the mice this way.

Silas Katana, farmer, Kilifi District, Kenya,
quoted in Porter *et al.*, (1991), p. 195

Participatory approaches and practices enable lowers to express and analyse their multiple realities. Many poor people's realities are local, complex, diverse, dynamic and unpredictable. For farming, forest-based and pastoral livelihoods they often seek security by complicating and diversifying activities, and multiplying linkages and supports to exploit varied and varying local resources and opportunities.

The values and preferences of poor local people typically contrast with those of the better off, outsiders and professionals. They need and want to be able to take a long view. They can, locally, manage greater complexity. Their values, preferences and criteria are typically numerous, diverse and dynamic, and often differ from those supposed for them by professionals. Local people are themselves diverse, with sharp contrasts of preferences and priorities by age, gender, social and ethnic group, and wealth.

Reversals of normal dominance to enhance diversity and complexity, to empower local people, the poor and other lowers, and to privilege their realities, expresses a new paradigm (Chapter 9) and requires changes in the behaviour and attitudes of uppers (Chapter 10).

Poor people's realities

Participation, empowerment and mutual respect enable lowers, and poor people in general, to express and analyse their individual and shared realities. The principles and practices of participatory appraisal facilitate this analysis and expression. The realities which are expressed differ, as do the environments, resources, experiences, values, cultures and livelihood strategies of individuals and groups. We can talk, then, empirically, as postmodernists do, of multiple realities; and we can talk normatively of privileging the multiple realities of lowers.

Any attempt by a person who is in most respects an upper (in my case male, white, from the North, middle class, formally 'educated' and senescent)[1] to describe the realities of lowers is open to many of the errors outlined in earlier chapters. A person who is not poor who pronounces on what matters to those who are poor is in a trap. Self-critical analysis, sensitive rapport and participatory methods can contribute some valid insight into the lives, values, priorities and preferences of poor people. We can struggle to reconstruct our realities to reflect what poor people indicate to be theirs. But there will always be distortions. We can never fully escape our conditioning. And the nature of interactions between the poor and the non-poor affects what is shared and learnt. In what follows, however much I try, I cannot avoid being wrong in substance and emphasis. For I am trying to generalize about what is local (and both rural and urban), complex, diverse, dynamic, personal and multidimensional, and to do this from scattered evidence and experience, perceived, filtered and fitted together in a personally idiosyncratic way. Error is inherent in the enterprise. There must always be doubts. But if the reality of poor people is to count more, we have to dare to try to know it better.

Help comes from field researchers, especially social anthropologists, from those who have been facilitating new participatory methods of appraisal and analysis, and increasingly from poor people themselves. When the roles and behaviour of outsiders change, so that they become facilitators, sitting down, respecting, listening, learning, not interrupting, in Raul Perezgrovas' terms 'being nice to people', then lowers, those who are normally dominated, begin to stand up and assert themselves; and then the methods of PRA enable them better to express, analyse and develop their realities and to act. They show that 'they can do it'. And when they do, the outcomes, again and again, differ from what uppers expect. When they express, share and analyse what they know, experience, need and want, they bring to light dimensions which normal professionals tend to miss or misperceive. In contrast with the universal, reductionist, standard, static, controlled and secure realities sought by normal professionals, the multiple realties which poor people know and show are local, complex, diverse, dynamic and uncontrollable.

Local livelihood strategies: complex and diverse

Contrary to normal professional prejudice, the livelihoods of most poor people are diverse and often complex. There is an Ancient Greek saying that 'The fox has many ideas but the hedgehog has one big idea'.[2] By analogy, most full-time employees found in the North and in industrial sectors in the South are hedgehogs, with one big idea, a job as source of livelihood. Other hedgehogs are those poor people, often powerless, desperate or exploited, who have but one survival strategy: slaves and bonded labourers, and many (though not all) of those who are outworkers tied to a single supplier-buyer, sex workers, beggars, vendors and occupational specialists.

Most poor people in the South, though, and more now in the North, are foxes. They have not one source of support but several. They maintain a portfolio of activities. Different members of the family seek and find different sources of food, fuel, animal fodder, cash and support in different ways in different places at different times of the year. Their living is improvised and sustained through their livelihood capabilities, through tangible assets in the form of stores and resources, and through intangible assets in the form of claims and access.

163

Fox strategies are rarely completely recognized by outsiders. They are unlikely to be fully revealed, if at all, by conventional questionnaire surveys. As we have seen (pp. 93–7) the schedules and questions, interactions, incentives and processes of questionnaire surveys tend to construct a standardized, short and simple reality. Also:

> Many aspects of rural livelihoods are not captured in either income or consumption-based survey data. This is because they are neither commoditized, nor evident enough to the researchers to be allocated 'imputed values' . . . Energy (fuelwood) and herbal medicines are two examples. A significant element of the 'safety net' for many rural people in times of stress consists of 'famine foods' which can be gathered from bush and fallow lands. (Norton *et al.*, 1994: 93)

The ingenuity and opportunism of poor people, and the diversity and complexity of their livelihood and survival strategies, can be illustrated by case studies and the accounts of social anthropologists and others (e.g. Beck, 1994; Breman, 1985; Davies, 1996; Griffith, 1994; Gulati, 1981; Hirway, 1986; Rahmato, 1987; Scoones, 1995c). Even within the same village, different social groups of the landless can have completely different strategies (e.g. Heyer, 1989). Usually an individual or a household engages in several or many livelihood activities over a year. Two of the most obvious and well recognized by professionals are cultivating field crops and keeping livestock, both for self-provisioning and for barter and cash income.

Additional sources of food, income, support and means of survival include:

○ *home gardening* (both rural and urban) and the exploitation of micro-environments. Seven studies in Indonesia reported the proportions of household income deriving from home gardens as being variously 10–30, 20–30, over 20, 22–33, 41–51, and 42–51 per cent, while another Indonesia study found the proportion higher among the poor, providing 24 per cent of their income compared with 9 per cent for the well off (cited in Hoogerbrugge and Fresco, 1993: 12);

○ *common property resources (CPRs)* – fishing, hunting, grazing, gathering, quarrying and mining variously in lakes, ponds, streams, rivers, the sea, shores, forests, woodlands, swamps, savannahs, hills, wastelands, fallows, roadsides, hedges, rocky places, quarries and mines . . .[3] for any of a vast range of fish, animals, birds, insects, fodders, wild foods, fibres, building materials, fuel, fertilizer, medicines, minerals such as gold, and much else. CPRs are often a major source of livelihood for the rural poor (see e.g. Jodha, 1990; Beck, 1994) and a safety-net fallback source of food and income in bad times (Moorehead, 1991; Davies, 1996: 242–3);

○ *scavenging* (mainly urban), *beachcombing* (sea and lakeside) and *gleaning* (mainly rural), including traditional rights and access to private residues (buttermilk, crop residues as fuel etc.);

○ *processing, hawking, vending and marketing*, including preparation and sale of food, beer, liquor, vegetables, other produce from home gardens and CPRs, and items scavenged.

164

o *share-rearing of livestock*, (see Beck, 1994: 142–56) where livestock are lent for herding in exchange for rights to some products and/or offspring (*mafisa* in Botswana, *poussani* in West Bengal). In West Bengal, share-rearing included cattle, goats, ducks and chickens, and was found by Beck (ibid. 146) to be much more important to the poorest than to other households;

o *transporting* goods by horse, donkey, mule, ox, cow, camel, llama or yak, by animal-drawn cart, by bicycle, by handcart, barrow or sledge, or by head or backloading;

o *mutual help*, including small borrowings from relatives and neighbours, and loans from savings groups;

o *contract outwork* – weaving, rolling cigarettes, making incense sticks etc.;

o *casual labour* and piecework especially in agriculture;

o *specialized occupations* – for example, barbers, blacksmiths, carpenters, sex workers, tailors;

o *domestic service* – especially by girls and women;

o *child labour* – domestic and agricultural work at home: fetching water, collecting fodder and fuel (leaves, twigs, branches, dung, grasses), weeding, picking coffee, tea or cotton, herding animals, removing stones from fields and ticks from livestock; and working away from home, in factories (for example, making carpets, candles, matches, fireworks), shops, restaurants, people's houses (see e.g. Johnson *et al.*, 1995);

o *craft work* of many sorts, making pots, baskets, carvings, ornaments, beadwork, toys, etc., especially in the off-seasons;

o *mortgaging and selling assets*, future labour and children;

o *family splitting*, including putting children out to others;

o *migration* for seasonal work in, for example, agriculture, brick-making, urban construction;

o *remittances* from family members who are employed away, child maintenance payments, and state pensions;

o *seasonal food-for-work, public works and relief*;

o *stinting*, in many ways, with food and other consumption;

o *begging*;

o *theft*; and

o *discrimination and triage*, especially with girl children and weaklings.

The point of this incomplete list is to illustrate, not to encompass the whole of the reality, which can perhaps never be done.

This is not 'employment' in 'a job' in 'a workplace', which is the Northern reality of most of those with 'work'. Employment, in the formal sense of having a job, is a reductionist Northern and industrial concept, and is a subset of livelihood, one means, but only one, by which livelihood can be secured. For many of the poor, the strategy is fox-like, along the lines of that presented by Alfred Stando in his livelihood matrix (Table 8.1). It is to do many things: to sniff around and look for opportunities, to diversify by adding enterprises and to multiply activities and relationships. It is to use not one but many means to gain food and cash, to reduce vulnerability and to improve the quality of life.

Partly because of the focus on formal employment, the diversity of activities of the urban poor has been underperceived. As Mitlin and

Table 8.1: Livelihood analysis by Alfred Stando, Chimontu, Zambia

Activity	J	F	M	A	M	J	J	A	S	O	N	D
Maize	3	3		2	3		2	3			1	1
Cotton	4	4	4	3		2	3				1	1
Groundnuts	2	2	3	3							1	1
Rape					4	3	2	2	2			
Cabbage				4	3	2	2	2	2	2		
Onion						4	2	2	2			
Tomato							5	3	3	2		
Farm income (normal year)	6		6		5	5	17	30				7
Farm income (this year)	6		6		5	5	17			27		7
Expenditure (farming)			9							18	7	8
Other expenditure	3	2	2	2	2	2	2	2	2	13	4	5
Other activities:												
Charcoal making					✓							
Woodcraft										✓	✓	✓
Honey collection					✓	✓	✓					
Bush meat				✓	✓	✓	✓					
Mushrooms		✓	✓								✓	✓
Ploughing others' land											✓	✓
Building houses							✓	✓				
Fishing	✓	✓	✓									✓

Note: The analyst used chalk, beans and seeds on the ground. The numbers against crops indicate the relative level of activity. 'Other activities' shows months of engagement in activities related to the bush. The year was not normal for income because of delays in the co-operative buying and paying for maize. Alfred Stando mentioned that his wives made mats but he did not have details. Chickens and goats were also sold to meet cash requirements.   Source, M.K. Shah, 1993

Thompson point out (1994: 5), the limited access of the urban poor to natural resources for fuel, fresh water and food makes diversity of income sources as important to them for reducing risk and uncertainty as diversity in agricultural practices for their rural counterparts.

Complexity and diversity in farming, pastoral and forest systems

Complexity and diversity are prominent in 'the third agriculture' (Chambers, Pacey and Thrupp, 1989; Scoones and Thompson, 1994). The first or industrial agriculture, found in the North and in plantations in the South, is standardized and simple. The second, or green-revolution agriculture, found in the South, is also relatively uniform and simple, with high-yielding packages of practices applied in stable or controlled conditions, especially with irrigation. The third agriculture, in contrast, is complex, diverse and risk-prone (CDR). It has been underestimated and misperceived.

Its significance is difficult to exaggerate. A recent estimate (Pretty, 1995a) of the numbers of people supported by industrial agriculture is some 1.2 billion, by green-revolution agriculture some 2.3–2.6 billion, and by CDR agriculture some 1.9–2.2 billion. For two reasons, CDR agriculture is now a priority: first, it must be supporting a majority of the poorest and most vulnerable people in the world; second, through what Pretty terms regenerative agriculture, much of it has a potential for two-fold or three-fold increases in production with little or no use of external inputs.

The strategies of CDR farmers differ from those of industrial and green-revolution farmers. The latter often seek to standardize, simplify, control and minimize management, substituting capital for labour. In contrast, CDR farmers often seek to reduce risk and increase food and income by complicating, diversifying and intensifying labour use in their farming systems, adding to their enterprises and maximizing management. Many are skilful engineers: they build bunds, confine, control and concentrate rainwater flows, flatten fields and shape land in a myriad of ways. They make, manage and exploit spatial niches such as silt-deposition fields, termite mounds, animal pens, and other pockets of fertility which contain, capture and concentrate nutrients, soil and water (Wilken, 1987; Premkumar, 1994; Scoones, 1995b; Carter and Murwira, 1995). They multiply the internal links and flows within their farming systems, through creating and exploiting micro-environments, through aquaculture, composting, cut-and-carry for stall-fed livestock, cover crops, manuring, multiple and serial cropping, agroforestry, home gardening, and the use of kitchen waste; and they bring in resources such as fodder, fuel, fibre, nutrients, soil and water from outside the boundary limits of their farms.

CDR farmers do not follow fixed procedures. They improvise and adapt continuously. Each season and year is different. What they do, how, when and where, depends on the life cycle of the household, on who is fit or sick, on who can do what, on what has already been done, on competing demands for the resources available, on past experience, social conventions and much else. Paul Richards (1989) has captured this in his description of farming as performance:

> The crop mix – the layout of different crops in the field – is not a design but a result, a completed performance. What transpired in that performance and why can only be interpreted by reconstructing the sequence of events in time. Each mixture is an historical record of what happened to

a specific farmer on a specific piece of land in a specific year, not an attempt to implement a general theory of inter-species ecological complementarity (as plant ecologists might suppose) . . . what matters to the Hausa farmer is sequential adjustment to unpredictable conditions.

Even more so, pastoralists have to be dynamic and adaptable (Scoones, 1995c, d, e and f). Both nomads and transhumants are alert and nimble in searching for, finding and exploiting transient resources. Even when patterns and timings of movements have regular rhythms, each day and season has its own idiosyncratic sequence of improvization. Herd management entails continuous appraisal, sensitive judgement, and at times very hard work. Management strategies and decisions cover herd composition, mix of species, choices of where and when to graze, browse, go for water, and go for salt, herding and protecting, preventing and dealing with disease, division of tasks and often intricate and extended social relations. There are many nicely poised trade-offs, choices and gambles to be made. The environment is diverse, uncertain and riddled with risks. Good decisions are matters of intensely concentrated judgement. Pastoralism is more than just a means of livelihood; as performance, it is an ecologically and socially complex and subtle art form.

Many livelihoods are forest-based or are diversified and supported by forests, woodlands and trees. The contribution of forest and woodlands to livelihoods is especially to be found through non-timber forest products (NTFPs) (see e.g. Amadi, 1993; Hobley and Shanks, 1993; Malhotra *et al.*, 1993; HSWG, 1995). NTFPs provide a rich range of resources for variegated livelihood strategies. The raw materials from forests often include many types of animals, bark, berries, birds, browse, buds, canes, caterpillars,[4] cocoons, creepers, dyes, eggs, fibres, flowers, fruits, fungi, gourds, grasses, gums, herbs, hides, honey, insects, leafy vegetables, leaves, locusts, nectar, nuts, paints, pods, raffia, rattans, reeds, resins, roots, saps, secretions, seeds, shoots, skins, soils, sticks, termites, tubers, twigs, vines, waxes, wood and worms. These are variously collected, shaped, prepared, and used, consumed or sold, as and for adhesives, agricultural tools, baits and traps, beehives, building, carvings, charcoal, cigarette wrappers, clothing materials, containers, cups, drinks, drums, dyes, fences, fertilizers, fibres, flavours, fodder, food, fuel, furniture, handicrafts (baskets, carvings, mats . . .), industrial raw materials, lubricants, medicines, mortars, musical instruments, narcotics, ornaments, plates, poisons, relishes, rituals, ropes, string, thatch, toothsticks, twines and utensils. No doubt this list is only an ignorant beginning, and could be lengthened further. For example, it omits the fact that forests and woodlands are also a source of wildings and wild species for domestication.

Forest and woodland-based livelihoods are many and varied. Some can be specialized and sustained for much of the year, for example carpentry and fuelwood sales. Many are seasonal. Using a combination of PRA and other methods, research in two villages in Zimbabwe listed 45 types of woodland products for sale, together with their prices (HSWG, 1995: 43–4).

Livelihoods are, though, often, perhaps usually, based on much more than cultivation, pastoralism or forests. They are more varied. The degree to which poor people, rural and urban, complicate and diversify their livelihood strategies can be illustrated in six dimensions: capability; person and activity; enterprise; social relationships; season; and interlinkages.

(1) *Capability*: family members gain different skills which enable them to be versatile in response to changing conditions. In reporting on a participatory poverty assessment in Ghana, Meera Kaul Shah (1993a: 23) wrote:

> Men mentioned that it has become important to acquire diverse skills like carpentry, masonry, plumbing or the skills of a mechanic to have a secure livelihood. Farming alone does not provide enough. Additional skills are important as a fall-back option during periods of financial stress or a bad agricultural year. A man not having these skills can be considered 'poor'.

(2) *Person and activity*: different members of a family, by gender, age, aptitude and skill, undertake different tasks, and secure food and income in different environments and in different ways. To illustrate: on any one day, one adult may be collecting firewood, another preparing food, cooking, cleaning and washing, another herding cattle, another mending an implement, another working for a neighbour, and another working in an office in a town, while the small children collect jungle greens as food, weeds and grass as fodder, and twigs and leaves as fuel.

(3) *Enterprise*: household and farm enterprises are multiplied, often with several types of livestock, several species of crop, many different vegetables and useful plants in home gardens, diverse food, fodder, fibre, medicines and other common property resources, the sale of a range of farm and garden products, craftwork, casual employment and remittances.

(4) *Social relationships*: people seek to maintain and extend personal relationships with neighbours, relatives, traders, moneylenders, local influentials, officials, teachers, priests, healers, politicians and others. Poor people need networks for small loans. Those with extended families have networks of mutuality and support. Those with few are 'poor in people' (Geof Wood, pers. comm.), like many refugees, displaced persons and those on settlement schemes.

(5) *Season*: seasonality is a pervasive dimension of the lives of the rural poor, and also of the urban. Labour demand, disease, mortality, the variety, quality and quantity of food, domestic violence, livelihood activities, conception, pregnancy and birth, prices, income, expenditure and debt are only a few of the dimensions of deprivation and well-being which vary seasonally.[5]

(6) *Interlinkages*: enterprises and activities are connected and sequenced so that they are mutually supporting, for example when waste products from one activity are used for another. This applies especially with gardening, cultivation and livestock, and farming systems generally. Interlinkages and synergistic sequences are multiplied, as with the addition of aquaculture to a farming system.

Complicating and diversifying in these ways requires labour and management. We find women and men evolving farming systems which are non-linear, multi-storey, sequential, interactive, and mixed and managed in many different ways, forming and fitting micro-environments, making their land more heterogeneous and its enterprises more diverse, and multiplying labour-intensive internal linkages. All these demand a continuity of intensive management. All move in a direction opposite to the simplifying, standardizing, management- and labour-sparing farming systems of industrial and green-revolution agriculture. Why, when so many of the urban workers and middle classes of the world are hedgehogs, with one employment, do so many of the poor seek to diversify and complicate their livelihoods and farming systems? What is there in such behaviour for the poor and resource-poor?

Complex and diverse for livelihood flows, security and well-being

The reasons are several and overlapping, but three stand out: livelihood flows – their number, size and spread; security; and well-being.

First, increased complexity and diversity in livelihood systems normally add to the number, size and spread of flows of food, income and other resources. Sometimes this is through the addition of enterprises or activities, and sometimes (often with complex small-farming systems) through synergies which increase the flows from existing enterprises. Intercropping, composting, animal fodders and manures, cover crops and many micro-environments present examples of synergies, which add to gross yields.

Increased diversity also often spreads livelihood flows more evenly across the seasons. Poor people pick enterprises and activities which fit their seasonal slacks. Activities in agricultural off-seasons can slow or avert the rundown of stocks or the build-up of debt, or even add to stocks and reduce debt. Food-for-work and other public works are often vital in filling in gaps in productive work. For many, sources of food and income during the rains and before harvest are critical, since this is when food is shortest and damaging debts and obligations most often incurred. For those who live near the margin, food and income flows at such times are often the key to a sustainable livelihood.

Second, complex and diverse livelihood and farming systems reduce vulnerability and enhance security. Security here means freedom from threats or loss. Livelihood security, the opposite of vulnerability, depends most obviously on the physical, social and economic environment, and on the means and ability to deal with stress and shocks without damaging loss. In this, livelihood capabilities, tangible (stocks) and intangible assets play their part. Less well recognized, security also depends on how complexity enhances stability and sustainability. Stability here refers to the steadiness and dependability of flows and sustainability, to ability to maintain or improve a level of living and quality of life, including managing stress and shocks. Failure to understand how complexity contributes to stability and sustainability may stem from the mental models of machines and the controlled tidiness of normal science.

170

A complex machine is vulnerable to a fault in any one of its parts. The motor car, as all garage mechanics know and most owners sooner or later learn, can go wrong in many ways. There is some redundancy in the spare wheel, the sparking plugs and cylinders, sometimes in a reserve fuel tank, and nowadays in rear-view mirrors, meaning that if one fails, another can take its place. But with the battery, cooling system, carburettor, steering and transmission systems, one fault is usually enough to stop the whole machine.

In contrast, redundancy is inherent in the complexity and diversity alike of ecosystems, and many farming and livelihood systems. With these, the more diverse their parts and the more complex their linkages, the more they are buffered against shocks and failures. If one enterprise or activity fails, another can take its place: when the bottom falls out of the market for one vegetable or livestock product, others can be substituted; if a crop fails as a whole, there are wild foods. Herders in Mongolia responded to new uncertainties in markets and prices for livestock which came with privatization by diversifying their herds in species and also in composition (Mearns et al., 1992). If one productive asset is lost or destroyed, others are a fallback: if the cattle die, there are sheep or goats; if the sheep or goats die, hens, eggs and honey can still be sold. If one internal linkage weakens, others can supplement it: when animals run out of grazing, or fish run short of feed, they can be fed crop stover, tree leaf fodder, weeds or other gathered organic material. So resource-poor farmers and herders seek to reduce risks by adding to their enterprises, accumulating varied assets and multiplying linkages. Faced with uncertain conditions, farmers and herders diversify.

Risk-reducing diversity and complexity can be misunderstood because they often look untidy. Staggered planting can appear haphazard and messy, but reduces losses if there is a dry spell. Micro-environments can look chaotic, but human-made microclimates tend to be stable and smoothing compared with the ambient, more uniform environment. Really intensive home gardens can seem shambolic, yet they often manifest the sensitive creation and management of niches which change as plants grow. Their diversity of plants is habitually underestimated: a rule of thumb is that the number of useful species in a home garden will be double the number guessed by the visitor before counting. With field crops, variability and diversity reduce the threat of pests,[6] while monocultures are more vulnerable. Intercropping, as with maize and beans, often reduces the risks of loss of either crop.

Neat standardization and straight lines are, in contrast, vulnerable. The straight lines or row planting of industrial and green-revolution agriculture, and even of allotment gardeners in temperate climates, sometimes make little sense to farmers in difficult tropical conditions. Farmers in Machakos District in Kenya were advised to plant their maize in rows, but reverted to their tradition of triangles in order to intercrop with their fall-back crop of cassava in the middle of the triangles (pers. comm. Daniel Mwayaya). And the farmer in Kilifi District quoted at the head of this chapter planted randomly because seeds in straight lines were more vulnerable to mice. For many farmers there is method in the muddle.

171

So we can conclude, with Francis Shaxon (1993: 129), that: 'The more diverse and complex an agricultural system, the more stable and sustainable it will be'. Diversity spreads risks by adding species, enterprises, linkages and activities; complexity reduces risks through redundancy.

A third aspect of diversity habitually overlooked by normal professionals is well-being. Increases in the number, size and spread of livelihood flows, and greater livelihood security contribute to well-being. Beyond these, diversity adds to independence and to the quality of experience.

Diversity serves economic and social independence. The more sources of food and income a household has, the less it has to rely on any single one. The more varied the employment or productive work available, the less the danger of exploitation by one provider, for example, a single patron or business. If a local employer gives a bad deal, there is work on construction in town or in the brick factory, or, elsewhere, harvesting. Such options improve bargaining power, and so wages and incomes. Socially and psychologically, too, diversity liberates: diversity for lowers diminishes domination by uppers and enhances independence and self-respect.

Diversity also enhances well-being through the quality of experience.[7] A variety of foods – fruits, grains, vegetables, meats, relishes and wild foods, of activities and festivals in their seasons, of places familiar and new for living and moving in and visiting, of friends, relatives and people met and known, of games, music, dance and celebration, of experience of many sorts – these mean much to most people. In most cultures these are a part of the good life. They are, however, no part of normal economic valuation.

Complexity, diversity and dynamism underperceived

This understanding of the complexity and diversity of livelihood strategies sharpens understanding of the contrasts between the knowledge of normal professionals and that of local people. Much diversity is unseen or undervalued by normal professionals.

The seasonal dimension and its significance are underperceived by season-proofed professionals (Chambers, 1993a: 51–3). An oversimple impression is given by visits concentrated at certain times of the year, notably in the dry season after harvest, which miss the intensive activities of the rains when there is more work, less food, more sickness and greater need to exercise ingenuity. In her study of livelihoods in the Malian Sahel, Susanna Davies has shown in detail not only the wide range of coping strategies but also how all of them, whether based on production, common property resources, reciprocity, assets, labour, exchange, migration or consumption, are seasonal, some not at first obviously so but with a 'hidden seasonality' (Davies, 1996: 246–53).

Other interlocking professional and personal biases focus their attention on what is larger-scale, uniform, accessible, marketed and modern. Agriculturalists tend to notice and concern themselves with field crops on flat fields, to the neglect of micro-environments on slopes, in hollows or in home gardens. NTFPs for the livelihoods of the local poor were for long described as 'minor' forest products, while timber and poles for the distant rich were 'major' (Chambers, Shah and Saxena, 1989: 143–69). Monocultures and plantations are accessible, large-scale, modern, marketed and easy to inspect. Non-timber forest products are dispersed, small-scale, often 'traditional' and consumed by households, and out of sight.

Male bias pervasively overlooks and undervalues diversity. Most outsider professionals are still men, and tend to meet and interact with men. Whatever is larger-scale, marketed and modern is more likely to be managed by men than women. Most local diversity, on the other hand, is managed by women. Home gardens are pre-eminently a domain of women, close to the home or hut, sometimes a source and haven of often astonishing biodiversity, with plants of many species and uses; NTFPs are mainly collected by women; domestic livestock, large and small, including chickens, are usually tended mainly by women. But these activities are small-scale and scattered. They are also unseen because their products are either not marketed, or are done so on a dispersed and intermittent small scale. It is also often women who physically manage the internal organic linkages of farming systems, variously cutting, carrying, feeding, tending and applying the fodder grasses, tree fodders, crop residues, domestic animals, organic manure and composting which complicate and diversify farming systems. To all these tendencies, exceptions can surely be found, where men are mainly concerned. But in most contexts, it is women, more than men, who manage and maintain biological and livelihood diversity.

Much change is underperceived, or not perceived at all, by outsiders. Much of it is not visible and inaccessible through questionnaires. Social change is often rapid. Gender roles may be changing in many parts of the world far faster than normal professionals realize. Figure 8.1 shows the shifts in gender responsibilities presented by Indian villagers, showing a sharp increase in women's responsibilities over ten years.

Local process is also underperceived by outsiders. The learning of scientists tends to be stepwise, that of local people incremental. Local people are continuously observing and experiencing. Farmers have a dynamic knowledge system 'which co-evolves with the dynamics of the complex biological systems which underlie agricultural technology and production' (Hall and Clark, 1995: 1611). They constantly learn and unlearn, disciplined by the rigour of struggle for livelihood. Scientists often rely on averages, which slows learning about change; the knowledge of local people is more dynamic and up-to-date, continually revised as conditions change. Patrick Sikana (1994: 81) found in Zambia that farmers' perception of the fertility status of a particular soil changed constantly, taking into consideration the factors which favoured or impeded crop performance, such as plot age, location and previous use, weed infestation and pest build-up. Similarly, Gerard Gill (1991b) in his analysis of 20 years of rainfall data presented by farmers in Nepal (p. 146) found that farmers' perceptions were weighted by recent experience. As with soils in Zambia, or rainfall in Nepal, so, too, generally, farmers' perceptions, compared with those of scientists, are more evolutionary and dynamic, changing as local realities change.

We are concerned here with different constructions of reality. To polarize, scientists and large farmers dominate their environments: they are able to value and apply principles and practices which are universal, simple, standardized, stable and controllable. Small and poor farmers, pastoralists and forest-dwellers have in contrast to adapt to their environments: their

173

Area of work	Men		Women	
	10 yrs ago	Now	10 yrs ago	Now
Agriculture	o o o o o o o o o o	o o o o o o	—	o o o o
Home-related	o o	o o o	o o o o o o o o	o o o o o o o
Credit-related	o o o o o o o o o o	o o o o o o o	—	o o o
Cattle-related	o o o o o o o o o o	o o o o o	—	o o o o o
Education	o o o o o o o o o o	o o o o	—	o o o o o o
Purchase of Assets	o o o o o o o o o o	o o o o o o	—	o o o o
Marriage of Children	o o o o o	o o o o o o	o o o o o	o o o o
Marketing / Selling	o o o o o o o o o o	o o o o o o o	—	o o o

Figure 8.1: Shifts in gender responsibilities over 10 years. Source: MYRADA, South India 1994. Separate interviews with men and women were later jointly reconciled after much argument. Matrices were developed on the ground using stones etc.

survival is a versatile performance, managing in conditions which are locally specific, complex, diverse, dynamic and difficult to control. Scientists learn intermittently in conditions which are simplified and controlled. Local people learn continuously in conditions which are complex and uncontrolled. The realities of the two differ.

The common belief of scientists and outsiders that their knowledge is superior is reflected in the title of Gill's paper: 'But what about the REAL data?' The question was asked by an outsider professional, but a Nepalese farmer might ask a scientist the same question. Whose reality counts? And whose priorities?

Whose priorities count?

Who takes the long view?

It is a common prejudice among those who are not poor that poor people are improvident and 'live hand-to-mouth'. In part this is seen as a moral defect, in part as a strategy for survival. Those who are indigent and desperate, who 'do not know where the next meal is coming from' cannot and do not take the long view of professionals and élites.

Much empirical evidence is strikingly contrary. To be sure, there are many – those who are displaced, refugees, destitute, abandoned, chronically sick and disabled – who are forced to focus on immediate survival. But they usually wish to take a long view, and struggle to do so by safeguarding their livelihoods and investing labour for the long term.

In practice, again and again poor people show tenacity and self-sacrifice in conserving the basis of their livelihoods. A desperately poor family in Bangladesh only cut down their two trees as a near-last resort (Hartmann and Boyce, 1983: 160–68). To get them through the hungry season, a household in Mali cut consumption to one meal a day in order to avoid having to sell a traction animal (Davies, 1996: 253). Alex de Waal (pers. comm.) found a woman in Darfur in Sudan, on leaving her village in a famine, preserving millet seed for planting on her hoped-for return by mixing it with sand to prevent her hungry children eating it. On the basis of extended fieldwork during famine, he concluded that 'avoiding hunger is not a policy priority for rural people faced with famine', and 'people are quite prepared to put up with considerable degrees of hunger, in order to preserve seed for planting, cultivate their own fields, or avoid having to sell an animal' (de Waal, 1989, and 1991: 68). It has been a widespread finding that as soon as food shortage threatens, people eat less and worse in order to protect their livelihood assets in the bad times to come (see e.g. Corbett, 1988). Hunger is how poor people take the long view.

Again and again, small farmers with a sense of security in land invest their labour for the long term. They do this in shaping land, terracing and creating fertile micro-environments; in harvesting water, silt and nutrients; and in planting and protecting trees. The astonishing terraced rice paddies on sloped land in many parts of Asia are spectacular evidence, so widespread that it is easily overlooked. Less visible, but equally striking, are silt-deposition fields throughout much of the semi-arid tropics. For these, farmers build up barriers of stones year by year which harvest silt to create protected, highly fertile micro-environments which provide much higher and stabler yields than other land (see e.g. Wilken, 1987). When conditions are right, farmers terrace rainfed land and plant trees, as in Machakos District and elsewhere in Kenya (Tiffen et al., 1993; Holmgren et al., 1994; see also pp. 24–6). The planting and protecting of trees as long-term savings (Chambers and Leach, 1989) is again widespread evidence of actions which take the long view.

Similarly, pastoralists and livestock herders have long-term strategies. They balance the composition of their herds and flocks. Breeding strategies can be very long term. High-altitude herders in the Himalaya–Karakorum region cross-breed yak and cattle to optimize balances of characteristics adapted to different altitudes. Desirable herd composition depends on many factors including markets, the availability of grazing and labour. Their strategies take account of characteristics of females and males, and whether these are yak, cattle or hybrids (of what sort), through to the sixth generation. As Patrick Robinson (1993: 148) observes:

When a major change takes place in the desired herd composition, it can take many years of investment with little return before a new balance of breeding and productive stock is developed locally or stimulated from other areas.

Benign caricature could mislead: there is a danger of portraying the perfectly rational poor person who always takes the long view, investing with foresight in distant income streams for the benefit of future generations. There are poor people, as there are rich, who are profligate, make mistakes and have bad luck. The point is that the penalties for them and their children are vastly higher. So much more is at stake than for the rich. The well-off can afford to be short-sighted; the poor cannot. It is then not surprising that so many, on so vast a scale, strive to safeguard assets and invest for their future livelihoods.

Contrary to popular belief, it is less the poor and weak and more the rich and powerful who take the short-term view. Economists discount future benefits: the further off benefits are, the less they are worth now. Commercial businesses seek early returns on capital invested. Contractors grab fast bucks by clear-felling forest and getting timber out quickly. Government officials strive to spend votes and achieve targets by the end of each financial year. Staff transferable between districts expect short assignments; lacking incentives to launch long-term development, and fearing their successors will neglect what they start, they opt for actions with early results. For their part, politicians constantly court popularity and set their sights no further than the next election.[8] In various ways, then, all these among the relatively rich and powerful are driven to take the short view: by professional methods and norms, by shareholders, by interest rates on loans, by the imperatives of capital, by government procedures and practices, by the frequency of transfers and elections, and by prudence, realism and greed. It is less the rich, secure and strong, and more the poor, vulnerable and weak, who struggle and strive to take the long view.

Income, wealth and well-being

As we saw in Chapter 3 (pp. 42–9), professionals often construct and use reductionist realities. For assessing economic welfare, this takes the form of per capita income, or per capita consumption as a proxy for income. Income or consumption is assessed through questionnaire surveys and related to income-poverty lines. Measuring or estimating income-poverty is difficult and flawed, and questionnaire surveys are often slow, costly, inaccurate and low in credibility. But the data are convenient. They allow, or purport to allow, comparisons between areas and over time. In addition, at the local level, proxy indicators for wealth and income like quality of housing are sometimes used. Though other measures are recognized, per capita income tends to be taken as the main measure not just of economic welfare, but of ill-being and well-being.

Local realities assessed and expressed through PRA methods have been more varied and multi-dimensional. In wealth or well-being ranking, local people sort household cards into piles. This is either preceded or followed, or both, by a discussion of criteria. The realities presented and analysed challenge and qualify both the use of proxy indicators for wealth and income and the primacy of income-poverty.

Proxy indicators have included quality of housing, tin roofs, numbers of rooms, occupation, number of items of clothing, furniture, and above all in rural surveys, land-holding size. PRA approaches and methods have revealed qualifications so numerous that they may be normal. In a slum in San Domingo, in the Dominican Republic, Hilary Cottam (pers. comm. 1993) found that those in better housing were considered worse off, having to rent, while those in cardboard boxes were considered better off, living on land they owned. In a careful and detailed investigation in South India, a questionnaire survey using 5 indicators chosen by professionals led to misclassification of over a third of households, the reasons for this including the bad fit of the indicators and the many other relevant factors overlooked (Rajaratnam *et al.*, 1993; see also p. 143). Again, in Sri Lanka in December 1994, a villager explained why a government programme to help the poor had often identified the wrong people: some had bad houses but were well off; one had inherited a nice looking house but was weak and poor; one very poor family was excluded because the surveyor recorded a radio cassette player given by a relative who had been to the Gulf. Outsiders' surveys often miss or misinterpret major elements in wealth and income. Local people's assessments are more knowledgeable and nuanced. They include, for example, remittances from relatives, differences in types of loan and debt and repaying capacity, different forms of ownership, mortgaging, loaning, borrowing and benefiting from land, and the same for livestock, repeated expenditures for health treatment, and multifarious access to common property resources. For income and wealth, outsiders' proxy indicators often misfit, miss much, and mislead.

Beyond this, the primacy of income-poverty has been challenged and qualified by sensitive research, and by wealth and well-being ranking. Local people value much besides income. The classic study by N.S. Jodha (1988) in two villages in Rajasthan has been much quoted as a source of this insight. He asked farmers and villagers in two villages for their own categories and criteria of changing economic status. They named thirty-eight. Comparing data from his fieldwork in 1964–66 with 1982–84 he found that the 36 households which were more than 5 per cent worse off in per capita real incomes were on average better off according to 37 out of 38 of their own criteria. The criteria included not having to migrate for work, not having to skip a third meal during the lean period, not residing on a patron's yard or land, and other indicators of social and economic independence.

Wealth ranking, and its successor well-being ranking, have since repeatedly illuminated and validated Jodha's insights. The wealth ranking (Grandin, 1988) which was seminal for much current practice was conducted in Kenya among Maasai, for whom wealth was a key concept reflected in numbers of cattle, meeting outsiders' preference for a single measure. But wealth is simpler than well-being. Elsewhere in the world, even when discussion has started with wealth, local analysts have repeatedly used a more composite criterion. In a ranking in Ghana, 'god-fearing' was a separate category from wealth, and included some from all wealth groupings – rich, medium, poor and assetless (pers. comm. Meera Shah, 1993). In Zimbabwe, Scoones (1995a: 85) found that 'prestige, respect, esteem, conduct, behaviour and local political influence may be significant in ranking a particular household and act to trade-off against potentially lower asset or income levels', and concluded that: 'Wealth and well-being are thus complex and dynamic, with multiple local meanings and interpretations'. In parts of North India the concepts of *sukhi* (with a meaning close to 'happy') and *dukhi* (with a meaning close to 'un-happy') are used. In Masaka District in Uganda the Luganda phrase used was 'embeera n'obulama bwabantu' which translates literally as 'the conditions of day-to-day life of people' (Seeley *et al.*, 1996: 14). Well-being ranking enables local people to express their own concepts and values.

Well-being is then shown to be a local, complex, diverse and dynamic reality. Parmesh Shah's research in a village in Gujarat found (1996: 218–20) that people's idea of well-being changed rapidly in parallel with other changes. In Mozambique, after the end of conflict, local people's criteria shifted sharply from security and peace to include, for example, access to services. Well-being means different things in different places to different people at different times.

Reports of well-being ranking consulted all confirm well-being as multi-dimensional. When local people first place cards for households in piles, and then give their reasons, they often reveal ten or more criteria and indicators (see e.g. Rajaratnam *et al.*, 1993; Redd Barna, 1993), others being added as the process continues. Even more come to light when reasons are given for putting individual households in particular piles. Many negative indicators are revealed: having to skip meals in the lean season, having more mouths to feed and fewer hands to help (the depend-ency ratio), being unable to send children to school, having to put children in employment, being dependent on common property resources, having to accept low-status or demeaning work, social isolation and being poor in people, or being unable decently to bury the dead. Repeatedly health and physical and mental well-being are significant. Bad habits like alcoholism and other addictions recur, as does the physical ill-being of the disabled or chronically sick. Income, the reductionist criterion of normal economists, has never, in my experience or in the evidence I have been able to review, been given explicit primacy. PRA analyses from Pakistan, Zambia and Bulgaria throw light on this issue.

In a PRA process in a Pakistani village in April 1994 (pers. comm. Rashida Dohad):

> the local people did a matrix of their existing sources of income to determine the preferred income source. Interestingly, for me, the cri-terion 'more income' was the 9th or 10th one listed (out of a total of about 10 criteria). 'More time at home', 'ability to get involved in neigh-bours' joys and sorrows' were listed earlier . . . the generally perceived-to-be preferred source of income (high-paying skilled/manual labour in the Middle Eastern countries, particularly Dubai) did not emerge as victor . . ., the reason worked out by the local analysts being that it did badly on their social criteria.

Reporting on a discussion with a rural household in Zambia, Delia Paul (World Vision, 1993) had this to say:

One of the things we found in the village which surprised us was people's idea of wellbeing and how that related to having money. We talked to a family, asking them to rank everybody in the village from the richest to the poorest and asking them why they would rank somebody as being well off, somebody as being less well off, and someone as poor. And we found that in that analysis money meant very little to the people. The person who was ranked as poorest in the village was a man who was probably the only person who was receiving a salary. But that did not count to the villagers because he did not have cattle, he was not married, and he did not have any children. So the money on its own did not sort of mean anything. What was important was that they could have a certain lifestyle, that they were able to entertain with generosity, and that there were many children around them.

In a community in Bulgaria a master builder who had been invited to rank people according to wealth:

. . . spontaneously enlarged the list of wellbeing criteria emphasizing the importance of children's education, good health and a good humoured nature. The villager then picked up the name cards and sorted the cards into three piles. Interestingly, the less well-off group included the most wealthy person of the village – an unhappy, bad tempered fellow put at the bottom of the pile along with the drunks and sick.

(BSCRM and WWF-International, 1995: 24)

None of this is to undervalue income as a means to achieving other objectives. But it shows that in local people's reality much matters besides income, and other criteria – sickness, disability, dependence, being unable to fulfil social obligations, being 'poor in people', and being a miserable sort – again and again come up. People's values and aspirations are complex, diverse and dynamic; and they cannot be known by outsiders without enquiry, without enabling local people freely to undertake and share their own analysis. When a poor rural woman in Zambia was asked what her dream was, she said it was to have time to go to the town and spend time with her friends.[9]

Whose preferences and criteria count?

Professionals and local people

Professionals and local people also differ more generally in their values and preferences. What local people, especially the poor, want and need is often not what they are thought by professionals to want and need, or what professionals themselves want. Six examples can illustrate:

O *Basic needs: whose list?* The ILO listing of basic needs (ILO, 1976: 7) was drawn up by professionals, not poor rural people. It included food, shelter, clothing, access to essential services such as safe drinking-water, sanitation, transport, health and education, and an adequately remunerated job for those able and willing to work. It did not include access to basic consumer goods. But a rural study in Tanzania carried out for a Basic Needs Mission found widespread non-availability of basic goods such as salt, sugar, soap, matches, batteries and blankets. The Mission concluded: 'There seems little doubt that if villagers were pressed to give priorities to their main needs the first place would have gone to the supply of essential consumer goods' (ILO, 1982: 285).

○ *Seed-breeding: whose criteria?* The contrasting physical, economic and social conditions of scientists and of resource-poor farmers have long been recognized. Scientists on research stations and in laboratories seek peer approval and promotion. Resource-poor farmers on their farms seek livelihoods and survival. They live in different worlds. Yet many scientists have assumed that they know best what farmers need. For many, much has now changed since the Green Revolution days when scientists competed for maximum yield with high inputs. It is questionable, though, how much scientists take note of the range and weightings of farmers' criteria for crop varieties in their 'baskets of choice', for farmers' criteria are typically many (see e.g. Ashby *et al.*, 1989; Women of Sangams Pastapur etc. and Pimbert, 1991; Drinkwater, 1993; Tamang, 1993; Manoharan *et al.*, 1993). Common criteria include early maturation (shortening the hungry season), pest resistance, ease of weeding, fodder quantity and quality, drought resistance, ease of processing, price, storability, cooking quality and taste.

Two examples of divergent preferences revealed through matrix-scoring can be cited. In Andhra Pradesh, after matrix-scoring pigeon-pea varieties against ten criteria, women farmers indicated that they would not again grow an ICRISAT-released variety, despite its higher yield and greater pest resistance, because of its bitter taste (Women of Sangams Pastapur etc. and Pimbert, 1991). In Botswana, when in 1992 farmers matrix-scored five varieties of sorghum, they included tillering (branching) as a positive criterion. The facilitating scientist was astonished. Scientists had been breeding to reduce or eliminate tillering. He said they could change their practice.

○ *Animals and neighbours: whose problems?* In Sulawezi, Indonesia, in 1992, five groups of livestock staff identified and matrix-scored characteristics of different domestic animals – ducks, chickens, goats, horses, buffalo and cattle. Subsequently, villagers repeated the exercise, identifying freely the characteristics that mattered to them. The staff had only one sort of duck, the villagers two. Their scores out of 10 differed for the same characteristic: staff gave chicken meat 6 against villagers' 10, and horse meat 4 against villagers' 7. There was one criterion critical for the villagers which none of the staff had listed: causing trouble or conflict with neighbours. Manila ducks were extreme for this, scoring 11 out of 10 against 6 out of 10 for local ducks; and goats were so bad that the village had banned them altogether.[10]

○ *Woodfuel: whose crisis?* In the 1980s, an acute woodfuel crisis was perceived by planners in many central places. In Tanzania, a professional

180

projection foresaw no trees by 1990 (see pp. 22–3). But an ILO (1982) Basic Needs Mission was surprised that field investigations indicated no danger of deforestation although at the national level this was seen as a problem. Some years later, in Mwanza District, the Tanzania Government, the World Bank and initially the ODA of the British Government all wanted a forestry project. A local NGO carried out a listening survey. Of 8000 village conversations recorded only three mentioned timber, fuelwood or other tree products (Flint, 1991).[11] In the Usambara mountains, even in the 1980s, the perception of outsiders was of forest being destroyed by local people under the pressure of population; the reality reported by a social anthropologist was of people eager and willing to plant trees, both on their own land and elsewhere to create forest (Johansson, 1992). For part of Guinea, 'Rural villagers rarely consider firewood availability to be a problem' and in one area women's access to fuelwood had improved (Leach and Fairhead, 1992: 10 and 27). Lack of woodfuel is indeed often a local problem. But in many parts of the world, it would seem, the response to loss of trees in forests has been agroforestry – trees on farms, planted and protected, often for other purposes, but also providing woodfuel (see e.g. Scherr, 1995). The crisis has been more in professional perceptions than in local lacks.

○ *Forest development: whose interests and priorities?* In Haryana in India, researchers asked foresters and community management groups to rank order their preferences for 23 forest-development investment strategies (SPWD, 1992: 83–4). Some of the contrast in priorities is summarized in Table 8.2.

Table 8.2: Ranking of priorities for forest development

	Forest dept. staff	Communities
Trenches	1	20
Checkdams	2	17
Gabion checkdams	3	18
Gully plugs	4	21
Jamun	23	5
Guava	22	4
Dholu/sarala fruit	19	3
Dholu/Sarala	13	2
Bhabbar	12	1

The foresters' first four options were physical works on the land, which they would construct: trenches, checkdams, gabion checkdams and gully plugs. These were all ranked near bottom by the communities. The first five preferences of the communities, were all useful plants – bhabbar grass, dholu/sarala, dholu/sarala + fruit, guava and jamun. These were ranked low by the foresters, whose bottom five choices were all trees, not trees for timber, which the foresters would market, but trees for fruit, which people would enjoy.

○ *Trees on farms: whose reality?* In a study over nearly four years in Pakistan, M.R. Dove (1992) compared foresters' beliefs about farmers with farmers' realities. The comparison (Table 8.3) went far to explain problems with a nation-wide social forestry project for tree-planting by farmers. Foresters believed that only large farmers would be interested, but small farmers already had trees on their land and wanted more. The foresters' beliefs and small farmers' realities contrasted comprehensively: over the types and numbers of trees wanted, the obstacles to tree planting, the uses of the trees, the preferred time of planting, and whether fuelwood would reduce dung-burning.

Table 8.3: Foresters' beliefs and small farmers' realities (Pakistan)

	Foresters' beliefs	*Small farmers' realities*
Farmers who would plant	Only large	Already with trees on their land and wanted more
Small farmers were	Opposed to planting trees	
Farmers' preferences	Only large blocks of market-oriented exotics	Small plantings of multi-purpose native trees
Major obstacles to tree planting by small farmers	Farmers' lack of interest	Lack of water Problem of protection against livestock Effect on nearby crops
Best time for planting	Monsoon	When labour was available
Farmers' fuel use	More fuelwood would not reduce dung-burning	More fuelwood would reduce dung-burning

Source: Adapted from Dove (1992).

These six sets of contrasts can be understood in terms of how the realities of the professionals had been formed. Few if any of those who drew up the ILO's list of basic needs can ever have been unable to buy basic goods. None of those who bred crops for high yield in high-input conditions is likely ever to have been a resource-poor farmer. The Sulawezi livestock staff were in an office, not living in villages and needing to keep on good terms with neighbours. Those who projected the woodfuel crisis are unlikely to have lived in a village and cooked with biomass. Forest department staff in Haryana preferred short-term physical works which might perhaps contribute to their unofficial incomes, not longer-term fruit-tree growing which would contribute to the livelihood flows of local people. Foresters in Pakistan derived their beliefs both from their professional training, and from meetings which were 'rigorously restricted to a tiny fraction of the rural population, namely the rural élite' (Dove, 1992: 32).

In each case, professionals projected and asserted their reality and interests, and ignored, failed to appreciate, or opposed those of local people.

182

Their normal professionalism, distance, dominance, selective perceptions, personal interests and life experiences combined variously to mislead. It is scarcely surprising, on reflection, that professionals at international conferences, on research stations and in laboratories, in offices with computers and working in a transfer-of-technology mode have had such different criteria and preferences from local people. Their life experiences, working environments, values, reward systems, livelihood strategies and personal interests all differ. Without major reversals, there is no way they could share the same realities.

Diversity within the community

Again and again, outsider professionals treat communities as homogeneous. Policy documents and project proposals advocate 'community participation' and go no further. Visitors to villages and slums assume that those whom they meet represent 'the community'. Within communities, though, there are many obvious differences. Following Alice Welbourn (1991), four major axes of difference can be seen: of age, gender, ethnic or social group, and poverty; and there are always others: of capability and disability, education, livelihood strategy, types of assets, and much else. Those whom outsiders meet and interact with are most likely to be middle-aged or youths, male, from dominant groups, and economically better off. And often their criteria, preferences and priorities are taken as those of the whole community; but the community also includes those who are weaker and worse off – children, the very old, females, social inferiors, subordinate groups, the disabled and those who are vulnerable and poor.

The use of PRA approaches and methods has repeatedly confirmed that different groups, households and individuals within a community have a variety of criteria, preferences and priorities. This has been demonstrated through combinations and sequences of participatory mapping, seasonal calendars, causal and linkage diagramming, matrix-scoring and ranking, Venn diagramming, well-being ranking and other methods, applied by different individuals and groups (see e.g. Welbourn, 1991; Swift and Umar, 1991; Redd Barna, 1993; Guijt *et al.*, 1994).

There are, of course, commonalities of interest. The illustrations which follow emphasize differences. The point is that until tests for difference have been made, commonalities or consensus cannot be assumed; and those who are younger or very old, female, of low-status groups and/or poor, deprived, disabled and weak will tend to be left out unless care is taken to find them and bring them in. The axes interlock. As Alice Welbourn has pointed out:

> If we speak to the 'women's group', we often fail to recognize that these women tend to be the wives of better-off, more influential men in the community. The single mothers, the divorcees, the poorer wives tend to be excluded from such groups on the basis of economic well-being, moral standing or just age.

On *age*, Welbourn (1991: 16–18) found that young and old express different realities and priorities. In Bangladesh young men mapped the paths and railway they used to go to find work, while the old men showed the boundaries of land lost to the river but to which they still laid claim. In a village in Sierra Leone, Welbourn intervened to stop young men leaving a meeting in disgust: old men were giving their priorities; the young men felt theirs would once again be neglected. They were persuaded to stay. It emerged later that the old men wanted a new bridge to get across the river to their land, and a new mosque; the young men wanted a school and football goal posts.

On *gender*, the different knowledge, perceptions and priorities of women and men have been extensively expressed through PRA methods (see e.g. Welbourn, 1991, 1992; Mukherjee, 1993: 104–8; Humble, 1994; Guijt and Shah, forthcoming). No generalizations are likely to be valid everywhere, but some contrasts are common. Women and men know and show in their diagrams and calendars much about what touches their lives and the activities they engage in: women usually know more about, and attach more importance to, people – who lives where, how many there are in a family, health status and the like – and show this in social maps; men know more about surrounding resources and towns, and show this in resource maps. In drawing maps of the same environment, those of women and men often differ significantly (Cornwall, 1991; Welbourn, 1991), showing the different places they visit and that matter to them, and their relative concerns and priorities. PRA procedures, using matrix scoring of trees, have been evolved to enable women and men in a community to state the relative numbers they would like of species of their choice. The sexes meet separately and allocate 100 seeds or stones to the species they want. A negotiation (often, it seems, good humoured) is then mediated between the two groups (M. Shah, 1995a).

Many gender differences have been expressed and illuminated through PRA methods: in Kenya, men's and women's rights of ownership and access; in Bangladesh, differences in type and amount of foods consumed by month for women and men, and for a girl child and boy child; in Zimbabwe, differences of weighting criteria in matrix-scoring of different grain crops (Scoones, 1995b: 89, 91); and cash flows, for which Meera Shah (1993b: 18) found in Ghana that 'not only are women's and men's cash flows separate and very different from each other, but they also face different points of seasonal stress in terms of their livelihoods'.

PRA methods have many similar applications for the hitherto rather opaque area of intra-household allocations and relations, and domestic violence.

Women and men also express different values in identifying those they consider poor or badly off. In an Indian village, men chose male-headed households when identifying the poorest; the women identified two widows, one of whom was blind in one eye (Mukherjee, 1993: 105). For the men, assets and employment opportunities were more important (the two widows had access to some land); for the women, physical and social conditions were more important.

On *ethnic or social group*, social mappers in India almost always try to show different households by caste. Ethnic and social groups are often

Table 8.4: Livelihood analysis of income flows (cash only) by men and women, Darko Village, Ashanti Region, Ghana, May 1993

						Month						
Item	J	F	M	A	M	J	J	A	S	O	N	D
Men												
Inflows												
Cocoa	3	1			1	1	2	4	7	14	7	4
Maize					2	4	5	7	9	11	5	
Leather work			3	4						6	10	12
Masonry										5	7	9
Carpentry										5	7	8
Agri. labour	3	7	8	3								2
Women												
Vegetables			2	5	7	5						
Cassava	3	1					1	2	3	5	7	9
Agri. labour				3	5	8	1					
Outflows												
Men									7	10	12	9
Women					7	3						22

Analysts: Mary Amponsah, Charles Nyantaki, Alex Bobie-Ansah and K.B. Abu.

Notes: Prepared on ground using chalk, local materials and beans for scoring. The numbers are of beans placed for each month. Men and women analysed separately. Men's and women's scores cannot, therefore, be compared in absolute terms.

Source: M. Shah, (1993a).

residentially clustered. Interests and priorities can be not just different, but antagonistic, as between cultivators and pastoralists in the same villages in parts of Gujarat in India. How much life for women in the same community can vary by social group can be illustrated from a participatory assessment of women's problems and concerns in Morocco (Shah and Bourarach, 1995) (Table 8.5). Three groups – Berber, Arab and Draoui lived in the same village. Of eleven activities, only two – housework and processing dates at home – were undertaken by women from all three groups.

On *poverty and deprivation*, Jeremy Swift and Abdi Noor Umar (1991) note that public meetings tend to be dominated by one or two people who are often not representative of the community as a whole, and that it would be wrong anyway to expect communities, stratified by wealth, age, gender and occupation, to have a single view of priorities. In their work with the pastoral Boran people in Kenya, wealth or well-being ranking was first used, and then focus-group discussions held with wealth groups – rich, middle and poor, using a problem-and-solution game with holes in the ground, similar to a traditional game familiar to the Boran. The results, from 24 groups of the rich, 17 of the middle, and 27 of the poor, are consolidated in Table 8.6. The contrast between rich and poor is sharp: for the rich, livestock management scored 87 out of 100 (and most of the 'other' was problems with lion and hyena), against only 7 for the poor. The

Table 8.5: Participation in activities by women of different social groups in Assrir Village, Ouarzazate, Morocco, 1994–95

Activities	Social groups		
	Berber	Arab	Draoui
Housework	Y	Y	Y
Harvesting cereals	Y	N	Y
Grazing cattle	Y	N	Y
Collecting fodder	Y	N	Y
Collecting dates	Y	N	Y
Processing dates at home	Y	Y	Y
Sewing	Y	Y	N
Knitting	Y	Y	N
Gathering fuelwood	Y	N	Y
Selling fuelwood	Y	N	Y
Selling fodder	Y	N	Y

Source: Shah and Bourarach, 1995: 102.

Table 8.6: Problems and solutions as seen by different wealth groups – Boran pastoralists in Isiolo District, Kenya, 1991 (% of total possible score)

	Rich	Middle	Poor
Livestock management	87	51	7
Lack of livestock	–	21	49
Agriculture	4	9	13
Alternative employment	2	4	10
Direct assistance	–	2	12
Other	7	10	9
	100	100	100

Source: Swift and Umar, 1991: 56.

problems and solutions of the poor were more diverse, the largest being lack of livestock (49 out of 100), which did not score at all for the rich.

Differences between communities and between types of communities are also often marked. Within the same district in South India, a comparison of 12 villages, all growing irrigated rice, found striking contrasts between all of them (Chambers and Harriss, 1977). More generally, types of community differ. In India, again, there is a common dichotomy between villages which are accessible, larger, with irrigated land, a mixture of castes and greater social inequalities, and those which are remote, smaller, with rainfed agriculture, less marked social inequalities and more homogeneity of castes (Dasgupta, 1975; Chambers, Shah and Saxena, 1989: 162). In rural Morocco, Meera Shah and Khadija Bourarach (1995: 125) found that the concerns and priorities of women separated villages into two types: those with basic infrastructure and facilities like safe drinking-water, healthcare and cooking fuel; and those which lacked them.

Differences between communities, and within communities by age, gender, social group and poverty and wealth, are almost universal, and universally significant. Being aware of them is part of good facilitation practice in participatory appraisal and analysis. There is a limit, though, to how far the analysis of difference can and should go. It may be essential to find those who are excluded, and to bring them into a participatory process, or help them to generate their own. It can also be part of a good strategy to find issues which Irene Guijt (pers. comm. 1995) calls catalytic, which are in everyone's interest and which can bring people together. In participatory processes the challenge is to sequence and balance a coming together around common interests, and recognize and support diversity, complexity and multiple realities to empower those who are weaker and excluded.

Reversals for complexity and diversity

The emerging consensus of objectives and values outlined in Chapter 1 combined responsible well-being, capabilities, livelihood security, equity and sustainability. The means are now clearer to make that vision practical. Responsible well-being for uppers includes commitment to empowering lowers, enhancing their capabilities and confidence, and so serving equity. And in a local, complex, diverse, dynamic and unpredictable context, livelihoods and sustainability are to be sought less by simplifying and standardizing, and more by complicating and diversifying links and relationships.

To achieve that vision requires reversals: of normal professionalism, from the universal and simple to the local and complex; of normal bureaucracy, from top-down and standard packages to bottom-up and diverse baskets of choice; of normal careers, from moving inwards to moving also outwards; of normal learning, from vertical and didactic to lateral and experiential; and of normal behaviour, from dominance to empowerment.

These reversals are the subject of the last two chapters of this book. They challenge all those who work in development. They imply and require a new paradigm (Chapter 9) and changes which are personal, professional and institutional (Chapter 10).

9

The New High Ground

Probably the single most prevalent claim advanced by the proponents of a new paradigm is that they can solve the problems that have led the old one to a crisis.

Thomas Kuhn, 1962

As the existing system crumbles around us, new and exciting alternatives are sprouting up in the rubble.

Daphne Thuvesson, 1995, 26–27

In an evolving paradigm of development there is a new high ground, a paradigm of people as people. Local, complex, diverse, dynamic and unpredictable, its conditions are difficult to measure and demand judgement. RRA fits a cybernetic model of fast feedback in conditions of rapid change. Good PRA goes further, in empowering lowers. Its principles, precepts and practices resonate with parallel evolutions in the natural sciences, chaos and complexity theory, the social sciences and post-modernism, and business management.

On the new high ground, decentralization, democracy, diversity and dynamism combine. Multiple local and individual realities are recognized, accepted, enhanced and celebrated. Truth, trust, and diversity link. Baskets of choice replace packages of practices. Doubt, critical self-awareness and acknowledgement of error are valued. Reversals, positive-sums and 'both–and' thinking are mutually reinforcing. To the new high ground the PRA experience adds empirical affirmations: that 'lowers can do it'; that social synergy and fun are a positive sum; and that uppers' behaviour, attitudes and personal responsibility are central. For the realities of lowers to count more, and for the new high ground to prevail, it is uppers who have to change.

Paradigms and development

In starting this chapter I have struggled not to say that current thinking about development is in crisis. The word crisis is overused. In a sense, thinking about the human condition always has been in crisis; and perhaps it would be wrong were it not. There may be no final or universal answers to the Great Questions of Life. What seems permanent is search, questioning, uncertainty and change.

Still, as noted in Chapter 1, change is accelerating, both in development itself and in thinking about development. Theories of universal economic growth as a unilinear main means to a better life are no longer tenable (see e.g. Ekins and Max-Neef, 1992; Sachs, 1992). As economic growth ceases to be a simple, universal objective, as it is recognized as environmentally harmful among the richer, and as economic resources are recognized as finite, so it matters more to seek responsible well-being and quality of life through more sustainable means. For the rich, the question is how to be better off with less; for the poor, it is how to gain more and be better off without repeating the errors of the rich. One way to serve these objectives is to enable local people to identify, express and achieve more of their own priorities. In line with this, the emergent paradigm for human living on and with the Earth brings together decentralization, democracy and diversity. What is local, and what is different, is valued. The trends towards centralization, authoritarianism and homogenization are reversed. Reductionism, linear thinking, and standard solutions give way to an inclusive holism, open-systems thinking, and diverse options and actions.

Development theory and practice are in constant flux. The speed with which key words come and go and fashions flourish and fade confuses, alarms and breeds cynicism. Some phrases have fallen from favour: calls for better co-ordination, better integration, better planning and better transfer of technology, once standbys for civil servants drafting ministers' speeches, now raise eyebrows. In their place in the latter half of the 1980s and in the 1990s have come other words: accountability, civil society, entitlement, governance, human rights, livelihood, ownership, participation, people-centred development, stakeholder, sustainability, transparency, well-being.

I have argued elsewhere (1986: 1993a: 1–14) that fashions conceal deeper continuities and shifts of paradigm. By paradigm, I mean a coherent and mutually supporting pattern of concepts, values, methods and behaviour, amenable to wide application. Two well-known contrasting paradigms are the top–down blueprint and bottom–up learning process approaches to development, first elaborated by David Korten and well documented (e.g. Korten, 1980, 1984; Rondinelli, 1983). Resonating with, and reinforcing this contrast, earlier chapters in this book have suggested other polar dimensions so that we have, putting them together:

things	*people*
top–down	bottom–up
blueprint	learning process
measurement	judgement
standardization	diversity

The things column corresponds with much normal professionalism, and the people column with much of a new professionalism.

Blueprint approaches are needed and are brilliantly successful in engineering. Blueprints, precise measurements and calculations, standardization and much that goes with normal professionalism, are essential for physical constructions; we need buildings and bridges which stand and are safe.

The problems arise because, as we saw in Chapter 3, those who work in the paradigm of things tend, professionally, to be high-status uppers, while those who work in the paradigm of people, tend to be low-status lowers. Economists, engineers and blueprint approaches usually dominate the early stages of new projects, when construction is a prominent goal and activity; and their norms and ways of working then set patterns which persist into the later project stages, with top–down, centrally planned targets even though the goals and activities have shifted to people. The problem is that the necessary paradigm which fits things and also people as things, has extended and gone out of bounds to structure the domain of people as people. Many of the errors of development have followed from trying to apply blueprint approaches, which work with controllable and predictable things, to processes with uncontrollable and unpredictable people.

The counter and complementary paradigm of people as people has, though, been evolving and gaining strength and coherence. Its reversals and changes in dominant concepts, values, methods and behaviours have found many expressions. Among international organizations UNICEF has been a leader in putting people first, and UNDP in its *Human Development Report* (HDR) has broken much new ground. Perhaps most significant have been movements within the World Bank. *Putting People First* was the title of a book edited by Michael Cernea and published for the World Bank in 1985. In December 1990 a bank-wide Learning Group on Participatory Development was launched, leading in 1994 to official endorsement of participatory approaches (World Bank, 1994b) which are contrary to much of the style and culture of that organization. In 1995 there were world summits for social development in Copenhagen and for women in and near Beijing. A new high ground of reversals of the normal has been taking shape – a high ground of people as people, of people first, and of lowers first of all.

The new high ground

In the opening sentences of his book *Educating the Reflective Practitioner* (1987), Donald Schon wrote:

> In the varied topography of professional practice, there is a high, hard ground overlooking a swamp. On the high ground, manageable problems lend themselves to solution through the application of research-based theory and technique. In the swampy lowland, messy, confusing problems defy technical solution. The irony of this situation is that the problems of the high ground tend to be relatively unimportant to individuals or society at large, however great their technical interest may be, while in the swamp lie the problems of greatest human concern. The practitioner must choose. Shall he (sic) remain on the high ground where we can solve relatively unimportant problems according to prevailing standards of rigor, or shall he descend to the swamp of important problems and nonrigorous inquiry?

The evolving paradigm turns this on its head, as Schon perhaps would wish. His high ground describes the conditions of normal professionalism, but a new professionalism is taking over. The imagery is upended: the swamp becomes new high ground.

190

So with new imagery, the old high ground of normal professionalism is now a flat plan surrounded by wooded hills. On the flat plain, tractors plough straight lines in large monocropped fields. Work is controlled, regular, repetitive and easy to measure. The people of the plain are specialists with jobs and narrow vision. In contrast, the new high ground of the wooded hills above is varied and irregular. Many sorts of plants, animals and people coexist and interact in a flux of change. Activities are diverse, complex, irregular, adaptive, and harder to measure. The people of the hills improvise and assure their livelihoods in many ways. They are versatile generalists with varied skills, and have many perspectives.

The plain is a domain of things and of people like things – simplified, standardized, regimented, controlled, predictable. The wooded hills are a domain of people and of things like people – complex, diverse, independent, uncontrolled, and unpredictable. On the plain, order has been imposed; in the hills, continuity is interactive.

The normal professional assumption has been that the modern pattern of the plains should be and will be extended to the hills. Disciplined hard work fits and supports the drive for regularity, order and control. A verse of Richard Henry Horne (1803–84) embodies virtues both Victorian and Stalinist:

> Ye rigid ploughmen! Bear in mind
> Your labour is for future hours
> Advance! Spare not! Nor look behind!
> Plough deep and straight with all your powers!

The great poetry of Isaiah, too, expresses the vision of a godly order through levelling and smoothing:

> The voice of him that crieth in the wilderness,
> Prepare ye the way of the Lord, make straight in the desert a highway for our God.
> Every valley shall be exalted, and every mountain and hill shall be made low: and the crooked shall be made straight, and the rough places plain.

Jehovah was an anthropomorphic and patriarchal figure.[1] And the drive for mastery of the physical environment has been deep in the human, and perhaps especially male, psyche. Until recently, these drives have been little questioned. In a world of where macho values prevailed, they seemed to make sense. The plains belong to the paradigms of uppers, of male dominance and control, imposing uniformity, of Man separate from and superior to nature.[2]

With awareness of spaceship earth, of the global village, of limits to growth, and of threats to the environment, the metaphorical hills have come into their own. It is less from simple uniformities imposed on plains, and more with complex diversities fostered in hills, that sustainable livelihoods and responsible well-being can be assured. The hills belong to the paradigm of managing diversity, of sharing and enabling, of humankind in symbiosis with the rest of nature. Still, the plains people are powerful, uppers in power if lowers in well-being and vision. As a rich and prosperous minority – scientists, politicians, bureaucrats, businesspeople, farmers and contractors – they colonize the hills, woods and forests. But resistance builds, and reversals begin. In counterflows, here and there, the plains are recolonized by the systems of the hills.

For on the high ground, the normal is reversed. People are not treated as things *manqués*, but as complex, diverse, dynamic, individual and idiosyncratic people. The values, uniformities and relationships of the plains are turned on their heads. People come before things, lowers before uppers, judgement before measurement, lateral and experiential South–South sharing and learning before vertical North–South lecturing and transfers of reality. Change is continuous. Realities are multiple and in constant flux.

Parallel evolutions

The new high ground has been emerging in different domains in which evolution has been parallel. The concepts, values, methods, behaviours and beliefs in one political system, profession, discipline, organization, or community interpenetrate with and influence others. There is an ambience of questioning former certainties; the unthinkable becomes less unthinkable. Now, with the communications revolution of the 1990s, this happens more than ever.

Words and phrases play their part in this. The effects of language are not trivial. New words and the concepts they carry change the way we think and act. They seem to be shared, borrowed and adopted between disciplines more than before. They lodge and embed themselves through repetition, and are manifest in thoughts and actions. Parallel shifts make times ripe for changes unimaginable earlier. So perhaps it has been with RRA and PRA. They seem so obvious that one wonders why we had to wait for them until the 1980s and 1990s. Part of the answer may be that in other domains old certainties had to be shaken and new ways opened up. Conditions had to be favourable for innovation and spread.

The paradigmatic significance of RRA has already been recognized and analysed. Neil Jamieson's (1987) paper to the International Conference on Rapid Rural Appraisal at Khon Kaen in 1985 was a milestone. Jamieson argued that RRA, with its rapid learning, fitted and supported a new and emerging paradigm of development. Despite their ideological conflicts, Marxists, socialists and capitalists had shared evolutionary, unilineal, universalistic, positivistic and utilitarian assumptions, and a fervent belief in progress. Another view of development, he said, was of human evolution as problem-solving under pressure, as adaptive change. This fitted better with a cybernetic systems approach, which included the concepts of feedback, of lead time (the time between receipt of information and when it is too late to use it), and of lag time (the time between receipt of information and the completion of action based on it) (see also Joseph, 1991). Jamieson argued that accelerating change and increased unpredictability made accurate and timely feedback more vital than ever for effective adaptive change.

Since 1985, these points of Jamieson have come to apply even more. Russel and Ison (1991) have gone on to link RRA with soft systems theory

(Checkland, 1981) and contextual science. RRA and PRA have been validated and reinforced, as modest partners, by parallel developments in the natural sciences, in chaos and edge-of-chaos theory, in the social sciences, and in business management, sharing with them a new high ground.

Natural sciences

In the natural sciences, conventional approaches, using hard systems and reductionist assumptions and methods, are in crisis when faced with many of our important problems (Mearns 1991; Appleyard 1992). Scientific method is not competent to predict or prescribe for the complex open systems which matter most. Global environmental issues involve huge uncertainties, and demand what Funtowicz and Ravetz (1990) call 'second order science' in which judgement plays a more recognized part. Precise understanding, prediction and prescription for local agro-eco-social systems can be similarly elusive. This is not a new discovery. Jeremy Swift wrote in 1981:

> a major World Bank livestock development project in Mali is based, for crucial calculations of sustainable grazing pressure, on the report of a highly competent ecologist in 1972; the calculations were redone in 1977/78 by a different, equally well-qualified ecologist, who halved the earlier carrying capacity. Nobody is to blame; the science is inexact. But the consequences could be disastrous for the project, and more so for the pastoralists involved. (Swift 1981: 487)

Perhaps no one was to blame then. But now we know more about what is not knowable using the standard methods of established disciplines. When so much is so unknowable and so unpredictable, it seems sensible to seek solutions through methodological pluralism, through flexible and continuous learning and adaptation. Here the new high ground is recognition of the need for, and limits to, the exercise of judgement.

Two relevant contributions from ecology stand out:

(1) With ecological systems, resilience increases with complexity. Simple systems with few links are vulnerable. If one part of a food chain disappears, a whole system can collapse. Conversely, in systems which are complex and diverse, there is redundancy. If one part disappears, others can substitute. The analogy with livelihood and farming systems is evident. Within the limits of labour, management and economics, complexity and diversity make systems more resilient, adaptable and secure. Here the new high ground is recognition that for many poor people there are gains in complicating and diversifying their livelihood systems.
(2) New ecological theory has introduced an understanding of non-equilibrium dynamics (Behnke *et al.*, 1995; Scoones, 1995c). Conventional theory is linear: ecological succession proceeds through a natural process of stages, leading to a climatic climax system. This applies generally in well-endowed and stable environments. It bears some

resemblance to Rostow's (1960) theory of stages of economic growth which was in vogue in the 1950s. In less well-endowed environments, such as those of much pastoralism in Africa, with low and highly variable rainfall, the succession model does not hold. There is no convergence on an equilibrium state. Instead there are multiple states with degrees of stability, and transitions between states, with thresholds, irreversibility and critical levels of variability as key concepts. To these dynamic and unpredictable conditions the opportunist strategies of pastoralists are well fitted. Here the new high ground is recognition of a nimble and versatile adaptability using a diverse repertoire of responses, as a key quality for those who seek livelihoods in uncertain and marginal environments.

Chaos and complexity theory

From chaos theory and complexity theory come further support. At the empirical level, as was suggested in Chapter 1, changes in local and global conditions – ecological, social and political – appear to be accelerating. At a theoretical level, chaos theory has now shown more clearly how patterns and directions of change can be sensitive to small differences in starting conditions (Gleick, 1988). This underlines even more the importance of quick learning and adjustments, and of personal responsibility and opportunity. In conditions of faster change and increasing unpredictability, prompt learning and rapid adaptive responses matter even more because of the bigger later effects they can have.

Those working on 'edge-of-chaos' theory (Waldrop, 1994), like their ecologist colleagues, challenge simplistic concepts of sustainability as convergence on an equilibrium. In the words of John Holland:

> You have to assume that the transitions are going to continue forever and ever and ever. You have to talk about systems that remain continuously dynamic, and that are embedded in environments that themselves are continuously dynamic.
>
> (Quoted in Waldrop, 1994: 356)

The world has to adapt itself to a permanence of transitions, a condition of perpetual novelty, at the edge of chaos. This edge of chaos is a zone of plurality. Located between, on the one side, a wooden, formal and predictable order and, on the other side, an unpredictable chaos, it nurtures complexity and creativity. Systems at the edge of chaos are found better able to respond to change. This may be so for individuals, populations or entire ecosystems. Here the emergent new high ground is a science of complexity, reinforcing the common sense of Arnold Toynbee's theory of challenge and response in history: that adaptive innovation flowers in the border zone between formal stability and anarchic chaos, where the challenges are strong enough to loosen constraints and evoke creative responses but not so strong as to destroy.

In computer simulations, complex behaviour is now generated through decentralized self-organization. Self-organization is 'the spontaneous emergence of nonequilibrium structural organizations on a macroscopic level due to collective interactions between a large number of simple, usually microscopic, objects' (Coveney and Highfield, 1995: 432). Simulations of flocks of birds flying, termites foraging, and traffic jams, are examples of self-organization, without leaders and without central control (Resnick, 1994). Their complex and apparently co-ordinated behaviour on the computer screen arises, as it were democratically, from a few simple rules of behaviour for a number of objects.

The analogy to be explored for human society is that not centralization and many complex rules, but decentralization and a few simple tendencies or rules, are the conditions for complex and harmonized local behaviour. Examples of spontaneous organization from tendencies might be an audience which starts by clapping chaotically and comes to clap in unison, or a group which starts singing a song in different keys but converges on one.[3] An example of spontaneous organization from simple rules might be small groups for savings and credit, where the key minimum is honest, accurate and transparent accounting, permitting each group then to evolve its own complex, diverse and unpredictable behaviour. The hypothesis here, by analogy with findings from computer explorations, is that diversity, complexity, creativity and adaptability will be greatest at the local level with an appropriate minimum of regulation to enable individuals to know what the rules are and what is happening, so that they can collaborate creatively.

Social sciences

The social sciences have contributed through questioning the past solid ground of universals. Post-modernism and some insights of Norman Uphoff (1992) deserve mention here.

Post-modernism (e.g. Harvey, 1990; Rosenau, 1992) has eroded some of the solid ground of the plain. It asserts philosophical relativism and multiple realities. Rosenau makes intelligible the inconsiderate obscurity (if it is not thought disorder) of some post-modern authors.[4] She separates them into the sceptical and the affirmative. Interpreting the view of the affirmative, less radical, post-modernists, she writes (ibid: 22):

The absence of truth . . . yields intellectual humility and tolerance. [The post-modernists] see truth as personal and community-specific: although it may be relative, it is not arbitrary . . . Some of them substitute a substantive focus on the local, on daily life, and on traditional narrative for the hegemonic theory of mainstream social science.

Norman Uphoff's (1992) study of participation in Sri Lanka and the conclusions he draws from it appears to have more to contribute, and more intelligibly, than post-modernism. His 'post-Newtonian social science' challenges reductionism and mechanistic models. Beyond this, his distinctive contribution is to recognize and rehabilitate altruism and co-operation, to stress positive sums and to identify the potentials of 'social energy' which is manifest when individuals and groups work for some common purpose.

195

Post-modernism, Uphoff's analysis and PRA have different starting points and trajectories: some post-modernism tends to a near-anarchic individualism of realities; Uphoff starts with empirical experience which then informs and interlinks with theory; and PRA sticks more with the action, with dispersed practitioners subject to the discipline of what works and what seems ethically right, trying to do better through action more than thinking about theory. But post-modern theory, post-Newtonian social science and the experience of PRA are mutually reinforcing. They share the common new high ground, for variously they affirm and celebrate multiple realities, local diversity and personal and social potentials.

Business management

In business management, the parallel shift has been from the values and strategies of mass production to those of post-Fordist flexible specialization (see e.g. Kaplinsky, 1991: 7). Standardization has been replaced by variety and rapid response, hierarchical supervision by trust, and punitive quality control by personal quality assurance at source. A highly successful Brazilian manager, when he took over a company, abolished norms, manuals, rules and regulations, put the company's employees 'in the demanding position of using their own judgement', and adopted the principle that a company should trust its destiny to its employees (Semler, 1989: 79; 1993). Much in Tom Peters' advice (1989, 1992, 1994) to business managers, especially in *Thriving on Chaos: Handbook for a Management Revolution* (1989), applies equally in PRA. He advocates, for example, achieving flexibility by empowering people, learning to love change, becoming obsessed with listening, and deferring to the front line.

The theme of local knowledge and action is also strong. In *The Fifth Discipline: The Art and Practice and the Learning Organisation* (1990: 228) Peter Senge writes 'Localness is especially vital in times of rapid change. Local actors often have more current information in customer preferences, competitor actions and market trends; they are in a better position to manage the continuous adaptation that change demands'.

The need for more flexible learning approaches has now been widely recognized in management. In problem-solving, Checkland (1981, 1989) has pioneered and thought through a shift from mechanistic, hard-systems thinking – part of and derived from systems engineering, systems analysis and operational research (1989: 275), to soft-systems methodology. Soft-systems methodology, he argues, is the general case of which systems engineering is a special case. The problem-solving approach derived from systems engineering failed when attempts were made to apply it 'to the messy, changing, ill-defined problem situations with which managers have to cope in their day-to-day professional lives' (ibid 288), where the notions of 'a problem' and 'a solution' are inappropriate, and what makes more sense is a process of learning which is never-ending (1981: 279).

Strikingly, writers on management stress paradox, reversals, and what to a linear reductionist thinker must appear irrationality. Charles Handy writes of *The Age of UNreason* (1989), with the Un emphasized in the original, and 'An Upside-down Society'. In his 1989 classic *Thriving on*

196

Chaos, Tom Peters writes about 'building systems for a world turned upside down'. His 1992 best-seller, *Liberation Management*, is subtitled *necessary* DISORGANIZATION *for the nanosecond nineties* (my emphasis), and concludes with a chapter on customerizing, in which customers produce, direct and star. This is different from customizing:

> Customizing, a good idea, is still pre-Copernican in slant. 'We' are still the center of the universe, presenting 'them' with a carefully crafted menu of offerings. It misses that huge Disney-leap into their creating us. Customer-as-initiator is the point. According to the new model, the factory, operating room or restaurant kitchen gets invented last, not first'. (Ibid. 742)

More surprising is the trend towards open sharing of information. In business this is, in 1996, largely in the North and between uppers. Secrecy is less secure with the ease of photocopying, as shown by information leaked to competitors or the press, and with the creation of cyberspace by computer and information technology, as shown by hackers. The Internet is a vast open-access voluntary co-operative for public sharing and linking, for those who have the technology and can afford the fee. It both opens up astonishing possibilities for sharing and interaction between 'uppers', among whom it is levelling, and creates a new class of excluded 'lowers'. Secrecy is also argued to be less efficient since it fosters centralization, stops exchanges and slows mutual learning. Tom Peters (1994: 191) urges business managers to: 'Reflect on the anthropological issues – a culture of knowledge-sharing versus hoarding, user-democracy versus authoritarianism'.

It has been the discipline of the market and opportunities and imperatives of new technology which have driven and drawn business management to decentralized flexibility, to diversification, towards a culture of sharing information, in order to keep ahead, to finding and exploiting transient niche markets. The ultimate discipline is sales and profits. For PRA and related approaches, the ultimate discipline is what works with people and communities. In both business management and PRA, value is placed on decentralization, open communications and sharing knowledge, empowerment, diversity and rapid adaptation. Error is embraced, 'failing forwards'. The one-sentence manual for PRA – 'Use your own best judgement at all times' (KGVK, 1991) – originates in North American business management (Peters, 1989: 378–9).[5] The new high ground in business management values trust and individual discretion and initiative.

Permanently provisional: the evolving paradigm

The evolving paradigm is permanently provisional. It differs from Thomas Kuhn's (1962) presentation of scientific paradigms. They somewhat resemble structures which are built up and built upon, with some of the solidity and ultimate fragility of a fixed physical thing. When finally challenged, they crumble and fall, to be replaced by a new structure. The evolving paradigm is more like a living thing which grows, changing form to fit its changing environment, flexible, able to yield and able to expand. To take another analogy (pers. comm. Sam Joseph), while the paradigm of traditional modern science is like a set symphony score for an orchestral concert, the evolving paradigm is more like a jazz performance, with improvisations around themes. Yet again, there is Uphoff's imagery derived from committed involvement in practical change: 'our experience in Gal Oya, once we were immersed in efforts to improve irrigation with farmer participation, made reality look ever more like a river and less like a rock' (ibid. 277).

But none of these analogies is exact. Things and people are what they are. The evolving paradigm is what it is – a mutually supporting pattern of concepts, values, methods and behaviours which is widely applicable and is neither fixed nor static.

The river analogy helps by bringing us closer to the turbulence of human experience. In chaos theory there are 'points of stability mixed with instability, and regions with changeable boundaries' (Gleick, 1988: 299). In the evolving paradigm in development thinking, one can ask whether it makes sense to search for concepts which can be like the 'basins of attraction' or 'strange attractors' of chaos theory. These, like the red spot on Jupiter, have a stability which emerges from the surrounding chaotic conditions. That is one way of seeing the suggestion in Chapter 1 of an emerging consensus on five concepts, each being both end and means (see Figure 1.1 and pp. 9–12). Readers will judge for themselves whether those, or other concepts they can propose, could serve as stable concepts in the flux of human change, or whether the idea of stable concepts is itself flawed, a contradiction of the paradigm.

Other parts of the new high ground can be sketched. Each of us would make a different chart. For me, in the context of development, five clusters or dimensions stand out, and seem to cohere:

○ *the 4 Ds* – decentralization, democracy, diversity and dynamism
○ *managing* complexity, diversity and dynamism
○ *diversity and choice*, from packages to baskets
○ *doubt and self-critical awareness*, and
○ *modes of thinking* – reversals, both–and, and positive sum.

To these can then be added four contributions from PRA experience:

○ *empowerment – lowers can do it*
○ *social synergy and fun*
○ *behaviour and attitudes*, and
○ *personal responsibility*.

All these imply reversals, shifts from current normal thinking and practice. A counter-magnetism of neutralizing normal upper–lower power relations informs and pervades them all.

The four Ds

In the evolving paradigm, one cluster of principles is reversals of normal upper–lower relationships which centralize, standardize, control and

198

stabilize. The changes can be described as the four Ds: decentralization, democracy, diversity, and dynamism.

Ds	normal tendency	reversal
decentralization	power in centre	power to periphery
	control	trust
democracy	unitary authority	dispersed
	dominance	equality
diversity	standardization	differentiation
dynamism	stabilization	change

Some of the gains from the four Ds are commonplaces of the experience and literature of participation. For example, it is recognized that with the four Ds ideally:

○ local knowledge is mobilized
○ local resources and energy are used
○ participation is enhanced
○ actions are better adapted and more sustainable
○ adaptation is fast and fitting to changes in local conditions
○ costs are reduced
○ central administration is reduced
○ political problems and conflicts are resolved locally.

Decentralization demands trust and permits and encourages diversity: different regions, organizations and people, when they have the discretion, do different things. Trust has to be two-way in a non-punitive culture: uppers trust lowers, and lowers trust uppers. With distrust, dominance and centralization, truth is distorted, as we saw in Chapter 5, and diversity muted and masked. Trust in contrast, diminishes misinformation. Lowers who are trusted and who trust their uppers are more likely to report the reality of local conditions, including bad news. Trust is a condition for sharing the truth about diversity. So it is that decentralization, trust, diversity and truth support each other.

Managing for diversity and complexity

As with integrated rural development projects (p. 17), top-down attempts to manage complex interrelations in several sectors at the local level have not worked. The view that more and better surveys would generate more and better data, allowing more and better planning, leading to more and better implementation, has been discredited. Centralized top-down planning for local conditions generates dependency, resentment, high costs, low morale, misinformation and actions which cannot be sustained. It is a problem, not a solution.

The computer-based science of complexity has reached the same conclusion: 'top-down systems are forever running into combinations of events they don't know how to handle. They tend to be touchy and fragile, and they all too often grind to a halt in a dither of indecision' (Waldrop, 1994: 279, citing Chris Langton). To achieve life-like behaviour, the key has been to start with a few simple rules, to use local control instead of global control, and to 'Let the behaviour emerge from the bottom up, instead of being specified from the top down' (ibid: 280).

A spectacular example is the computer-simulation 'boids' devised by Craig Reynolds (Waldrop, 1994: 241–3). Birdlike agents on a screen are given three rules of behaviour: to maintain a minimum distance from other boids and other objects; to try to match the velocities of nearby boids; and to try to move towards the centre of mass of boids in their neighbourhood. These three rules lead invariably to boids flocking about the screen like birds. A top-down rule to 'form a flock' would have been impossibly complex. The rules which worked were simple, local, bottom-up, and the system self-organizing and emergent. In the computer simulation, simple rules generate behaviour which is complex, diverse and, for practical purposes, in its detail unpredictable.

Computers are one thing, social systems another. How transferable principles and experience are from one to the other is hard to judge. The parallels are, though, intriguing. Development projects can be paralysed by overload at their centres of control. But they differ from boids. Projects deal with varied environments and with idiosyncratic people as independent agents. The simple rules which then work have to go further, allowing and enabling people to manage in many ways with their local, complex, diverse, dynamic and unpredictable conditions, and facilitating not the uniform behaviour of flocks but the diverse behaviour of individuals.

This runs counter to the administrative reflex to control. Caution calls for care to guard against all imaginable error or deviation, and for uniform and universal regulations to prevent these. In March 1992, I asked a group of Indian administrators what would be the basic minimum to standardize and regulate the setting-up of village-level savings and credit societies. Their list included rates of savings, application forms, eligibility, purposes of loans, rates of interest, repayment, penalties for default and credit ratios.

In contrast, the programme of some 2500 savings and credit societies initiated and supported by MYRADA, an NGO in South India, are diverse in their practices, entrusting rule-making to individual societies. Each society is free to meet its needs and its members' needs in its own way. Each makes its own rules for how much each member should save and at what intervals, what loans can be for, interest rates, conditions for repayment, penalties for defaulters, and so on. MYRADA insists on only two operating requirements: (i) transparent, accurate and honest accounting; and (ii) that those with special responsibility are regularly rotated through democratic election, and are not called presidents or secretaries but 'representatives' (pers. comm. Aloysius Fernandez, 1996).

These minimal rules or controls permit behaviour which is complex and locally diverse. The striking resonance by analogy with the few simple rules of non-hierarchical self-organizing systems in computer simulations poses the question whether we have here a deep paradigmatic insight, an interesting parallel or an insignificant coincidence. Whatever the answer, provisionally it would seem that with both computers and people the key is to minimize central controls, and to pick just those few rules which promote or permit complex, diverse and locally fitting behaviour. The practical conclusion is to decentralize, with minimum rules of control, to enable local people to appraise, analyse, plan and adapt for local fit in their necessarily different ways.

Diversity and choice, from packages to baskets

The solution of many scientists, bureaucrats and other upper professionals to the problem of local complexity and diversity has been to simplify and standardize, and then to transfer their reality in the form of Model-T packages (pp. 67–70 and Figure 4.2). Poor, local people are believed to be unable to handle complexity. Norman Borlaug, has criticized 'the new complicated and sophisticated' low-input, low-output technologies of sustainable agriculture as 'impractical for the farmer to adopt'. There is much counter-evidence (see e.g. Chapter 8 and Pretty, 1995a) and a different view of farmers' capabilities. Local conditions are too complex, diverse and uncontrollable for Borlaug's simple top-down packages to serve. Poor farmers need to improvise each season. Their environments are CDR (complex, diverse and risk-prone). They want an à la carte menu, with choices, not a fixed package. They can then adapt and fit what they do to their varied and unpredictable conditions.

Figure 4.2 (p. 69) and Table 9.1 contrast the normal professional and bureaucratic system of breeding and generating packages for the transfer-of-technology approach with the alternative farmer-first approach to generate a basket of choices from which farmers can choose to fit their needs and conditions. The principle of diversity and choice for local fit and adaptability is paradigmatic across the board. It applies not only to varieties and species of crops, but also to livestock, fish and trees; to farming practices; to organizations; and to methods and approaches.

One illustration can suffice. With organizations, the top-down tendency is to prescribe the same form of organization everywhere: all collectives, all co-operatives, all savings groups, all watershed committees, and so on. But Scoones, in considering appropriate organizations to provide support for pastoralism in difficult conditions, concludes that

> A diversity of different organizations may be appropriate to tackle complex challenges found in pastoral areas. Pastoral organizations, service NGOs, producers' federations, government – all may have roles. Do not get stuck in one organizational model. (1994: 30)

The fifth D: doubt, and self-critical awareness

The fifth D is doubt. This encompasses self-critical awareness, doubting one's perceptions and realities, and being able to embrace and learn from error. Many uppers are cursed by lack of self-doubt. Priests, politicians, bureaucrats, doctors, lecturers and other powerful professionals all too commonly go through life sure they are right, denying ignorance and hiding error. A new Labour member of Parliament in the UK said she found it astonishing and tiresome that hardly ever did anyone in the House of Commons admit to ignorance on any point or to being wrong.[6] Strong

Table 9.1: Transfer-of-technology and Farmer-first compared

	Transfer-of-technology	Farmer-first
Farming conditions to which applied or more applicable	Simple Uniform Controlled	Complex Diverse Risk-prone
Main objective	Transfer technology	Empower farmers
Analysis of needs and priorities by	Outsiders	Farmers facilitated by outsiders or other farmers
Transferred by outsiders to farmers	Precepts Messages Package of practices	Principles Methods Basket of choices
The 'menu'	Fixed	À la carte
Farmers' behaviour	Hear messages Act on precepts Adopt, adapt or reject package	Apply principles Use methods Choose from basket and experiment
Outsiders' desired outcomes	Widespread adoption of package	Wider farmers' choice and enhanced benefits and adaptability
Roles of outsider	Teacher Trainer Supervisor Service provider	Convenor Facilitator Consultant Searcher for and provider of choice

Source: Adapted from Chambers, 1993a: 68.

through its other virtues may be, parliamentary politics is often marred by a culture of bullshit, the downside of democratic debate. Paradoxically, within limits, admission of error adds to credibility.

Fundamentalisms are worse. To any pluralist it is mystifying how the followers of so many fundamental faiths can separately assert that only they are right, and all others wrong. They are mutually exclusive. Only one, if any, can be right. Each faith is its own isolated fortress. Each then has to believe that the great majority of humankind outside their walls are wrong, damned, infidels, lost souls, inferior. Many with faiths are not fundamentalists. But there are fundamentalists, in this sense, who are variously Christian, Fascist, Hindu, Marxist, Muslim, or racist, or any one of hundreds of political and religious sects. They all share the false security of being certain about the unknowable. Their motto might be, in Hilaire Belloc's whimsical lines:

> Oh! let us never, never doubt
> What nobody is sure about![7]

Quite apart from the intolerance, violence, cruelty and upper–lower dominances which they sustain, fundamentalisms disable. Inability to admit ignorance or error inhibits learning. It is hard for the know-all to know more, or the always right to improve.

In contrast, eclectic pluralists for whom doubt is a way of life are better placed to learn and do better. Self-critical epistemological awareness – examining and reflecting on how and what one learns – is the key. The spirit of mutual enquiry advocated by Karl Popper fits here: 'You may be right, and I may be wrong. And by an effort together we may get closer to the truth'.[8] Learning and doing better are then social, joint efforts; and one person, by admitting he or she may be wrong, makes it easier for others to have the confidence to make similar admissions.

This spirit of self-critical awareness can go yet further in reflecting on one's own partial perception of the realities and meanings of others. Ray Ison expressed this well in presenting his interpretations of some conference papers:

> I am conscious that what I am engaged in is 'mirroring' back my interpretations of what it is that I have read. Of course my interpretations are based on my own experiential history and theories of the world and thus my interpretations may not convey the meanings intended by the authors. My invitation therefore is to accept my interpretations, for which I accept responsibility, as a basis for dialogue, for making meaning, and hopefully for moving towards effective action. (Ison, pers. comm. 1994)

To be able to make such a statement requires a certain confidence, as do admissions of error which are not abject. Paradoxically, the value of self-critical doubt then depends on sense of personal security. For those who lack confidence and feel insecure, self-doubt can disable. For those who feel confident and secure, self-doubt can be enabling. Both face circular traps. The insecure, doubting their abilities, may not dare to try and so not learn what they can do. The secure, sharing their self-doubt and embracing errors, run the risk of self-righteous complacency. For both groups, it helps to recognize that there is a threshold of security and confidence. Above that threshold, self-critical questioning and doubt become means to learning and doing better. The challenge for those below the threshold is to gain the confidence to pass above it; the challenge for those already above it is to help others to join them.

Above all, doubt and self-critical awareness open up to the realities of others. Self-doubt implies that others may know or may be right. Understanding that realities are multiple, and that others' realities differ from one's own and from each other, then becomes a way forward, a means of learning and of doing better.

Reversals

Reversals of the normal, and especially of normal power relations, are a recurrent theme of this book. Much of the analysis and presentation has relied on contrasts and polarization. If the weak are to be empowered, big shifts must occur. Usually both poles of contrasts are needed; for example, both things and people, both top-down and bottom-up, both blueprint and learning process. But the normal imbalances are so extreme that one has to apply great weight on the weaker side for even a slight shift to a better balance. So reversals of the normal are necessary, and especially of upper-lower power relations. Only when reversals are deep and widespread can diversity be expressed and the realities of lowers begin to count as they should.

Reversals of the normal tendencies for uppers' behaviour, professionalism, bureaucracy, careers and modes of learning are shown in Table 9.2. In the magnetic analogy (pp. 58–9), the reversals sought are not absolute, for that simply replaces N–S with a similar S–N. Rather it is that hierarchical fields need to be weakened to give individuals freedom to spin and move and to relate with others in all directions. These are moves into a new space, a meta-paradigm of uncertainty, autonomy, adaptation and multiple interactions, surviving and thriving in and on a permanence of change.

Table 9.2: Reversals for diversity and realism*

	Normal tendencies	Needed reversals
Behaviour	Dominating Lecturing Extracting	Facilitating Listening Empowering
Professionalism	Things first Men before women Professionals set priorities Transfer of technology – packages Simplify	People first Women before men Poor people set priorities Choice of technology – baskets Complicate
Bureaucracy	Centralize Standardize Control	Decentralize Diversify Enable
Careers	Tying down (family) Inwards (urban) Upwards (hierarchy)	Also releasing Also outwards Also downwards
Modes of learning	From 'above' Rural development tourism Questionnaire surveys Measurement and statistics	From 'below' (rapid, relaxed and participatory appraisal etc.) RRA and PRA methods
Analysis and action more by	Professionals, outsiders	Local people, insiders

* The reversals are not absolute but to offset normal bias and so achieve an optimal balance.

Both-and, and positive-sum

As a complement to reversals, Uphoff's analysis of 'both-and' and positive-sum thinking help. Both-and thinking contrasts with the either-or of a forced choice of only one of a contrasted pair. Positive-sum thinking contrasts with negative-sum where a gain for one party is a loss for another. It often makes sense to look for applications of thinking which are both-and (see Uphoff, 1992: 280–84 and below, pp. 235–6) and positive-sum, where all gain.

Local knowledge and scientific knowledge are examples of both-and. The knowledge of local people, variously described as indigenous technical knowledge and rural people's knowledge, has a comparative strength with what is local and observable by eye, changes over time, and matters to people. It has been undervalued and neglected. But recognizing and empowering it should not lead to an opposite neglect of scientific knowledge. Modern science, with its comparative strength with whatever is very large and the very small, has a huge potential part to play in making things better for those who are poor and weak. The key is to know whether, where and how the two knowledges can be combined, with modern science as servant not master, and serving not those who are central, rich and powerful, but those who are peripheral, poor and weak, so that all gain.

An illustration of the complementarity of the two knowledges comes from Latin America. Participatory mapping has enabled indigenous Indian peoples to assert their rights to land, especially forests, and to protect them (see e.g. Denniston, 1995). But this does not mean that satellite imagery cannot also help. The Norwegian Rainforest Foundation raises funds to support a Brazilian NGO, OEDI (the Oecumenical Documentation and Information Centre), which buys satellite photographs and makes them into maps which show roads, deforested areas and forest areas altered by logging. These maps are then passed to Indian communities in Amazonia so that they can monitor the approach and spread of roads, ranches and logging near the boundaries of their territory (pers. comm. Lars Løvold, 1994). In cases like this both-and knowledge, mediated by uppers' altruism, empowers the weak.

Positive-sum thinking overlaps with both-and. Negative-sum thinking applies where all lose, as often in conflicts, and zero-sum thinking applies where one party's gain is another's loss, as often with fixed resources. But there are also many conditions in which all gain, as in the Chinese saying that when the tide comes in 'all boats float higher'. From conflict all may lose; from peace all may gain. In some conditions in irrigation management, all irrigators can gain from changes in water distribution (Chambers, 1988b: 117–24). The management of common property resources to avoid over-exploitation and to distribute benefits equitably is another case where all can often be better off.

The question is whether both-and and positive-sum thinking can contribute to reversals in power. Most uppers see their power in zero-sum terms: if they have less, others will have more, and they will then be worse off. This view is embedded in common usage. We talk of 'giving up power' and 'abandoning' it, implying loss, and 'losing' and 'gaining power' implying a zero sum. The question to be asked again and again, and to which we will turn in Chapter 10, is whether changes between uppers and lowers can be positive-sum, with both gaining through a reduction in the power of uppers.

Practical reflections from PRA

The PRA experience draws on, resonates with, and contributes to the new paradigm. Many of the links and synergies will be evident from Chapters 6, 7 and 8. But four deserve further mention, since they do seem, however modestly, to add something. All are practical and action-oriented. These concern: the capabilities of lowers; social synergy and fun; the behaviour and attitudes of uppers; and personal responsibility.

Empowerment: lowers can do it

The PRA discovery that 'they can do it' has been a startling revelation to many outsiders. Many of the activities which we though only outsider professionals could so, can be done by local people, and done better. As we have seen (pp. 131–3), a sequence of dominoes has fallen. Empowered in a PRA mode, local people have proved able to:

○ map, model, observe on transect walks, list, estimate, rank, score, compare, diagram, and interview, appraising and analysing their conditions;
○ plan and act;
○ monitor, evaluate and conduct their own research;
○ facilitate PRA in other communities and groups; and
○ host and train outsiders.

That poor and weak people can have the ability to undertake their own research has been known for decades. Some of the better known examples are Paulo Freire and his followers in Latin America and elsewhere; the work of the Highlander Center in Appalanchia in enabling poor communities to research on waste dumped on their land (Gaventa, 1980); the research by landless poor people in Bangladesh into how they were exploited, facilitated by BRAC (1979).

What is perhaps new is the way methods, behaviours and sharing have come together to reinforce each other. Visualization is one strong part. It can empower those who are not literate or who otherwise would be marginalized or excluded. Participatory activities in sequences, often starting with visualizations, build on each other. There is something new in intensity, synergy and scale.

The paradigmatic significance of these approaches and capabilities extends to other lowers. In a PRA context children, women, those who are not literate, those of low social status and other lowers have again and again shown abilities beyond normal uppers' expectations. Nor is this at all unique to PRA: workers sit on companies' boards, mental patients speak at psychologists' conferences, and sex workers conduct research into their lives and conditions (Franklin, 1993). Lowers also deceive uppers by feigning incapacity and incapacitate themselves by internalizing uppers' beliefs in their inabilities. The key to realizing and developing capabilities is then belief. When outsiders in PRA believe, and act out their belief, that they can do it, then local people usually find and show that they can indeed do it. Generalizing, the PRA principle of 'they can do it' becomes 'lowers can do it' if uppers show that they believe they can.[9] Believing is enabling.

Social synergy and fun

Normal Uphoff has argued that positive sums can be achieved through the release of what he calls social energy. In PRA activities this is often synergistic, meaning that the sum becomes greater than the parts. There are two sides to this:

(1) *Conflict resolution.* Conflict burns up energy, much of it in negative sums in which all parties lose, materially, morally, in peace of mind and in well-being. Negotiation, agreement and common action can often lead to gains by all, as the energies which were previously destructive and self-cancelling become mutually enhancing. Conflict resolution, especially through agreed visualizations, is one frontier of PRA.

(2) *The flowering of group-visual synergy* (pp. 159–60). This is a repeated experience with PRA methods. The interaction of local people with their visual representations, especially on the ground, with cumulative cross-checking, the addition and correction of detail, and commitment to completeness, often take off into self-sustaining activity. Interpersonal relations change. Participants learn what they are capable of individually and as a group. They learn what they and others know. They analyse. They take pride in what they create. So the process empowers, and often it is enjoyed. The development vocabulary cannot any longer do without the word 'fun', a sense of the creative energy of a spirit of play.

The paradigmatic significance is the power and potential of combinations of: lowers' group activities and analysis; visualizations; the democracy of the ground (pp. 151–2); and a spirit of play. Understanding this has tended to be confined to children. The PRA experience in many countries, however, indicates that these combinations have wide applications for neutralizing verbal dominance among adults, and for empowering lowers.

Uppers' behaviour and attitudes

As PRA approaches and methods spread, the prime importance of facilitators' behaviour and attitudes became clear. Again and again, outsiders wagged their fingers, criticized, lectured, interrupted, suggested what should be done, put forward their own ideas, and contradicted and put down local people. All these were inhibiting. All made local people appear, to outsiders and to themselves, incapable.

So the new imperatives became to establish rapport, to sit down, listen and learn, to be patient, to respect, to facilitate, to 'be nice to people', to learn not to interview, to know when not to speak and when not to be present. The task for outsiders became to hand over the stick, to empower

207

local people, to enhance their confidence, to enable them to define, express and analyse their reality, and not to reflect that of the upper.

The need for such changes of behaviour has been neglected in development. Personal behaviour is rarely a topic in university courses on development. Still less is what sort of people we are. But behaviour and attitudes, what sort of people we are, how we relate to one another are so universally significant that their neglect is bizarre. Perhaps they are personally embarrassing as subjects; to raise them draws attention to one's own defects, to personal hypocrisy, to the personal need to change.

The paradigmatic significance is the reversal of making not lowers, but uppers, the focus: their behaviour, attitudes and beliefs, and what sort of people they are. It is making the powerful the centre of attention for analysis, action and change.

Personal responsibility

With PRA proper, outsiders do not, as in RRA, primarily gather or extract data; they facilitate. Data are expressed and analysed by local people and used by them for their own planning, action, monitoring and evaluation. The dominant values concern less the quality of the data, and more the quality of interaction and process. As Webber and Ison (1995: 110) have put it, in the shift from RRA to PRA 'responsibility replaces objectivity' as a major concern. The issues are ethical more than epistemological. The implications are personal more than methodological.

So, empirically, we find that personal responsibility has emerged as central to PRA. This can be understood from its evolution. PRA is experiential, not metaphysical. It springs from actions in the field, not analyses in academe. Theory has been induced from practice, not deduced from propositions. Good performance has been achieved through practical improvisation, not abstract invention. Discipline has come from the struggle to find what works, and rigour from the demands of interaction, people with people. Guidance has come not from written rules, regulations and procedures but from personal self-critical reflection and judgement. In this mode, each PRA experience has been unique, the outcome of local conditions and personal interactions between local people and facilitators. Authority has resided not in a bible or manual, not in set sequences, but in personal interactions, judgements, improvizations and adaptations. 'Use your own best judgement at all times' has been a sort of meta-manual.

Personal responsibility on the part of uppers is central, not just to PRA, but to the new high ground. It implies self-critical reflection. Paradigmatically, it validates and justifies decentralization, democracy and trust; it permits and requires improvization, invention, and local and individual diversity. It includes responsibility to enable others, lowers, to be responsible. It endorses and expresses multiple realities.

These four reflections cohere. Personal responsibility supports changes in behaviour and attitudes among uppers and outsiders. This enables the capabilities of lowers and local people to be expressed and synergy released. It is when outsiders 'hand over the stick' that it is shown that 'they

208

can do it'. It may be through these experiences that PRA has most to contribute to the evolving paradigm both for development, and in wider contexts.

PRA and development discourse

PRA has been described by some as a movement. Others have talked of a PRA philosophy. Neither word should be allowed to permit pretensions, nor to fix or freeze what is fluid and evolving and has permeable boundaries. There is no linear progression, but rather a continuous process of experiencing, questioning, learning and sharing, of streams flowing, separating, merging and spreading into new domains.

All the same, in PRA experience and writing, and in the orientation of this book, there are commonalities in concerns and concepts. In part, these are signposted in the words which are used and seem to make sense. Some are quite widespread in the development discourse of the mid-1990s. They include: capabilities, complexity, decentralization, democracy, diversity, dynamism, empowerment, equity, ownership, participation, pluralism, process, sustainability and well-being.

In different ways in different places, practitioners of PRA have been putting flesh on the bones of these words. PRA experience also goes further, and points towards other words and concepts, emerging but not yet so current: commitment, disempowerment, doubt, embracing error, fulfilment and fun,[10] generosity,[11] responsibility, self-critical awareness, sharing, trust. These have had little place in the literature of development. None features as a chapter heading in the *Development Dictionary* (Sachs, 1992),[12] which is perhaps not surprising given its generally negative orientation. But all have emerged as significant in PRA experience. Strikingly, all apply to the powerful, to uppers, and to how they behave. All point to changes in uppers' behaviour and attitudes as a way forward.

209

10

Putting the First Last

If PRA as a longer-term process is to have a meaningful influence on mainstream development practice, radical institutional, personal and professional changes are necessary.

Andrea Cornwall and Sue Fleming, 1995: 11–12

It is not that we should simply seek new and better ways for managing society, the economy and the world. The point is that we should fundamentally change how we behave.

Vaclav Havel, 1992

The new high ground presents challenges. Nested in other changes, PRA confronts the dominance of uppers. Rapid spread top-down as a fashion has brought bad practice: dominant and superior behaviour, rushing, upper-to-upper bias, taking without giving, and arousing expectations which are not met. PRA done well generates synergies: the three pillars – methods, behaviour and attitudes, and sharing and partnership – reinforce each other; participatory training sets the style for participation in the field; and adoption of the behaviour and principles of PRA, like the methods, can spread and catalyse other good changes. Empowerment is through identifying the weak and enabling them to gain in skills, confidence and knowledge. They then analyse, monitor and evaluate, make presentations, become consultants and trainers, organize themselves, and negotiate resolution of conflicts.

PRA and the evolving paradigm imply and demand changes which are institutional, professional and personal. Institutional change needs a long-term perspective, with patient and painstaking learning and reorientation. Professional change needs new concepts, values, methods and behaviours, and new curricula and approaches to learning. Personal change and commitment have primacy, and can be sought experientially. Learning to change, and learning to enjoy change, are fundamental.

Responsible well-being for uppers can be sought through altruism and generosity, putting the last first, and through disempowerment, putting the first last. To many uppers, disempowerment seems loss; but often all can gain. As in PRA, disempowerment can liberate uppers from professional prisons and personal stress. More ways are needed for the powerful to gain from less power. For new behaviour, there is no need to wait. There is a vanguard to join and new high ground to explore.

The challenge

The challenge presented by this book is to uppers, to the powerful, to the structures of power. It is to upend the normal, to stand convention on its head, to put people before things, and lowers before uppers. Imbalance is needed to establish balance. So children come before adults, women before men, the poor before the rich, the weak before the powerful, the vulnerable before the secure. The personal, professional and institutional changes implied entail reversals of much that prevails as normal. The changes are radical. For they are not just to put the last first, which is altruism; they are to put the first last, which is disempowerment.

Reversals would be absurd if pushed to anarchy, dismantling the state, abolishing bureaucracy, removing all rules and controls. They would be improbable if uppers had always to lose. They would be immoral if driven to extremes which made lowers into new uppers. But what is sought is not revolution. it is reorientation, retaining some hierarchy while loosening constraints and freeing actors. The final theme of this book is that reversals are not stupid but sane, not improbable but practicable, not the low ground, but the high.

The experience and philosophy of PRA are part of this, and a source of learning, insight and inspiration. PRA has spread with alarming speed, across boundaries of disciplines, professions, organizations, communities, countries and continents. In doing so, it has repeatedly confronted the relations of uppers and lowers. Issues have been raised concerning concepts, values, beliefs, methods, behaviours and cultures. And there has been much bad practice.

Bad practice

The first-generation problems were to establish and spread PRA. The main second-generation problems are bad practice with proliferation. With rapid spread, many practitioners have been early and low on the learning curve. Many PRA practitioners have expressed alarm (see e.g. Osuga and Mutayisa, 1994; Absalom *et al.*, 1995; Backhaus and Wagachchi, 1995; Gueye, 1995; Guijt and Cornwall, 1995; Guijt, 1995; Leurs, 1996). At national and international meetings, the dominant concern has repeatedly been how to improve and assure quality.

Bad practice can be analysed under three heads: top-down fashion and spread; behaviour, attitudes and training; and field practice and ethics. These are not unique to PRA but have been highlighted by it.

Top-down fashion and spread

PRA has become an instant fad, demanded by donors in projects and introduced in programmes of NGOs and government departments. It has been made to go to scale too fast. Label has spread without substance. Quality has suffered from the very top-down centralized system which PRA seeks to modify and reverse. The 'old paradigm has co-opted and contorted the new. The behavioural, professional and institutional implications of PRA have not been understood, or if understood, not internalized.

Demand has created its own supply. When donors demand that 'PRA will be used', PRA trainers and practitioners appear. Some trainers have been excellent, other opportunists. A Northern consultant said he did not believe in PRA but had put it in his bid for a ten-year contract in an African country because the bilateral donor required it. Consultants are easily criticized; not all are guilty. But some are the chameleons of development, making themselves up with the latest instant tints:

Consultants with contracts to win
wear colours they know to be 'in'.
  Chameleons, they
  fake a fashion display
Camouflaging for cash is no sin.

or so they would seem to believe. As a genus, chameleon consultants have a wide distribution. There are tropical species, but many are from the temperate North.

Some sponsors of PRA have been slow to realize that most good PRA trainers are in and from the South. At times, inexperienced Northerners have been recruited to conduct training. Northern students have been sent into the field for insensitive extractive research. At least one Northern university has included PRA in a course where the 'students' from the South knew much more than the 'teacher' from the North. But not all these faults have been in the North.

Behaviour, attitudes and training

In good PRA, participatory behaviour and attitudes matter more than methods. Facilitators have to learn not to dominate. This learning is not easy. Many trainers find it difficult (I do). To confront behaviour and attitudes is harder than to teach methods. The power and popularity of the methods is such that some results can come in the field even with bad, top–down, dominating facilitation.

Two traps have been common:

(1) Training has been didactic rather than participatory, in classrooms and hotels rather than in and with communities, through teaching rather than experience, and through lectures rather than practice. PRA methods, especially of visualization, can be 'taught' in a traditional and non-participatory manner. Not to lecture comes hard to seasoned academics. One PRA training was two weeks of lectures on a university campus. Another was three days in a hotel with no field experience, and certificates issued at the end. But good PRA training has itself to be participatory and experiential, and to stress behaviour and attitudes more than methods.

(2) Manuals have been written. Source-books with examples and ideas can be useful. Stepwise sequences also make sense for some topic PRA processes (see e.g. M.K. Shah, 1995a). But the formalism of manuals with set procedures can fossilize and stultify. With any innovation there is an urge to standardize and codify, often in the name of quality. Manuals are called for and composed. Paragraphs proliferate as intelligent authors seek to cater for every condition and contingency.[1] As texts lengthen, so too does training. The more there is on paper, the

212

more reading and lecturing become the norm, and the more inhibited and inflexible participants become in the field. Big manuals and bad training go together.

Field practice and ethics

Many errors occur in field practice. All processes are imperfect. Each of us repeatedly makes mistakes. I have been guilty of all the following common and serious errors of practice and ethics:

Dominating. Dominant and superior behaviour is the most widespread error. No upper can be free from it. We start with unavoidable marks and signals which send upper or lower messages, as with colour, sex, language, accent and age. The issue is also complicated because dominant action can be needed, for instance to stop someone being beaten up, to insist on sound accounting or to combat corruption. Decisive leadership has its time and place. All that said, uppers are disabled by their dominant behaviour: verbally, through lecturing, shouting down, interrupting, criticizing, contra-dicting, preaching, pontificating and putting forward their own ideas, tell-ing lowers what they ought to think, and being boring and overbearing;[2] and non-verbally, through dress, accoutrements, body language, facial ex-pressions or hiding behind dark glasses. Again and again, dominant and superior behaviour damages participatory processes.

Rushing. The word 'rapid' may have been needed in the late 1970s and early 1980s to offset the long-drawn-out learning of traditional social an-thropology and counter that of the large-scale questionnaire. RRA came to be seen as a short cut.[3] But by the late 1980s 'rapid' had become a liability. Rapid is often wrong. Relaxed is better. In practice, PRA facilitators often, perhaps usually, take too little time: they fail to explain who they are, why they have come, what they can do, and what they cannot do; they hurry to get on with 'the methods', not taking time to earn trust and gain rapport; and later they fail to take time to 'interview the map' or 'interview the diagram'.

Routines and ruts. Especially in going to scale, repetition breeds regular habits. Routines dig ruts. There are many ways local people can map, model, do transects, diagram, rank and score. But rigidity easily sets in, with the idea that there is only one right way. PRA facilitators in any organization, or even region, have shown signs of slipping into unvarying standard practices, overlooking other options and missing the creativity of inventive interaction.

Gender and upper-to-upper bias. It is notorious that the community mem-bers who can most freely interact with visitors are usually men, and those who are better off and older (see e.g. Mosse, 1993, 1995).[4] Under pressure of time, and for convenience, it is easier to encounter and consult only them, or only a few others. Unless carefully offset, the familiar bias to élites will manifest itself. If it is offset only by a generalized and populist concern for 'the poor', gender-blindness can still neglect women and girls (Jackson, 1996). Differences between genders, groups, ages and occupations are easily overlooked. Those left out are the lowers – women, the poor, the very old, children, those of inferior status, the marginal, the destitute, the disabled, refugees, outcasts. It is then the reality of local uppers that comes to count.

Taking without giving. PRA methods have frequently been used for 'extractive' research. As uppers, outsiders can often induce local people to give up time to processes from which it is the upper who will mainly benefit. It is true that the lowers, the analysts, may enjoy and be empowered by discovering their own abilities and knowledge. But as with all research involving local people, there are ethical questions about unequal relationships and the cost of people's time.

Arousing unmet expectations. PRA methods and processes can engage local people for long periods in intense and creative activities. Again and again, these lead to expectations of future action, especially where appraisal and planning are involved. Again and again, outsiders and outside agencies have been unable to respond, or have failed to honour their pledges. While this is not a new experience to most communities, and not peculiar to PRA, it remains an issue for continuous concern and self-questioning among facilitators.

Third-generation problems have also began to emerge: providing training for financially challenged small NGOs; overcoming the language élitism of English, French, Spanish and Portuguese; changing donor and government procedures; networking and sharing South–South; approaches and methods for training in behaviour and attitudes; and above all, in Ramesh Singh's (1996) words, moving from a 'doing phase' to a 'being phase'.

Other criticisms have less force:[5] that PRA is nothing new, impractical, unrigorous, or narrow in scope. Much depends on the definition of PRA and the quality of practice. If old methods are relabelled PRA, it will be nothing new; if it is facilitated badly, it will be impractical; if it is used sloppily, it will be unrigorous; if it is seen as little more than appraisal using group visualizations, it will be narrow in scope. As Parmesh and Meera Shah (1995) have pointed out, most writing on these issues has been by academics who use PRA methods only briefly and who neglect process. Many experienced practitioners are striving to achieve another reality of PRA which is inventive through interaction, practical in application, rigorous through self-criticism, and empowering through process.

Synergies

Reviewing these problems and traps fosters pessimism. Images come to mind of vicious circles and downward spirals. Upper–lower magnetism can seem so strong that it will repeatedly reassert itself. 'Success' in the high-level acceptance of PRA is then self-destructive: the embrace of the powerful, demanding PRA, stifles spontaneity and ruins quality. It is easy then to slip into the fatal despair of thinking 'nothing can change unless everything changes' and 'nothing can change everything'.

Such a view overlooks the incrementalism of positive interactions. There are synergies between the three pillars of PRA, in participatory training, and in the principles and precepts of PRA, and these have led to the good experiences and the many and widespread applications noted in Chapter 6.

The three pillars

The three pillars of PRA (page 105) – sharing and partnership, methods, and behaviour and attitudes – are mutually reinforcing. And each provides a point of entry.

Sharing between organizations supports and spreads a culture of openness. The possessive territoriality of government departments, NGOs and university departments, insulates, inbreeds and inhibits learning and change. When NGOs conduct PRA training, and invite participants from other organizations, they set a precedent of sharing which affects behaviour and attitudes. Again, when interactions with villagers are in a spirit of sharing – of food, of living together, of learning – so rapport and the process of PRA and its methods are strengthened.

When local people use PRA methods, outsiders are often amazed. Simply observing participatory mapping or matrix scoring by local people who are little educated or illiterate affects outsiders' beliefs, behaviour and attitudes. Similarly, group activities entail sharing of knowledge, ideas and values between participants. Group-visual synergy (pp. 159–60) generates commitment, cross-checking, enthusiasm and even fun, and a cumulative expression of knowledge, judgement and analysis in which information tends to be readily shared both between participants and with facilitators and observers.

The third pillar, behaviour and attitudes, is the key. Good facilitators avoid dominant behaviour. They are respectful, relaxed, unhurried, interested, able to establish rapport, and able to listen, learn, initiate a process, and then not interrupt. Such behaviour facilitates the methods. It also engenders a spirit of sharing.

Participatory training

There are synergies too in participatory training. Training is never easy, and we all stumble and stub our toes. If fieldwork is to be participatory, so too must be the modes of training. Where training is not through lecturing, but through learning by doing and experiencing, a culture or style is set which can carry over into fieldwork, into organizations, and even into the family. An example was set by the large-scale training programme for trainers for watershed management in India conducted by the organization MANAGE. In a four-week training experience, there were to be only two lectures: an inaugural, and a final. All other activities were to be interactive, and in a different style (J.K. Arora, pers. comm.).

In much PRA training, sequences of activities seek to create a culture of self-critical awareness and of participation. The range of activities is expanding (see e.g. Pretty *et al.*, 1995; IDS – Behaviour and Attitudes 1996). It includes games or exercises with names like saboteur and dominator which then lodge as words, often used jokingly by participants. Shoulder-tapping (A. Shah, 1991) is another, where participants agree to tap each

215

others' shoulders whenever something wrong is done. 'What would you do if . . .?' entails groups discussing how they would deal with difficult situations in their teams or in the field. Group contracts drawn up by field teams list agreed norms of behaviour. Reflection on experience and lessons learnt is another element. And other activities exist, and more are needed.

Precepts and principles

Most simply, behaviour and attitude change can be captured in precepts and principles which have become current in PRA:

o *Sit down, listen, watch and learn.* Change behaviour. Learn not to dominate, not to wag the finger, not to interview, and not to interrupt.
o *Use your own best judgement at all times.* Rely on personal judgement, not manuals and rules, fostering flexible and adaptable responses, and accepting responsibility.
o *Unlearn.* Be open to discarding beliefs, behaviours and attitudes, including many inculcated through formal education and rewards.
o *Be optimally unprepared.* Enter unknown, participatory situations with a repertoire but without a detailed preset programme, so allowing for creative improvization and an open interactive process the course of which cannot be foreseen.
o *Embrace error.* Be positive about mistakes. Do not bury them. Recognize, share and learn from them. Fail forwards.
o *Relax.* Do not rush. Take time. Enjoy things with people.
o *Hand over the stick.* Facilitate. Hand over the stick, chalk or pen. Initiate participatory processes, and then step back, listen, and observe, without interrupting.
o *They can do it.* Assume that people can do something until proved otherwise.
o *Ask them.* Ask local people for information and advice, including advice on how they would wish us (outsiders) to behave.
o *Be nice to people.* Adopt the triple principle of Raul Perezgrovas: Rule No. 1, Be nice to people; Rule No. 2, Repeat rule no 1; and Rule No. 3, Repeat rule no. 2.

Together, the three pillars, participatory training, and the precepts and principles outlined above are therapeutic in liberating from personal and professional prisons, and opening up new ranges of experiences and relationships, and they mutually reinforce one another. A hope and hypothesis is that they will be like benign viruses, seeding change for the better as they spread.

Empowerment

PRA can be empowering for lowers, and especially, when gender-sensitive, it can be and has been empowering for women (Guijt and Shah, forthcoming). Empowerment in the PRA context has four angles: differences within communities; methods and process; community-level organization; and conflict and negotiation.

216

Differences within communities

Differentiating groups and interests can empower the poorer in several ways. It can give them collective awareness and confidence to confront others and argue their case. AKRSP (India) has convened groups of women and men separately to choose the numbers of trees of different sorts they want in their nursery, and then helped them reconcile their differences (M.K. Shah, 1995a). Differentiation through wealth or well-being ranking can help an outside organization select and deselect those with whom it will work: MY-RADA in South India, and ActionAid in Ethiopia, India, Nepal and Pakistan are among the NGOs which have used PRA methods to identify the poorer with whom to work in their programmes.

Whether empowerment is good depends on who are empowered, and how their new power is used. If those who gain are outsiders who exploit, or a local élite which dominates, the poor and disadvantaged may be worse off. Whether PRA is equitable and good depends then on whom it involves. The natural tendency is for this to be men rather than women, the better-off rather than the worse-off, and those of higher-status groups rather than those of lower status. The challenge is so to introduce and use PRA that the weaker are identified and empowered and equity is served.

Fortunately, the tools available suit this task. Sequences such as participatory mapping – household listing – well-being ranking – livelihood analysis can identify groups distinguished according to local values. Focus-group discussions can then be convened to identify the priorities and interests of different categories of people, including those who are disadvantaged. The contrasts can be sharp. Drawing on applications of PRA techniques in Sierra Leone, Ghana, Malawi and Bangladesh, Alice Welbourn (1991) has shown how significant can be differences of ethnic group, age, gender and economic status, and combinations of these. With pastoralists in Kenya, Jeremy Swift and Abdi Noor Umar (1991: 56) found striking differences of priority according to wealth group (see pp. 185–6).

Methods and process

People can learn through PRA, expressing and sharing what they know but earlier had not expressed and shared. Through diagramming, mapping, investigating and observing, they can add to their knowledge. Through their analysis, they become yet more aware and reach new understanding. Those who plan and then implement what they have planned take command, and further learn through the experience of action.

People also gain in skills and confidence. They learn that they can do things they did not know they could. The second map is more detailed than the first, and the third more detailed than the second. PRA processes often throw up new leaders in communities, people with aptitudes expressed in the free context of PRA activities.

In good practice, these gains in confidence and capability are enhanced by honouring those who have made maps or conducted analysis, recording their names as mappers or analysts on the outputs. Villagers invited to Colombo, Gaborone and Dhaka to present their analyses were treated as consultants, and in the two latter cases paid as such. Villagers' knowledge has also been recognized in the authorship of academic papers such as that of Chidhari *et al.* and Louise Fortmann (1992) where the outsider's name came last, and in the video produced by the Women of Sangams Pastapur etc. and Michel Pimbert (1991).

Changing and reversing roles, handing over the stick, has taken many forms. These can be expressed as questions, such as: who appraises? who makes maps, lists, matrices, diagrams? who analyses? who plans? who implements? with the answer in each case that local people do, facilitated by outsiders. Beyond these, other dominoes have fallen. For example:

Who monitors and evaluates? Traditional M&E has been conducted by outsiders, using their criteria and measures. This has been turned on its head. Farmers in Gujarat in India have conducted their own monitoring of soil- and water-conservation works, recording changes on their own maps (P. Shah *et al.*, 1991). In participatory evaluation of watershed development in Karnataka, farmers demonstrated the physical technology of their stone anti-erosion structures, jumped up and down on them to show how robust they were, and went to a meeting in Bangalore with the Secretary of Agriculture, showed him slides of their technology, explained why it was superior to that of the government, and were successful in securing a change in the official norms (Sommer, 1993; see also Premkumar, 1994). Village organizations in Sri Lanka and Gujarat (P. Shah 1996: 242–3) have assessed their performance at intervals according to criteria they themselves have drawn up. Participatory M&E is a major frontier.[6]

Who makes, edits and uses video? Video made with and by local people can be a powerful tool. It can empower more than the written (and often badly written) word. It provides a visual medium for confident presentation of local realities to other levels. In Tanzania, a video made with and by local people presented damage done by dynamiting fish (Johansson, 1995: 62–3). The video was shown to other villages and to local and national policy-makers. No plans were put on paper, but committees started in forty villages, local government allowed villages to organize police patrols, ministers made commitments and dynamite dealers were prosecuted. In Nepal, a committee of Bhutanese refugees involved with an OXFAM programme planned and scripted the material they wished to film. The woman who co-ordinated the filming was then invited to Cambridge to be involved in the editing, when key decisions are taken on what to include and exclude (pers. comm. Rachel Hinton).

Who is the consultant? Local people's knowledge and skills often qualify them as consultants. Outsiders, though, often act and think as though local people's time is a costless resource at their service. But now local people have been recruited as paid consultants, both by outsiders to demonstrate PRA-type analyses, and by other communities to act as facilitators (pers. comm. M. and P. Shah).

Who is the trainer? Villagers now train outsiders. Sam Joseph of ActionAid, India has pioneered an approach in which villagers familiar with PRA host outsiders who stay in their village, share in village tasks, and are shown PRA methods and analysis in practice. The outsider trainees pay fees, and these are used at the discretion of the host villagers for public purposes or as remuneration for their time and trouble. All gain. Appropriately, the issue of *Participation in Action* (PIA, 1995) which describes examples of this approach is headed 'Win–Win Trainings', for everyone gains.

Community-level organization

Empowerment can be weak and short-lived unless it is embodied in institutions. PRA has often been regarded as a one-off activity. But for many practitioners it affects and is part of stages in processes which lead to and empower community-based organizations (see e.g. P. Shah, 1996). The need for new or transformed organizations at the group or community level has been increasingly recognized by NGOs and governments, and increasingly become the reality. They can have many functions, such as savings and credit, income-earning activities, natural-resource management, maintaining group or community solidarity, preparing proposals and negotiating with outside agencies. They can maintain group or community solidarity and negotiating power in relation to threats. They can deal with other community-based organizations. They can mobilize countervailing power to meet and match the power of the hierarchies of NGOs and the state.

Conflict and negotiation

PRA approaches and methods can change the attitudes of dominant groups. Gender relations provide examples. When both women and men, separately, have made their own maps, men have exclaimed that they did not know the women could do it. Women have again and again made social maps with more detail, and as it has turned out, more accurate detail, than men: in Sri Lanka a group of women identified 44 households to men's 42 in a village, and the men then conceded that they should add the two they had missed. More directly, PRA approaches have been used to enable men to appreciate the hard life and conditions of women. Meena Bilgi (pers. comm. 1992) of the Aga Khan Rural Support Programme (India) found men in one village in Gujarat hostile to her work with women and to drudgery-sparing technology for women. She asked the men to diagram and discuss women's time use. They first doubted the information which they themselves had given. Then they became defensive, saying that men's work was harder. Finally they analysed women's activities, listing the difficulties and problems which they faced. In the end, the men's attitudes changed towards new technologies to benefit the women.

PRA methods such as diagramming can also be brought into play to clarify and resolve conflicts. Agroecosystem diagramming was used in the Philippines to make explicit the differences of interests between groups after the construction of a small dam at Lake Buhi and to achieve consensus about priorities (Conway *et al.*, 1989; Conway, 1989). In the approach of the Neighbourhood Initiatives Foundation in the UK, a large model of a

219

neighbourhood allows people to address conflicts by putting down suggestions, and using markers to agree or disagree without needing to identify themselves. This 'depersonalises conflicts and introduces informality where consensus is more easily reached' (Gibson, 1992). Diagrams are promising as a means to defuse tension by making agreed fact visible and differences explicit, focusing public debate on a physical thing rather than on individual people. The identification, expression and resolution of conflicts of interest is another frontier for participatory methods.

Empowerment, unless abused, serves equity and well-being. It is not a static condition. It is a process not a product; it is not something that is ever finished. There is no 'empowerment' box which can be ticked as complete. It entails enhanced capabilities and wider scope for choice and action. Nor is it just something that happens among lowers. It is interactive, between lowers, peers and uppers. Especially, it requires and implies changes in power relations and behaviour. These can be analysed under three heads: institutional; professional; and personal.

These are linked, as in Figure 10.1. They interact with the three pillars of PRA: sharing with institutional change; methods with professional change; and behaviour and attitudes with personal change. All present points of entry; all are capable of provoking and reinforcing changes in the others.

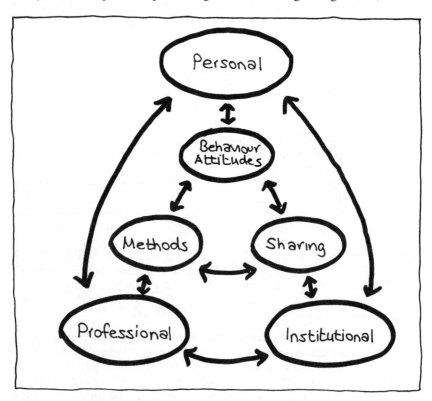

Figure 10.1: Dimensions and linkages of change

PRA used well stimulates and supports these broader changes. PRA is, then, one point of entry or leverage.

To change institutions

'Institution' is used here (following Thompson, 1995: 1545) conveniently with two meanings: organization, referring to a particular organization, such as an NGO, government department, university or training institute; and rules-in-use, referring to working rules, procedures and norms expressed in repeated activities and relationships between individuals in organizations.

The PRA experience is that the institutional challenge is formidable. Normal bureaucracies, of NGOs as well as of government departments and donor agencies, are confronted by participatory approaches in many ways: by revealing local people's priorities to differ from those supposed for them; by generating diverse actions and demands to which top-down packages do not fit; by making planned targets hard to meet; by slowing disbursements of funds; by spending more on personnel and logistics, and less on hardware; by generating benefits like capabilities which are hard to inspect, measure or count. Good participatory processes at the grassroots have impacts upwards on reward systems, upper–lower relationships between levels, budgeting, planning and procurement procedures, and values and personal interactions. The challenge is to transform the incentives, procedures, and cultures of organizations, large and small, at all levels.

Hierarchical upper–lower institutions are a starting point for understanding the obstacles to change.

Upper–lower institutions

Many institutions are hierarchical and sustain and reinforce upper–lower dominance, with multiple uppers over multiple lowers. Most marked are states and organizations based on fundamentalisms, whether political or religious or both together. But other organizations, like donor agencies in development, or government departments, have similar if less extreme features. Four common factors deserve comment:

(1) *Sacred texts* can be, and often are, used to legitimize or require upper–lower and insider–outsider distinctions. These may be God over humankind, priests over laity, men over women, believers and the saved over pagans and the damned. Das Kapital, the Christian Bible, and the Koran can be interpreted either as eternally true or as historical documents reflecting the cultures and mores of past times and places. One can reflect and speculate on whether their inspired originators would, if alive today, endorse or disown the literal reverence with which they are sometimes interpreted. The upper–lower view of men and women in parts of the Bible and of the Koran is an example. In parts of each, divine authority is used to justify the dominance of men over women. The relevant texts are addressed, not to humankind, but to married

men, telling them how to treat their wives as lowers. To lesser degrees, organizations have books of rules which lay down authority, of managers over managed, of seniors over juniors, of those qualified over those not qualified.

(2) *Manuals and rituals* enjoin set sequences and procedures. Texts are conservative. In established religions, litanies and rituals endure for centuries. In teaching and training for development, the same textbooks and manuals (for questionnaire surveys, for social-cost-benefit analysis, for logical framework analysis and ZOPP) have been reused year after year. They express and reinforce upper-lower distinctions, elevating those who know and perform the sequences of actions over those who do not. Whether it is a priest celebrating mass, an economist celebrating cost-benefit analysis, or a consultant celebrating ZOPP, preset ritual is consummated in transubstantiation – bread and wine into the body and blood of Christ, guesstimates into a benefit-cost ratio, or social and physical complexity and diversity into a single core problem. The upper is master (mistress never[7] with the bread and wine, though sometimes with the others) of the arcane process, performs the observances, and validates the myth.

(3) *Hierarchy and control* are so commonplace that little comment is needed. Weberian bureaucracy, though a threatened species in some places, flourishes in most contexts. Levels of seniority, ladders of promotion, distinctions of grade, privilege, dress, workplace, place of eating and food, and top-down punitive controls for standardized activities – these Fordist features, though discredited in business management, are alive and well where multiple upper–lower relations persist.

(4) *Privileged access and secrecy*, supposed, pretended or actual, are a key to dominance by uppers. Priests have a direct line to God. Senior officials have the ear of the Minister. Cabals conspire together. Secrecy hides error and abuse and protects uppers from lowers. That knowledge is power is one of the most worn and valid clichés of the English language.

At worst, these four factors combine. Fundamentalist and totalitarian states and male-dominated authoritarian bureaucracies are not yet fossils of the past. Men are empowered and protected by holy text, ritual, hierarchy and secrecy and perpetuate their dominance. More generally, age, class, caste, education, seniority, wealth and other distinctions legitimize and perpetuate upper–lower relations. Women are trapped; but so too are men. Lowers are trapped, but so too are uppers. Uppers rarely recognize that the system is a prison for them too.

Reversals

To reverse these four factors is to neutralize normal North–South dominance and to liberate both lowers and uppers. The PRA experience illustrates a form of liberation with parallels in other domains.

(1) Individual responsibility replaces a sacred text or manual as source of authority. The one-sentence manual 'Use your own best judgement at

all times' makes the individual the authority. A much wider parallel is the idea of consciously designing your own religion (Forsyth, 1991).

(2) Action does not have to follow fixed sequences. Each time can be different. There are contexts in which broad sequences make sense (for community planning, for forest nurseries, for focused programmes). But generally, the lack of ritual and formal procedure gives space for freedom of interaction, inventiveness, creativity and fun.

(3) Power and control are decentralized. Hierarchy is flattened and weakened. Controls and rules from above are minimized. Uppers facilitate, enabling lowers to generate their own power and control, to fit local conditions and needs, and taking different forms in different places.

(4) Transparency replaces secrecy. Facilitators explain who they are, their purposes, and what they can and cannot do. Local people are encouraged to share their knowledge and analysis with each other and with uppers. Trust replaces suspicion.

These are statements of ideals. The problem is how in the real, messy, magnetized and hierarchical world to work towards them, and to do so on a growing scale. Two thrusts are complementary: pressures from participation below, from groups and communities; and strategies and tactics from within.

Pressures from below: lowers versus uppers

PRA at the level of communities and groups has repeatedly challenged upper-lower priorities and institutions. When communities and groups are facilitated freely to conduct their own appraisal and analysis, their preferences and priorities have again and again been diverse and different from those supposed for them by Government departments, donor-aided projects, and even NGOs which say they are participatory.

Questions of 'whose reality counts?' are raised by the misfit between logical framework analysis (LFA, and its incarnation ZOPP) and participatory approaches including PRA (see also pp. 42–4). LFA and ZOPP can be instruments for the imposition of uppers' realities. In Indonesia, participatory exercises in villages identified villagers' core problems as 'low income'. At a subsequent ZOPP none of the 45 representatives was from village or subdistrict level. The core problem came out as 'natural resources in the project area are not used by the local population and government agencies in a sustainable way' (Wentzel, 1994: 86).

In other cases, PRA has challenged the priorities and programmes predetermined by LFA and ZOPP. In Kilifi District in Kenya, a ZOPP exercise in August 1993 identified water and sanitation as the main priorities, and the resulting project was entitled KIWASAP, the Kilifi Water and Sanitation Programme; but when a year later Kenyan officials and German students stayed in villages and facilitated participatory appraisal and analysis, people's priorities proved much more diverse. The programme was then transformed (Schubert *et al.*, 1994), the goal becoming 'An increasing number of communities in Kilifi District . . . empowered to manage their own development activities which aim at exploiting unused potential to solve problems given priority by the communities' (ibid. Vol. 1: 93).

In the Lindi and Mtwara regions of southeast Tanzania, Lars Johansson has written of the process of evolution of an on-going project, (1995: 62, 63) that there was a

> not very constructive period of trying to write up and appraise a five year plan according to the logical framework format. Making pro- gramme and project documents had become increasingly traumatic to all involved. The more we learned the more important it seemed not to mystify development and take the initiative away from local people through abstract concepts of objectivity like outputs and indicators. The strategies that proved to work did so because they were locally intelli- gible and based on subjective representations of reality, so that they could be negotiated in spoken Swahili during village workshops amongst people with different perspectives and interests. Personal commitments to a coalition of people proved much more important than scientifically adequate project logics, but required a totally different approach to planning.

Examples could be multiplied from other countries. Participation gener- ates unexpected and diverse demands which pressure normal bureaucracy to turn on its head, and respond with differentiated support and services. Participation lower down is insecure without participation higher up. The implications of PRA go right to the top of government departments and donor agencies, including the World Bank. All are challenged to change at all levels.

In summary, the institutional challenge for all development agencies is to become learning organizations (Senge, 1990; Pretty and Chambers, 1993a): to flatten and soften hierarchy, to develop a culture of particip- atory management, to recruit a gender and disciplinary mix of staff com- mitted to people, and to adopt and promote procedures, norms and rewards which permit and encourage more open-ended participation at all levels. Project procedures, textbooks and training all require revision. Top–down targets, drives to disburse funds fast, rewards to big spenders, and rushed visits, meetings and decisions, have all to be restrained and reversed.

Perhaps the most damaging is the drive to disburse and to achieve phys- ical targets. These destroy participation. Agencies compete to spend and give away. In Sri Lanka and Vietnam, patient participatory programmes, encouraging self-reliance, have been undermined by donor-funded pro- grammes rushing in to spend money in neighbouring villages. In an IFAD- funded programme in Sri Lanka, the manager was called in to report every three months on how many villages have been covered, and to account for shortfalls. Such top-down targetry substitutes dependence for particip- ation. But in multilateral banks, donor agencies, and even government departments, staff are rewarded by how much they spend. So a donor might plead to the poor, and reveal the system:

Beneficiaries here I come
Donor with a tidy sum
Father Christmas is my name
Spending targets are the game
All will gain, that is the notion
You get cash, I get promotion.

Help me be a good provider
Open up your mouths much wider
What I bring is sure to please
Sacks with stacks of free goodies
All you have to do is take'em
Evaluations? We can fake'em.

Make disbursements, that's the must
Where they go we will adjust
Take a lot and quickly spend
Financial Year is near its end
For accounting, we can fudge it
All that matters – spend the budget!

Retained consultants will report
Contractors acted as they ought
None of the structures was defective
Monies spent were cost-effective
All the data that're obtainable
Show the project is sustainable.

Shun the mean facilitator
What he brings is less and later
PRA is but a con
Make your map, and they move on
Their approach will make you sick
All they hand you is a stick.

Participation too's a mess
You do more and they do less
What good calling you clients and actors?
Better cash from benefactors
You, the poor, should never spurn
Gifts you do not have to earn.

Then the poor might reply:

Donor, we reject your song
Top-down targetry is wrong
Floods of funds as in your verse
Corrupt and spoil and make things worse.
Keep your money. We will show
True development's from below.

Or they might not. However damaging they may be, free gifts are hard for the hard up to refuse. It is too much to expect the poor to send Father Christmas home heavy-laden with ungiven gifts. Besides, he might lose his job. It is the institutions behind Father Christmas, their ideologies, cultures, norms, rewards and procedures that have to change.

Strategies and tactics for institutional change

Strategies and tactics to enable upper–lower organizations to loosen up, to stand on their heads, to foster participation and to put people first have received much attention in the management literature (e.g. Peters, 1989, 1992, 1994; Handy, 1989). In Peter Senge's terms, the organizations which excel in the future will be those 'that discover how to tap people's commitment and capacity to learn at *all* levels in an organization' (emphasis in original: Senge, 1990: 2). In these 'learning organizations', people are continually learning to learn together. While these may be ideals to aim for, change in upper–lower organizations has in practice often been piecemeal and painful.

In large central organizations, like FAO and the World Bank, one approach has been action by committed individuals, at first meeting informally. In FAO for years an informal group met to discuss and share experience with RRA, but without high-level commitment this did not lead to major institutional change. In the World Bank, high-level commitment was secured for the establishment of a bank-wide Learning Group on Participatory Development in December 1990. With support from allies in bilateral agencies and NGOs, this group gradually gained acceptance for mainstreaming participation in the Bank (see e.g. World Bank, 1994a), produced a comprehensive sourcebook (World Bank, 1995), and then received the enthusiastic support of the new president of the World Bank.

Large field organizations of government have also sought transformations which seek to put communities and people first. The experiences which have been analysed and from which lessons can be learnt include the National Irrigation Administration in the Philippines (Bagadion and Korten, 1991; Thompson, 1995) and the Gal Oya Project in Sri Lanka (Uphoff, 1992). Both these preceded the use of PRA. Others, since then, have involved PRA.[8]

From the many lessons of these experiences, six prescriptions stand out:

(1) *Commit with continuity.* Enabling conditions include a favourable policy environment, and staff stability. Where there is a donor agency involved, or a training NGO, it needs to hang in with its host organization, often a government department, for years, sometimes perhaps decades. One big danger is a change of top executive: cases are multiplying where an organization has led outstandingly in the development and spread of participatory approaches, and then ceased to do so almost instantly on the appointment of an unsympathetic new head. Changes take time to root and grow and need sustained support from the top. Donor agencies and training NGOs also need their own long-term commitment to being learning organizations themselves.

(2) *Network with allies.* In the early stages often only a few favour change. Within and between organizations, and between levels in organizations, the like-minded can support one another. Change in one organization can help others learn. A strong combination can be two key people, one in a donor agency or NGO, and one in a government organization, who work together over a period of years, as Frances Korten of the Ford Foundation and Benjamin Bagadion of the National Irrigation Administration did in the Philippines.

(3) *Start small and slow.* Learning comes from doing. New approaches and methods meet resistances. Gradual evolution, establishing and securing small bridgeheads of learning, works better than going abruptly to scale.

(4) *Fund flexibly.* Fixed targets for spending, and rewards to staff who make big loans, spend fast and achieve high physical targets, propagate Model-T programmes and dependence. In their early years, participatory programmes and projects need to spend most on exploration, training, learning, capacity-building and processes of institutional change. Flexible funding allows more or less to be spent, according to emerging needs and opportunities, and for directions and priorities to change.

(5) *Train, encourage and support grass-roots staff.* The front-line staff – those in direct working contact with communities, farmers and people – are central to participation. Like other lowers, they are more capable than their seniors suppose. As they change their roles from transferers of technology to facilitators of participation, they can gain in enthusiasm and commitment (see e.g. Uphoff, 1992; Johansson, 1995).

(6) *Build out and up from grass-roots success.* In every success, the start has been small, local, experimental and risky. Inventiveness, errors and adaptation have provided the learning and examples for spread. Lateral transfer and adoption, peer to peer, have been strong. Free funds have been few. Cosseted pet pilot projects are trapped in their privileged cocoons and costly to replicate. In contrast, truly participatory approaches cost less, and later spread more easily through example and enthusiasm.

Within organizations, points of leverage and change are many. Formal rules can be changed to allow flexibility. Committee and team memberships can be democratized. Separate eating can be abolished. Senior staff can practice MBWA (management by wandering around). Seating at meetings can be made informal and egalitarian. Suggestions can be encouraged and rewarded. Distinctions of dress can be reduced. Though changes seem small, together they can gradually transform the culture of an organization.

What is not yet (1996) known is whether the cultures of hierarchical organizations can in due course be transformed by going to scale rapidly with participatory approaches. In the mid-1990s, PRA-based programmes in several countries, including India (GOI, 1994), Indonesia (Mukherjee, 1996), Kenya and Vietnam, are being rapidly and massively extended. Not all are basing expansion on earlier slow and experimental learning. The trade-offs between scale and quality are not easy to assess, and present ethical dilemmas. Whatever happens, there will be much to learn. At worst, PRA approaches will be discredited and abandoned and communities disillusioned, making later participation harder; at best, PRA will be like a benign virus or Trojan horse, infiltrating and eventually transforming the citadels of hierarchical institutions. Most likely, the outcomes will be mixed, demanding patient and long-term commitment. Much will depend on parallel changes, which are professional and personal.

New professionalism

As we saw in Chapter 3, normal professionalism – the ideas, values, methods and behaviours accepted and dominant and professions and disciplines – is a part of the problem. The challenge is to shift the balances: to put people before things; to make reductionism, measurement and economics servants not masters; to put the weak before the powerful; to value judgement and commitment. It is to break out of the prison of the old fixed, linear, unitary professionalism of things. It is to establish participatory approaches, bottom up, privileging local, complex, diverse, dynamic and unpredictable realities as not just respectable but vital, not Schon's insalubrious swamp, but new high ground in mainline professionalism.

The moving frontier

Professions are, though, conservative. Eminent authorities are often too old to question their normal professionalism. Those in the middle ranks of organizations, owing their positions to one set of norms, are threatened by alternatives. New curricula, new styles of training and of helping people learn, and new less-controlled experiences, all demand more work and risk for teachers and trainers. Professional norms are embodied in textbooks and manuals, with a common currency of concepts, language and methods. To seek to change these can entail confrontation, argument, and being marginalized. Students find it hard to use PRA methods when their supervisors do not know them or disapprove. Modern science and questionnaires, in contrast, are respectable and safe.

What seems to constitute a new professionalism also itself evolves. An earlier attempt to articulate it (Chambers, 1983: 168–89) stressed reversals of normal tendencies: spatial reversals, through decentralizations from cores to peripheries, and through choices of where to live and work; reversals of normal professional values and concerns; reversals into gaps between disciplines, professions and departments; and the mobilization of management and law as missing professions in rural development. These points still seem valid, though some of what was 'last' in 1983 is now more accepted.

Other perspectives have evolved since then (see e.g. Pretty and Chambers, 1993; Pretty, 1995b). Modern science is increasingly seen as only one among many systems of knowledge, with its own emic values (Scoones and Thompson, 1994). To these can be added the new high ground of openness to multiple realities, to the local, complex, diverse, dynamic and unpredictable, and of the evolution of participatory approaches, such as PRA, which enable multiple realities to be expressed.

The professionalism of the new high ground has its own evolving ideas, values, epistemology, methods, and behaviours. The ideas and values inter-link. Concepts which bear on human relations have implicit values. In the new professionalism, underlying values are not hidden in assumptions of objectivity, but made explicit. An eclectic pluralism values doubt, self-critical awareness and open-mindedness; respect for the views of others; and respect for the views and values of lowers.

Each of us has a personal set of values and beliefs. In a spirit of plural tolerance and mutual learning it is better for each to articulate these and share them than for one set to be accorded primacy or to prevail. Beyond certain core human values, there is then a meta-value of value diversity which tolerates all values except those that will not tolerate others.

Epistemology and methods refer to both learning and unlearning. Epistemologies and their methods for learning which support the new professionalism have many forms and origins besides those more obviously adopted and evolved in PRA. Some key assumptions and principles are:[9]

o Pluralism is inclusive, and asks 'what else?', 'what else?', recognizing the existence and value of many, not few, realities, epistemologies, values, agendas, and behaviours;
o Realities are multiple and socially constructed, and personal, local, com-plex, diverse, dynamic and unpredictable;
o Epistemologies are multiple and complementary. Modern scientific method is only one among many means of learning, suitable for well-defined problems when system uncertainties are low. Holistic and participatory methodologies are needed for lcddu conditions, and to combine, reconcile and evolve multiple realities;
o Values are implicit in epistemologies, in principles of enquiry and in methods, requiring commitment to trying to make them explicit;[10]
o Agendas, priorities, values and criteria in research and action are evolved interactively, respecting and privileging those of lowers;
o Interaction between lowers and uppers is part of learning. The nature of mutual perceptions and interactions is a key question in research and in assessing trustworthiness.
o Relationships between uppers and lowers are sensitive to uppers' be-haviour and attitudes. These need to be enabling, building trust and starting with the empowerment of lowers before joint analyses and negotiation;
o Quality assurance and evaluation are based on self-critical awareness, embracing error, and criteria of trustworthiness, and the judgement of both uppers and lowers, enabling lowers as feasible to be primary actors.

Plural professionalisms: whose realities?

It is mainly through behaviour, through what they do, that professionals, and uppers generally, express their ideas, values, epistemologies and methods, and influence each other. So it is possible to outline the behaviours expected of a new professional.

In research, radical change is entailed, from the common dominant modes of interaction between 'investigators' and the people who are the 'objects' of research. Researchers become facilitators, and part of an interactive process.

In hierarchies of development bureaucracies another, but parallel and overlapping, set of behaviours can be suggested. Here is one written earlier:

> The challenge can be expressed as the paragon new professional. She is committed to the poor and weak, and to enabling them to gain more of what they want and need. She is democratic and participatory in management style; is a good listener; embraces error and believes in failing forwards; finds pleasure in enabling others to take initiatives; monitors and controls only a core minimum of standards and activities; is not threatened by the unforeseeable; does not demand targets for disbursements and achievements; abjures punitive management; devolves authority, expecting her staff to use their own best judgement at all times; gives priority to the front-line; and rewards honesty. For her, watchwords are truth, trust and diversity. And throughout this paragraph she can also be a he.
>
> (Chambers, 1995: 32–3)

There is a twist in the tail. This statement was a product of time, context and person. It is what was written in a paper, at a particular time, with a particular purpose, and by me. By what right, with what authority, dare I say what is or what ought to be for others? Is this not contrary to pluralism, doubt and self-critical awareness? The logic is a trap. Too much doubt and self-criticism leads to paralysis, ultimately to immobility, itself a choice. The answer perhaps, as so often, is to seek to optimize: to present one's own view, inviting criticism and encouraging others to present theirs. Then each can be responsible.

In this pluralism, new professionalisms are multiple; they differ not just by discipline but by individual. Each of us invents our own. Each is responsible for evolving, articulating and sharing our own ideas, values, methods and behaviours. Whether to explore and develop a new professionalism, and what it should be, is then a personal choice.

Strategies and tactics for change

Much of the problem is the process of professional socialization. 'By the time they leave university, the damage has been done' was a remark at an IDS workshop in 1980. As we saw in Chapter 4, top-down teaching about things and about people treated like things orients, magnetizes and narrows the frames and views of those 'taught'. Often, the more education people have, so the more they think they know, the more vulnerable they are to simplistic reductionism, and the less open they are to multiple epistemologies and realities. Unlearning for many will never occur, or it can be traumatic. In the words of a demographer:

> PRA is difficult; it is more than application. It is a process of 'unlearning' from being the 'knower' to sharing and learning new ideas. To a demographer, this is an extremely painful exercise which challenges the conventional process of gathering demographic data.
>
> (Marindo-Ranganai, 1995: 61)

Direct field experience of interactions in a PRA mode provides one means of unlearning; but we need to invent and use more. In the long term, more important is preventing the damage in the first place, and instead creating learning environments and processes which foster new professionalisms.

The institutions most concerned are universities and training institutes, and the processes most concerned are teaching, learning and experiencing. None of what follows is to undermine the values of accuracy, scholarship, honesty and intellectual rigour. It is rather to change curricula and modes of learning. From PRA experiences and other sources, five prescriptions stand out.

(1) *Shift from didactic teaching to participatory learning.* Optimize modes of teaching and learning by limiting lecturing, making interactive learning the key, learning from and with peers. Teachers become facilitators, and students become teachers and facilitators for other students.
(2) *Shift from classroom and things to field and people.* Make more learning experiential, with direct contact with field realities.
(3) *Learn through empowering lowers.* In curricula, include learning how to empower lowers, how to enable them to learn, and learning from and with them.
(4) *Stress the personal and interpersonal.* In curricula include workshops for personal awareness, reflection and change in behaviour and attitudes.
(5) *Value diversity, creativity and dissent.* Make pluralism central, recognizing multiple epistemologies and methods, encouraging discovery and invention, and valuing and rewarding constructive critical dissent.

These five prescriptions apply widely. They can be seen as shifts, not slot-rattling. But the agenda they present is radical and opens up a wonderful world of learning and experience.

The primacy of the personal

The primacy of behaviour and attitudes in PRA has deeper significance. Behaviour is only the outward show of what a person is like. It is not just behaviour, but the sort of people we are that counts.[11]

The personal

The personal dimension is a bizarre blind spot in development. Behaviour and attitudes have simply not been on the development map. As for beliefs, they have been debated almost entirely in the publicly contested areas of ideology and fundamentalisms, whether Marxist, neo-classical or more overtly religious. Personal responsibility for actions and non-actions has not been a subject. Yet what powerful uppers do determines much of the form and direction of change. When personal responsibility is given primacy, authority resides not in texts, manuals or sequences of observance or procedure, but in individual judgements, choices and actions. Improving those becomes the focus.

Personality seems to be a factor in our preferences for paradigms, between things–certainty–standardization–equilibrium and people–uncertainty–diversity–dynamism. On the exploration of complexity, W.B. Arthur is quoted as saying:

> I think there's a personality that goes with this kind of thing. It's people who like process and pattern, as opposed to people who are comfortable with stasis and order. I know that every time in my life that I've run across simple rules giving rise to emergent, complex messiness I've just said, 'Ah, isn't that lovely!' And I think that sometimes, when other people run across it, they recoil. (cited in Waldrop, 1994: 334)

People differ in the ease or difficulty with which they take to participatory approaches and behaviours. Some who have been brought up strictly, who have been 'magnetized' into a strong N–S orientation, who 'stand to attention' and expect others to do so, who are given to lecturing and wagging the finger, find participation hard. It is not their fault. Others who are more flexible and open, and freer to spin, take to it with enthusiasm. For some, the damage of earlier experience is deep.[12]

The personal dimension applies to interactions and mutual perceptions. Rapport is less a matter of behaviour and technique and more one of empathy. Each of us senses what sort of people others are. As an experienced mental patient said: 'I could tell by one look at a doctor and one sound of his voice as to whether he was going to do me any good' (Karle, 1992: 249). In PRA training one can usually tell within a few moments who will take to it readily and who will find it difficult.

Personal belief, behaviour and being are then the crux. If whole systems are to shift and transform, it will be because of the sum and interaction of innumerable personal actions and changes in what sort of people we are. Given this primacy of the personal, psychological studies of uppers have been oddly absent from development studies. Political scientists have had the field largely to themselves, interviewing élites and interpreting their behaviour (e.g. Leonard, 1991). Perhaps the most neglected aspect of development is the personal psychology of what powerful professionals believe and do.

Strategies and tactics for change

Personal change is a minefield, the subject of much evangelism, mythology, popular writing, and psychological and managerial lore. It is value-laden. It concerns what sort of people we are and become: closed or open, fearful or

232

secure, callous or caring, hating or tolerant, violent or peacemaking. It raises the question: whose values count? Do we, the relatively powerful, have an obligation to enable lowers to express their values, to question and doubt our own, and to discuss them with others who differ? Do we also have a right or duty, with whatever reserve and caution, to present and act on our own values?

As strategies and tactics for personal change, PRA experiences suggest four thrusts, to which I have added a fifth:

(1) *Facilitate lowers.* Facilitating others, as with PRA methods and processes, demands changes in normal behaviour, especially learning to shut up, keep quiet, and not interrupt; done well, it also changes uppers' perceptions of lowers as their capabilities are shown and their realities are expressed.

(2) *Change behaviour.* It is easier, quicker and less dominating to provide opportunities for new behaviour and experiences, than frontally to challenge belief systems. Changed behaviour leads to changes in relationships, experiences and insights, which then in turn influence beliefs.

(3) *Make training experiential and interactive.* Preaching and lecturing seek to impose knowledge, meaning and values. Experiential and interactive training can be patterned, but provides opportunities for participants to learn through personal experience, and to come to their own conclusions. Staying in communities, with community members as hosts, guides and teachers, is one example.

(4) *Reflect and share.* Reflecting on others' realities, personal reflection on experiences, and then mutual sharing with colleagues and peers, helps learning and insight, a process of giving and receiving in which all gain and grow.

(5) *Transform through children.* Family relationships of adults and children are hugely formative. What sort of people we are depends so much on that extreme relationship of powerlessness to which we are all exposed as children. Of all the points of entry for change, none may be as powerful in the long term as changing the way we treat children. Those who are violent and intolerant as adults are often those against whom violence was done when they were young and defenceless: Hitler, Stalin and Ceausescu all endured gross violent abuses as children (Miller, 1991). It is odd that the treatment of children by their parents is not a matter of massive global public concern, analysis, critical learning and sharing; that organizations like UNICEF and PLAN International, so committed to children, do not make this more a priority.

These five injunctions do not advocate uniformity. We will always remain irreducibly diverse. Each of us has a different reality, each a different kaleidoscopic and dynamic definition of well-being, and each a different definition of responsibility. We also have multiple cultures to recognize, embrace and celebrate.

The bottom line is to be nice to people. This is close to 'love thy neighbour as thyself'. Courtesy, respect, patience consideration, generosity, reflecting on and being sensitive to others' realities . . . such virtues seem the core of personal and interpersonal well-being.[13]

Putting the first last

Thirteen years ago it was as far as I could get to argue for putting the last first (Chambers, 1983). This meant putting first those who are poor, physically weak, isolated, vulnerable and powerless, and their priorities and the things that matter to them. Norman Uphoff (1992) has taken this further, making a case for rehabilitation of the concept of altruism and generous behaviour. He has identified a continuum of orientations toward self and others (Table 10.1) from aggressive behaviour (destructive of others), through selfish behaviour (in which one's gain is another's loss), to generous behaviour (in which all gain) and finally sacrificial behaviour (which is self-destructive). The generous or altruistic person gains either from the satisfaction of seeing the welfare of others improve, or from action which is seen to be inherently good. Putting the last first is generous or altruistic behaviour in either or both of these senses. It has a positive-sum orientation in which all can gain.

Table 10.1: Continuum of orientations toward self and others

(a)	(b)	(c)	(d)
Aggressive behaviour *(destructive of others)*	Selfish behaviour *(zero-sum orientation)*	Generous behaviour *(positive-sum orientation)*	Sacrificial behaviour *(self-destructive)*

Source: Uphoff, 1992: 343.

Disempowerment as loss

Putting the first last goes further. It confronts issues of power. With altruism and generous behaviour, the first remain first: uppers remain uppers. Putting the first last is more radical. For it means that those who are uppers and powerful step down, disempower themselves, and empower others. It means putting the first (oneself) last, or at least lower. It implies that uppers have to give up something and make themselves vulnerable. It sounds like sacrificial behaviour, a zero-sum in which uppers, the powerful, have to lose.

That such loss could be accepted on any scale may seem improbable. In personal terms, it looks contrary to normal self-regard and self-protection. Ideologically, it conflicts with the pervasive ethos of the neo-liberal market and of the materialism and global greed of the mid-1990s. The very language we use expresses a zero-sum mindset. It treats power as a commodity where one's gain is another's loss: it is something we lose, surrender, give up, are stripped of, or hand over. If we are socialized into wanting more of everything, then we want more power.

Professionally, reversals can also be seen as threat. For professional uppers, 'lowers can do it', and 'ask lowers' can be sensed to imply loss of self-esteem, status and control. To recognize and privilege lowers' realities can seem a Pandora's box: the expression of complex and multiple realities, criteria, categories and demands might cause the simple standard bricks of central citadels to crumble. The fear of freedom afflicts not only fascists. It can also daunt those whose dominance is grounded in denials of democratic diversity. Many professionals need the solid structures of their realities, their prisons.

Politically and personally, those most reluctant to give up power are often those who have done wrong. They fear exposure, punishment and revenge, and feel that to protect themselves they must retain control. They are then victims of their own wrongdoing, trapped by fear of retribution for what they have done and been. For them, disempowerment is dangerous. The challenge is to find ways uppers can free themselves from these traps.

Disempowerment as gain: effectiveness, liberation, fulfilment and fun

Fortunately, disempowerment is often a positive sum, in which all gain. This can take several forms.

Effectiveness. Instrumentally, disempowerment offers new roles with new effectiveness in development. To facilitate the participation of others is often practical and cost-effective. The errors of 'all power deceives' diminish. Local realities which are complex, diverse, dynamic and unpredictable can be better expressed and local needs better met. Equity can be served in empowering the weak. Good change can be more sustainable when it is locally owned. In many ways, uppers can gain because empowering lowers is so practical. Against expectations, it so often works.

Liberation. Power on a pinnacle is lonely. Centralized control of more than the minimum is stressful. In contrast, decentralization, spreading responsibility and enhancing trust can defuse tension. In a participatory mode, a boss is not isolated but a team member as well as leader. Relationships are then more equal, with mutual exchanges, learning, partnership, friendship and collegiality. Openness, honesty and realism are foundations of peace of mind.

A striking contemporary example is the extraordinary forgiveness of black Africans manifested in Kenya, Zimbabwe and South Africa after colonial and white domination. Before independence in Kenya, and before majority rule in Zimbabwe and South Africa, many whites in those countries were consumed with fear. They could not believe that 'giving up and handing over' power and control could lead to anything but violence and revenge. As of 1996, they were almost completely wrong. So far, in several senses, almost all have gained from the disempowerment of the whites. A great gift of Africa to humankind has been to make manifest the healing powers of magnanimity. Like Mahatma Gandhi earlier, so Nelson Mandela today towers as an inspiration.

One can ask then, in how many other conditions and places, in political systems, organizations, communities and families, similar fears may be tragically unnecessary, perpetuating pain for lowers and fear for uppers; and how often there is an alternative of positive synergy where lowers' forgiveness generates uppers' relief and gratitude, where disempowerment liberates.

Fulfilment and fun. As many teachers know, enabling others to learn, grow and fulfil themselves is itself fulfilling. So too, in a PRA mode, is empowering others through facilitating their analysis, planning and action. Some of the fulfilment, too, comes from processes which people enjoy. Until recently with PRA, the word 'fun' has scarcely been used in development. Faced with the horrors of war and extremes of cruelty and deprivation, fun may sound self-regarding or even frivolous. But creativity, play and laughter are part of what most people value and wish for themselves and for others; and they are quite often part of PRA processes.

The most seminal learning from the PRA experience comes from going beyond the altruism and generosity of putting the last first to the exhilaration of putting the first last: to responsible disempowerment, eased by the forgiveness of lowers and enhanced by the fulfilment of uppers. In reversals of dominance – stepping down, handing over the stick, facilitating – uppers have means and opportunities for taking pleasure in empowering lowers. To do that, putting the first last, is not a threat but a fulfilment, a liberation, a gain.

For well-being which is sustainable, equitable and responsible, the prison of power is one problem, material possessiveness another. A great methodological challenge for the twenty-first century is to find good ways to enable those with more to be better off with less.

So what? Start!

Development professionals today have access to a different space, open to new insights and behaviours, compared with ten, or even only five years ago. We now know better what local people and lowers can do. It is more than we supposed. We have to hand powerful and popular behaviours, approaches and methods. We know that these are one way to development as better change, to gains by the weaker in ways they will welcome. We know they can enable those in power to be more in touch and up-to-date. We know these behaviours, approaches and methods can enable poor people, women, children, the vulnerable and the marginalized, to express their knowledge and enhance their confidence and capabilities.

As a result, the question 'Whose reality counts?' can be answered more and more with 'Theirs'. The issue is whether we, as development professionals, have the vision, guts and will to change our behaviour, to embrace and act out reversals, and:

○ as economists and bureaucrats to decentralize, destandardize and support local diversity;
○ as staff in NGOs to continue to evolve, apply, share and spread participatory approaches and methods;
○ as teachers in universities, training institutes and colleges, to go with our students to local people to learn, to revise our curricula, to rewrite our textbooks, to teach and lecture less, and more to help others learn;
○ as staff in government organizations, not to talk down but to listen, learn and facilitate, and to provide choices and responsive services;

o as political leaders, to promote and sustain decentralization, democratic values, tolerance, peace and the equitable rule of law;
o as people, to be self-critically aware, to respect others, and to value truth, trust and diversity;
o as uppers, to disempower ourselves, controlling only the minimum, handing over the stick, devolving discretion, encouraging and rewarding lowers' initiatives, and finding fulfilment and fun in enabling others to express, analyse and act on their diverse realities.

We can all think for ourselves, use our personal best judgement, and help others to do the same. We can all define responsible well-being in our own ways for ourselves. We can all celebrate local and personal diversity. Whatever the constraints, most of us, in different ways, some small, some big, can challenge the excesses of centralized power, convention, and uniformity. And most of us have ways to empower others, lowers, the weak, poor and vulnerable, to express their realities and make them count.

Good change flows from personal decisions and action. There is no need to wait. There is a vanguard to join and new high ground to explore.

Postscript: Past and Future: what might have been, and what might be

The book would not be complete without reflecting back on the errors of Chapter 2. We can ask what might have happened if the participatory approaches and methods described had been applied. Readers will make their own judgements. Let us suppose the following actions had been taken:

○ *Macro-policies for structural adjustment.* Participatory poverty appraisals were undertaken before structural adjustment policies were decided. They identified the need for safety-nets for the poor, the importance of recurrent support for health and education services, the seasonal dimensions of deprivation, other aspects of the realities of the poor, and actions to meet their low-cost priorities. These were brought home to policymakers in national governments, the IMF and the World Bank.

Is it reasonable to suppose that:

deprivation and suffering on a vast scale would have been avoided?

○ *Integrated rural development projects.* Participatory approaches and methods in proposed project areas identified poor people's local priorities. These challenged the top–down special project approach which was then abandoned in favour of a programme of decentralization, accommodating local diversity, and providing support and baskets of choice for small farmers and the poor. The World Bank and Governments abstained from top–down pressures to disburse funds, and diverse participatory actions with good local fit resulted.

Is it reasonable to suppose that:

tens of billions of dollars would have been saved, the debts of poor countries would now be far less and the poor of the countries affected would be better off in their own terms?

○ *Model-Ts.* All proposed top-down standardized programmes were screened for local fit, and reformulated in a participatory mode. Seed-breeding practices and procedures generated baskets of choices and practices for farmers to try, not standard packages. Agricultural extension staff were trained not for T&V but for facilitating farmers' own analysis and trials, and searching on their behalf for technology and materials to serve their needs. Systems of farm-level canal irrigation water distribution were evolved locally by farmers and staff.

Is it reasonable to suppose that:

motivation would have replaced demoralization among field-level staff, government services would have gained in credibility and poor farmers would have been better served, for a more diverse, complex, less risky and more sustainable agriculture?

○ *Beliefs about famine and famine deaths.* Decades earlier, detailed and sensitive participatory fieldwork carried out before and during famines revealed the crucial but neglected importance of entitlements – being able to command and obtain food, of disease prevention to save lives, and of early interventions to safeguard livelihoods.

Is it reasonable to suppose that:

changes in policy and practice would have saved the lives of hundreds of thousands, and would have reduced the suffering and impoverishment of millions?

○ *Village-level post-harvest losses.* Policy was based on careful, cross-checked and credible estimates made in a PRA mode by small farmers based on their conditions, practices and experience.

Is it reasonable to suppose that:

fewer funds, staff and organizations would have focused on field-level post-harvest losses, releasing resources for activities with higher benefits?

○ *Multipurpose wheeled toolcarriers.* Engineers and scientists began in a participatory way learning from and with farmers about their problems and priorities, and worked in the field to support them in developing technologies which met their perceived needs.

Is it reasonable to suppose that:

many millions of dollars, much demoralization, and hundreds of years of staff time would have been saved, and useful self-spreading technologies would have been developed and at a lower cost?

○ *The woodfuel crisis.* Assessments were based on participatory analyses at the village level, and on field experience. Local people's priorities determined policy. The species and proportions of trees grown in nurseries were based on local analyses and preferences of local groups.

Is it reasonable to suppose that:

the largely failed drive for village fuelwood lots in many countries would not have been undertaken, and instead of trees for fuelwood, where these were low priority or unwanted, local people would have planted and protected trees they did want, for fodder, fruit and the like?

○ *People and the environment.* Professionals of all departments, disciplines and agencies, and politicians, listened to, believed and learnt from rural people about their history and environment and understood the nature

239

and rationale of their practices, including their priorities for security of land, water and tree tenure.

Is it reasonable to suppose that:

Draconian, self-defeating controls would have been abandoned, local communities would have taken more control of their resources, and farming households would have developed more sustainable agricultural systems with more trees, terraces and long-term investments on their land?, that in particular, secure land and tree tenure in Ethiopia would have led to massive terracing and tree planting as in Kenya, reducing vulnerability and famines, and enhancing well-being on a huge scale?

Whatever answers these questions merit, most readers would probably agree that the benefits gained and the suffering averted if participatory approaches and methods had been applied would have been simply vast. And these errors and examples are but a fraction of the total.

The approaches, methods and insights which might have led to these scenarios had not come together in those earlier years. Now they have. We can have a vision of a future where such errors are no longer made; where responsible well-being for uppers means privileging and respecting the realities of lowers; where development means change that is good for the poor in their terms, where it is their reality that counts.

Why not?

PRA Contacts and Sources of Information

CONTACTS AND SOURCES OF INFORMATION

For information about PRA and PRA-related networks in many countries contact:

PRA, Institute of Development Studies, University of Sussex, Brighton BN1 9RE, UK. Telephone (44) 1273 606261. Fax (44) 1273 621202. E-mail qdfe9@sussex.ac.uk

For information about *PLA Notes* contact:

Sustainable Agriculture Programme, International Institute for Environment and Development, 3 Endsleigh Street, London WC1H 0DD, UK. Telephone (44) 171 388 2117. Fax (44) 171 388 2826. E-mail iiedagri@gn.apc.org

Notes

Chapter 1   The Challenge to Change

1. Some people have difficulty with this title, like a tipsy reveller who once came up to me at a party: 'I have jusht been reading your book . . . ah, putting the . . . putting the . . . putting the cart before the horshe'.
2. As so often, polarization leads to two categories – 'us' and 'them' – when the reality is a continuum with ambiguities and crossings over. At the field and community level there are usually people who belong both to 'us' and to 'them'. So 'us' can include a village volunteer or official when acting for an outside agency, and 'them' can include the same person when acting as a local inhabitant.
3. The word 'females', rather than women, is deliberate and descriptive. Much of the discrimination against females occurs before adulthood. 'Women' misses girls, girl babies, and female foetuses.
4. The 'missing women' (actually missing females) point has been made forcefully by Dreze and Sen (1989: 52–53) who for 1986 figures calculated 37 million for India and 44 million for China. I have taken the total population and used the sex ratio (93 females for every 100 males for India) to estimate the number of females and males. I have then multiplied the number of males by the sex ratios for sub-Saharan Africa (102) and the industrialized countries (104) to find the number of females there would have been for that number of males. Subtracting the actually reported number of females then gives the missing millions.

    Tim Dyson (pers. comm. 1996) has correctly described these figures as 'sound-bite demography' (see also Dyson 1987; 1994). The assumptions and figures are subject to much detailed qualification, especially regarding census undercounts of females. Even so, my best judgement is that there is still here evidence of massive discrimination against females. Though flawed, the calculation, as Dreze and Sen put it, 'reveals in quiet statistics a gruesome story of anti-female bias' (ibid: 53). A footnote to this footnote is to invite the reader to estimate missing people, taking average life expectancy (1992) as reported to be 63.2 for the 4.61 billion people in low- and middle-income developing countries and 74.4 (for the 0.83 billion) in the high-income countries (WDR, 1995: 162–3).
5. I have added these categories of 'too many', 'about right' and 'too few'. There is nothing precise about this. Klatzmann (1983) cited in Uvin (1994a: 69–70) esti- mated in 1983 that about 20 per cent of the world's population engaged in excessive consumption (more than 2800 calories and 40 grams of protein a day) and 1.5 billion were undernourished (less than 2000 calories and 10 grams of animal protein a day). Klatzmann later stood by these earlier estimates except that he widened the ranges, implying greater polarization.
6. For further discussion of livelihoods, including sustainable livelihoods, see Chambers 1988a, Conroy and Litvinoff 1988, Swift 1989, Bernstein, Crow and Johnson 1992, Chambers and Conway 1992, and Davies 1996.
7. I have hesitated to use the word 'capability' since Amartya Sen, and others following him, have given it special meanings. I am using capability in its diction- ary sense of 'the quality of being capable; ability' (*The Collins English Diction- ary*, second edition 1986).

241

8. Offence might be caused by mentioning Soros in the same paragraph and context as people like Gandhi and Mother Theresa. The point, though, is that it is good when those who are rich and powerful make good things happen, even if their wealth and power have questionable origins, much is misused, they could do much more, their own levels of living are unaffected, and their egos are not diminished by being benefactors.

9. The need and opportunity for change in the World Bank can be put in various ways. For example:

> The global village had its day
> but rapidly has shrunk away
> So now we find ourselves instead
> together in a global bed
>
> Enjoying patriarchal rank
> we know our Father is the Bank
> And up till now we had to learn
> when Father turns, so we all turn
>
> No more. Upend him. Master fate
> and make him change before too late
> reorienting in the bed
> not side to side, but on his head.

There are promising indications that James Wolfensohn, the most recent president of the World Bank, has some ideas of standing on his head.

Chapter 2   Normal Error

1. Any reader who is sceptical is referred to Swift's analysis, which I have read only in the late stages of writing this book. The belief in widespread human-made desertification in the Sahel was based on scanty and erroneous evidence, over-generalizations from bad years, conceptual confusion, and the repetition and embedding of wrong statistics, all of these serving strong institutional vested interests and constituting and sustaining a worldwide professional illusion.

Chapter 3   Professional Realities

1. For further analysis of normal professionalism, see Chambers (1993a), Chapters 1, 5 and 6, parts of which are summarized in the first paragraphs of this chapter.
2. Bob Lack, from Auckland in New Zealand, in a letter published in the *Guardian Weekly* of 5 September 1993, disagreed with Professor Lester Thurow's view that real per capita GDP was the best over-all measure of standard of living. He wrote:

'If, after writing his article, Prof. Thurow had eaten a healthy meal of home-grown vegetables, gone to bed, made love with his partner and then enjoyed a good night's sleep he would have contributed precisely nothing to GDP. If, on the other hand, he had driven to a casino, got drunk, crashed his car on the way home and injured himself and some passing pedestrians he would have increased his country's GDP by thousands of dollars. The fuel, the liquor, the tow truck and the ambulance, the car repairs and the hospital bills: all contribute to GDP and hence, by his reasoning, to the standard of living.
What nonsense! . . .

3. This is no criticism of the legendary punctuality of Swiss trains, which I appreciate. The trick is to know where exact prediction and targeting make sense and

where they do not. The logical framework conflicts with the flexibility needed for participation (see e.g. Schubert *et al.*, 1994; Johansson, 1995).

4. Some of the better known early manuals and works on social cost benefit analysis were McKean, 1965; King, 1967; ODA, 1972; OECD, 1973, Little and Mirlees, 1974; and Squire and van der Tak, 1975. Gittinger (1982) is a more recent classic which has been widely distributed and taught, including translation into Russian.

5. The critical reader will properly ask for evidence of this assertion. It is not surprising that practising economists do not provide written evidence about how they actually perform SCBA. It might cost them, if not their jobs, at least some of their credibility. The evidence on which this is based is of the sort which is shared over a drink in the evening.

6. This guess may encourage someone to come up with a better figure. In the Overseas Development Administration of the British Government by 1996 the ratio was very different, of the order of only two economists to one non-economist social scientist (mainly social development advisers).

7. In mid-1996, there is a momentum within the Bank to mainstream social development, recognizing the shift of emphasis from physical infrastructure to what in Bank language is known as social infrastructure. It remains to be seen how far this shift from things to people can go.

8. Five of the six Nobel prizes for economics awarded to date in the 1990s have been to economists at the University of Chicago: Merton Miller (corporate finance, 1990), Ronald Coase (property rights, 1991), Gary Becker (non-market behaviour, 1992), Robert Fogel (economic history, 1993) and Robert Lucas (rational expectations, 1995). Earlier Nobel prizewinners from Chicago were Friedrich von Hayek (1974), Milton Friedman (1976), Theodore Schultz (1979) and George Stigler (1982) (*The Economist* (London) 30 March 1996).

9. These were American economists and economics students. Economists of other nationalities may differ. It is, though, American economists who have the most influence. More generally, let me warn against the stereotyping implicit in the generalizations in this section. Many, many economists are fine, generous, humane people, perhaps in spite of the conditioning of their professional training and experiences.

10. Pavlovian here refers not to the dancing of the Russian ballerina, nor to the cake named after her, made of meringue and topped with cream and fruit, but to the Soviet physiologist and Nobel prize winner, Ivan Petrovich Pavlov, who conditioned dogs to salivate at the sound of a bell, regardless of whether there was food, and so founded the science of behaviourism.

11. Though critical of some of Freud's work elsewhere in this book, I acknowledge his contribution to understanding the quirks of the mind (and in my case, fingers) in *The Psychopathology of Everyday Life* (1901). I first typed not dog, but god, chasing its (hers? his?) tail. A flattering interpretation might take this as an unconscious comment on the stabilizing circularities of much theology as well as secular ideology, and of belief systems in general; less flattering is to apply this to the argument of this book. Am I also a mad dog chasing its tail, also with my lamp-post and pool of light? Must any coherence and consistency be at the cost of circularity, selecting what fits and discarding the discordant? Are reductionist roundabouts necessary for progress with understanding? Perhaps there is no escape, only a willingness to recognize the roundabouts, to get off them from time to time, to look at them from outside, to seek and puzzle over evidence that does not fit, to reflect critically, and to doubt, question and be open to change. All positions are then permanently provisional; in human affairs there is then no final reality, no final truth.

12. I know this sentence should have been deleted, but my better judgement has not prevailed.

Chapter 4   The Transfer of Reality

1. Throughout I shall use the word 'personal' rather than 'subjective'. Subjective is value-laden, implying unreliable and biased, in contrast with objective which implies a superior lasting truth. It follows then that personal experience and judgement (subjective) are not to be trusted as much as anything that is measured or observed in controlled conditions (objective). But the way we live and learn values both, and it seems sensible to treat them evenly, recognizing their different strengths and weaknesses.

2. Upper–lower bias is reflected in language, usage and differentiation of meanings, with more categories and nuances among uppers than lowers. For example, the Oxford Thesaurus (Urdang, 1991) gives 12 synonyms or entries for the adjective 'upper', including '(more) northerly, northern', but only 2 for the adjective 'lower' neither of which is southerly or southern. 'Upper-class' has 19 entries, 'upper crust' 7, and 'upper hand' 11, but lower-class is not included in the Thesaurus, and lower crust and lower hand are not even common usage.

3. The deep embedding of a Northern, rather than Southern geographical orientation, at least among mountaineers, is illustrated by Peter Cliff in his best-selling book *Mountain Navigation*. He points out that 'If you ask someone what the main use of a compass is, the answer will probably be: to find North. But in itself, this is not a great help, unless you happen to be on the way by direct route to the North Pole' (Cliff, 1991: 17). Neither South nor the South Pole come into it. However, N–S maps are not quite universal. Happily, some have been made in the South, notably in Australia, with South at the top. The way they startle brings home how education and convention condition us to see the arbitrary as normal and natural. Interestingly, most people's local mental maps do not have North at the top. Invited to draw quick sketch maps of the neighbourhood where they live, on average only 10–15 per cent of people in different countries put North at the top. Exceptionally, North is put at the top by most students in London (perhaps influenced by N–S maps used to find their way around) and men in Finland who wear suits (influenced by I know not what, but the sample was small).

4. Changes have indeed taken place in the teaching of mathematics, notably with what in the United States was known at first as 'new math', which taught mathematical understanding through other bases besides the base ten. Like all changes this was at first a threat to teachers set in old ways. As Tom Lehrer had it in his song, new math was 'so simple, so very simple, that only a child can do it'.

5. The effect can be maddening or sometimes, for the antiquarian, an entrancing delight. In 1989 courteous and helpful officials of the government of Andhra Pradesh issued Jenny and me with International Driving Permits. The contracting states for which these were valid included a litany from my stamp-collecting childhood – French India, Curaçao, Lithuania, Sambilan, Pahang, Colony of Gold Coast and Ashanti, and Free City of Dantzing (sic) [annexed by Hitler in 1939], as well as Saar Territory [annexed by Hitler in 1935] and Isle of Men (sic). To the duplicated list of countries had been added the United States of America and Canada; but no country, it would seem, had been deleted or updated. An Indian friend visiting Indonesia in 1990 was worried how Indonesian police would react to his permit to drive in the Dutch East Indies.

6. I have done this in Kenya. There was a special problem there. The end of the Government financial year came just before the long rains. It was a costly lesson that cement had to be safely banked to avoid conversion into a currency so hard as to be almost valueless.

7. This approach is more commonly referred to as 'Fordist', but when I used that term in an earlier paper, colleagues and friends in the Ford Foundation were upset. They pointed out not just that the Ford Foundation has no connection with the Ford Motor Company or Henry Ford's descendants, but that the approaches to development supported by the Ford Foundation are very different from standardized batch production. The term Model-T is more acceptable: it is anchored in history, avoids misunderstanding, and is a close analogy with the phenomenon of standardized supply which is being described.

8. Henry Ford may or may not have said this. Scanning half a dozen biographies has not revealed a source; nor does this remark appear in any of the dictionaries of quotations consulted. One wonders how many other sayings have become well known without apparently having been said. However, in the words of one historian (Lewis, 1976: 57): 'The statement "The public can have any color it wants so long as it's black", if not actually made by Henry Ford, at least expressed his attitude regarding the opinions of customers during the years the Model T dominated the auto market'. Significantly, in the 1920s he eventually bowed to public pressure and manufactured automobiles in other colours.

9. This point is elaborated in Chambers and Ghildyal (1985) and Chambers and Jiggins (1986).

10. For assessments and evaluations of the system, see e.g. Cernea *et al.*, 1984; Moore, 1984; Howell, 1988; and Hulme, 1991. Antholt (1993) reviews earlier evaluations.

11. Expressed differently:

In classic Model T and V
conveyor belt machinery
presents its stock delivery
of packages by TOT.

12. A fuller statement of the evidence and argument on which this section is based can be found in Chambers 1988b: 92–9.

13. With hindsight, I am appalled at my own, if minor, part in this. I was personally involved in the subdivision of the El Barta Plains and part of the Ndoto mountains in Samburu District in Kenya into four grazing blocks. The four-month rotation was attempted but never fully adopted. The sage Samburu took the long view and accepted the boundaries in exchange for improved water supplies. The temporary inconvenience of 'grazing control' was abandoned with the approach of Independence. I have been back and apologized. They were generously forgiving.

14. Searching my memory I can think of nothing that could be described as a success. But my knowledge is limited. 'Almost always' is a necessary caution. T&V is believed to work in some places. It is also quite possible, for example, that somewhere in India outside the Northwest *warabandi* is working. If so, I would welcome information about the conditions in which this has proved possible. I am more confident about the rigid ranch model. It seems unlikely that it would be implemented in any risk-prone environment unless by a totalitarian government or a rich psychotic.

Chapter 5 All Power Deceives

1. Myth is used here and elsewhere to mean misguided belief.
2. The reference is to Lord Acton's aphorism: 'Power tends to corrupt, and absolute power corrupts absolutely', in a letter to Mandell Creighton, 5 April 1887.
3. Claims have been made by some parents accused of abuse by their adult children of a 'False Memory Syndrome'. The claims are that therapy has led to the

recovery of false memories of abuse. This is a contested area which does not affect the points being made here. That child sex abuse is widespread, at least in the North, is not in dispute: a conservative estimate of the incidence in the UK is 10 per cent of children and of adults. For what reads as a balanced review, see Toon *et al.*, 1996.

4. An impressive number of women have been prominent psychoanalysts, including Helen Deutsch, Anna Freud, Freda Fromm-Reichmann, Karen Horney, Margaret Mahler, Hanna Segal and Melanie Klein, who founded a major school of psychoanalysis. But overall, as in most professions, more psychoanalysts were men than women, and being a woman did not necessarily mean being more sympathetic. Kleinians, for example, tend to 'blame the baby' (pers. comm. Jenny Chambers).

5. No doubt I have fallen into this trap in this book. It is how some academics establish their credentials and impress some others. It is always tempting to use a longer, more obscure word, when a shorter, clearer one will do. To readers mystified in consequence, especially those for whom English is not their first language, I can only apologize.

6. I may just be badly read and ignorant. Non-fiction books about the behaviour of development professionals may exist. If they do, I shall be grateful to anyone who can bring them to my notice.

7. New posts and new organizations are often only allowed on marginal 'territory', and are regarded as a threat by those already established. Examples in East Africa in the 1950s and 1960s included planning organizations, and departments for community development, co-operatives and settlement. The resources required for them to fight for 'territory' are among the costs of setting up new organizations where claimants to their functions already exist (Chambers, 1977).

8. The status significance of location is, though, not always sequentially straightforward. Also in Khartoum, but in the 1960s, on entering the ministry of planning the signs encountered announced, in sequence, LADIES, GENTLEMEN, ECONOMISTS.

9. Many other ways will be found for dismissing scrupulous research that has significant but discordant results. Ignoring it is one, discounting its origins another. One wonders whether the editor of *Nature* would take seriously the work of Lepes and Argibay (1994) of the internationally perhaps not particularly well-known Instituto Argentino de Parapsicologia who found evidence of psi (extra-sensory) effects with the fruit fly Drosophila melanogaster.

10. Any curious reader can consult the tedious text which argues this (Chambers, 1988b, pp. 54–9).

11. This is a time-honoured technique, often effective, as so many civil servants know. At one time I had a tray on my desk marked TIME MAY SOLVE. I had to remove it after a complainant was outraged when he saw his file in that tray. All the same, 'Time may solve' may be no worse than the common 'Your file has been lost' or 'Your file is in transit' of the British and Indian (and no doubt other) Civil Services.

12. Catechism is defined as 'instruction by a series of questions and answers, especially a book containing such instruction on the religious doctrine of a Christian church . . . rigorous and persistent questioning . . .' (*The Collins English Dictionary*, 1986). It stems from a Greek word meaning 'to shout down'.

13. I owe the insights in this paragraph, and of much of this chapter, to Jenny Chambers. But as elsewhere, responsibility for opinions and errors remains mine alone.

14. I am indebted to Meera Shah for this account. She alone, as facilitator, had to struggle against the false consensus of planners and displaced people to make

space for the people to conduct their own participatory analysis and recognize the implications of their choices. In most such situations, the false consensus would prevail.

15. L.W. Kingsland's translation from the Danish, quoted here, has more character than the clipped basic English of the Penguin 60s version published in 1995.

16. The Egocentric Reminiscence Ratio (ERR) is relevant here. This is the proportion of a person's speech devoted to personal recollections of the 'When I was . . .' sort. Expatriates in Botswana have been known as the WaWenwe, those who say 'When we were in Kenya . . . When we were in Zambia . . .'. Working hypotheses are that the ERR is higher among men than women, and seniors than juniors, rises with age, on retirement leaps to a new high level, is higher in the evening than the morning, and rises sharply with the consumption of alcohol. My limited self-awareness includes recognition that my ERR is high in parts of this book. Also, as in some respects a multiple upper, I am guilty of hubris and hypocrisy in pronouncing on a range of subjects, about some of which I know less than others. I have painted myself into a no-win corner. The only defence is to doubt and to invite criticism.

17. This section draws on experience in India in the early 1980s, especially in the irrigation sector, and is in danger of treating the past as the present. The World Bank and governments in the South do change and the reader is asked to judge to what extent the analysis still applies. Detailed evidence is given in *Managing Canal Irrigation* (Chambers, 1988b).

18. According to a consultant with much experience of working with the Bank: 'Until the Bank gets away from spending targets it will go on doing bad work', 'We have got good things we can do but we can't get them in because they do not involve new lending', and 'It is a totalitarian system, and it is more totalitarian on the Bank side' (pers. comm. 1995).

19. The World Bank has not acted on the suggestion that a training video be made to show the pressures on staff and how they behave on their brief country visits. Yet the research needed for such a video would open up the black box of face-to-face interactions which are at the core of so much good and bad development practice.

20. There was a large body of evidence suggesting that distribution of water on the main canal system was indeed the main issue and opportunity, but the Bank and the Indian Government persisted in a series of large-scale standard programmes which did not tackle this problem; in the meantime they were continuously misled about their success (See Chambers, 1988b: chs 3, 4, 5 and 6).

21. ZOPP was relabelled OOPP (Objectives Oriented Project Planning) for use in Chad. The task manager explained: 'As we described ZOPP, I noticed that people were giggling and laughing. I asked what was the matter. They explained, good naturedly, that in Chad, the word 'Zopp' was a slang expression with sexual connotations – and we all had a good laugh about it. But they had a more serious problem. They said we were acting in a typical Bank manner by prescribing how to do things' (Ndao, 1995: 29).

Chapter 6   Learning to Learn

1. The phrases in this sentence are combined from the cover of Fals-Borda and Rahman *Action and Knowledge* (1991).

2. RRA as Rapid Rural Appraisal is not to be confused with RRA as the Rhino Reintroduction Area designated in the Dudhwa National Park in North India (Aziz, 1993) although both sorts of RRA have faced problems with dominant participants brought in by air – foreign experts and rhino bulls respectively.

3. Any listing of the NGOs in India that took pioneering initiatives at an early stage would include (in alphabetical order) ActionAid, Bangalore; Activists for

247

Social Alternatives, Trichy; the Aga Khan Rural Support Programme (India); Krishi Gram Vikas Kendra, Ranchi; MYRADA, Bangalore; Seva Bharati, Midnapore District; SPEECH, Madurai; and Youth for Action, Hyderabad. Among others, government organizations in India that received and promoted training included the Drylands Development Board, Karnataka, the District Rural Development Agencies, Andhra Pradesh, and several Forestry Departments. PRA methods were adopted by the National Academy of Administration, Mussoorie for the fieldwork of its 300-odd Indian Administrative Service probationers each year, and by the Xavier Institute of Social Services, Ranchi, which introduced PRA for the fieldwork of its students.

4. The larger international foundations, agencies and NGOs active in supporting and promoting activities described as PRA have included ActionAid, the Aga Khan Foundation, CARE, DANIDA, FAO, Farm Africa, FINNIDA, the Ford Foundation, Forests Trees and People, GTZ, Helvetas, IDRC, IFAD, Intercooperation, IIED, Irish Aid, the Near East Foundation, NOVIB, ODA, OXFAM, the Paul Hamlyn Foundation, Redd Barna, SAREC, Save the Children (UK), Swiss Development Cooperation, SIDA, UNDP, UNICEF, Winrock International, the World Bank, the World Resources Institute, and World Neighbours.

5. As at June 1996, PRA-related activities had taken place in at least the following: Albania, Argentina, Armenia, Australia, *Bangladesh*, Belize, Bhutan, *Bolivia*, Botswana, *Brazil*, Bulgaria, *Burkina Faso*, Cambodia, Cameroon, *Canada*, Cap Verde, Chile, *China*, Colombia, Costa Rica, Ecuador, *Egypt*, El Salvador, *Eritrea*, Estonia, *Ethiopia*, *Finland*, the Gambia, Germany, *Ghana*, Guatemala, Guinea, Honduras, *India*, *Indonesia*, Ireland, Jordan, *Kenya*, Lao PDR, Lebanon, *Lesotho*, Malawi, Malaysia, Maldives, *Mali*, Mauritania, *Mexico*, Mongolia, Morocco, *Mozambique*, *Namibia*, *Nepal*, Nicaragua, *Niger*, *Nigeria*, *Norway*, Pakistan, Palestine, Panama, Papua New Guinea, Paraguay, Peru, *the Philippines*, *Senegal*, Sierra Leone, Somaliland, *South Africa*, Spain, *Sri Lanka*, Sudan, Switzerland, Tanzania, Thailand, Turkey, Uganda, *UK*, Uruguay, USA, Uzbekistan, Venezuela, Vietnam, Zambia and Zimbabwe. (Italics indicate a known active PRA-related network or networks.)

6. This menu draws on Box 3 in Chambers and Guijt, 1995: 9. This is an empirical listing, using the terms for some of the more common methods and approaches. For an analysis of the components of visual methods, which opens up a wider range of potential combinations, see Chapter 7 of this book, pp. 135–6. Much invention and adaptation continues. For example, *The REFLECT Mother Manual* (Archer and Cottingham, 1996b) contains a full and often original menu of methods and applications, some additional to those listed here.

7. Grandin's classical method entailed individual interviews, followed by mathematical analysis of scores. This has evolved into card sorting by groups which has been used with well over 100 000 households (including in Ethiopia, India, Pakistan and Sri Lanka).

8. A late addition at the time of going to press is the potential for applications of PRA visualizations (Venn diagramming, matrix scoring, linkage diagramming etc.) in psychotherapy (pers. comm. Fiona Chambers).

9. For a good example of the use of PRA methods in a research mode see HSWG, 1995. Largely in two weeks, a multi-disciplinary team of 27 persons worked in two villages in Zimbabwe, leading to a full and convincing review of the diversity and value of local-level savannah woodland resources, how they are perceived, and how they contribute to livelihoods.

10. Participatory seasonal calendars in Scotland have also shown the timing of payment of school expenses to fall at a bad time of year (pers. comm. Carolyn Jones), but this cannot be linked with the rains. The reported realities of the Scots are that it rains all round the year.

11. For general overviews of PPAs see Norton and Stephens, 1995 and Robb, 1996. For urban applications in Ghana and Zambia see Norton, 1994. For Ghana see Norton *et al.*, 1995, Dogbe, 1996, and Norton 1996; for Zambia, Norton *et al.*, 1994, Milimo, 1996, and Norton and Owen, 1996; for Tanzania, Narayan, 1996; for South Africa, Attwood, 1996; and for Mozambique, Owen, 1996.

12. International meetings for sharing and building on parallel innovations in RRA and PRA modes have included those for RRA at the Institute of Development Studies at the University of Sussex in 1979, at Khon Kaen University in 1985 (KKU, 1987), and again at IDS jointly with IIED in 1988; that for PRA at Bangalore in 1991 (Mascarenhas *et al.*, 1991); four subsequent South–South PRA Exchange Workshops, three in India and the latest (1995) in the Philippines; and a Latin American meeting at the Isla de Mujeres in Mexico in August 1995 (de Toma, 1996). In addition there have been national workshops in at least Bangladesh, Ethiopia, Kenya, Indonesia, Nepal, the Philippines, Sri Lanka, Uganda, Vietnam, and Zambia. From 1991 through 1996 IDS and IIED held a series of PRA workshops on topics such as well-being ranking, health, training, gender, children, policy, scaling up and ethics, PRA and policy, and PRA and institutions.

Chapter 7　What Works and Why

1. Yet another domino is local people writing their own training manual. There is already positive experience from India (Meera and Parmesh Shah, pers. comm.), Namibia (Pat Norrish, pers. comm.) and Sri Lanka (Norrish and Best, 1994) of training participants writing their own manuals rather than adopting or translating those of the trainers.

2. In my view, patient and painstaking social anthropological fieldwork over extended periods can lead to understandings unlikely to be accessible through PRA approaches and methods. At the same time, PRA processes (e.g. mapping, matrices, linkage diagrams) express realities which social anthropologists would otherwise miss.

3. Ordinal has two meanings which both apply here: the first concerns a position in a sequence, as in ranking; the second comes from biology, where it means relating to or characteristic of an order in biological classification. Ordinal thus combines the activities of comparing and of classifying.

4. In the work of the Agricultural Research Planning Team in Central Province, Zambia, participatory mapping has been a stage in identifying key informants. Using the map they have made: people help select who should be involved in the interviewing process; the selection can be made representative; and those not selected can better understand how and why the choices have been made (pers comm. Simon Kandela Tunkanya, 1995).

5. Values varied by age-group even for the same category, '. . . cover and camouflage were mentioned as important in the context of warfare. During the liberation struggle, the villagers had used the woodlands as hiding places. The boys, unable to remember the war, interpreted cover as a useful value as a hiding place from adults when they are with their girlfriends!' (HSWG, 1995: 59).

6. In her classic study, Barbara Grandin (1988) found that correlations (Spearman's Rho) across informants in 12 instances of wealth ranking (using a total of 41 informants) averaged 0.77 (range 0.59–0.96). The correlations of each informant with the final score averaged 0.91 (range 0.84–0.98).

7. The questionnaire survey, with a pretested structured schedule was administered to 412 households by five very experienced investigators, collecting data on type of house, caste, education, occupation, ownership of assets, number of

dresses per person, and yearly income. A 'professionals' classification' was then compiled, based on a composite index calculated for each household. A separate community classification was facilitated, and conducted by groups of knowledgeable local women and men. The two classifications were compared, and about half of the discrepancies were investigated by senior researchers in careful detail, including home visits. The conclusions about validity were based on these investigations of discrepancies.

8. These generalizations are supported by the ranking of the value of 30 browse plants as feed for cattle by pastoralists in Nigeria (Bayer, 1987, 1988). The rankings for the most important plants were found to correspond closely between different groups of pastoralists.

9. A tantalizing finding from a study in Nepal (UNICEF, 1975, cited in Bradley, 1995: 84) was that villagers who did not recognize other pictures recognized and could interpret a diagram of tuberculosis transmission which a medical team had shown and explained to them some time earlier. This opens up the question whether diagram literacy is more general and widespread (perhaps a more general faculty) than visual literacy for understanding pictures. One factor may be the relative lack of cultural baggage carried by diagrams compared with pictures (but see Gill (1993b) on slicing pies versus tearing chapattis).

10. In the process which led to 'Sharing Our Concerns' (*PLA Notes* 22: 5–10) the 20 participants first wrote their ideas of principles anonymously on cards. These were placed on the ground and sorted by everyone into what came to be six groups. Anyone who disagreed with a card or felt it should be discussed turned it over. Those not turned over were taken as agreed. Those which had been turned over were then put on a board and discussed, with one person facilitating. Without the flexible use of the ground, the process would have been more difficult, long-drawn-out and exhausting; and in my judgement would have led to a lower quality of consensus and output.

11. 'Tous les participants expriment le vif désir de continuer ce travail et de l'approfondir.'

12. In her account of demographic data collection in the Zambezi Valley in Zimbabwe, Ravai Marindo-Ranganai (1995) wrote: 'The villagers had a sense of humour. After the researcher's hut was destroyed by a gas fire, the villagers made a small fire on the model of the village. The children went as far as dramatizing the fire, shouting "my papers, my papers, leave the clothes, bring out the papers".'

13. I am in no position to throw stones. Though not a social anthropologist, I have conducted field research in which my motivation was more to get a degree than to do good.

14. I would have liked to have stood on higher moral ground, and adopted a stricter line, that no outputs should ever be taken away from those who create them. But I have sinned, even though in the arguably good cause of familiarizing others with what PRA can generate, in borrowing outputs to show to others before being returned.

15. I slightly prefer credibility to trustworthiness. In common usage, the meanings of the two words are close. But in constructivist literature (e.g. Lincoln and Guba, 1985; Guba and Lincoln, 1989) credibility is given a meaning as a subset of trustworthiness. I have decided not to confuse things further and to accept trustworthiness. For a review and elaboration including a longer list of 'goodness criteria' see Pretty, 1995b: 1255–6. What one does to assure goodness matters more than what words are used.

Chapter 8 Poor People's Realities: Local, Complex, Diverse, Dynamic and Unpredictable

1. It may be lack of self-insight which makes me prefer senescent ('growing old') to senile ('mentally or physically weak or infirm on account of old age'). Physically, I have passed the watershed of being described as sprightly but not yet, at least in my hearing, as decrepit. The mental dimension is harder (from inside) to assess.
2. Hedgehogs and foxes are lamentably Eurocentric, a form of North–South domination by metaphor. Readers from other continents, please substitute porcupines and jackals, or other equivalents.
3. This list of CPRs picks up only some of the main spatial sources to which poor people can have access. There are many others, such as railway lines, canal banks and road reserves. Convention often allows access to certain items such as wild fruits on private land (e.g. blackberries and mushrooms in the UK). In some African cities people collect and eat the insects which fall to the ground under lamp-posts after dark.
4. Caterpillars and locusts are both insects, but I have included them because they are noted in the literature, and it is nice to have them in the list.
5. Seasonal dimensions of rural poverty have a substantial literature, some of which is briefly reviewed in Chambers, 1993a: 57–9. See e.g. Schofield, 1974; Chambers *et al.*, 1981; Longhurst, 1986; Huss-Ashmore *et al.*, 1988; Sahn, 1989; Walker and Ryan, 1990; Gill, 1991a; Chambers, 1993a: 40–59; and Ulijaszek and Strickland, 1993.
6. A counter-case is how pests can build up with staggered cultivation, whereas with synchronized cultivation they lack time to multiply before their chances are over.
7. As a boy I had huge pleasure in picking, storing and selling some 40 varieties of apples from an orchard (now a housing estate). There was delight in the diversity of names (Newton Wonder, Charles Ross, Beauty of Bath, Worcester Permain, Allington Pippin, Russet, Bramley, Blenheim . . .), and in their differences of shape, size, colour, taste, time of ripening, ease of picking, ease of bruising, storability, ease of sale, and the prices I could get for them.
8. Galbraith, in *The Culture of Contentment* (1992: 20–22) points out that for politicians 'In the briefest word, short-run public inaction, even if held to be alarming as to consequence, is always preferred to protective long-run action'. Present cost and taxation are specific; the benefits are future and dispersed, and those who might benefit are 'later and different individuals'.
9. The source is a moving account by a PRA-training participant in the video *The PRA Report*, based on a PRA experience in Zambia, and produced by World Vision Australia.
10. This may prove a costly paragraph. I have asked people in the course of PRA familiarization to guess what criteria local people had that none of the staff thought of, offering prize money to anyone guessing the answer. I have only twice had to pay up. It will test whether anyone reads this book to see if I now start to lose more often.
11. ODA did not fund the project.

Chapter 9 The New High Ground

1. I have not researched recent Hebrew theology and cannot say whether the sex of the deity has changed or, as it were, been neutralized. In the syntax of the

Old Testament of the Bible, on which I was brought up, God was unequivocally male.

2. The imagery is also literal. Americans who tamed the plains of the west were, and still are, honoured as pioneers: the cowboys who herded their cattle and settlers who cleared their fields endure as folk heroes. But today the poor Africans, Asians and Latin Americans who graze their animals and make their fields in the hills and forests are branded as encroachers and their animals as destroyers. The poor herders and settlers of the South have become scapegoats for the global rich. Until recently, the rich and powerful who bulldoze, cut and construct have escaped largely scot-free. But that is changing.

3. For this example I am indebted to the fellow revellers who sang 'Auld Lang Syne' at the 1995/96 New Year party in the village of Kingston, near Lewes, East Sussex, UK.

4. One wonders, for example, whether it is worth wondering what this means:

> Many such views of the classical, modern and post-modern scholars may be cited for establishing the fact that respective appraisals of social reality follow from different value premises envisaging the prime mover of society by particular gamuts of social processes. The processual attributes entering into these gamuts for defining culture as a dependent, intervening or symbiotic variable of different kinds (and thus compose the human groups) may not be mutually exclusive. However, as evident from the views quoted, the attributes would form distinctive gamuts of social processes by their absence from one or another gamut or the nature and extent of their presence in these gamuts.

(Mukherjee, 1991: PE–29)

5. 'Use your own best judgement at all times' was (and may still be) the one-sentence policy manual of the large North American retailer Nordstrom. Tom Peters (1989: 379) reports that at Nordstrom the chief duty of supervisors is to coach salespersons on exactly what it means 'to use your own best judgement', and that 'The absence of childish rules shifts the employee's focus of innovation to precisely where the firm wishes it to be: in pursuit of serving the customer better, rather than in pursuit of evasion of the rules about toilet breaks'. In PRA the application is deeper and wider, extending to personal growth and responsibility in diverse domains.

6. Let me admit to doubt and possible error myself here, since I am recalling this from memory, without the source, and I may well have embellished or fashioned her remark to fit the purpose of the point I want to make.

7. Belloc's lines come from *The Microbe*.

8. Fallibly quoted from memory. I have not been able to bring myself to pore through Popper's voluminous works to find the source.

9. Uppers almost always underestimate the capabilities of lowers. In an earlier draft I partially excepted those who are brain damaged or severely mentally defective. But recovery from brain damage and unusual capabilities among the mentally defective are common enough to justify the principle also with them: assume lowers can do something until proved otherwise.

10. In this list, fun is an apple among oranges. The other words are serious and moral. Fun looks frivolous. That fun is out of reach for so many – the desperately sick, suffering and poor, those who are abused, trapped, victims of violence, those fleeing in terror from war – may make it seem obscene in a development vocabulary. But it is as important as the others. With play and fun come creativity, laughter, the breakdown of barriers, the expression of realities, new insights, and the weakening of defences and of structures of power. That it is out of reach for so many is an outrage. Should fun be a basic human right?

11. In an earlier draft I used 'altruism'. But altruism is an austere, unsmiling word with overtones of do-gooding. I am grateful to Norman Uphoff (1992: 341) for

pointing out that altruism and generosity can be used interchangeably. His Chapter 12 is exciting and essential reading on this.

12. There is, however, a chapter by Marianne Gronemeyer on 'Helping' which is close to altruism. She analyses the modernizing of the idea of help. This, she argues, has evolved from spontaneous response to a cry of need to an instrument for the sophisticated exercise of power, in which neediness is determined not by the cry of the afflicted (lower) but by the diagnosis of the development establishment (upper).

Chapter 10   Putting the First Last

1. Some farming-systems research gave rise to manuals the weight and size of which became problems. On our kitchen scales, the four volumes of the Farming-Systems Support-Project manuals weighed approximately 3.6kg, raising the spectre of the day when some of the less robust professionals might require a porter in the field.

2. My children tell me that I do all these things. This is, of course, a total fabrication.

3. I was too slow off the mark to prevent a World Bank editor changing the title of something I wrote in the early 1980s. 'Short-cut' was inserted in the title, and it has remained there ever since. It is an unfortunate word: it implies a second-best; and for good reason it is part of the folklore of mountaineers and motorists that short-cuts are often not short at all.

4. Mosse also argues that distortions are introduced by the public nature of PRA activities. Being aware of this matters, and where appropriate, convening separate groups, as has become widely recognized as good practice by the mid-1990s. Group-visual synergy (pp. 159–60) also tends towards honesty and accuracy.

5. In an earlier draft I phrased this as 'perceived as a threat by some people'. To describe resistance or criticism as reflecting a threat is a classical put-down and defence by those criticized. As in psychoanalysis, it can be part of a circular system in which the critic or victim cannot win. The reader who has survived Chapter 5 will realize that I have to point the finger at myself.

6. For abstracts of sources on participatory M&E, see McPherson (1995).

7. This applies to the Catholic church, but no longer to some Protestant churches.

8. These are now numerous. Early adopters included the Drylands Development Board, Karnataka in India; the Soil and Water Conservation Branch, Ministry of Agriculture in Kenya (Thompson, 1995); some of the Integrated Rural Development Projects (Thompson, 1995) and the North Western Province Dry Zone Participatory Development Project (Kar and Backhaus, 1994; Backhaus and Wagachchi, 1995; Thompson, 1995), both in Sri Lanka; the RIPS in Tanzania (Johansson, 1995); and the Smallholder Development Project in the Copperbelt in Zambia (Drinkwater, 1994). For NGOs see Samaranayake, 1994.

9. This section draws on and modifies Pretty and Chambers (1993) and Pretty (1995b). For other sources see e.g. Schon, 1983, 1987; Lincoln and Guba, 1985; Erlandson et al., 1993; and others in the references in Pretty, 1995b: 1259–63.

10. The reader will judge whether I have made my values explicit enough in this book. I am not sure.

11. Although an Englishman practised in hypocrisy, I am uneasy writing this. But it has an empirical base in common experience.

12. Difficult participants in PRA training may be victims of their life experiences and deserve sympathetic understanding. A religious fundamentalist who was a resistant saboteur on a training told me that when he was a boy at school discipline was so strict that, quite apart from physical abuse, pupils were not allowed to look at teachers' faces, only at their shoes.

13. I am embarrassed to be writing this moralizing stuff, especially having some sense of my own hopeless impatience, lack of respect for others, meanness etc. But it would be wrong for this embarrassment to stop these things being said. For they matter. And there is anyway a less moralizing empirical dimension to all this. It is observable, verifiable and common experience that these good qualities enhance most people's sense of well-being.

References

Absalom, Elkanah *et al.* (1995), 'Participatory Methods and Approaches: sharing our concerns and looking to the future', *PLA Notes* 22: 5–10.

ActionAid (1994), *The Reality of Aid 94: an Independent Review of International Aid*, ed. Judith Randel and Tony German, ActionAid, London.

ActionAid (1995), *The Reality of Aid 95: an Independent Review of International Aid*, ed. Judith Randel and Tony German, ActionAid, London.

ActionAid-Nepal (1992), *Participatory Rural Appraisal Utilization Survey Report Part 1, Rural Development Area Sindhupalchowk*, Monitoring and Evaluation Unit, ActionAid-Nepal, PO Box 3198, Kathmandu, July.

Adiseshiah, Malcolm (1983), 'Education, Doing or Not Doing the Job? The Answer is No, it is Not, but Yes, it Could!', *Yojana* (Special Issue on Scientific Temper or Bondage of Traditions), 27: 60–63, 15 August.

Adriance, David (1995), 'PRA in a Health Education, Water and Sanitation Project in Kenya', *PLA Notes* 22: 41–4.

Ahluwalia, Montek S. (1986), 'Rural Poverty, Agricultural Production, and Prices: a re-examination', in John W. Mellor and Gunvant M. Desai (eds), *Agricultural Change and Rural Poverty: Variations on a Theme by Dharm Narain*, Oxford University Press, Dehli.

Amadi, Ruth Malleson (1993), 'Harmony and Conflict Between NTFP Use and Conservation in Korup National Park', *Rural Development Forestry Network Paper* 15c, ODI, London, Summer.

Ammer, Christine (1992), *The Methuen Dictionary of Clichés*, Methuen, London.

Ampt, P.R. and Ison, R.L. (1989), 'Rapid Rural Appraisal for the Identification of Grassland Research Problems', Proceedings of the XVI International Grassland Congress, Nice, France: 1291–2.

Andersen, Hans (1984), *Hans Andersen's Fairy Tales: a Selection*, translated from the Danish by L.W. Kingsland, World's Classics Paperback, Oxford University Press ('*The Emperor's New Clothes*' first published 1837).

Antholt, Charles H. (1993), *Getting Ready for the Twenty-First Century: Technical Change and Institutional Modernization in Agriculture*, World Bank Technical Paper Number 217, Asia Technical Department Series, World Bank, Washington.

Appleton, Judith (1992), Notes from a Food and Nutrition PRA in a Guinean Fishing Village, *RRA Notes* 16: 77–85, July.

Appleton, Judith (1995), 'PRA, Social Tremors and Rolling Heads: thoughts on PRA and empowerment', *PLA Notes* 24: 43–7.

Appleyard, B. (1992), *Understanding the Present: Science and the Soul of Modern Man* (London: Picador, published by Pan Books).

Archer, David (1995) 'Using PRA for a Radical New Approach to Adult Literacy', *PLA Notes* 23: 51–5, June.

Archer, David and Sara Cottingham (1996a), *Action Research Report on REFLECT: the Experiences of Three REFLECT Pilot Projects in Uganda, Bangladesh, El Salvador*, ODA Education Papers No. 17, ODA, London, March.

Archer, David and Sara Cottingham (1996b), *The REFLECT Mother Manual: Regenerated Freirean Literacy Through Empowering Community Techniques*, ActionAid, London, March.

Argyris, Chris, Robert Putnam and Diana McLain Smith (1985), *Action Science: Concepts, Methods and Skills for Research and Intervention*, Jossey-Bass Publishers, San Francisco and London.

ASEAN (1985), *Food Handling Newsletter*, 18 October.

Ashby, J.A. (1990), *Evaluating Technology with Farmers: a Handbook*, IPRA Projects, Centro Internacional de Agricultura Tropical (CIAT), AA 6713, Cali, Colombia, December.

Ashby, Jacqueline A, Carlos A. Quiros and Yolanda M. Rivers (1989), 'Experience with Group Techniques in Colombia', in Chambers, Pacey and Thrupp (eds) *Farmer First*: 127–132.

Assefa, Taye and Alemayehu Konde (eds) (1996), *Proceedings of the National Conference on PRA, 12–15 February 1996, Addis Ababa*, Farm-Africa, PO Box 5746, Addis Ababa, April.

Attwood, Heidi (1996), *South African Participatory Poverty Assessment Process: Were the Voices of the Poor Heard?* Paper for the PRA and Policy Workshop, IDS, Sussex, 13–14 May.

Aziz, Tariz (1993), 'Nepal Rhinos Walk Over South', *The Independent (Calcutta)*, 7 July.

Backhaus, Christoph and Rukman Wagachchi (1995), 'Only Playing with Beans? Participatory Approaches in Large-scale Government Programmes', *PLA Notes* 24: 62–5.

Bagadion, Benjamin U. and Frances F. Korten (1991), 'Developing Irrigators' Organizations: a learning process approach', in Cernea, *Putting People First* 2nd ed. (1991): 73–112.

Baker, Rachel (1996), 'PRA with Street Children in Nepal', *PLA Notes* 25: 56–60.

Bakirya, Judith (1994), 'Language, Literacy and Change', *Education Action*, No. 2, July, ActionAid, London.

Baldwin, K.D.S. (1957), *The Niger Agricultural Project: an Experiment in African Development*, Harvard University Press, Cambridge, Mass.

Bandyopadhyay, J., N.D. Jayal, U. Schoettli and Chhatrapati Singh (eds) (1985), *India's Environment: Crises and Responses*, Natraj Publishers, Dehra Dun, India.

Bardhan, Pranab (ed.) (1989), *Conversations between Economists and Anthropologists: Methodological Issues in Measuring Economic Change in Rural India*, Oxford University Press, Delhi, Oxford, New York.

Baumol, William J. (1991), 'Toward a Newer Economics: the future lies ahead!', *Economic Journal*, 101: 1–8, January.

Bayer, W. (1987), 'Browse Quality and Availability in a Farming Area and a Grazing Reserve in the Nigerian Subhumid Zone', Report to the ILCA Subhumid Zone Programme, Kaduna, Nigeria, Gottingen, May.

Bayer, W. (1988), 'Ranking of Browse Species by Cattlekeepers in Nigeria', *RRA Notes* 3: 4–10, December.

Beaton, G.H., R. Martorell, K.A. L'Abbe, B. Edmonston, G. McCabe, A.C. Ross and B. Harvey (1993), *Effectiveness of Vitamin A Supplementation in the Control of Young Child Morbidity and Mortality in Developing Countries, Summary Report*, International Nutrition Program, University of Toronto.

Beck, Tony (1994), *The Experience of Poverty: Fighting for Respect and Resources in Village India*, Intermediate Technology Publications, London.

Beebe, J. (1987), 'Rapid Appraisal: the evolution of the concept and the definition of issues', in KKU (1987): 47–68.

Beeching, Henry Charles (late 1870s), *The Masque of Balliol*, composed and current among members of Balliol College, Oxford, in the late 1870s.

Behnke, Roy H. Jr, Ian Scoones and Carol Kerven (eds) (1995), *Range Ecology at Disequilibrium: New Models of Natural Variability and Pastoral Adaptation in African Savannas*, ODI, IIED and the Commonwealth Secretariat, London.

Belshaw, D. (1981), 'A Theoretical Framework for Data-enconomizing Appraisal Procedures with Applications for Rural Development Planning', in Longhurst (ed.) *IDS Bulletin*: 12–22.

Benor, Daniel and James Q. Harrison (1977), *Agricultural Extension: the Training and Visit System*, World Bank, Washington, May.

Bentley, Margaret E., Gretel H. Pelto, Walter L. Straus, Debra A. Schumann, Catherine Adegbola, Emanuela de la Pena, Gbolahan A. Oni, Kenneth H. Brown and Sandra L. Huffman (1988), 'Rapid Ethnographic Assessment: applications in a diarrhea management program', *Social Science in Medicine*, Vol. 27, No. 1: 107–16.

Bernadas, C.N. Jr (1991), 'Lessons in Upland Farmer Participation: the case of enriched fallow technology in Jaro, Leyte, Philippines', *Forests, Trees and People Newsletter*, No. 14 (October): 10–13.

Bernstein, Henry, Ben Crow and Hazel Johnson (eds) (1992), *Rural Livelihoods: Crises and Responses*, Oxford University Press in association with the Open University.

Biggs, S.D. (1980), 'Informal R and D', *Ceres*, Vol. 13, No. 4: 23–6.

Binns, Tony (ed.) (1995), *People and Environment in Africa*, Wiley, Chichester, UK.

Binswanger, H.P., R.D. Ghodake and G.E. Thierstein (1979), 'Observations on the Economics of Tractors, Bullocks, and Wheeled Tool-carriers in the Semi-arid Tropics of India', in Ryan (ed.) (1979): 199–212.

Bishop, Josh and Ian Scoones (1994), *Beer and Baskets: the Economics of Women's Livelihoods in Ngamiland, Botswana*, Hidden Harvest Project Research Series Vol. 3, No. 1, IIED and Biodiversity Unit, WWF, Gland, Switzerland.

Bleek, W. (1987), 'Lying Informants: a fieldwork experience from Ghana', *Population Development Review*, 13(2): 314–22.

Booth, David (1995), 'Bridging the Macro–Micro Divide in Policy-oriented Research: two African experiences', *Development in Practice*, Vol. 5, No. 4.

Booth, David, John Milimo, Ginny Bond, Silverio Chimuka, Mulako Nabanda, Kwibisa Liywalii, Monde Mwalusi, Mulako Mwanamwalye, Edward Mwanza, Lizzie Peme and Agatha Zulu (1995), *Coping with Cost Recovery: A Study of the Social Impact of and Responses to Cost Recovery in Poor Communities in Zambia*, Report to SIDA, commissioned through the Development Studies Unit, Department of Social Anthropology, Stockholm University.

Borlaug, Norman E. (1992), 'Small-scale Agriculture in Africa', *Feeding the Future* (Newsletter of the Sasakawa Africa Association): 4(2).

Borlaug, Norman E. (1994), Testimony before the United States House of Representatives Committee on Agriculture, Subcommittee on Foreign Agriculture and Hunger, 1 March.

Borlaug, Norman E. and Christopher R. Dowswell (1995), 'Mobilising Science and Technology to Get Agriculture Moving in Africa', *Development Policy Review*, Vol. 13, No. 2: 115–29, June.

Bourne, Malcolm C. (1977), *Post-harvest Food Losses – The Neglected Dimensions in Increasing the World Food Supply*, Department of Food Science and Technology, Cornell University, Ithaca, New York.

BRAC (1979), *Peasant Perceptions: Famine*, Bangladesh Rural Advancement Committee, Dhaka.

BRAC (1983), *The Net: Power Structure in Ten Villages*, Bangladesh Rural Advancement Committee, Dhaka.

Bradley, P.N. (1991), *Woodfuel, Women and Woodlots, Volume 1: The Foundations of a Woodfuel Development Strategy for East Africa*, Macmillan Education, London and Basingstoke.

257

Bradley, P.N., N. Chavangi and A. van Gelder (1985) 'Development Research and Energy Planning in Kenya', *Ambio*, Vol. 14, nos 4–5: 228–36.

Bradley, Sarah Murray (1995), *How People Use Pictures: an Annotated Bibliography and Review for Development Workers*, IIED Participatory Methodology Series, IIED, London.

Breman, Jan (1985), *Of Peasants, Migrants and Paupers: Rural Labour Circulation and Capitalist Production in West India*, Oxford University Press, Delhi.

Brokensha, D., D. Warren and O. Werner (eds) (1980), *Indigenous Knowledge Systems and Development*, University Press of America, Lanham, Maryland.

Brown, Lester (1970), *Seeds of Change*, Pall Mall, London.

BSCRM and WWF-International (1995), *Planning for Conservation: Participatory Rural Appraisal for Community Based Initiatives*, Report on the Participatory Rural Appraisal (PRA) training workshop held in Ostritza, Bulgaria 14–22 June 1993, Bulgarian Society for the Conservation of the Rhodopi Mountains, 2 Gagarin Street, 1113 Sofia, Bulgaria and The World Wide Fund for Nature, Avenue du Mont-Blanc, CH-1196, Gland, Switzerland.

Buchanan-Smith, M. *et al.* (1993), 'Finding Out How People Prioritise Their Food Security Problems in Chad: the challenges of RRA at national level', *RRA Notes* 18: 33–43.

Bunch, R. (1985), *Two Ears of Corn: a Guide to People-centered Agricultural Improvement*, World Neighbors, 5116 North Portland, Oklahoma City, Oklahoma 73112.

Burkey, Stan (1993), *People First: A Guide to Self-reliant Participatory Rural Development*, Zed Books, London and New Jersey.

Campbell, J. Gabriel, Ramesh Shrestha and Linda Stone (1979), *The Use and Misuse of Social Science Research in Nepal*, Research Centre for Nepal and Asian Studies, Tribhuvan University, Kirtipur, Kathmandu.

Camus, Albert (1956), *The Fall* (cited in the International Thesaurus of Quotations under 'power').

Carey, John (ed.) (1995), *The Faber Book of Science*, Faber and Faber, London.

Carlin, John (1996), 'Downsizing: the backlash begins', *Independent on Sunday* (London), 19 May.

Carruthers, Ian and Robert Chambers (1981), 'Rapid Appraisal for Rural Development', *Agricultural Administration* 8(6): 407–22.

Carruthers, Ian and Eric Clayton (1977), 'Ex-post Evaluation of Agricultural Projects – its implication for planning', *Journal of Agricultural Economics*, Vol. 28, No. 3.

Carson, B. (1992), *The Land, the Farmer and the Future: A Soil Fertility Management Strategy for Nepal*, International Centre for Integrated Mountain Development (ICIMOD), Occasional Paper 21, Kathmandu.

Carter, A.S., and D.A. Gilmour (1989), 'Increase in Tree Cover on Private Farm Land in Central Nepal', *Mountain Research and Development*, Vol. 9, No. 4: 381–91.

Carter, Simon E. and Herbert K. Murwira (1995), 'Spatial Variability in Soil Fertility Management and Crop Response in Mutoko Communal Area, Zimbabwe', *Ambio*, Vol. 24, No. 2: 77–84, March.

Case, D'Arcy Davis (1990), *The Community's Toolbox: The Idea, Methods and Tools for Participatory Assessment, Monitoring and Evaluation in Community Forestry*, Community Forestry Field Manual 2, FAO: Rome.

Cassen, Robert and Associates (1986), *Does Aid Work?*, Clarendon Press, Oxford.

Cernea, Michael M., John K. Coulter and John F.A. Russell (eds) (1984), *Agricultural Extension by Training and Visit: The Asian Experience*, World Bank, Washington DC.

Cernea, Michael (ed.) (1985), *Putting People First: Sociological Variables in Development Projects*, Johns Hopkins Press, Baltimore.

258

CESEN (1986), *The Rural/Urban Household Energy Survey*, Technical Report No. 7, CESEN (for the Ministry of Mines and Energy, Ethiopia, May), Genoa, Italy.

CGIAR (1993), The Ecoregional Approach to Research in the CGIAR, TAC Secretariat, FAO, Rome, March.

Chadha, O.P. (1981), 'Irrigation System Management and Research Priorities', in Tamil Nadu Agricultural University, *Field Research Methodologies for Improved Irrigation System Management*, 65–75.

Chambers, Robert (1973), 'The Perkerra Irrigation Scheme: a contrasting case', in Chambers and Moris (eds) (1973): 344–64.

Chambers, Robert (1974), *Managing Rural Development: Ideas and Experience from East Africa*, Scandinavian Institute of African Studies, Uppsala.

Chambers, Robert (1977), 'Creating and Expanding Organisations for Rural Development', in L. Cliffe, J.S. Coleman and M.R. Doornbos (eds) *Government and Rural Development in East Africa: Essays on Political Penetration*, Martinus Nijhoff, The Hague, 119–38.

Chambers, Robert (1981), 'Rapid Rural Appraisal: rationale and repertoire', *Public Administration and Development*, Vol. 2, No. 2: 95–106.

Chambers, Robert (1983), *Rural Development: Putting the Last First*, Longman, Harlow.

Chambers, Robert (1986), 'Normal Professionalism, New Paradigms and Development', *IDS Discussion Paper* 227, IDS, University of Sussex, December.

Chambers, Robert (1988a), 'Sustainable Livelihoods, Environment and Development: putting poor people first', *IDS Discussion Paper* 240, IDS, University of Sussex, January.

Chambers, Robert (1988b), *Managing Canal Irrigation: Practical Analysis from South Asia*, Oxford and IBH, New Delhi, and Cambridge University Press, Cambridge, UK.

Chambers, Robert (1992), 'The Self-deceiving State', in Robin Murray (ed.), *New Forms of Public Administration, IDS Bulletin* 23(4): 31–42.

Chambers, Robert (1993a), *Challenging the Professions: Frontiers for Rural Development*, Intermediate Technology Publications, London.

Chambers, Robert (1993b), 'Methods for Analysis by Farmers: the professional challenge', *Journal for Farming Systems Research-Extension*, Vol. 4, No. 1: 87–101.

Chambers, Robert (1994a), 'The Origins and Practice of Participatory Rural Appraisal', *World Development*, Vol. 22, No. 7: 953–69, July.

Chambers, Robert (1994b), 'Participatory Rural Appraisal (PRA): analysis of experience', *World Development*, Vol. 22, No. 9: 1253–68, September.

Chambers, Robert (1994c), 'Participatory Rural Appraisal (PRA): challenges, potentials and paradigm', *World Development*, Vol. 22, No. 10: 1437–54, October.

Chambers, Robert (1995), 'Poverty and Livelihoods: Whose Reality Counts? *IDS Discussion Paper* 347, IDS, University of Sussex, January.

Chambers, Robert and Jon Moris (eds) (1973), *Mwea: An Irrigated Rice Settlement in Kenya*, Afrika-Studien Nr. 83, Weltforum Verlag, Munchen.

Chambers, Robert and John Harriss (1977), 'Comparing Twelve South Indian Villages', in Farmer (ed.), 301–22.

Chambers, Robert and B.W.E. Wickremanayake (1977), 'Agricultural Extension: myth, reality and challenge', in Farmer (ed.): 155–67.

Chambers, Robert, Arnold Pacey and Richard Longhurst (eds) (1981), *Seasonal Dimensions to Rural Poverty*, Frances Pinter, London.

Chambers, Robert and B.P. Ghildyal (1985), 'Agricultural Research for Resource-poor Farmers: the farmer-first-and-last model', *Agricultural Administration and Extension*, 20: 1–30.

Chambers, Robert and Janice Jiggins (1986), 'Agricultural Research for Resource-poor Farmers: a parsimonious paradigm', *Discussion Paper* 228, IDS, University of Sussex.

Chambers, Robert, Arnold Pacey and Lori Ann Thrupp (eds) (1989), *Farmer First: Farmer Innovation and Agricultural Research*, Intermediate Technology Publications, London.

Chambers, Robert, Tushaar Shah and N.C. Saxena (1989), *To the Hands of the Poor: Water and Trees*, Oxford and IBH, New Delhi, and Intermediate Technology Publications, London.

Chambers, Robert and Melissa Leach (1989), 'Trees as Savings and Security for the Rural Poor', *World Development*, Vol. 17, No. 3: 329–42 (short updated version, Chambers, Leach and Czech Conroy, *Gatekeeper Series*, No. 3, IIED, 1993).

Chambers, Robert, and Gordon Conway (1992), 'Sustainable Rural Livelihoods: practical concepts for the 21st century', *Discussion Paper* 296, IDS, University of Sussex.

Chambers, Robert and Irene Guijt (1995), 'PRA – Five Years Later. Where are we Now?' *Forests, Trees and People Newsletter* 26/27: 4–14.

Chandramouli, K. (1991), 'Pass on the Pen' Approach: Identifying the Poorest of the Poor Families', *RRA Notes* 14: 29–32, December.

Checkland, Peter (1981), *Systems Thinking, Systems Practice*, Chichester: John Wiley.

Checkland, Peter B. (1989), 'Soft Systems Methodology', *Human Systems Management* 8: 273–89.

Chidhari, Gift *et al.* and Louise Fortmann (1992), 'The use of Indigenous Trees in Mhondoro District', Centre for Applied Social Sciences, Harare.

Cliff, Peter (1991), *Mountain Navigation*, Bookmag, Henderson Road, Inverness, UK.

Cline, William R. (1992), *The Economics of Global Warming*, Institute for International Economics, Washington DC.

Cocks, Joan (1989), *The Oppositional Imagination: Feminism, Critique and Political Theory*, Routledge, London.

Colaco, P. and Bostock, T. (1993), 'Post-Harvest Goes Participatory: Participating and Learning in a Fishing Village', *Bay of Bengal News*: 6–11, September.

Colaco, P. and P. Gururaja (1993), The Second South–South Exchange, Part 2: South India, OUTREACH, Bangalore, 12–22 September.

Colletta, Nat J. and Gillian Perkins (1995), *Participation in Education*, Environment Department Papers, Participation Series No 001, World Bank.

Collinson, Michael (1981), 'A Low-cost Approach to Understanding Small Farmers', *Agricultural Administration* 8(6): 433–50.

Conroy, Czech and Miles Litvinoff (eds) (1988), *The Greening of Aid: Sustainable Livelihoods in Practice*, Earthscan in association with IIED, London.

Convergence (1975), Vol. 7, No. 2; (1981), Vol. 14, no. 2; and (1988), Vol. 21, nos 2 and 3, special issues on participatory research.

Conway, G. (1985), 'Agroecosystem Analysis, *Agricultural Administration* 20: 31–55.

Conway, G. (1986), *Agroecosystem Analysis for Research and Development*, Winrock International Institute for Agricultural Development, PO Box 1172, Nana Post Office, Bangkok 10112.

Conway, G. (1987), 'Rapid Rural Appraisal and Agroecosystem Analysis: a case study from Northern Pakistan', in KKU *Proceedings*: 228–54.

Conway, G. (1988), 'Rainbow over Wollo', *New Scientist*, 5 May.

Conway, G. (1989), 'Diagrams for Farmers', in Chambers, Pacey and Thrupp (eds.) *Farmer First:* 77-86.

Conway, G., P. Sajise and W. Knowland (1989), 'Lake Buhi: resolving conflicts in a Philippines development project', *Ambio*, Vol. 18, No. 2: 128–35.

Corbett, Jane (1988), 'Famine and Household Coping Strategies', *World Development*, Vol. 16, No. 9: 1099–112.

Cornwall, Andrea (1991), 'Modelling Different Concerns', *ILEIA Newsletter* 23: 23.

Cornwall, A. (1992), 'Body Mapping in Health RRA/PRA', *RRA Notes* 16: 69–76, July.

Cornwall, Andrea and Sue Fleming (1995), 'Context and Complexity: anthropological reflections on PRA', *PLA Notes* 24: 8–12.

Cornwall, Andrea and Rachel Jewkes (1995), 'Participatory Research', *Social Science and Medicine*, Vol. 41, No. 12: 1667–76.

Cornwall, Andrea, Irene Guijt and Alice Welbourn (1994), 'Acknowledging process: challenges for agricultural research and extension methodology', in Scoones and Thompson (eds) (1994): 98–117.

Coveney, Peter and Roger Highfield (1995), *Frontiers of Complexity: The Search for Order in a Chaotic World*, Faber and Faber, London.

Daane, J.R.V. (1987), 'Quelle Méthode pour l'Analyse de Systèmes de Production en Zone Rurale Tropicale? Le dilemme entre démarche quantitative peu fiable et démarche qualitative peu généralisable', Contribution au 8ème Seminaire d'Economie Rurale, 14–18 Septembre, CIRAD, Montpellier.

Daniels, P.W., S. Holden, E. Lewin, and Sri Dadi (eds) (1993), *Livestock Services for Smallholders: a Critical Evaluation*, Proceedings of a Seminar held in Jogjakarta, Indonesia, November 1992.

Darling, P.J. (1993), 'Updating Some African Population Myths', Paper for the First World Optimum Population Congress, 8–11 August 1993 (Natural Resources Institute, Chatham, UK).

Dasgupta, Biplab (1975), 'A Typology of Village Socio-economic Systems from Indian Village Studies', *Economic and Political Weekly*, Vol. 10, nos 33–5: 1394–414, August.

Davies, Susanna (1996), *Adaptable Livelihoods: Coping with Food Insecurity in the Malian Sahel*, Macmillan, Basingstoke and London.

de Koning, Korrie and Marion Martin (eds) (1996), *Participatory Research in Health*, ZED Books, London and New Jersey.

de Padua (1976), Rice Post-production Handling and Processing: its significance to agricultural development', Paper presented at the International Workshop on Accelerating Agricultural Development, SEARCA, Laguna, Philippines, April (cited in Greeley 1986, 1987).

de Toma, Costanza (1996), 'Sharing Experiences of Participation in Latin America: a workshop report', *PLA Notes* 25: 4–5.

de Waal, Alexander (1989), *Famine That Kills: Darfur, Sudan, 1984–1985*, Clarendon Press, Oxford.

de Waal, Alexander (1991), 'Emergency Food Security in Western Sudan: What Is It For?', in Maxwell (ed.) (1991).

Denniston, David, with Andrew Leake (1995), 'Defending the Land with Maps', *PLA Notes* 22: 36–40.

Dent, Judith (1996), 'Stumbling Towards Gender-aware Training in Indonesia', *PLA Notes* 25: 19–22.

Devavaram, John, Nalini J. Vimalnathan, Abdul Sarkar, Krishnan, A.P. Mayandi and Karunanidhi (1991), 'PRA for Rural Resource Management', *RRA Notes* 13: 102–11.

Dewees, Peter (1989a), 'Aerial Photography and Household Studies in Kenya', *RRA Notes* 7: 9–12.

Dewees, Peter (1989b), 'The Woodfuel Crisis Reconsidered: observations on the dynamics of abundance and scarcity', *World Development*, Vol. 17, No. 9: 1159–72.

Dickens, Charles (1854), *Hard Times* (Rupa and Co, Calcutta, 1981).

Dogbe, Tony (1996), 'The One Who Rides the Donkey Does Not Know the Ground is Hot', Paper for the PRA and Policy Workshop, IDS, Sussex, 13–14 May 1996.

Dove, M.R. (1992), 'Foresters' Beliefs about Farmers: a priority for social science research in social forestry', *Agroforestry Systems* 17: 13–41.

Dreze, Jean (1990), 'Poverty in India and the IRDP Delusion', *Economic and Political Weekly* 29 September, A95–A104.

Dreze, Jean and Amartya Sen (1989), *Hunger and Public Action*, Clarendon Press, Oxford.

Drinkwater, Michael (1993), 'Sorting Fact from Opinion: the use of a direct matrix to evaluate finger millet varieties', *RRA Notes* 17: 24–8, March.

Drinkwater, Michael (1994), 'Participatory Needs Assessment in the Peri-urban Areas of Lusaka, Zambia, *RRA Notes* 21: 33–6.

Duangsa, Dusit (1995), 'A Participatory Approach to Promoting AIDS Awareness in Thailand', *PLA Notes* 23: 66–8.

Dunn, Tony and Allan McMillan (1991), 'Action Research: the application of rapid rural appraisal to learn about issues of concern in landcare areas near Wagga Wagga, NSW'. Paper presented to a conference on Agriculture, Education and Information Transfer, Murrumbigee College of Agriculture, NSW, 30 September–2 October, 1991.

Durning, Alan Thein (1992), *How Much is Enough? The Consumer Society and the Future of the Earth*, W.W. Norton and Company, New York and London.

Dyson, Tim (1987), 'Excess Female Mortality in India: uncertain evidence of a narrowing differential', in Srinivasan and Mukerji (eds) (1987): 351–81.

Dyson, Tim (1994) 'On the Demography of the 1991 Census', *Economic and Political Weekly*, Vol. 29, Nos 51 and 52: 3235–9, December 17–24.

EA (1994–), *Education Action/Acción Educativa*, nos 1–5 (continuing), ActionAid, London.

Ekins, Paul and Manfred Max-Neef (eds) (1992), *Real Life Economics: Understanding Wealth Creation*, Routledge, London and New York.

ERCS (1988), *Rapid Rural Appraisal: A Closer Look at Rural Life in Wollo*, Ethiopian Red Cross Society, Addis Ababa and IIED, London.

Erlandson, David A., Edward L. Harris, Barbara L. Skipper and Steve D. Allen (1993), *Doing Naturalistic Inquiry: A Guide to Methods*, Sage, London and New Delhi.

Euler, Claus (1995), 'Women Prefer Lunchtime', *PLA Notes* 22:28.

Fairhead, James and Melissa Leach, with Dominique Millimouno and Marie Kamano (1992a), 'Forests of the Past? Archival, Oral and Demographic Evidence in Kissidougou Prefecture's Vegetation History', COLA Working Paper 1, Connaissance et Organisation Locales Agro-ecologiques, BP 4100 Conakry, Guinea, October.

Fairhead, James and Melissa Leach with Dominique Millimouno and Marie Kamano (1992b), 'Managed Productivity: technical knowledge used in local natural resources management in Kissidougou Prefecture', COLA Working Paper 2, Connaissance et Organisation Locales Agro-ecologiques, BP 4100 Conakry, Guinea, December.

Fairhead, James and Melissa Leach (1994), 'Contested Forests: modern conservation and historical land use in Guinea's Ziama Reserve', *African Affairs* 93: 481–512.

Fairhead, James and Melissa Leach (1995), 'Reading Forest History Backwards: the interaction of policy and local land use in Guinea's forest-savanna mosaic, 1893–1993', *Environment and History*, Vol. 1: 55–91.

Fairhead, James and Melissa Leach (forthcoming), 'Reframing Forest History: a radical reappraisal of the roles of people and climate in West African vegetation change', in G. Chapman and D. Driver (eds), *Timescales of Environmental Changes*, Routledge, London.

Fals-Borda, Orlando and Mohammad Anisur Rahman (eds) (1991), *Action and Knowledge: Breaking the Monopoly with Participatory Action-Research*, Intermediate Technology Publications, London.

262

Farmer, B.H. (ed.) (1977), *Green Revolution?: Technology and Change in Rice-growing Areas of Tamil Nadu and Sri Lanka*, Macmillan, London and Basingstoke.

Farrington, John (ed.) (1988), *Experimental Agriculture*, Vol. 24, Part 3.

Farrington, John and Adrienne Martin (1988), 'Farmer Participation in Agricultural Research: a review of concepts and practices', *Agricultural Administration Occasional Paper*, No. 9, ODI, London.

FCO (1993), *Foreign and Commonwealth Office including Overseas Development Administration Department Report 1993, The Government's Expenditure Plans 1993–94 to 1995–96*, Cm. 2202, Her Majesty's Stationery Office, London.

Flint, Michael (1991), 'Contribution to Question Time Debate', in Johnson (ed.) (1991): 46.

Forsyth, Richard S. (1991), 'Towards a Grounded Morality', *Changes*, Vol. 9, No. 4: 264–78, December.

Fox, Jefferson (1993), 'Forest Resources in a Nepali Village in 1980 and 1990: the positive influence of population growth', *Mountain Research and Development* 13: 1: 89–98.

Francis, S., J. Devavaram and A. Erskin (1992), 'Training Workshop on Participatory Rural Appraisal for Planning Health Projects', *RRA Notes* 16: 37–47, July.

Frank, Robert, Thomas Gilovich and Dennis Regan (1993), 'Does Studying Economics Inhibit Co-operation?', *Journal of Economic Perspectives*, Spring (as reviewed in *The Economist* 29 May 1993: 71).

Franklin, Barbara (1993), *The Risk of AIDS in Vietnam*, an audience analysis of risk factors for HIV/AIDS amongst men and commercial sex workers in Hanoi and Ho Chi Minh City, Monograph Series No 1, CARE International in Vietnam, 130A Thuy Khue, Hanoi, June.

Freire, Paulo (1970), *Pedagogy of the Oppressed*, The Seabury Press, New York.

Freire, Paulo (1974), *Education for Critical Consciousness*, Sheed and Ward, London (original edition Editora Paz e Terra, Rio de Janeiro, 1967).

Freud, Sigmund (1901), *The Psychopathology of Everyday Life*, Hogarth Press and the Institute of Psycho-Analysis, London.

Freudenberger, Karen Schoonmaker (1994), *Tree and Land Tenure: Rapid Appraisal Tools*, Community Forest Field Manual 4, FAO, Rome.

Freudenberger, Karen Schoonmaker (1995), 'The Historical Matrix – Breaking Away from Static Analysis', *Forests, Trees and People Newsletter* 26/27: 78–9, April.

Freudenberger, Karen Schoonmaker (1996), 'The Use of RRA to Inform Policy: some personal observations', Paper for the PRA and Policy Workshop, IDS Sussex, 13–14 May, 1996.

Freudenberger, Karen Schoonmaker and Mark Schoonmaker Freudenberger (1994), 'Livelihoods, Livestock and Change: the versatility and richness of historical matrices', *RRA Notes* 20: 144–8.

Freudenthal, K. and Narrowe (1991), *Focus on People and Trees: A Guide to Designing and Conducting Community Baseline Studies for Community Forestry*, Report No. 20, Development Studies Unit, Department of Social Anthropology, Stockholm University, Stockholm.

Frey, Bruno S., Werner W. Pommerehne, Friedrich Schneider and Guy Gilbert (1984), 'Consensus and Dissension Among Economists: an empirical enquiry', *American Economic Review*, Vol. 74, No. 5: 986–94, December.

FSRU (1991), *Structural Adjustment and Communal Area Agriculture in Zimbabwe: Case Studies from Mangwende and Chivi Communal Areas: A Report of a Rapid Rural Appraisal Exercise*, Farming Systems Research Unit, Department of Research and Specialist Services, Ministry of Lands, Agriculture and Rural Settlement, Ministry of Lands, Harare, Zimbabwe: November.

FSSP (1987), *Diagnosis, Design and Analysis in Farming Systems Research and Extension*, volumes I, II and III, and *Trainer's Manual*, Farming Systems Support Project, Institute of Food and Agricultural Sciences, University of Florida, Gainesville, Florida 32611, December.

Funtowicz, S.O. and J.R. Ravetz (1990), *Global Environmental Issues and the Emergence of Second Order Science*, Commission of the European Communities, Luxembourg.

Galbraith, John Kenneth (1992), *The Culture of Contentment*, Penguin Books, London.

Gaventa, John (1980), *Power and Powerlessness: Rebellion and Quiescence in an Appalachian Valley*, University of Illinois Press, Chicago.

Gaventa, John and Helen Lewis (1991), *Participatory Education and Grassroots Development: The Case of Rural Appalachia*, Gatekeeper Series No. 25, IIED.

Gibbs, Christopher (1987), 'Rapid Rural Appraisal: an overview of concepts and applications', in KKU (1987): 193–206.

Gibson, Tony (1992), 'Changing Neighbourhoods', in Ekins and Max-Neef (eds) (1992): 388–92.

Gibson, Tony (1995), 'Showing What You Mean (Not Just Talking About It)', *RRA Notes* 21: 41–7.

Gichuki, F.N. (1991), *Environmental Change and Dryland Management in Machakos District, Kenya, 1930–90: Conservation Profile*, ODI Working Paper No. 56, ODI, London.

Giddens, Anthony (1990), *The Consequences of Modernity*, Polity Press, Cambridge, UK.

Gilbert, E.H., D.W. Norman, and F.E. Winch (1980), *Farming Systems Research: A Critical Appraisal*, MSU Rural Development Paper No. 6, Department of Agricultural Economics, Michigan State University, East Lansing, Michigan 48824.

Gill, G.J. (1991a), *Seasonality and Agriculture in the Developing World: A Problem of the Poor and Powerlessness*, Cambridge University Press.

Gill, Gerard J. (1991b), 'But How Does It Compare with the REAL Data?' *RRA Notes* 14: 5–13.

Gill, Gerard, J. (1992), *Policy Analysis for Agricultural Resource Management in Nepal: A Comparison of Conventional and Participatory Approaches*, Research Support Series No. 9, HMG Ministry of Agriculture/Winrock International, Kathmandu, July.

Gill, Gerard J. (1993a), *OK, The Data's Lousy, But It's All We've Got (Being a Critique of Conventional Methods)*, Gatekeeper Series 38, IIED, London.

Gill, Gerard J. (1993b), 'Are Some "Participatory" Techniques Culturally Biased? (Or: Are We Hooked on Mom's Apple Pie?)' *RRA Notes* 18: 12–14.

Gill, Gerard J. (1995), *Major Natural Resource Management Concerns in South Asia*, Agriculture and Environmental Discussion Paper 8, IFPRI, Washington DC, November.

Gill, Gerard J. (1996a), *Using PRA for Agricultural Policy Analysis in Nepal*, Paper for the PRA and Policy Workshop, IDS Sussex, 13–14 May 1996.

Gill, Gerard J. (1996b), *Maintaining the Granary: Foodgrain Production and Productivity in the Nepal Tarai*, Winrock International, Kathmandu.

Gilmour, D.A. (1988), 'Not Seeing the Trees for the Forest: a re-appraisal of the deforestation crisis in two hill districts of Nepal', *Mountain Research and Development*, Vol. 8 No. 4: 343–50.

Gilmour, D.A. (1989), *Forest Resources and Indigenous Management in Nepal*, Working Paper No. 17, Environment and Policy Institute, East-West Center, Honolulu, Hawaii 96848.

Gittinger, J. Price (1982), *The Economic Analysis of Agricultural Projects* (2nd ed.), Economic Development Institute, World Bank, Washington DC.

Gleick, James (1988), *Chaos: Making a New Science*, Sphere Books, Penguin Group, London.

GOI (1985), *Seventh Five-Year Plan 1985–90*, Vol. 2, Planning Commission, Government of India.

GOI (1994) *Guidelines for Watershed Development*, Ministry of Rural Development, Government of India Press, New Delhi.

Good, Mary-Jo DelVecchio and Byron J. Good (1989), 'Disabling Practitioners: hazards of learning to be a doctor in American medical education', *American Journal of Orthopsychiatry*, Vol. 59, No. 2: 303–9, April.

Gosselink, Paul and Pierre Strosser (1995), 'Participatory Rural Appraisal for Irrigation Management Research: lessons from IIMI's experience', Working Paper No. 38, IIMI, Colombo.

Gould, P., and R. White (1974), *Mental Maps*, Penguin Books, Harmondsworth, UK.

Grady, H., A. Daqqa, *et al.* (1991), 'Assessing Women's Needs in Gaza Using Participatory Rapid Appraisal Techniques', *RRA Notes* 10: 12–19, February.

Grandin, Barbara (1988), *Wealth Ranking in Smallholder Communities: A Field Manual*, Intermediate Technology Publications, London.

Grandstaff, Somluckrat W., Terry B. Grandstaff and George W. Lovelace (1987a), Summary Report in KKU, (1987): 3–30.

Grandstaff, Terry B. and Somluckrat W. Grandstaff (1987a), 'A Conceptual Basis for Methodological Development in Rapid Rural Appraisal', in KKU (1987): 69–88.

Grandstaff, Somluckrat W. and Terry B. Grandstaff (1987b), 'Semi-structured Interviewing by Multidisciplinary Teams in RRA', in KKU (1987): 129–143.

Greeley, Martin (1980), 'Farm-level Post-harvest Food Losses: the myth of the soft third option', Paper presented at the Post-production Workshop on Food Grains, 12–14 December, 1980, Dacca.

Greeley, Martin (ed.) (1982), 'Feeding the Hungry: a role for post-harvest technology?', *IDS Bulletin* 13(3), IDS, University of Sussex, June.

Greeley, Martin (1986), 'Food, Technology and Employment: the farm-level post-harvest system in developing countries', *Journal of Agricultural Economics* 37(3): 333–47, September.

Greeley, Martin (1987), *Post-harvest Losses, Technology and Employment*, Westview Press, Boulder CO and London.

Griffith, Geoff (1994), *Poverty Alleviation for Rural Women*, Avebury, Aldershot.

Groenfeldt, David (1989), *Guidelines for Rapid Assessment of Minor Irrigation Schemes in Sri Lanka*, IIMI, Colombo.

GTZ (1988), *ZOPP (an introduction to the method)*, Deutsche Gesellschaft für Technische Zusammenarbeit (GTZ) GmbH, Postfach 5180, D-6236 Eschborn 1 bei Frankfurt am Main, Germany.

Guba, Egon, G. and Yvonna, S. Lincoln (1989), *Fourth Generation Evaluation*, Sage Publications, London and New Delhi.

Gueye, Bara (1995), 'Development of PRA in Francophone Africa: lessons from the Sahel', *PLA Notes* 24: 70–73.

Gueye, Bara et Karen Schoonmaker Freudenberger (1990), *Introduction à la Méthode Accélérée de Recherche Participative (MARP)*, Centre de Recherches pour le Développement International, BP 2435, Dakar, Senegal, Octobre.

Gueye, Bara and Karen Schoonmaker Freudenberger (1991), *Méthode Accélérée de Recherche Participative*, IIED, London, August.

Guijt, Irene (1994), 'Making a Difference: integrating gender analysis into PRA training', *RRA Notes* 19: 49–55, February.

Guijt, Irene (1995), *Moving Slowly and Reaching Far: Institutionalizing Participating Planning for Child-centred Community Development*, IIED and Redd Barna–East Africa, Uganda, August.

265

Guijt, Irene, and Jules N. Pretty (eds) (1992), *Participatory Rural Appraisal for Farmer Participatory Research in Punjab, Pakistan*, IIED, London, September.

Guijt, Irene, Andreas Fuglesang and Tony Kisadha (1994), *It is the Young Trees that make a Thick Forest*, Report on Redd Barna Learning Experiences with Participatory Rural Appraisal, Kyakatebe, Masaka District, Uganda, 7–17 March 1994, Redd Barna, PO Box 12018, Kampala and IIED, London, September.

Guijt, Irene and Andrea Cornwall (1995), 'Editorial: critical reflections on the practice of PRA', *PLA Notes* 24: 2–7.

Guijt, Irene and Meera Kaul Shah (eds) (forthcoming), *The Myth of Community: Gender Issues in Participatory Development*.

Gujja, Biksham, Michel Pimbert and Meera Shah (1996), *Village Voices Challenging Wetland Management Policies: PRA Experiences from Pakistan and India*, Paper for the PRA and Policy Workshop, IDS Sussex, 13–14 May 1996.

Gulati, Leela (1981), *Profiles in Female Poverty: A Study of Five Poor Working Women in Kerala*, Hindustan Publishing Corporation (India), Delhi 110007.

Gypmantasiri *et al.* and Gordon Conway (1980), *An Interdisciplinary Perspective of Cropping Systems in the Chiang Mai Valley: Key Questions for Research*, Multiple Cropping Project, Faculty of Agriculture, University of Chiang Mai, Thailand, June.

Hahn, H. (1991), *Apprendre avec les yeux, s'exprimer avec les mains: des paysans se forment à la gestion du terroir*, AGRECOL, Oekozentrum, CH-4438 Langenbruck, Switzerland.

Hall, Andrew and Norman Clark (1995), 'Coping with Change, Complexity and Diversity in Agriculture – The Case of Rhizobium Inoculants in Thailand', *World Development*, Vol. 23, No. 9: 1601–14.

Handy, Charles (1989), *The Age of Unreason*, Business Books Limited (Arrow Books, London ed. 1990).

Hanger, Jane and Jon Moris (1973), 'Women and the Household Economy', in Chambers and Moris (eds) (1973): 209–44.

Harriss, John (1989), 'Knowing About Rural Economic Change: problems arising from a comparison of the results of "macro" and "micro" research in Tamil Nadu', in Bardhan (ed.) (1989): 137–73.

Hartmann, Betsy and James Boyce (1983), *Quiet Violence: View from a Bangladesh Village*, Zed Press, London.

Harvey, David (1990), *The Condition of Postmodernity: an Enquiry into the Origins of Cultural Change*, Blackwell, Cambridge MA and Oxford UK.

Harwood, R. (1979), *Small Farm Development: Understanding and Improving Farming Systems in the Humid Tropics*, Westview Press, Boulder, Colorado.

Havel, Vaclav (1992), Condensation of a speech to the Davos Development Conference, reported in *New York Times*, 1 March 1992.

HDR (1993), *Human Development Report 1993*, published for UNDP by Oxford University Press, New York and Oxford.

HDR (1994, 1995, 1996), as above.

Heyer, Judith (1989), 'Landless Agricultural Labourers' Asset Strategies', in *Vulnerability: How the Poor Cope, IDS Bulletin* 20(2): 33–40, April.

Hill, Polly (1972), *Rural Hausa: A Village and a Setting*, Cambridge University Press, Cambridge.

Hill, Polly (1986), *Development Economics on Trial: The Anthropological Case for a Prosecution*, Cambridge University Press, Cambridge.

Hinchcliffe, Fiona, compiler (1995), *The Hidden Harvest: Wild Resources and Agricultural Systems*, summary of a review and planning workshop, IIED, London.

Hinchcliffe, Fiona, Irene Guijt, Jules N. Pretty and Parmesh Shah (1995), *New Horizons: the Economic, Social and Environmental Impacts of Participatory Watershed Development*, Gatekeeper Series No. 50, IIED, London.

Hinton, Rachel (1995), 'Trades in Different Worlds: listening to refugee voices', *PLA Notes* 24: 21–6.

Hirschman, Albert O. (1967), *Development Projects Observed*, Brookings Institution, Washington DC.

Hirway, Indira, 1986, *Abolition of Poverty in India with Special Reference to Target Group Approach in Gujarat*, New Delhi: Publishing House.

Hobley, Mary and Edwin Shanks (1993), Editorial, *Rural Development Forestry Network Newsletter* 15, ODI, London, Summer, 1993.

Holmgren, Peter, Edward Juma Masakha and Hakan Sjoholm (1994), 'Not All African Land is Being Degraded: a recent survey of trees on farms in Kenya reveals rapidly increasing forest resources', *Ambio* 23(7): 390–95.

Hoogerbrugge, Inge D. and Louise O. Fresco (1993), 'Home Garden Systems: agricultural characteristics and challenges', *Gatekeeper Series*, No. 39, IIED, London.

Howell, John (1988), *Training and Visit Extension in Practice*, Agricultural Administration Unit, Occasional Paper 8, ODI, London.

Howes, Mick and Chris Roche (1995), 'A Participatory Organisational Appraisal of ACORD', *PLA Notes* 22: 69–73.

HSWG (1995), *Local-level Economic Evaluation of Savanna Woodland Resources: Village Cases from Zimbabwe*, Hot Springs Working Group (B. Campbell, J. Clarke, M. Luckert, F. Matose, C. Musvoto and I. Scoones), *Research Series*, Vol. 3, No. 2, Sustainable Agriculture Programme, IIED, London.

Hudson, Norman and Rodney J. Cheatle (eds) (1993), *Working with Farmers for Better Land Husbandry*, Intermediate Technology Publications, London.

Hudock, Ann (1996), 'Facilitating PRA Amidst War: experiences from Sierra Leone', *PLA Notes* 25: 27–9.

Hulme, David (1991), 'Agricultural Extension Services as Machines: the impact of the training and visit approach', in W.R. and Dan Gustafsen (eds), *Agricultural Extension: Worldwide Institutional Evolution and Forces for Change*, Elsevier, New York.

Humble, Morag E. (1994), 'Implementing Gender and Development Theory: assessing participatory rural appraisal as a GAD technique', MA thesis, Department of Political Science, Carleton University, Ottawa, Ontario, 21 December.

Huss-Ashmore, Rebecca, with John J. Curry and Robert J. Hitchcock (eds) (1988) *Coping with Seasonal Constraints*, MASCA Papers in Science and Archeology Vol. 5, 1988, University Museum, University of Pennsylvania, Philadelphia.

IDS (1979), 'Whose Knowledge Counts?', *IDS Bulletin*, Vol. 10, No. 2.

IDS Agriculture (1996), Agriculture Pack, PRA, IDS, Sussex.

IDS Behaviour and Attitudes (1996), Behaviour and Attitudes Pack, PRA, IDS, Sussex.

IDS Coastal and Fisheries (1996), Coastal and Fisheries Pack, PRA, IDS, Sussex.

IDS Emergencies (1996), Emergencies Pack, PRA, IDS, Sussex.

IDS Gender (1996) Gender Pack, PRA, IDS, Sussex.

IDS Health (1996), Health Pack, PRA, IDS, Sussex.

IDS People and Parks (1996), People and Parks Pack. PRA, IDS, Sussex.

IDS Sexual and Reproductive Health (1996), Sexual and Reproductive Health Pack, PRA, IDS, Sussex.

IIRR (1993), *Indigenous Knowledge and Sustainable Development*, 25 selected papers presented at the International Symposium at the International Institute of Rural Reconstruction, 20–26 September 1992, IIRR, Silang, Cavite, Philippines.

ILO (1976), *Employment, Growth and Basic Needs: A One-World Problem*, International Labour Office, Geneva.

ILO (1981), *First Things First: Meeting the Basic Needs of the People of Nigeria*, International Labour Office, Jobs and Skills Programme for Africa, Addis Ababa.

267

ILO (1982), *Basic Needs in Danger: A Basic Needs Oriented Development Strategy for Tanzania*, report to the Government of Tanzania by a JASPA Basic Needs Mission, International Labour Office, Jobs and Skills Programme for Africa, Addis Ababa.

Inglis, Andrew Stewart (1990), 'Harvesting Local Forestry Knowledge: a field test and evaluation of rapid rural appraisal techniques for social forestry project analysis', dissertation presented for the degree of Master of Science, University of Edinburgh.

Inglis, Andrew Stewart (1991), 'Harvesting Local Forestry Knowledge: a comparison of RRA and conventional surveys', *RRA Notes* 12: 32–40.

Inglis, Andy (1992), *A Tale of Two Approaches: Conventional Questionnaire Surveys vs PRA*, Rural Development Forestry Network Paper 14c, ODI, London, Winter.

Inglis, Andy and Susan Guy (1996), *Scottish Forest Policy 'U-turn' – Was PRA in Laggan Behind It?* Paper for the PRA and Policy Workshop, IDS. Sussex, 13–14 May, 1996.

Ives, Jack D. (1987), 'The Theory of Himalayan Environmental Degradation: its validity and application challenged by recent research', *Mountain Research and Development*, Vol. 7, No. 3: 189–99.

Jackson, Bill, Michael Nurse and Hukum Bahadur Singh (1994), *Participatory Mapping for Community Forestry*, Rural Development Forestry Network Paper 17e, ODI, London, Summer: 1–9.

Jackson, Cecile (1996), 'Rescuing Gender From the Poverty Trap', *World Development* 24(3): 489–504.

Jamieson, N. (1987), 'The Paradigmatic Significance of RRA', in KKU (1987): 89–102.

Jayal, N.D. (1985), 'Emerging Pattern of the Crisis in Water Resource Conservation', in Bandyopadhyay *et al.* (1985): 78–90.

Jayaratne, K.A. and Amasiri de Silva (eds) (1995), *Proceedings of the Consultative Meeting on Participatory Research in Urban Asia*, Sevanthal – Urban Research Centre, Colombo.

Jodha, N.S. (1988), 'Poverty Debate in India: a minority view', *Economic and Political Weekly,* Special Number: 2421–28, November.

Jodha, N.S. (1990), 'Rural Common Property Resources: growing crisis', *Gatekeeper Series* 24, IIED, London.

Johansson, Lars (1992), 'When Teacher Becomes Student', *Sveriges Natur* (Magazine of the Swedish Society for Nature Conservation), 30–33, special issue.

Johansson, Lars (1995), 'Reforming Donor Driven Projects and State Bureaucracies through PRA', *Forests, Trees and People Newsletter* 26/27: 59–63, April.

Johansson, Lars, and Allan Hoben (1992), 'RRA's For Land Policy Formulation in Tanzania', *Forests, Trees and People Newsletter,* 14/15, February: 26–31.

Johnson, Victoria (ed.) (1991), *Lifestyle Overload? Population and Environment in the Balance,* Report of the ActionAid seminar, London, 20 November, ActionAid Development Report No. 5, ActionAid, Chard, Somerset UK.

Johnson, Victoria (1995), 'Linking PRA-based Research to Policy', *PLA Notes* 24: 52–6, October.

Johnson, Victoria, Joanna Hill and Edda Ivan-Smith (1995), *Listening to Smaller Voices: Children in an Environment of Change*, ActionAid, London.

Joseph, S. (1991), 'Lead Time, Lag Time: RRA/PRA in ActionAid', ActionAid, Bangalore.

Joseph, S. (1992), 'Participatory Rural Appraisal in Identifying Major Illness, Healthcare Providers and Costs', *RRA Notes* 16: 53–56, July.

Joseph, Sam (1994), 'Drinking Water and Sanitation: a participatory model', in de Koning and Martin (eds) *Proceedings*: 140–43.

268

Joseph, Sam *et al.* (1994), *Programme Review/Evaluation October 1994*, ActionAid Somaliland.

Kabeer, Naila (1994), *Reversed Realities: Gender Hierarchies in Development Thought*, Verso Press, London, New York.

Kabutha, Charity, and Richard Ford (1988), 'Using RRA to Formulate a Village Resources Management Plan, Mbusanyi, Kenya', *RRA Notes*, 2: 4–11, October.

Kamarck, Andrew (1983), *Economics and the Real World*, Blackwell, Oxford.

Kane, Eileen (1995), *Seeing for Yourself: Research Handbook for Girls' Education in Africa*, EDI Learning Resources Series, Economic Development Institute of the World Bank, Washington.

Kane, Eileen, Lawrence Bruce, Haddy Sey and Mary O'Reilly-de Brun (1996), *Girls' Education in The Gambia*, Paper for the PRA and Policy Workshop, IDS Sussex, 13–14 May, 1996.

Kaplinsky, R. (1991), 'From Mass Production to Flexible Specialisation: a case study from a semi-industrialised economy', *IDS Discussion Paper*, 295, IDS, University of Sussex, Brighton, November.

Kar, K. (1993), *PRA on Village Area Development Planning for East Java Rainfed Agricultural Project*, Indonesia: East Java Rainfed Agricultural Project.

Kar, Kamal and Christof Backhaus (1994), Old Wine in New Bottles? Typescript.

Karle, Helmut (1992), *The Filthy Lie: Discovering and Recovering from Childhood Abuse*, Hamish Hamilton, London.

Kasivelu, S., Rupert Howes and John Devavaram (1995), 'The Use of PRA in Rehabilitating Minor Irrigation Tanks', *PLA Notes* 22: 49–52.

Kassam, Yusuf, and Kemal Mustafa (eds.) (1982), *Participatory Research: An Emerging Alternative Methodology in Social Science Research*, Society for Participatory Research in Asia, 45 Sainik Farm, Khanpur, New Delhi 110 062.

Kenyon, John (1983), 'When a Community Describes Itself, *Together*, October–December: 21–6.

Kerr, J.M. (ed.) (1991), *Farmers' Practices and Soil and Water Conservation Programmes*, Summary proceedings of a workshop, June 19–21, ICRISAT Center, Patancheru, India.

KGVK (1991), *Management Training Manual*, Krishi Gram Vikas Kendra, Ranchi, Bihar.

Kievelitz, Uwe and Rolf-Dieter Reineke (1993), 'Rapid Appraisal of Organisational Cultures: a Challenge for Field Work', *RRA Notes* 17: 57–63, March.

King, J.A. Jr. (1967), *Economic Development Projects and Their Appraisal: Cases and Principles from the Experience of the World Bank*, Johns Hopkins University Press, Baltimore.

Kingsley, M. and P. Musante (1996), *Developing Farmer Field Schools and Farmer Networks: Case Study of an NGO-Coordinated Integrated Pest Management Project in Indonesia*, World Education, Jakarta.

KKU (1987), *Proceedings of the 1985 International Conference on Rapid Rural Appraisal*, Rural Systems Research and Farming Systems Research Projects, University of Khon Kaen, Thailand.

Klamer, Arjo and David Colander (1990), *The Making of an Economist*, Westview Press, Boulder, San Francisco, London.

Klatzmann, B. (1983), *Nourrir dix milliards d'hommes?* PUF (Le géographe: 16), 2nd ed. (original 1975).

Korten, D.C. (1980), 'Community Organization and Rural Development: a learning process approach', *Public Administration Review*, Vol. 40: 480–510, Sept–Oct.

Korten, D.C. (1984), 'Rural Development Programming: the learning process approach', in Korten and Klauss (eds), *People-centered Development*, Kumarian Press, West Hartford, Connecticut, pp. 176–88.

Korten, David (1995), 'Sustainability and the global economy: beyond Bretton Woods', *Forests, Trees and People Newsletter* 29: 4–10, November.

Korten, Frances (1993), 'The High Costs of Environmental Loans', *Asia Pacific Issues* (Analysis from the East-West Center) No. 7, September.

Kuhn, Thomas (1962), *The Structure of Scientific Revolutions*, University of Chicago Press, Illinois.

Leach, Gerald and Robin Mearns (1988), *Beyond the Woodfuel Crisis: People, Land and Trees in Africa*, Earthscan Publications, London.

Leach, Melissa and James Fairhead (1992), 'Whose Social Forestry and Why? People, Trees and Managed Continuity in Guinea's Forest-Savanna Mosaic', Connaissance et Organisation Locales Agro-ecologiques, BP 4100, Conakry, Guinea, November.

Leach, Melissa and James Fairhead (1994), 'Natural Resource Management: The Reproduction and Use of Environmental Misinformation in Guinea's Forest-Savanna Transition Zone', in Davies (ed.) *Knowledge is Power?* pp. 81–7.

Leach, Melissa and James Fairhead, with Dominique Millimouno and Marie Kamano, (1994), *The Forest Islands of Kissidougo: Social Dynamics of Environmental Change in West Africa's Forest-Savanna Mosaic*, Report to ESCOR of the Overseas Development Administration, July.

Leach, Melissa and Robin Mearns (eds) (1996), *The Lie of the Land: Challenging Received Wisdom on the African Environment*, The International African Institute in association with James Currey, Oxford and Heinemann, Portsmouth (N.H.).

Leonard, David K. (1991), *African successes: Four Public Managers of Kenyan Rural Development*, University of California Press, Berkeley, Los Angeles, Oxford.

Leonard, H. Jeffery (1989), *Environment and the Poor: Development Strategies for a Common Agenda*, Transaction Books, New Brunswick (USA) and Oxford (UK).

Lepes, Ivan T. and Juan C. Argibay (1994), 'Possible Psi Effect with Drosophila Melanogaster' *Journal of the Society for Psychical Research*, Vol. 60, No. 837: 78–85.

Leurs, Robert (1996), 'Current Challenges Facing Participatory Rural Appraisal', *Public Administration and Development*, Vol. 16: 1–16.

Lewis, David L. (1976), *The Public Image of Henry Ford*, Wayne State University Press, Detroit.

Leyland, Tim (1993), 'Participatory Rural Appraisal in Afghanistan', in Daniels *et al.* (eds), *Livestock Services for Smallholders*: 140–3.

Lightfoot, Clive *et al.* (1991), *Training Resource Book for Participatory Experimental Design*, Narendra Dev University of Agriculture and Technology, Faizabad, UP, India; International Center for Living Aquatic Resources Management, Manila, Philippines; International Rice Research Institute, Manila, Philippines.

Lightfoot, Clive and D.R. Minnick (1991), 'Farmer-first Qualitative Methods: farmers' diagrams for improving methods of experimental design in integrated farming systems', *Journal of Farming Systems Research-Extension*, 2(1): 57–69.

Lightfoot, Clive, Reg Noble and Regina Morales (1991), *Training Resource Book on a Participatory Method of Modelling Bioresource Flows*, International Center for Living Aquatic Resources Management, Manila, Philippines.

Lightfoot, Clive and Reg Noble (1993), 'Participatory Experiment in Sustainable Agriculture', *Journal for Farming Systems Research-Extension* Vol. 4, No. 1: 11–34.

Lincoln, Yvonna S. and Egon G. Guba (1985), *Naturalistic Enquiry*, Sage Publications, London and New Delhi.

Lipton, Michael and Martin Ravallion (1993), 'Poverty and Policy', monograph for Chapter 42 in Jere Behrman and T.N. Srinivasan (eds), *Handbook of Development Economics*, Vol. 3, North-Holland, Amsterdam.

Little, I.M.D. and J.A. Mirlees (1974), *Project Appraisal and Planning for Developing Countries*, Heinemann Education Books, London.

Longhurst, Richard (ed.) (1986), 'Seasonality and Poverty', *IDS Bulletin*, Vol. 17, No. 3, July.

Malhotra, S.P. (1982), *The Warabandi System and Its Infrastructure*, Central Board for Irrigation and Power, Malcha Marg, New Delhi 110021.

Malhotra, K.C., Debal Deb, M. Dutta, T.S. Vasulu, G. Yadav and M. Adhikari (1993), 'The Role of Non-timber Forest Products in Village Economies of South-West Bengal', *Rural Development Forestry Network Paper* 15d, ODI, London, Summer 1993.

Manoharan, M., K. Velayudham and N. Shunmugavalli (1993), 'PRA: an approach to find felt needs of crop varieties', *RRA Notes* 18: 66–8, June.

Maranga, Stella (1993), 'Participatory Information Collection in Kenya and Zimbabwe', in Daniels *et al.* (eds), *Livestock Services for Smallholders*: 137–9.

Marindo-Ranganai, Ravai (1995), 'Diagrams for Demographic Data Collection: examples from the Tembomvura, Zimbabwe', *PLA Notes* 22: 53–61.

Marindo-Ranganai, Ravai (1996), 'A Zimbabwean Case' in de Koning and Martin (eds) (1996): 177–90.

Mascarenhas, J. (1990), 'Transects in PRA', *PALM Series* IV E, MYRADA, 2 Service Road, Domlur Layout, Bangalore 560 071.

Mascarenhas, James (1991), 'PRA and Participatory Learning Methods: Recent Experiences from MYRADA and South India', *RRA Notes* 13: 49–57, August.

Mascarenhas, J. and R. Hildalgo (1992), *Experience of a Participatory Rural Appraisal Exercise*, paper for International Course on Regenerative Agriculture, IIRR, Silang, Cavite, Philippines, 21–23 October.

Mascarenhas, James (1996), *The Participatory Watershed Development Implementation Process: Some Practical Tips Drawn from OUTREACH in South India*, Outreach Series Paper 1, Bangalore.

Mascarenhas, J. and P.D. Prem Kumar (1991), 'Participatory Mapping and Modelling: user's notes', *RRA Notes*, 12: 9–20.

Mascarenhas, James, Parmesh Shah, Sam Joseph, Ravi Jayakaran, John Devavaram, Vidya Ramachandran, Aloysius Fernandez, Robert Chambers and Jules Pretty (eds) (1991), *Proceedings of the February 1991 Bangalore PRA Workshop, RRA Notes* 13, August.

Mason, John J. and Elijah Y. Danso (1995), 'PRA for People and Parks: the case of Mole National Park, Ghana', *PLA Notes* 22: 76–9.

Masson, Jeffrey (1989), *Against Therapy*, Collins, London.

Masson, Jeffrey (1992), *The Assault on Truth: Freud and Child Sexual Abuse*, Fontana, London (first published 1984, by Farrar, Straus and Giroux Inc).

Maxwell, Simon (ed.) (1990), 'Food Security in Developing Countries', *IDS Bulletin*, Vol. 21, No. 3, July.

Maxwell, Simon (ed.) (1991), *To Cure All Hunger: Food Policy and Food Security in Sudan*, Intermediate Technology Publications, London.

Maxwell, Simon and Bart Duff (1995), 'Beyond Ranking: Exploring Relative Preferences in P/RRA', *PLA Notes* 22: 28–35.

May, Julian (1996), *Kicking Down Doors and Lighting Fires: Participating in Policy: The SA-PPA Experience*, Paper for the PRA and Policy Workshop, IDS, Sussex, 13–14 May 1996.

Mayer, Thomas (1993), *Truth versus Precision in Economics*, Edward Elgar, Aldershot and Vermont.

McCracken, J.A. (1988), *Participatory Rapid Rural Appraisal in Gujarat: a trial model for the Aga Khan Rural Support Programme (India)*, IIED, London, November.

McCracken, J.A. (1990), 'BOBP tries out RRA in Chinnamedu, Tamil Nadu', *Bay of Bengal News*, June 1990: 2–5.

McCracken, J.A., Jules N. Pretty and Gordon R. Conway (1988), *An Introduction to Rapid Rural Appraisal for Agricultural Development*, IIED, London.

McKean, R.N. (1965), *Efficiency in Government Through Systems Analysis*, John Wiley and Sons, New York.

McPherson, Sam (1995), *Participatory Monitoring and Evaluation: Abstracts of Sources*, IDS, University of Sussex.

Mduma, E.K. (1982), 'Appropriate Technology for Grain Storage at Bwakira Chimi Village', in Kassam and Mustafa (eds): 198–213.

Mearns, R. (1989), 'Aerial Photographs in Rapid Land Resource Appraisal, Papua New Guinea', *RRA Notes*, 7: 12–14A.

Mearns, R. (1991), 'Environmental Implications of Structural Adjustment: reflections on scientific methods', *IDS Discussion Paper* 284, IDS, University of Sussex, Brighton, February.

Mearns, Robin (1995), 'Institutions and Natural Resource Management: access to and control over woodfuel in East Africa', in Binns (ed.) (1995): 103—14.

Mearns, Robin, D. Shombodon, G. Narangerel, U. Turul, A. Enkhamgalan, B. Myagmarzhav, A. Bayanjargal and B. Bekhsuren (1992), 'Direct and Indirect Uses of Wealth Ranking in Mongolia', *RRA Notes* 15: 29–38.

Mikkelsen, Britta (1995), *Methods for Development Work and Research: A Guide for Practitioners*, Sage Publications, New Delhi, Thousand Oaks, London.

Milimo, John (1996), *A Note on the Use of PRA Approaches and Methods and their Impacts on Policy and Practice in Zambia*, Paper for the PRA and Policy Workshop, IDS, Sussex, 13–14 May, 1996.

Miller, Alice (1991), Interview by Alix Kirsta, *Observer* (London), 15 September 1991: 52.

Mishler, Elliot (1986), *Research Interviewing: Context and Narrative*, Cambridge, Mass.

Mitlin, Diana and John Thompson (1994), 'Addressing the Gaps or Dispelling the Myths? Participatory approaches in low-income urban communities', *RRA Notes* 21: 3–12.

Mook, B. (1974), 'Value and Action in Indian Bureaucracy', *IDS Discussion Paper* 65, IDS, University of Sussex.

Moore, Mick (1984), 'Institutional Development, the World Bank, and India's New Agricultural Extension Programme', *Journal of Development Studies* Vol. 20 No. 3: 303–17.

Moorehead, Richard (1991), Structural Chaos: community and state management of common property in Mali, D. Phil Thesis, University of Sussex.

Moris, Jon R. (1970), 'Multi-subject Farm Surveys Reconsidered: some methodological issues', Paper for the East African Agricultural Economics Society Conference, Dar es Salaam, 31 March–4 April.

Morse, Bradford and Thomas R. Berger (1992), *Sardar Sarovar: Report of the Independent Review*, Resource Futures International Inc., One Nicholas Street, Ottawa, Canada K1N 7B7.

Mortimore, Michael (ed.) (1991), *Environmental Change and Dryland Management in Machakos District, Kenya 1930–90*, Working Paper 53, ODI and the University of Nairobi, December.

Moser, C.A. and G. Kalton (1971), *Survey Methods in Social Investigation*, (1st ed. 1958), Heinemann Educational Books, London and elsewhere.

Moser, Caroline and Jeremy Holland (1995), *A Participatory Study of Urban Poverty and Violence in Jamaica: Analysis of Research Results*, Urban Development Division, World Bank, Washington, December.

Moser, Caroline and Jeremy Holland (1996), *Can Policy-focused PRAs be Participatory? Recent Policy-focused Research on Violence and Poverty in Jamaica using PRA Methods*, Paper for the PRA and Policy Workshop, IDS Sussex, 13–14 May 1996.

Mosse, David (1993), *Authority, Gender and Knowledge: Theoretical Reflections on the Practice of Participatory Rural Appraisal*, ODI Network Paper 44, ODI, London.

272

Mosse, David (1995), 'Social Analysis in Participatory Rural Development', *PLA Notes* 24: 27–33.

Mukherjee, Neela (1992), 'Villagers' Perceptions of Rural Poverty through the Mapping Methods of PRA', *RRA Notes* 15: 21–6.

Mukherjee, Neela (1993), *Participatory Rural Appraisal: Methodology and Applications*, Concept Publishing Company, New Delhi 110059.

Mukherjee, Neela (1995), *Participatory Rural Appraisal and Questionnaire Survey: Comparative Field Experience and Methodological Innovations*, Concept Publishing Company, New Delhi 110059.

Mukherjee, Nilanjana (1996), 'The Rush to Scale: lessons being learnt in Indonesia', Paper for the Workshop on Institutionalising Participatory Approaches, IDS, Sussex, 16–17 May.

Mukherjee, Ramkrishna (1991), 'Social and Cultural Components of Society and Appraisal of Social Reality', *Economic and Political Weekly*, 26: PE21–PE36, January.

Murphy, Carol (1995), *Implications of Poverty for Black Rural Women in Kwazulu/ Natal*, Report for the South African Participatory Poverty Assessment, Institute of Natural Resources, P. Bag X01, Scottsville, South Africa 3209.

Myrdal, Gunnar (1968), *Asian Drama: An Inquiry into the Poverty of Nations*, Penguin Books, Harmondsworth.

Narayan, Deepa (1993), *Participatory Evaluation Tools for Managing Change in Water and Sanitation*, Washington: UNDP-World Bank Water and Sanitation Program.

Narayan, Deepa (1996), *The Poverty Experts: A Participatory Poverty Assessment in Tanzania*, video, World Bank and Fast Forward Facilities, Nairobi.

NARC-ADB (1991), 'Nepal Agricultural Research Study', Study Team Report prepared for the National Agricultural Research Council and the Asian Development Bank, Kathmandu.

NCAER (1993) *Comparative Study of Sample Survey and Participatory Rural Appraisal Methodologies*. National Council for Applied Economic Research, 11 Indraprastha Estate, New Delhi 110 002, November.

Ndao, Makha (1995), 'Chad: Education V', in *World Bank Participation Sourcebook*, pp. 29–32.

Neefjes, Koos, with Hanneke Meijers, Pouk Sok, Pok Panha *et al.* (1993), *Participatory Environmental Assessment and Planning for Development*, Report on a workshop in Cambodia, November/December 1992, Oxfam, Oxford.

Nelson, Nici and Susan Wright (eds) (1995), *Power and Participatory Development: Theory and Practice*, Intermediate Technology Publications, London.

NES (1990), *Participatory Rural Appraisal Handbook*, National Environment Secretariat, Kenya; Clark University; Egerton University; and the Center for International Development and Environment of the World Resources Institute, February.

Norman, D.W. (1975), 'Rationalizing Mixed Cropping under Indigenous Conditions: the example of Northern Nigeria', *Samaru Research Bulletin* 232, Institute for Agricultural Research, Samaru, Ahmadu Bello University, Zaria, Nigeria (also *Journal of Development Studies* nd: 3–21).

Norrish, Patricia and John Best (1994), 'Sri Lanka: a writing workshop', *The Rural Extension Bulletin* 6: 33–5, (AERDD, University of Reading, Reading, UK) December.

Norton, Andy (1994), 'Observations on Urban Applications of PRA Methods from Ghana and Zambia: Participatory Poverty Assessments', *RRA Notes* 21: 55–6.

Norton, Andy (1996), *The Ghana Participatory Poverty Assessment: Some Notes on the Process and Lessons Learned*, Paper for the PRA and Policy Workshop, IDS, Sussex, 13–14 May 1996.

Norton, Andy, Dan Owen and John Milimo (1994), *Zambia Participatory Poverty Assessment: Volume 5: Participatory Poverty Assessment*, Report 12985-ZA, Southern Africa Department, World Bank, Washington, 30 November 1994.

Norton, Andy, David Kroboe, Ellen Bortei-Dorku and D.K. Tony Dogbe (1995), *Ghana Participatory Poverty Assessment. Consolidated Report on Poverty Assessment in Ghana Using Qualitative and Participatory Research Methods: Draft Report*, AFTHR, World Bank.

Norton, Andrew and Thomas Stephens (1995), *Participation in Poverty Assessments*, Environment Department Papers Participation Series, Social Policy and Resettlement Division, World Bank, Washington, June.

Norton, Andy and Dan Owen (1996), *The Zambia Participatory Poverty Assessment: Notes on the Process and Lessons Learned*, Paper for the PRA and Policy Workshop, IDS Sussex, 13–14 May 1996.

ODA (1972), *A Guide to Project Appraisal in Developing Countries*, HMSO, London.

ODA (1995), *Participatory Rural Appraisal: Matching Agricultural and Natural Resources Development to People's Needs in Nigeria*, Seminar Proceedings 25–7 April 1995, Kaduna, Nigeria, Overseas Development Administration, London.

OECD (1973), *Methods of Project Appraisal in Developing Countries*, OECD, Paris.

Okali, Christine, James Sumberg and John Farrington (1994), *Farmer Participatory Research: Rhetoric and Reality*, Intermediate Technology Publications, London.

Okumu, B.E.N. (1994), 'Systematizing Participation in Water and Sanitation Projects', in de Konings and Martin (eds) *Proceedings*: 138–40.

Omolo, E.O., J.W. Ssennyonga, A. Ngugi, F. Kiros and C. Okali (1995), *Community Mapping Exercises: An Evaluation*, Agricultural Administration (Research and Extension) Network, Network Paper 52, ODI, London, January.

Osuga, Ben and David Mutayisa (1994), *PRA Lessons and Concerns: Experiences in Uganda*, Uganda CBHC Association, PO Box 325, Entebbe, February.

Otterbein, Keith F. (1990). 'Two Styles of Cross-Cultural Research', *CAM (Cultural Anthropology Methods) Newsletter* Vol. 2 Issue 3: 6–7, November.

Owen, Dan (1996), *The Mozambique Participatory Poverty Assessment – Lessons from the Process*, Paper for the PRA and Policy Workshop, IDS, Sussex, 13–14 May 1996.

Pacey, Arnold and Philip Payne (eds) (1985), *Agricultural Development and Nutrition*, Hutchinson, London.

Parpia, H.A.B. (1977), 'More Than Food Would Be Saved' *Ceres* 10(6): 19–24.

Patel, C.C. (1981), 'Warabandi: Problems, Needs and Suggestions', in K.K. Singh (ed.) (1981): 7–10.

Payne, P.R. (1990), 'Measuring Malnutrition' in Maxwell (ed.) (1990): 14–30.

Pelto, Pertti, J., and Gretel H. Pelto (1978), *Anthropological Research: the Structure of Inquiry*, Second edition, Cambridge University Press.

Pembroke, Louise Roxanne (1994), 'Louise Roxanne Pembroke', in Louise Roxanne Pembroke (ed.) *Self-Harm: Perspectives from Personal Experience*, Survivors Speak Out, 34 Osnaburgh Street, London NW1 3ND.

Pennycuick, C.J. (1992), *Newton Rules Biology: A Physical Approach to Biological Problems*, Oxford University Press.

Persson, Reidar (1995), 'Myths and Truths on Global Deforestation', *IRDC Currents* 10 (IRDC, Swedish University of Agricultural Sciences, Uppsala): 4–6 May.

Peters, Thomas J. and Robert H. Waterman (1982), *In Search of Excellence: Lessons from America's Best-run Companies*, Harper and Row, New York.

Peters, Tom (1989), *Thriving on Chaos: Handbook for a Management Revolution*, (London: Pan Books).

Peters, Tom (1992), *Liberation Management: Necessary Disorganization for the Nanosecond Nineties*, Alfred Knopf, New York and Macmillan, London.

Peters, Tom (1994), *The Tom Peters Seminar: Crazy Times Call for Crazy Organisations*, Macmillan, London.

PIA (1994), *Participation in Action*, Issue 1, September 1994, PRA Unit, ActionAid, 3 Rest House Road, Bangalore 560 001, India.

PIA (1995), *Participation in Action*, Issue 5, August.

PID and NES (1989), *An Introduction to Participatory Rural Appraisal for Rural Resources Management*, Program for International Development, Clark University, Worcester, Mass. and National Environment Secretariat, Ministry of Environment and Natural Resources, Nairobi, November.

Pido, Michael D. (1995), 'RRA in Coastal Resource Planning: Malampaya Sound, the Philippines', *PLA Notes* 22: 45–8.

Pimbert, Michel (1993), 'The Making of Agricultural Biodiversity in Europe', in Vithal Rajan (ed.), *Rebuilding Communities: Experiences and Experiments in Europe*, Green Books in association with WWF, pp. 59–82.

Pimbert, Michel, with others (1996), *Community Based Planning for Wetland Conservation: Lessons from the Ucchali Complex in Pakistan*, Report on the Participatory Rural Appraisal (PRA) Training Workshop held in Ucchali Complex, Pakistan, 10–21 December 1994, WWF-Pakistan, World Wide Fund for Nature, CH 1196, Gland, Switzerland, and Punjab Wildlife Department, Pakistan.

Pinstrup-Andersen, Per and Rajul Pandya-Lorch (1995), *Food Security Now and for the Future*, Paper for the Conference on Tough Remedies-Silent Tragedies, NGO Forum, Copenhagen, 8 March 1995.

Plato (n.d.) *The Republic*, Penguin Books, Harmondsworth (1955).

Poate, C.D. and P.F. Daplyn (1993), *Data for Agrarian Development*, Cambridge University Press, Cambridge.

Pocknell, Sarah and Danny Annaly (1995), 'The Use of RRA in Conservation Expeditions: Experiences from Sierra Leone', *PLA Notes* 22: 80–83.

Porter, Doug, Bryant Allen and Gaye Thompson (1991), *Development in Practice: Paved with Good Intentions*, Routledge, London and New York.

Posadas, Adora (1995), 'Participatory Evaluation of Rice', *Organic Matters*, Journal on Philippine Low External Input Sustainable Agriculture, No. 18: 40–45, March.

Potten, David (1985), *Rapid Rural Appraisal – Emergence of a Methodology and Its Application to Irrigation: A Bibliographical Review*, International Irrigation Management Institute, Sri Lanka.

Pottier, Johan (1992), 'Agrarian Change at the Household Level: investigative styles in research on Mambwe agriculture', in Preben Kaarsholm (ed.) *Institutions, Culture and Change at Local Community Level*, International Development Studies Occasional Paper 3, Roskilde University Centre, Denmark, pp. 61–74.

Pottier, Johan and Patrick Orone (1995), 'Consensus or Cover-up? The Limitations of Group Meetings' *PLA Notes* 24: 38–42.

Premkumar, P.D. (1994), *Farmers are Engineers: Indigenous Soil and Water Conservation Practices in a Participatory Watershed Development Programme*, edited by Blaise Humbert-Droz, Pidow-Myrada, Kamalapura – 585 313, Gulbarga, Karnataka, India.

Preston, Lewis T. (1993), Foreword, in *Implementing the World Bank's Strategy to Reduce Poverty: Progress and Challenges*, World Bank, Washington, April.

Pretty, Jules N. (1990), *Rapid Catchment Analysis for Extension Agents: Notes on the 1990 Kericho Training Workshop for the Ministry of Agriculture, Kenya*, Sustainable Agriculture Programme, IIED, London, November.

Pretty, Jules N. (1995a), *Regenerating Agriculture: Policies and Practice for Sustainability and Self-reliance*, Earthscan Publications, London.

Pretty, Jules N. (1995b), 'Participatory Learning for Sustainable Agriculture', *World Development*, Vol. 23, No. 8: 1–17.

Pretty, Jules and Robert Chambers (1993), 'Towards a Learning Paradigm: new professionalism and institutions for agriculture', *IDS Discussion Paper* No. 334 (Brighton: Institute of Development Studies, University of Sussex, December.

Pretty, Jules, Irene Guijt, John Thompson and Ian Scoones (1995), *A Trainer's Guide for Particpatory Learning and Action*, IIED Participatory Methodology Series, IIED.

Price, M. (1992), 'National Inventories of the Sources and Sinks of Greenhouse Gases', Report on the initial mission to Senegal 30 November – 3 December 1992, United Nations Environment Programme.

Rahman, Md Anisur (ed.) (1984), *Grassroots Participation and Self-reliance*, Oxford and IBH, New Delhi.

Rahmato, Dessalegn (1987), 'Peasant Survival Strategies', in Angela Penrose (ed.) Beyond the Famine: an examination of the issues behind famine in Ethiopia, International Institute for Relief and Development, Food for the Hungry International, Geneva.

Rajaratnam, Jolly, C. Gamesan, Helen Thasian, Navamoni Babu and Abel Rajaratnam (1993), *Validating the Wealth Ranking of PRA and Formal Survey in Identifying the Rural Poor*, RUHSA Department, Christian Medical College and Hospital, Vellore, Tamil Nadu.

Ramachandran, Vidya (1990), A Workshop on Participatory Learning Methods, 8 to 12 January 1990, MYRADA Talavadi Project, *PRA/PALM Series* No. 1, MYRADA, Bangalore.

RDWSSP (1994), *PRA Reference Guide*, Rural Domestic Water Supply and Sanitation Project, II/PAT, PO Box 1137, Kisumu, Kenya.

Redd Barna (1993), *NOT ONLY the Well Off BUT ALSO the Worse Off*, Report of a Participatory Rural Appraisal Training Workshop, 4–22 October 1993, Chiredzi, Zimbabwe, Redd Barna Regional Office Africa, PO Box 12018, Kampala, Uganda.

Repetto, Robert (1986), *Skimming the Water: Rent-seeking and the Performance of Public Irrigation Systems*, World Resources Institute Research Report 4, WRI, 1735 New York Avenue, NW, Washington DC.

Resnick, Mitchell (1994), *Turtles, Termites, and Traffic Jams: Explorations in Massively Parallel Microworlds*, MIT Press, Cambridge, Mass and London, England.

Reusen, Rene and Jan Johnson (1994), 'Linking Government Agents and Local Users: PUA for artisanal fishing port development' *RRA Notes* 21: 57–69.

Rhoades, Robert (1982), *The Art of the Informal Agricultural Survey*, International Potato Center, Apartado 5969, Lima.

Rhoades, Robert (1990), 'The Coming Revolution in Methods for Rural Development Research', User's Perspective Network (UPWARD), International Potato Center (CIP), PO Box 933, Manila.

Rhoades, Robert (1992), 'The Coming Revolution in Methods for Rural Development Research', in Scrimshaw and Gleason (eds) (1992): 61–78.

Richards, Janet Radcliffe (1992), Foreword, in Karle, 1992.

Richards, P. (1985), *Indigenous Agricultural Revolution*, Hutchinson, London and Westview Press, Colorado.

Richards, Paul (1989), 'Agriculture as Performance', in Chambers *et al.* (eds) (1989): 39–43.

Robb, Caroline (1996), *Participatory Poverty Assessment: Key Issues*, Paper presented at the PRA and Policy Workshop, IDS Sussex, 13–14 May 1996.

Robinson, Eva (1993), 'Women's PRA in Hindupur' *RRA Notes* 17, 46–8.

Robinson, Patrick (1993), 'Indigenous Knowledge in Yak/Cattle Cross-breeding Management in High Altitude Nepal', in Tamang *et al.* (eds) (1993): 139–48.

Robinson-Pant, Anna (1995), 'PRA: a new literacy?' *PLA Notes* 24: 78–82.

Rocheleau, Diane, Kamoji Wachira, Luis Malaret and Bernard Muchiri Wanjohi, (1989), 'Local knowledge for agroforestry and native plants', in Chambers, Pacey and Thrupp (eds), pp. 14–24.

276

Roling, Niels (1992), 'Facilitating Sustainable Agriculture Changes Policy Models', Paper for IIED/IDS Beyond Farmer First: Rural People's Knowledge, Agricultural Research and Extension Practice Workshop, IDS, University of Sussex, 27–9 October 1992.

Rondinelli, D.A. (1983), *Development Projects as Policy Experiments: An Adaptive Approach to Development Administration,* Methuen, London and New York.

Rosenau, Pauline Marie (1992), *Post-Modernism and the Social Sciences: Insights, Inroads and Intrusions,* Princeton University Press, Princeton, New Jersey.

Rostow, W.W. (1960), *The Stages of Economic Growth: a Non-Communist Manifesto,* Cambridge University Press, Cambridge, UK.

Rowe, Dorothy (1989), Foreword, in Masson, 1989.

Roy, S.B. and Mitali Chatterjee (1994), *Joint Forest Management: A Training Manual,* Inter-India Publications, D-17, Raja Gardens, New Delhi 110015, India.

RRA Notes 1–21, subsequently *PLA Notes* 22–6 (continuing), Sustainable Agriculture Programme, International Institute for Environment and Development, 3 Endsleigh Street, London WC1H 0DD.

Russell, David B., and Raymond L. Ison (1991), 'The Research-Development Relationship in Rangelands: an opportunity for contextual science', Plenary paper for Fourth International Rangelands Congress, Montpellier, France, April 22–6.

Ryan, J.G. (ed.) (1979), Socioeconomic Constraints to Development of Semi-arid Agriculture, ICRISAT, India.

Sachs, Wolfgang (ed.) (1992), *The Development Dictionary: A Guide to Knowledge as Power,* Zed Books, London and New Jersey.

Sadomba, Wilbert Z. (1996), 'Retrospective community mapping: a tool for community education', *PLA Notes* 25: 9–13.

Sahn, D.E. (ed.) (1989), *Seasonal Variability in Third World Agriculture: The Consequences for Food Security,* Johns Hopkins Press, Baltimore.

Samaranayake, Mallika (1994), 'Institutionalizing Participatory Approaches', Paper presented at the 'Dare to Share' Fair, Participatory Learning Approaches in Development Cooperation, 20–21 September 1994, GTZ, Eschborn, Germany.

Sanderson, Christiane (1990), *Counselling Adult Survivors of Child Sexual Abuse,* Jessica Kingsley Publishers, London and Philadelphia.

Sandford, Dick (1989), 'A Note on the Use of Aerial Photographs for Land Use Planning on a Settlement Site in Ethiopia', *RRA Notes,* 6: 18–19.

Satterthwaite, David (1996), 'The Scale and Nature of Urban Change in the South', rejected by *Development and Change* (manuscript available from IIED).

Scherr, Sara J. (1995), 'Economic Factors in Farmer Adoption of Agroforestry: patterns observed in Western Kenya', *World Development,* Vol. 23, No. 5: 787–804.

Schofield, Susan (1974), 'Seasonal Factors Affecting Nutrition in Different Age Groups and Especially Preschool Children', *Journal of Development Studies* 11(1) October.

Schon, Donald, A. (1983), *The Reflective Practitioner: How Professionals Think in Action,* Basic Books Inc.

Schon, Donald A. (1987), *Educating the Reflective Practitioner,* Jossey-Bass, San Francisco.

Schonhuth, Michael and Uwe Kievelitz (1994), *Participatory Learning Approaches: Rapid Rural Appraisal, Participatory Appraisal. An Introductory Guide,* GTZ-Verlagsgesellschaft mbH, Postfach 1164, D-64373 Rossdorf, Germany.

Schubert, Berndt *et al.* (1994), *Facilitating the Introduction of a Participatory and Integrated Development Approach (PIDA) in Kilifi District, Kenya:* Vol. 1, *Recommendations for Institutionalising PIDA Based on Four Pilot Projects*: Vol. 2 *From Concept to Action: A Manual for Trainers and Users of PIDA,* KIWASAP, POB 666, Kilifi, Kenya and CATAD, Podbielskiallee 66, D-14195 Berlin, Germany.

Schumacher, E.F. (1973), *Small is Beautiful: A Study of Economics as if People Mattered*, Blond Briggs, London.

Scoones, Ian (1994), *Living with Uncertainty: New Directions for Pastoral Development in Africa*, Drylands Paper No. 6, IIED, London, April.

Scoones, Ian (1995a), 'Investigating Difference: applications of wealth ranking and household survey approaches among farming households in Southern Zimbabwe', *Development and Change* Vol. 26: 67–88.

Scoones, Ian (1995b), *Hazards and Opportunities. Farming Livelihoods in Dryland Africa: Lessons from Zimbabwe*, Zed Books, London.

Scoones, Ian (ed.) (1995c), *Living with Uncertainty: New Directions in Pastoral Development in Africa*, Intermediate Technology Publications, London.

Scoones, Ian (1995d), 'New Directions in Pastoral Development in Africa', in Scoones (1995c): 1–36.

Scoones, Ian (1995e), *Range Management for the 21st Century: Challenges for a New Professionalism*, Commentary on the session Integrating the Social Sciences into Rangeland Management, Vth International Rangelands Congress, Salt Lake City, July 1995.

Scoones, Ian (1995f), 'Policies for Pastoralists: New Directions for Pastoral Development in Africa', in Binns (ed.) (1995): 23–30.

Scoones, Ian, Mary Melnyk and Jules Pretty (1992), *The Hidden Harvest: Wild Foods and Agricultural Systems. A Literature Review and Annotated Bibliography*, IIED, London.

Scoones, Ian and John Thompson (eds) (1994), *Beyond Farmer First: Rural People's Knowledge, Agricultural Research and Extension Practice*, Intermediate Technology Publications, London.

Scrimshaw, Nevin and Gary R. Gleason (eds) (1992), *RAP Rapid Assessment Procedures: Qualitative Methodologies for Planning and Evaluation of Health Related Programmes*, International Nutrition Foundation for Developing Countries, PO Box 500, Charles Street Station, Boston MA 02114–0500, USA.

Scrimshaw, S., and E. Hurtado (1987), *Rapid Assessment Procedures for Nutrition and Primary Health Care: Anthropological Approaches for Improving Programme Effectiveness*, United Nations University, Tokyo; UNICEF/UN Children's Fund; and UCLA Latin American Center, Los Angeles.

SDN (1993), *Social Development Newsletter* (ODA, London) Vol. 2, No. 1, August.

Seeley, Janet, Januario Nabaitu, Lorraine Taylor, Ellen Kajura, Tanance Bukenya, Elizabeth Kabunga and Fatuma Ssembajja (1996), 'Revealing Gender Differences through Well-being Ranking in Uganda', *PLA Notes* 25: 14–18.

Self, P. (1975), *Econocrats and the Policy Process: The Politics and Philosophy of Cost-Benefit Analysis*, Macmillan, London.

Semler, R., 'Managing Without Managers', Harvard Business Review (September–October 1989), 76–84.

Semler, Ricardo (1993), *Maverick! The Success Story Behind the World's Most Unusual Workplace*, Century, London.

Sen, Amartya (1981), *Poverty and Famines: An Essay on Entitlement and Famines*, Clarendon Press, Oxford.

Senge, Peter (1990), *The Fifth Discipline: The Art and Practice of the Learning Organisation*, Doubleday, USA (1992 ed. Random House, London).

SEWA-Rural Research Team – Gayatri Giri, Ashok Patel, Lata Desai, S. Sridhar, Pankaj Shah and others (1996), 'An Experience in the Use of PRA/RRA Approach and Methods for Health Needs Assessment in a Remote Rural Community of Northern Gujarat, India', in de Koning and Martin (eds) 1996: 130–40.

Shah, Anil C. (1991), 'Shoulder-tapping: a technique of training in participatory rural appraisal', *Forests, Trees and People Newsletter* 14: 14–15.

Shah, Anil C. (1996), 'Challenges in Influencing Public Policy', Paper for the PRA and Policy Workshop, IDS, Sussex, 13–14 May 1996.

278

Shah, Meera Kaul (1993a), 'Using Participatory Methods to Understand Gender Differences in Perceptions of Poverty, Well-being and Social Change: people's perspective from a village in Ghana', typescript, IDS, Sussex, June.

Shah, Meera Kaul (1993b), *Training Workshop on Participatory Appraisal Methods for Participatory Poverty Assessment in Zambia*, 9–20 September 1993, Report submitted to the World Bank, October.

Shah, Meera Kaul (1995a), 'Participatory Reforestation: experience from Bharuch District, South Gujarat, India' *Forests, Trees and People Newsletter* 26/27: 53–8, April.

Shah, Meera Kaul (1995b), 'Training Workshop on Participatory Appraisal Methods for Participatory Assessment of Urban Poverty and Violence in Jamaica', September 1995' Report submitted to the World Bank, October.

Shah, Meera Kaul (1996), 'Participatory Planning with Disaster Victims: experience from earthquake-hit areas of Maharashtra, India', *Refugee Participation Network*, Refugee Studies Programme, Oxford, UK, No. 21: 15–17, April.

Shah, Meera Kaul and Khadija Bourarach (1995), *Participatory Assessment of Women's Problems and Concerns in Morocco*, Report submitted to the World Bank, first draft, February.

Shah, Parmesh (1993), 'Participatory Watershed Management Programmes in India: reversing our roles and revising our theories', in *Rural People's Knowledge, Agricultural Research and Extension Practice, Asia Papers*, IIED Research Series, Vol. 1, No. 3: 38–67.

Shah, Parmesh (1995), 'Farmers as Analysts, Facilitators and Decision-makers', in Nelson and Wright (eds) (1995): 83–94.

Shah, Parmesh (1996), 'Participatory Village Resource Management: case study of Aga Khan Rural Support Programme (AKRSP) India', D. Phil. thesis submitted to the University of Sussex, April.

Shah, Parmesh, Girish Bharwaj and Ranjit Ambastha (1991), 'Participatory Impact Monitoring of a Soil and Water Conservation Programme by Farmers, Extension Volunteers and AKRSP', in Mascarenhas *et al.* (1991): 127–31.

Shah, Parmesh and Meera Kaul Shah (1995), 'Participatory Methods: precipitating or avoiding conflict?' *PLA Notes* 24: 48–51.

Shaner, W.W., P.F. Philipp and W.R. Schmehl (1982), *Farming Systems Research and Development: Guidelines for Developing Countries*, Westview Press, Boulder, Colorado.

Shaxson, T.F. (1993), 'A Strategy for Better Land Husbandry at Thabana Morena', in Hudson and Cheatle (eds) (1993): 126–30.

Sheldrake, Rupert (1981), *A New Science of Life: the Hypothesis of Formative Causation*, Blond and Briggs, London. (Second edition, Paladin, London (1987).)

Shrestha, Rajesh B. (1996), 'Trees: farmers' response to change', *ILEIA Newsletter, Mountains in Balance* 12(1), April: 20–21.

Siegman, Gita (1992), *World of Winners* (2nd ed.), Gale Research International, Detroit and London.

Sikana, Patrick (1994), 'Indigenous Soil Characterization in Northern Zambia', in Scoones and Thompson (eds) (1994): 80–82.

Silverman, Sydel F. (1966), 'An Ethnographic Approach to Social Stratification: prestige in a central Italian community', *American Anthropologist* 68(4): 899–921 (quoted in Pelto and Pelto (1978): 82–4).

Singh, K.K. (ed.) (1981), *Warabandi for Irrigated Agriculture in India*, Publication No. 146, Central Board for Irrigation and Power, Malcha Marg, New Delhi 110021.

Singh, Ramesh (1996), 'PRA in Nepal: talking, doing, being', *Face to Face* (Kathmandu), No. 7: 7–9, March.

Slim, Hugo and Paul Thompson (1993), *Listening for a Change: Oral Testimony and Development*, Panos Publications, London.

Slim, Hugo and John Mitchell (1992), 'The Application of RAP and RRA Techniques in Emergency Relief Programmes', in Scrimshaw and Gleason (eds) (1992): 251–6.

Sommer, Martin (1993), *Whose Values Matter? Experiences and Lessons from a Self-Evaluation in PIDOW Project, Karnataka,* India, Swiss Development Cooperation, Bangalore Field Office.

Sonaiya, E.B. (1993), 'An Integrative Approach to the Definition of Problems and Opportunities for Smallholder Rural Poultry Farmers in Nigeria', in Daniels *et al.* (eds) *Livestock Services for Smallholders:* 130–2.

Sperling, Louise (1992), 'Farmer Participation and the Development of Bean Varieties in Rwanda', in J.L. Moock and R. Rhoades (eds), *Diversity, Farmer Knowledge, and Sustainability,* Cornell University Press, Ithaca and London.

Sperling, Louise and Urs Scheidegger (1995), *Participatory Selection of Beans in Rwanda: Results, Methods and Institutional Issues,* Gatekeeper Series 51, IIED, London.

Sperling, Louise, Michael E. Loevinsohn and Beatrice Ntambomvura (in press), 'Rethinking the Farmer's Role in Plant Breeding: local bean expert and on-station selection in Rwanda', *Experimental Agriculture.*

SPRA (1982), *Participatory Research: An Introduction,* Society for Participatory Research in Asia, 45 Sainik Farm, Khanpur, New Delhi 110062.

SPWD (1992), *Field Methods Manual Volume 1: Diagnostic Tools for Supporting Joint Forest Management Systems,* prepared for the joint Forest Management Support Program, and *Vol. 2. Community Forest Economy and Use Patterns: Participatory Rural Appraisal (PRA) Methods in South Gujarat,* India Society for Promotion of Wastelands Development, 1 Copernicus Marg, New Delhi 110001.

Squire, L. and H.G. van der Tak (1975), *Economic Analysis of Projects,* Johns Hopkins University Press, Baltimore and London.

Srinivasan, K. and S. Mukerji (eds) (1987), *Dynamics of Population and Family Welfare,* Himalaya Publishing House, Bombay, Nagpur, Delhi.

SSP (1992), *We Could Do What We Never Knew We Could,* video, Self-Help Support Programme, 92/2 D.S. Senanayake Mawatha, Colombo 8, Sri Lanka.

Starkey, Paul (1988), *Animal-Drawn Wheeled Toolcarriers: Perfected yet Rejected,* Friedrich Vieweg & Sohn, Braunschweig/Wiesbaden.

Stocking, Michael (1993a), 'The Rapid Appraisal of Physical Properties Affecting Land Degradation', in Carl Christiansson, Annika Dahlberg, Vesa-Matte Loiske and Wilhelm Ostberg (eds), *Environment Users Scholars: Exploring Interfaces,* Environment and Development Studies Unit, School of Geography, Stockholm University, pp. 20–23.

Stocking, Michael (1993b), 'Soil Erosion in Developing Countries: where geomorphology fears to tread', *Discussion Paper* 241, School of Development Studies, University of East Anglia, Norwich, UK.

Stocking, Michael (1996), 'Challenging Conventional Wisdoms about Soil Erosion in Africa', in Leach and Mearns (eds): 140–54.

Swift, Jeremy (1989), 'Why are Rural People Vulnerable to Famine?' in *Vulnerability: How the Poor Cope, IDS Bulletin* 20(2): 8–15.

Swift, J. (1981), 'Rapid Appraisal and Cost-effective Research in West Africa', *Agricultural Administration,* Vol. 8: 485–92, 6 November.

Swift, Jeremy and Abdi Noor Umar (1991), *Participatory Pastoral Development in Isiolo District,* Final Report, Isiolo Livestock Development Project, EMI ASAL Programme, Kenya.

Swift, Jeremy (1996), 'Desertification: narratives, winners and losers', in Leach and Mearns (eds): 73–90.

Tabatabai, Hamid (1995), 'Poverty and Inequality in Developing Countries: a review of evidence', in Rodgers and van der Hoeven (eds) (1995): 11–32.

280

Tamang, Devika (1992), *Indigenous Soil Fertility Management in the Hills of Nepal: Lessons from an East-West Transect*, Research report Paper No. 19, Winrock International, Kathmandu (also in IIRR, 1993: 469–94).

Tamang, Devika (1993), *Living in a Fragile Ecosystem: Indigenous Soils Management in the Hills of Nepal*, Gatekeeper Series 41, IIED, London.

Tamang, Devika, Gerard J. Gill and Ganesh B. Thapa (eds) (1993), *Indigenous Management of Natural Resources in Nepal*, HMG Ministry of Agriculture/ Winrock International, Kathmandu.

Teixeira, Lynne and Fiona Chambers (1995), *Child Support in Small Towns in the Eastern Cape*, Black Sash Advice Office, Port Elizabeth, October.

Thakur, D.S. (1985), 'A Survey of Literature on Rural Poverty in India', *Margin*: 32–49, April.

Theis, J. and H. Grady (1991), *Participatory Rural Appraisal for Community Development: A Training Manual Based on Experiences in the Middle East and North Africa*, IIED and Save the Children Federation.

Thomas, D.B. (1991), 'Soil Erosion' in Mortimore (ed.) *Environmental Change and Dryland Management in Machakos District, Kenya 1930–90*, pp. 24–43.

Thompson, John (1995), 'Participatory Approaches in Government Bureaucracies: Facilitating the Process of Institutional Change', *World Development*, Vol. 23, No. 9: 1521–54, September.

Thompson, Paul (1988), *Voice of the Past: Oral History*, 2nd ed., Oxford University Press.

Thuvesson, Daphne (1995), Editorial in *Forests and People Newsletter*, 26–27 April.

Tiffen, Mary (1992), *Environmental Change and Dryland Management in Machakos District, Kenya 1930–90: Farming and Incomes Systems*, ODI Working Paper 59, ODI, London.

Tiffen, Mary (1993), 'Productivity and Environmental Conservation under Rapid Population Growth: a case study of Machakos District', *Journal of International Development* 5(2): 207–23.

Tiffen, Mary (1994), 'Land, Capital and Management: blind spots in the study of the resource poor farmer', Paper for the workshop Escaping Orthodoxy: Environmental Change Assessments, Local Natural Resource Management and Policy Processes in Africa, IDS, Sussex, 13–14 September 1994.

Tiffen, Mary and Michael Mortimore (1992), 'Environment, Population Growth and Productivity in Kenya: a case study of Machakos District', *Development Policy Review* 10: 359–87.

Tiffen, Mary, Michael Mortimore and F.N. Gichuki (1993), *More People, Less Erosion: Environmental Recovery in Kenya*, John Wiley and Sons, Chichester, New York, Brisbane, Toronto, Singapore.

Tillmann, Hermann J. (1993), *VIPP: Visualisation in Participatory Programmes: A Manual for Facilitators and Trainers in Participatory Group events*, UNICEF, PO Box 58, Dhaka 1000, Bangladesh.

Tolley, E. and M. Bentley (1992), 'Participatory Methods for Research on Women's Reproductive Health', *RRA Notes* 16: 63–68, July.

Toon, Kay, Jon Fraise, Mark McFetridge and Nic Alwin (1996), 'Memory or Mirage? The FMS Debate', *The Psychologist* 9(2): 73–7, February.

Townsend, Peter (1993), *The International Analysis of Poverty*, Harvester Wheatsheaf, New York and London.

TriPARRD (1993), *A Manual on the Estate/Barangay-level Productivity Systems Assessment and Planning (PSAP) Methodology*, TriPAARD Technical Committee, Tripartite Partnership for Agrarian Reform and Rural Development and PhilDHRRA, 59 C. Salvador St. Loyola Heights, Quezon City, Philippines.

Turk, Carrie (1995), 'Identifying and Tackling Poverty: ActionAid's Experiences in Vietnam', *PLA Notes* 23: 37–41, June.

Tyler, Peter S. and Robin A. Boxall (1984), 'Post-harvest Loss Reduction Programmes: a decade of activities – what consequences', *Tropical Stored Products Information*, 50: 4–13.

Ulijaszek, S.J. and S.S. Strickland (eds) (1993), *Seasonality and Human Ecology*, 35th Symposium Volume of the Society for the Study of Human Biology, Cambridge University Press.

UNICEF (1975), *Communicating with Pictures*, UNICEF, Nepal.

Uphoff, Norman (1992), *Learning from Gal Oya: Possibilities for Participatory Development and Post-Newtonian Social Science*, Cornell University Press, Ithaca and London. (Note paperback edition with new introduction (1996), IT Publications, London.)

Urdang, Laurence (1991), *The Oxford Thesaurus*, Oxford University Press.

Uvin, Peter (1992), *Second Report on the World Nutrition Situation*, Vol. 1: *Global and Regional Results*, UN ACC Subcommittee on Nutrition, Geneva.

Uvin, Peter (1994), *The International Organization of Hunger*, Kegan Paul International, London.

Vigoda, Marcy (1994), 'Participatory Rural Appraisal in a Women's Health Education Project in Bangladesh', *RRA Notes* 19: 70–74, February.

Vigoda, Marcy, with Cathy Plume, Kirsten Johnson and PN-23 project team (1994), *Central Chuquisaca Renewable Natural Resources Project (PN-23) Baseline Study*, CARE Internacional, Sucre, Bolivia, October.

Vochten, Piet and Agus Mulyana (1995), 'Reforestation, Protection Forest and People – Finding Compromises through PRA', *Forests, Trees and People Newsletter* 26/27: 32–6, April.

Waldrop, M. Mitchell (1994), *Complexity: the Emerging Science at the Edge of Order and Chaos*, Penguin Books, Harmondsworth (first published by Simon and Schuster, USA, 1992).

Walker, T.S. and J.G. Ryan (1990), *Village and Household Economies in India's Semi-arid Tropics*, Johns Hopkins Press, Baltimore and London.

Ward, Pene, Veronica Scott, Jasper Hatwiinda and Charles Maseko (1995), *A Participatory Appraisal and Needs Assessment in Two Copperbelt Informal Settlements*, CARE Zambia, PO Box 36238, Lusaka, August.

Waters-Bayer, Ann and Wolfgang Bayer (1994), *Planning with Pastoralists: PRA and More. A Review of Methods Focused on Africa*, GTZ division 422 Working Paper, Druckerei Kinzel, Göttingen.

WDR (1995), *World Development Report 1995,* Oxford University Press.

Webber, Lynn M. and R.L. Ison (1995), 'Participatory Rural Appraisal Design: conceptual and process issues', *Agricultural Systems* 47: 107–31.

Webster, Richard (1995), *Why Freud Was Wrong: Sin, Science and Psychoanalysis*, Harper Collins, London.

Welbourn, Alice (1991), 'The Analysis of Difference', *RRA Notes* 14: 14–23, December.

Welbourn, Alice (1992), 'Rapid Rural Appraisal, Gender and Health – Alternative Ways of Listening to Needs', *IDS Bulletin*, Vol. 23, No. 1: 8–18.

Welbourn, Alice (1993), 'PRA, Gender and Conflict Resolution: some problems and possibilities', Paper for IIED/IDS PRA and Gender Workshop, 6 and 7 December 1993, IDS, Sussex.

Welbourn, Alice (1996), *Stepping Stones: A Training Package on HIV/AIDS, Gender Issues, Communication and Relationship Skills*, ActionAid, London.

Wentzel, Sandra (1994), 'Comparative Assessment of Experiences with Participatory Village Development Planning in the Context of GTZ-Supported Projects in Indonesia', draft, Indonesian-German Governmental Cooperation, Department Dalam Negeri and GTZ.

Whyte, A.V.T. (1977), *Guidelines for Field Studies in Environment Perception*, UNESCO, Paris.

Whyte, William Foote (1991), *Participatory Action Research*, Sage Publications, London.

Wild, Robert (1994), 'Community Participation in Planning Resource Utilization from Within a National Park – Bwindi Impenetrable National Park Uganda', typescript 4p., Development through Conservation Project, CARE Uganda, P.O. Box 7280, Kampala.

Wilken, Gene C. (1987), *Good Farmers: Traditional Agricultural Resource Management in Mexico and Central America*, University of California Press, Berkeley, Los Angeles, London.

Winrock International (1995), *The Tarai Research Network*, Paper No. 22, December, Winrock International, Kathmandu.

Women of Sangams Pastapur, Medak, Andhra Pradesh and Michel Pimbert (1991), 'Farmer Participation in On-farm Varietal Trials: multilocational testing under resource-poor conditions', *RRA Notes* 10: 3–8, February.

Woo, Henry (1986), *What's Wrong with Formalization in Economics?* Victoria Press, Newark, California.

Wood, Alan (1950), *The Groundnut Affair*, Bodley Head.

World Bank (1988), *Rural Development: World Bank Experience 1965–86*, Operations Evaluation Department, The World Bank, Washington DC.

World Bank (1992), *Effective Implementation: Key to Development Impact*. Report of the World Bank Portfolio Management Task Force (Wapenhans Report), World Bank, Washington, October.

World Bank (1994a), *The World Bank and Participation*, Operations Policy Department, World Bank, September.

World Bank (1994b), *Zambia Poverty Assessment Vol. V: Participatory Poverty Assessment*, Report No. 12985-ZA, 30 November.

World Bank (1995), *World Bank Participation Sourcebook*, Environment Department Papers, World Bank, June.

World Vision (1993), *The PRA Report: Walking in Their Shoes* (video), World Vision, Australia.

WSSD (1995), World Summit for Social Development, Declaration and Programme of Action.

Young, John (1993) 'Alternative Approaches to the Identification of Smallholder Problems and Opportunities', in Daniels *et al.* (eds) *Livestock Services for Smallholders*: 123–30.

Index

abilities 131, 206
  see also capabilities
Abu, K.B. 185
abuse 6, 77, 82, 83, 84, 233
academic/theory-practical/applied 34–5,
  51–4
accuracy 43, 143, 144, 158, 200
ActionAid 114, 121, 123–4, 133, 217–8,
  247–8
Activists for Social Alternatives 247–8
Acton, Lord 77, 245
adaptability/adaptation 167, 168, 192,
  194–5, 197, 199
adaptation to environment 174
Adiseshiah, Malcolm 61
Adjebeng-Asem, Selina 124
aerial/satellite survey/photographs 25,
  27, 82, 118, 205
afforestation 23–7, 66, 82, 90, 175,
  181
Afghanistan 3
Africa 22–3, 29, 31, 71–2, 74, 87, 98,
  112, 114, 194, 235
  East 246
  South 93, 114, 121, 127, 235, 248–9
  Sub-Saharan 6, 7, 16–17, 72–3, 241
  West 27–8, 82–3
Aga Khan Foundation 248
age 184
agriculture 34, 68–70, 109, 120
agro-ecosystem analysis 108–9, 112
Ahluwalia, Montek 46
aid *see* donors; funds; loans
AKRSP (Aga Khan Rural Support
  Programme] 109, 113, 132–3
Albania 248
altruism 13, 195, 211, 234
ambition 34
Amponsah, Mary 185
analysis of difference 44, 118–19, 187
analysis 46, 95, 132, 135–6
Angola 3, 7
Antholt, Charles 72
apologies owed 83, 84
approaches 102–4, 106, 108, 113–16

see also bottom-up; methods;
  paradigms; repertoire of; top-
  down; participatory approaches
approximation 41, 143
Argentina 248
Armenia 248
arrogance 50, 51, 63, 74, 174, 201,
  202
Arthur, W.B. 232
Ashby, Jacqueline 110
Asia 21–2, 72, 87, 108, 114, 175, 192
  South 6, 41, 112
  South-East 21, 109, 112
Asian Development Bank 28, 66
assets 164, 165, 175
assumptions 23, 48, 53, 72, 133, 201,
  235
attitudes 129, 162, 207–8, 209, 212, 215,
  219
  see also behaviour; conditioning
Australia 112, 157, 244, 248, 251
Austria 52
authority 58, 61–2, 63, 77, 79, 91–2
  see also patriarchy; powers; uppers
avoidance 80, 86

bad practice 43, 44, 90, 115, 142, 145,
  161, 211–14
Bagadion, Benjamin 227
balancing/equalizing/levelling 11, 104,
  149, 151, 152, 155, 204, 211
Bangladesh 6, 47, 108, 121, 123, 132,
  175, 184, 206, 217, 248–9
basic needs 10, 11, 47–8, 179–80, 181,
  182
basket of choices 68, 70, 180, 201
Baumol, William J. 5
Bayer, Woldgang 153
BBC 4
Becker, Gary 243
behaviour 79, 129, 133–4, 155, 157, 163,
  207–8, 215
  studies 50, 57, 194–5, 200
  see also attitudes' conditioning;
    human nature

285

293

WHO 3, 19
Winrock International 114, 126, 248
Wolfensohn, James 54, 242
Women of Sangams Vastapur 218
women & girls 37–8, 63, 126–7, 133,
140, 148, 149, 155, 173, 186, 217, 236
discrimination/abuse/violence 6, 58,
77, 83, 132
woodfuel & 'crisis' 22–3, 80, 180–1,
239
working environments 31, 36, 37, 38,
52, 53, 80
works, what 67–8, 146–7, 156
World Bank 2–4, 12–14, 17, 22, 49–50,
54, 60, 66–7, 71–2, 76, 81–2, 85, 92,
97–100, 113, 121, 127, 138, 181, 190,
193, 224, 226, 238, 242, 247–8, 253
shifts in 54, 190
World Neighbours 248

World Resources Institute 114, 248
World Vision 179, 251
wrong, being 29–31, 91–3
WWF-International 120, 179

Xavier Institute of Social Services,
India 248

yields 46, 47, 68
Youth for Action 248
Yugoslavia 3, 7

Zambia 47, 70, 121, 126–8, 136, 138,
142, 166, 173, 178–9, 247–9, 251, 253
zero-sum game/thinking 12, 205–6, 234
Ziama Reserve 27
Zimbabwe 114, 124–5, 130, 133, 143,
168, 178, 184, 235, 248, 250
ZOPP 42–4, 49, 54, 99–100, 223, 247